Oglethorpe and Colonial Georgia

Oglethorpe and Colonial Georgia

A History, 1733–1783

DAVID LEE RUSSELL

McFarland & Company, Inc., Publishers
Jefferson, North Carolina, and London

ALSO BY DAVID LEE RUSSELL

The American Revolution in the Southern Colonies (McFarland, 2000)

Victory on Sullivan's Island (Infinity, 2002)

LIBRARY OF CONGRESS CATALOGUING-IN-PUBLICATION DATA

Russell, David Lee, 1947–
     Oglethorpe and colonial Georgia : a history, 1733–1783 /
David Lee Russell.
          p.   cm.
     Includes bibliographical references and index.

     ISBN 0-7864-2233-5 (illustrated case binding : 50# alkaline paper)

     1. Oglethorpe, James Edward, 1696–1785.   2. Governors—
Georgia — Biography.   3. Georgia — History — Colonial period, ca.
1600–1775.   4. Georgia — History — Revolution, 1775–1783.   I. Title.
     F289.O37R87   2006
     975.8'02092 — dc22   2006000208

British Library cataloguing data are available

On the cover: Background www.clipart.com; British flags
©2006 PhotoSpin; portrait of James Edward Oglethorpe
courtesy Oglethorpe University

Manufactured in the United States of America

McFarland & Company, Inc., Publishers
  Box 611, Jefferson, North Carolina 28640
   www.mcfarlandpub.com

To inspired leaders like James Edward Oglethorpe,
who strived to make the
world a better place for everyone,
and to the loving memory of
my father, Luther, and my mother, Betty

Table of Contents

That worthy gentlemen Mr. Oglethorpe ... opened to me a scheme he had formed, to which I was before a perfect stranger but which I very much supported, to settle a hundred miserable wretches, lately relieved out of jail, on the continent of America, and for that end to petition His Majesty for a grant of a suitable quantity of acres, whereon to place these persons.

— Earl of Egmont, John Viscount Percival, Feb. 13, 1730

Preface

This book presents a most incredible story of the founding and emergence of colonial Georgia, the last of the British colonies in North America. As my research effort began in earnest, I was most intrigued with the background and unique contributions of a relatively unacknowledged English aristocrat and founder of colonial Georgia, James Edward Oglethorpe. He was a hands-on leader who saw his vision to establish a colony in the New World come to reality.

I was likewise impressed with the character and leadership of the three British royal governors of Georgia — Captain John Reynolds, Henry Ellis, and James Wright. Likewise unacknowledged, these men created the base legacy of colonial rule in Georgia and unknowingly helped to give these British subjects all they needed to muster the courage to move toward independence.

The contributions of the patriot leadership emerged just in time to deliver Georgia to the American cause. I have included the detailed events of the American Revolution in Georgia to complete the historical transition from colonial province to self-governed state. The military engagements in Georgia, which occurred mostly around Savannah and Augusta, were quite interesting, and though the province did not regain control over its territory until the British evacuated after the war, the spirited patriots who fought for liberty under difficult circumstances were worthy of respect and admiration.

My primary research material was gathered at the William Russell Pullen Library of Georgia State University at 100 Decatur Street in downtown Atlanta. I also found important material from various used history books and journals covering colonial Georgia and the Revolution which I purchased. For those like me, who spend hundreds of hours reading reference material, to find just the right reference text one needs on a particular topic is to feel a certain excitement that only authors experience.

My thanks go out to those who assisted me in obtaining the colonial maps and portrait images for this book. Those persons who helped me included Nelson Morgan of the Hargrett Rare Book and Manuscript Library at the University of Georgia, Lucy Waitt at the Picture Library of the National Maritime Museum at 8 Park Row in London; Mandi D. Johnson, the interim director of Library and Archives at the Georgia Historical Society in Savannah; and Joanne Yendle and Anne Salter at the Philip Weltner Library at Oglethorpe University in Atlanta.

As my research carries me to places and times of long ago, I am ever more intrigued by those early colonists who settled, built and fought for the South during the colonial period. Though we are all rightly focused on the challenges of our present day, there is great curiosity and some comfort in learning more about these special people and all they sacrificed. The incredible history they wrote day by day in their time in the Georgia of the 1700s is now set in the pages of this book.

David Lee Russell
Alpharetta, Georgia

Introduction

It is a most improbable, little known, yet true story that came to yield the last of the British colonies in North America. The 50 years of colonial Georgia (1733–1783) were the most profound, and, perhaps, the most unusual among all the 13 original American colonies. The story which is colonial Georgia is one that is forever tied to the vision of its founder, the stewardship of its three British royal governors, and the patriot leadership of those who fought to create a new government and engage the British in the American Revolution.

But the context of the story began with the earliest days of exploration. The origins of Georgia as we understand it began with the European explorations led by the Spanish in 1521, 29 years after an Italian, sailing under a Spanish flag, Christopher Columbus, first landed in the Bahamas (1492). The Spanish were in North American waters attempting to discover a route to the West Indies. Soon that effort switched to one of exploration and conquest.

Juan Poncé de León in 1513 sailed up the Florida coast and probably touched the area of coastal Georgia before 1520. Colonization began in 1526 on the coast of Carolina and Georgia by Lucas Vasquez de Ayllon. While the location is unknown, historians have come to believe it was near St. Catherine's Island. The colony ended in disaster with Vasquez and others dead as a few escaped.

Hernando deSoto visited Georgia in 1540 and was credited with participating in the destruction of much of the native culture. Other visitors of this era include Tristan de Luna in 1560 and Juan Pardo in 1566, exploring the interior. Pardo established a colony and Jesuit mission on San Pedro (St. Catherine's) near the Creek town of Guale early that year. More exploration continued. In 1586, Englishman Francis Drake came and raided St. Augustine, and two years later Drake would defeat the Spanish Armada. Soon, Franciscan monks came to Georgia to convert the native Indians until 1597, when a war broke out over an argument between a cleric and an aspiring chief and destroyed much of the Franciscans' work. After some ten years the missions regained their work and continued to operate for the next century.

In 1607, the English colony of Virginia was established at Jamestown, which served as the primary English base of operations along the southern frontier until the 1670 founding of Charles Town and the colony of Carolina. Ultimately, St. Augustine and Charles Town would become the centers of English and Spanish exploration and colonial expansion during the late 17th and early 18th centuries. The conflict for control of this area

1

between Florida and Carolina would be a central focus in the effort to establish the successful colony of Georgia.

Though the Spanish and French had explored most of Georgia, the first English explorer of Georgia was Dr. Henry Woodward. In the 1670s, from Carolina Dr. Woodward headed west to the falls of the Chattahoochee, near Coweta, which was the center of the Creek Nation. Woodward desired to lure the Indians away from the Spanish missionaries, who feared an outright English attack. Such an attack came in 1680, led by Woodward, whose ranks were swollen by the Indians whom he had worked with for ten years. The Spanish withdrew to Sapelo Island and by 1684 the Spanish were gone from the coast of Georgia.

In the early 18th century, conflict escalated between the English in Carolina and the Spanish in Florida as a result the War of Spanish Succession (Queen Anne's War). In 1715, members of the Creek Nation, including the Yuchi and the Yamassee, attacked the South Carolina frontier, driving the settlers back to Charles Town. Ten months later, the Creek were defeated and forced to move farther south.

With the coastal area of Georgia, the first attempt at controlling the territory between the Savana and Altamaha Rivers was with the establishment of the margravate of Azilia, an idyllic early representation of the Georgia colony. Another attempt came in 1721 with Fort King George, near present-day Darien, Georgia. In 1724 Jean Pierre Purry proposed a settlement named Georgina, in honor of newly crowned King George II, on the 33rd parallel.[1]

It is in this period of conflict in the early 1700s between the English and Spanish that the story of colonial Georgia begins. And it would seem like such an impossible story, for it is essentially a story that began with the vision of one man. In England, an aristocrat and member of Parliament would show compassion for the unfortunates held in debtor's prison. Eventually, this man was able to free thousands of debtors. Then, he petitioned the king to allow him to take some of them to a land of opportunity across the Atlantic Ocean. To ensure that the new colony was successful, this man sailed with them to the New World and lived for nearly a year in a tent. When he landed he coordinated the building of a new town, built forts, and fought off the Spanish intruders. To make sure his settlers maintained a moral focus and did not get lazy, he forbade rum and did not allow them to acquire slaves. He even spent his own money on the colonists after the trustee government funds ran out. Could a man like this really have existed? He did exist, and his name was James Edward Oglethorpe.

After the era of Oglethorpe, the colony of Georgia would enter the period of royal leadership and then on to the turmoil of the American Revolution. The story of colonial Georgia is one of ambition, religious settlement, death, native Indian displacement, altruism, failed dreams, turmoil, territorial greed, naive moral utopianism, military engagement, missionary fervor, nationalism, sacrifice, brutality, patriot spirit, vision, and achievement. In these pages you will travel through time, from the founding of an altruistic colony to the reality of a political independence as part of what would become the United States of America. This is the truly incredible story of colonial Georgia.

1

Oglethorpe and the Georgia Inspiration

"Not for ourselves, but for others."

The pilgrims bowed their heads in prayer before the altar and priest in the parish church at Milton, on the banks of the Thames. As the words of divine wisdom flowed around them on their last Sunday morning in England, their minds wandered to the mysteries of their new beginning and all that their future would hold. They may never see their mother country again, or feel the warm springs or behold the beauty of the damp green meadows they had known from their youth. As they raised their heads together and departed the sanctuary, they entered the open sunshine of the world of their adventure.

These pilgrims were about to take a grand voyage to a new world of the British North American colonies. For weeks the sergeants of the guards had drilled the men as the stores were loaded aboard the 200-ton chartered galley, *Anne*. Stationed at Deptford, some four miles below London, Captain John Thomas prepared his ship for departure with his cargo of material and humans. The band of pilgrims, and soon to be colonists, was made up of 114 "sober, industrious, and moral persons" from 35 families. There were "two merchants, five carpenters, two wig-makers, two tailors, a miller and baker, a writer, a surgeon, one gardener, five farmers, an upholsterer, a basket-maker, two sawyers, an apothecary, a vintner, a wheelwright, one stocking-maker, a reduced military officer." There was a Reverend Henry Herbert, D.D., to maintain their religious faith. And there was their most remarkable and important of leaders, James Edward Oglethorpe.[1]

James Edward Oglethorpe was no average man for he was among the privileged class. Oglethorpe came from a family distinguished for over six centuries for their powerful station in Britain. Tracing a lineage to Ligulfe, theane of Oglethorpe, in St. Edward the Confessor's reign, his ancestors had demonstrated a loyalty to the Crown at their own peril. For centuries they maintained their residence at their Yorkshire estate at Bramham, but the military tradition manifested in the civil wars of the seventeenth century left several Oglethorpe men dead on the battlefield near Oxford in defense of the monarchy. Sutton Oglethorpe suffered "for his loyalty to King Charles I and was fined by the Parliament in the sum of £20,000 for which his Estates were sequestered and afterwards forfeited."

During the two decades succeeding the Restoration, Sutton's son, Theophilus, rose through the ranks to become lieutenant colonel of Charles II's Lifeguard Dragoons. Eventually knighted, Sir Theophilus Oglethorpe became brigadier general to King James II and was rewarded enough to acquired the manor of Westbrook Estate in Godalming, Surrey. Sadly for Sir Theophilus, his king was thrown out in the 1688 Revolution. Sir Theophilus then became a Jacobite and joined his old master in exile in France. Later, when James II insisted that his supporters must be Catholics, he returned home, pledged his allegiance to William III and soon became MP for his local borough of Haslemere. This became a family parliamentary seat which James Oglethorpe himself would hold for 32 years.

When Sir Theophilus died in 1702, Lady Eleanor Wall Oglethorpe was left to bring up seven children, of whom the youngest, James, was age six. She was a beautiful Irishwoman from Tipperary who had been laundress to King Charles II, a rather well-paid office. As a dedicated Jacobite plotter, she eventually sent all her daughters to the exiled Stuart court in France; three of them married French aristocrats and the fourth became a Jacobite countess. Of James's two surviving older brothers, one became aide-de-camp to the Duke of Marlborough and was killed in the wars of Queen Anne, and the other fled in exile and secured a Jacobite peerage. That left James heir to the family estate in Godalming.

The date of his birth was December 22, 1696, in London. As befitting his station, he was baptized by the Archbishop of Canterbury the next day at St. Martin's-in- the-Fields. His boyhood was spent both in London and at Westbrook Estate. In London he became used to the activity of the streets and all that was part of the largest metropolis of Europe, where the population was nearly 500,000. Thirty-five miles away south was Godalming, spread up on two picturesque hills separated by the River Wey, above the Lammas Lands flood plain. Chartered by Queen Elizabeth I in 1576, Godalming was a village just over the hill from Westbrook, where the spire of the church of Sts. Peter and Paul dominated the landscape.

Not unexpected for the ambitious Lady Oglethorpe, she had young James appointed by Marlborough as an ensign in the 1st Foot Guards at age 13. Four years later the "paper commission" would be torn up as James was commissioned at Windsor on November 21, 1713, as lieutenant unassigned and with the rank of captain of the Foot.[2] Though he certainly had aspirations of a life in the army, at age 17 James went off to Eton College where he stayed just long enough to gain admittance to the Corpus Christi College at Oxford in July of 1714.

Within weeks of his arrival at Oxford, the country was in turmoil over the political activity surrounding Queen Anne's death. Rebellion broke out and James III landed at Peterhead in a futile attempt to recapture his throne. George I, a German-speaking prince descended from James I, gained the crown in conflict with the Jacobite loyalties of the Oglethorpe family and many others in England who believed the crown belonged to the Stuarts. Before long, Oxford was the site of brawls and riots started by Jacobites who refused to celebrate King George I's birthday. Though his army commission was renewed in 1715 by George I, who assigned him to the first troop of the Queen's Guards, James resigned his commission in 1716 to go abroad. Taking the example of his sisters and brothers, James left England for France in March. He ended up in a military academy in Paris.

With a thirst for action and adventure, James defied the French embargo on foreign service and joined the army of the Holy Roman Emperor, serving as an aide-de-camp to Prince Eugene of Savoy. It was in this role that he became involved in his first known public altercation. At a dinner table the Prince of Wurtemburg flipped wine in Oglethorpe's face. With a youthful smile and cool objectivity, James exclaimed, "That's a good joke, but we do it much better in England," where upon he proceeded to pour a full glass of wine over the astonished royal prince to the amusement of all in company. Only a man of confidence and distinguished upbringing would have had the courage to deal with the event with such flair.

James saw action with campaigns against the Turks. Soon, Oglethorpe was to gain some distinction from his superiors in the Battle of Belgrade on August 3, 1717. In what his sister Fanny described as "very bloody and sharpe," and though "his servant that was next to him is killed," Oglethorpe was unhurt.[3] With this Austrian victory and the campaign against the Turks ended, Oglethorpe at age twenty-two set out to visit his brother Theophilus in Turin, Italy. While there, James, in the company of his brother, made a visit to the court of the exiled James III at Urbino. The Old Pretender noted that James was "a pretty youth" and clearly a devoted Jacobite follower. Fanny wrote that her brother James was "a very good youth and has a true foundation of honest principles." After a stay with his sisters in Paris, James returned to England in early 1719, and away from the influences of the Jacobite world he was so close to.

Back at Westbrook, he settled in to live a quiet life with his mother and sister Molly. In 1722, Oglethorpe emerged from obscurity to announce that he was a candidate for Parliament from Haslemere. The days leading up to the election brought out the partisan passions of the villagers. After evening services on Sunday, March 25, four rather vocal opponents drew swords on Oglethorpe at a chance meeting. Heated words were exchanged and, showing his temper, Oglethorpe wounded a Mr. Sharpe in the stomach, and disabled Captain Onslow in his left hand and thigh. Oglethorpe then helped "bound up Captain Onslow's Wounds and sent for a Surgeon to him." Oglethorpe's letter of the event appeared four days letter in the *London Daily Journal*. With four candidates up for the two seats, Oglethorpe won the election on March 28 with 46 votes, with second-place finisher Peter Burrell getting 45. They were both off to the House of Commons.

James was a man from a family where the males could be a violent bunch. He was hyperactive and hot-tempered. His brother had been in duels and his father had killed a man in a brawl. Tensions over the election were still high on April 24 when a drunken Oglethorpe wandered into a tavern at 6 o'clock in the morning in "a night-house of evil repute" and engaged in an argument with a linkman, employed to carry a torch to light the streets. In this altercation Oglethorpe "drew his Sword and gave the Fellow a mortal Wound in the Breast." The newly elected MP from Haslemere was taken to the Gaol. Through the influence of a powerful friend, Oglethorpe was released from confinement to take his seat on October 9 as a Tory.[4]

As a thin, tall man with a rather shrill voice, Oglethorpe was soon to become a social reformer. During his first five years in Parliament he served on 42 different committees, focusing on the unprivileged class. His first assignment was on the "Committee to Inquire into pretended Privileged Places and the best means to abolish them." From this effort he became familiar with the plight of the debtor. The next committee involved the relief of insolvent debtors. Over the years he would tackle work with the poor of Gloucester, impressments into service of youths under the age of 16 for work as boatmen on the Thames, public safety, shipwrecked sailors, land reclamation, and more.[5]

In 1728, Oglethorpe published an unsigned pamphlet of 52 pages called *The Sailors Advocate*, which was an attack on the common British practice of forcibly recruiting men for the Royal Navy with the use of press gangs. In that pamphlet he wrote, "It is not the Timber nor the Iron of the Ships of War ... but the Sailors who mann them, who are the strength of the NATION...." Though no immediate or dramatic reform resulted, it did arouse the public, and the pamphlet was still being reprinted 50 years later.[6] He also called attention to paying sailors with promissory notes that could be redeemed only at the London Pay Office. With Oglethorpe's support, he was able to press Parliament to pass an act which put the payment of naval wages on a more modern footing. Soon he turned his attentions to another serious problem in England.[7]

This incredible voyage to America that was now about to begin was yet another dream of Mr. Oglethorpe's. It came about as the result of a most ordinary assignment from the House of Commons' leadership. Having reached the status as a distinguished member of Parliament and a reformer, it was not surprising that Oglethorpe was made the chairman of a committee to investigate the conditions of the debtor prisons or "gaols" of England on February 25, 1729.

The existence of debtor prisons was a result of literal interpretations of the earliest English law, which made the case for the obligation of debt as a personal matter, where the body of the person could be taken by the creditor. This sanctioning of incarceration of debtors, in many cases in the dungeon of a dirty prison, was just such a situation that confronted a friend of Oglethorpe, Robert Castell. Castell was an aspiring architect who wrote a book entitled *The Villas of the Ancients Illustrated*. As was the practice in those days, Castell decided to print the book at his own expense and sell them to his patrons and friends. Though Oglethorpe purchased a few copies of the book, not many were sold. As a result of his unsuccessful attempt as an author and publisher, Castell fell into debt, evaded his creditors for a short while, and was eventually sent to prison until the debt was paid.

In June of 1728, Castell was committed to the most renowned debtor's prison in England, know as "The Fleet." The Fleet prison warden was Thomas Bambridge, who had purchased the lucrative position for a £5,000 fee. He was able to charge a £5 fee to every prisoner who entered the prison, and exacted other charges for special living conditions. When Castell entered the prison he paid Bambridge a bribe to get comfortable spaces. When the money ran out, the warden moved Castell into quarters where deadly smallpox was raging. Soon, Castell contracted the disease and died, leaving "all his affairs in the greatest confusion, and a numerous family of small children in utmost distress."[8]

With Castell's death, Oglethorpe took action to push a resolution before the House of Commons, bypassing the custom of review of these types of cases in the House of Lords, to establish the committee to review "the State of the Gaols of this Kingdom." He proceeded to get himself made chairman of the committee of 14 rather distinguished men. The inquiry began with Fleet Prison, where the committee interviewed various imprisoned debtors who gave compelling evidence against the prison officials. The initial report presented shocking conditions which led the King to ask the attorney general to prosecute six officials, including Bambridge.

Work continued as the examinations moved to the prison of the Court of Marshalsea, the King's Palace Court of Westminster, and to the King's Bench Prison. As a result of these investigations, three reports were presented to the House of Commons detailing acts of prison officials selling offices, breaches of trust, extortion, and the highest crimes and misdemeanors. In the last report Oglethorpe declared, "If this be law, all England may be made one extended prison." The House of Commons accepted the proposals for reform and, thus, preventing the "Judges, their clerks and servants, from receiving any Fees, Gifts, Presents, or any gratuities whatsoever." Though reforms were passed, it was Oglethorpe who watched all the trials of the accused prison officials, only to see these unworthy and corrupt men ultimately acquitted.[9]

While the recommendations of the committee eventually led to the release of some 10,000 prisoners, the real significant and benevolent imagination came when Oglethorpe made a curious proposal to a fellow committee member and the future Earl of Egmont,

Portrait of James Edward Oglethorpe (courtesy of Oglethorpe University).

John Viscount Percival. Percival recorded of the event, "That worthy gentlemen Mr. Oglethorpe ... opened to me a scheme he had formed, to which I was before a perfect stranger but which I very much supported, to settle a hundred miserable wretches, lately relieved out of jail, on the continent of America, and for that end to petition His Majesty for a grant of a suitable quantity of acres, whereon to place these persons." With his fellow parliamentary prison reformers and those interested in church libraries and spreading the word of God, Oglethorpe joined forces to establish a debtor colony.

The full scope of the effort to acquire funding for Oglethorpe's grand adventure was manifested in a number of incremental steps and a worthy effort. With the releasing of thousands of prisoners from debtor's prison, Oglethorpe complained that no provision had been made for these unfortunate "miserable wretches ... let out of Gaol" in the Act of 1729. They were "starving about the town for want of employment." Oglethorpe's plan of relieving London's surplus of employment initially came from two sources, and later a collateral one. When a haberdasher named King died, he left his estate of £15,000 to be entrusted to three trustees. When Oglethorpe aided two of these trustees in forcing the third trustee to honor the will in a lawsuit, he was awarded a grant of £5,000 for his project. The terms of the grant required Oglethorpe to seek additional funding.[10]

Britain in these days was place of sharp contrast between the haves and the have-nots. On the upper rungs of the financial ladder were some 400 great landlord families whose annual income was £3,000 or more. Next were the 15,000 or so shopkeepers and landed gentry, which included the Oglethorpe's, who had high social standing and considerable property, but more limited median annual incomes of around £500. Just below them were the freeholders of perhaps 100,000 families with small tracts of land. The males in this group were allowed to vote in parliamentary elections.

On the bottom of the social-economic ladder were the masses of wretched poor. These families attempted to survive on the lowest of wages. A maid could make around 30 to 40 shilling (a shilling is equal to one-twentieth of a pound) per year, and they were better off than many of the farm laborers who flocked to the cities in the hope of a better life. As the numbers of urban poor increased, the attitudes towards them descended. The poor were born into their condition and they would never ascend, as the most powerful showed callous indifference. Oglethorpe was one of those men who did care, and he was determined to reveal his ideals in deeds.[11]

By 1730, Oglethorpe had gained more financial support for his dream of a debtor colony in the New World from the estate of philanthropist the Reverend Thomas Bray. The decision of America as the destination of the colonial adventure was actually set on April 1 of that year, and June 26 was the date the area south of Carolina was selected as the best place in America to establish the new colony. Oglethorpe's reformers gathered at Bedford Arms Tavern in London to draft the petition for a grant in America. As a veteran of the Spanish War, Oglethorpe recognized the potential of a new colony to become a buffer colony for the defense of Carolina from the Spanish in Florida. From as early as the sixteenth century, and nearly 100 years before the first permanent British settlement in North America at Jamestown, Spain had established camps in this part of the world and held claims on Carolina. Certainly a colony would serve as a place to market English goods as it provided a source of raw materials. From this southern environment England could acquire silk, flax, linen, pitch, tar, hemp, turpentine, and even wine.[12]

With Percival and others' support, the "petition to the King and Council for obtaining a grant of lands on the southwest of Carolina for settling poor persons of London, and having ordered it to be engrossed fair, we signed it, all who were present, and the other

Associates were to be spoke also to sign it before delivered." The petition for a charter was presented to the Privy Council on September 17. Unfortunately, it lay there for a year and a half.[13]

Oglethorpe and Percival used all their political skills to get the council to act. Minister Sir Robert Walpole was reluctant to approve the charter. The Board of Trade had to approve it, and even the last of the Carolina Proprietors, Lord Carteret, also had to agree. It was also necessary to get Walpole's promise to allow the effort to receive proceeds from the existing state lottery.

New problems arose. The first draft of the charter that had been submitted by the attorney general required "a new election of Councillors every three years which we apprehend is to take the power out of our hands and put it into new ones." The colonial militia was to be put under the control of the governor of Carolina. The two leaders continued to plead their case for revisions in the charter but the Whigs added their delay to the release.

Though the king had "put the fiat to our Carolina Charter" on January 26, 1732, the Duke of Newcastle then held up the signing. Finally, with the determined action from Oglethorpe, Percival and his supporters, King George II signed the charter and approved the colonial venture in June of 1732.[14] The Charter of the Colony of Georgia, named in honor of the king, read as follows:

George the Second,

By the grace of God, of Great Britain, France, and Ireland, King, Defender of the Faith, &c, To all to whom these presents shall come, greeting. Whereas we are credibly informed, that many of our poor subjects are, through misfortunes and want of employment, reduced to great necessity, insomuch as by their labour they are not able to provide a maintenance for themselves and families; and if they had means to defray their charges of passage, and other expenses incident to new settlements, they would be glad to settle in any of our provinces in America; where, by cultivating the lands at present waste and desolate, they might not only gain a comfortable subsistence for themselves and families, but also strengthen our colonies, and increase the trade, navigation, and wealth of these our realms. And whereas our provinces in North America have been frequently ravaged by Indian enemies; more especially that of South Carolina, which in the late war, by the neighboring savages, was laid waste by fire and sword, and great numbers of the English inhabitants miserably massacred; and our living subjects who now inhabit there, by reason of the smallness of their numbers, will, in case of a new war, be exposed to the like calamities; inasmuch as their whole southern frontier continueth unsettled, and lieth open to the said savages; and whereas we think it highly becoming our crown and royal dignity, to protect all our loving subjects, be they never so distant from us; to extend our fatherly compassion even to the meanest and most infatuate of our people, and to relieve the wants of our above mentioned poor subjects; and that it will be highly conductive for accomplishing those ends; that a regular colony of the said poor people be settled and established in the southern territories of Carolina; and whereas we have been well assured, that we would be graciously pleased to erect and settle a corporation, for the receiving, managing and disposing of the contributions of our loving subjects ... by the name of The Trustees for the establishing the Colony of Georgia in America ... and grant to the said corporation and their successors ... all those lands, countries and territories situate, lying and being in that part of South Carolina, in America, which lies from the most northern part of a stream or river there, commonly called the Savannah, all along the sea coast to the southward, unto the most southern stream of a certain other great water or river called the Alatamaha, and westerly from the heads of the said rivers respectively, in the direct lines to the South Seas; and all that share, circuit and precinct of land within the said boundaries, with the islands on the sea lying opposite to the eastern coast of the said lands, within twenty leagues of the same...."[15]

Now Oglethorpe and 19 associates, who were mostly from his committee of the gaols, were the "Trustees for establishing the colony of Georgia in America." The Trustees began to take charge of their new duties quickly. The focus was in two key areas—publicity of the new venture and obtaining adequate funding. At the August 3 meeting of the Trustees, Oglethorpe was appointed as the publicity agent. His mission was to advertise the effort in the newspapers and to "censor all undesirable articles relating thereunto." Before long, articles in the *Gentlemen's Magazine* were comparing the adventure to Georgia to the Roman concept of colonization as "among the noblest of their works."

Oglethorpe soon published *An Essay on Plantations* and created a prospectus, *A New and Accurate Account of the Provinces of South Carolina and Georgia*. In this document, Oglethorpe declared the philanthropic purposes of the colony: "The unfortunate will not be obliged to bind themselves to a long servitude to pay for their passage, for they may be carried grants into a land of liberty and plenty, where they immediately find themselves in possession of a competent estate in a happier climate than they knew before; and they are unfortunate indeed, if here they cannot forget their sorrows."[16]

Oglethorpe and the Trustees created perhaps the most grandiose promotional campaign in colonial history. They declared the new colony was "the most delightful country of the universe." With suggestions that Georgia lay at the same latitudes as the Garden of Eden, the Trustees told of a land of noble rivers filled with fish, and lands with minerals abounding, covered with beasts and birds of plenty. One early settler recorded that he expected Georgia to be "the promised land," and another told of considering himself as "one setting out to begin the founding of a new world." Poets wrote of the work of the colonists as they "fell the trees ... th'eternal woods admit the day ... sunny hills afar ... future harvests wave in ev'ry breast."[17]

With these promotional announcements, Oglethorpe was to receive hundreds of people who wanted to join him. The selection process required that no debtor could be taken without the consent of the creditor. Contrary to an enduring, yet false legacy, no criminal or "wicked" person was ever accepted. The debtor prisons were carefully examined and the worthiest poor were given the opportunity to sail to Georgia. Oglethorpe and the Trustees had established the charter for the most noble of causes in the eighteenth century. These debtors would never be able to pay back their debts locked up in prison, and there was little hope that even as they were set free from confinement that they would ever prosper in the England of that day. The motto selected for the new colony of Georgia said it all—"Non sibi sed aliis" or "Not for ourselves, but for others."[18]

Oglethorpe and a few colleagues interviewed some 600 heads of families to fill the agreed-upon 35 family limit. In truth, the families selected were by no means the poorest of London. Within three weeks they had narrowed the list to some 100 families, paying special attention to those judged most likely to be successful colonists. The 114 selected persons were for the most part "in decayed Circumstances, and therefore disabled from following any Business in England; and who, if in Debt, had leave from their Creditors to go, and such as were recommended by the Minister, Church-wardens, and Overseers of their respective Parishes."[19]

With royal charter in hand, adequately funding the adventure was now feasible. The directors of the Bank of England subscribed £300 and before long the East India Company directors gave a sum of £600. By September 14 1732, the Trustees had gathered over £2,000 for the Georgia project.

On June 19, Oglethorpe's mother, Lady Eleanor Wall Oglethorpe, died leaving James "without any domestic ties or encumbrances" to hold him back. It was then that Oglethorpe decided to "cast his lot" with the Georgia colonists. This decision to join the colonists received the congratulations of the proprietor of Pennsylvania, Thomas Penn. Though the governor of Massachusetts, Jonathan Belcher, wrote a Trustee, Thomas Coram, to warn that the southern areas of the North American continent "have been graves to the people of England," he, likewise, issued his congratulations to Oglethorpe.[20]

Attached to Oglethorpe's offer to accompany the colonists was a stipulation that the voyage must sail at once. Egmont and others were opposed to moving too quickly on the grounds that they were unprepared, Percival later wrote, "that Mr. Oglethorpe would go, for my great pain was that although we were ever so well prepared, it would be difficult to find a proper Governor, which post he has accepted of." With the continued insistence of Oglethorpe, on October 18 the Trustees agreed to allow the colonists to sail immediately. After some delays, the Georgia adventure was off the next month.[21]

On November 16, a contingent of seven Georgia Trustees came to visit Oglethorpe and the colonists at Deptford "to see nothing was wanting, and to take leave." They gave the voyagers an opportunity to back out of the trip, as one man did when he learned that his wife was sick at home at Southwark. Then they closed their visit with "an affectionate farewell." The *Anne* and her voyagers sailed at 8:00 A.M. the next day, November 17, 1732. The *Gentlemen's Magazine* wrote of the quaint event as the colonists sailed with "10 tons of Alderman Parson's best beer ... for the service of the colony."[22] From Gravesend they skirted along the southern coast of England and then headed out in the open Atlantic to America and their new lives in Georgia. The grand experiment was begun.[23]

The next day, Oglethorpe observed that many of the colonists were seasick but that he had been spared. The *Anne* sailed on westward as a routine set in for the colonists. Each family slept in one of the 35 wooden cradles separated from one another by canvas curtains. The men drilled with small arms as the women knitted and sewed. The food was dispensed according to a precise schedule; Thursdays and Sundays they had pork and peas; Saturday was for fish and butter; and the remaining days were beef and pudding days.

Oglethorpe took charge even at sea and did his best to make his fellow voyagers comfortable. He inspired confidence as the shipmates gained respect for their uncommon leader, a man who had given up his personal comfort to support them on their quest. Peter Gordon, a man named by the Trustees as one of the colonial officials for Georgia, wrote of the crossing of the *Anne*. Though he became sick a month into the voyage, his journal entries confirm that he was well attended to by Oglethorpe and the Reverend Henry Herbert, who were "constantly" in his cabin. The recorder for the colony, Thomas Christie, told of Oglethorpe's visits to the settlers "in the hold" where the living spaces were located. Oglethorpe became the godfather to the Warrens' son who was born at sea and christened Georgius Marinus.

Oglethorpe set the rhythm of the voyage as he did his best to keep the colonists busy as they endured the tedium of congested living. He issued orders that lights must be out by eight o'clock. Smoking was not allowed "unless with a Cap on the Pipe & then on the deck." Sadly, on the evening of November 24, in rather misty weather, Oglethorpe's dog was lost, supposedly "flung Over board by some of the Sailors."

After a month at sea Oglethorpe "caught a Dolphin" and after hearing that a "Bigbellyd. Woman" on the *Anne* had admired the catch, he presented it to her as a gift. A fishing party was also formed later with Oglethorpe, Herbert and others huddled "undr. an Umbrella" to protect themselves from the fierce sun. To celebrate their leader's 36th birthday "a sheep and some other fresh provisions was dress'd for our people, and a quantity of liquor given to drink the health of the day. After dinner we were diverted with cudgel playing and riding of skimingtons on account of Mrs. [Anne] Coles having beat her husband."

There were some sobering events. Sadly two children, James Cannon and James Clark, died on the voyage and were buried at sea. After the second funeral ceremony Oglethorpe was forced to resort to exceptional means to keep order. During the ceremony someone threatened to "throw water on them." Oglethorpe "came behind him & gave him a good kick on ye arse." After another event later on Oglethorpe released "a pint of Bumbo" for everyone "to Drink & be friends together." The trip had getting on everyone's nerves as the days at sea continued.[24]

As the *Anne* approached the coast of South Carolina, Oglethorpe looked on at the trees on the horizon with some sense of pleasure noting that it was "No disagreeable sight to those who for seven weeks have seen nothing but Sea and Sky." He had declared the voyage "a very favourable Passage." Finally, on January 13, 1733, they sailed into Rebellion Roads and anchored off Charles Town in the colony of Carolina.

All had survived the voyage except the youngest sons of Robert Clarke and Richard Cannon, who had both come on board in poor condition at Deptford. The anticipation in South Carolina of the new colonial visitors had been in evidence as early as October 7 when the oldest of southern newspapers, the *South Carolina Gazette,* had proclaimed, "we are very impatient here to know the Particulars of the Charter." That interest was maintained until Oglethorpe in his packet boat rowed to the shore at Charles Town. There the royal governor, Robert Johnson, and the speaker of the Assembly received him with every expression of respect.

After a short visit of only ten hours, the colonists sailed away on the *Anne* with the local king's pilot aboard, Mr. Middleton. On the 14th the colonists sailed over the bar at Port Royal, some 16 miles below Beaufort Town. Four days later, Oglethorpe went on shore at Trench's Island (Hilton Head Island). He left a guard unit at John's, which was a point on Trench's Island commanding the channel, and located halfway between Beaufort and the Savannah River entrance.

From there the colonists went to Beaufort Town, arriving on the 20th at one o'clock in the morning to the sound of cannon salute from the military unit. With the assistance of Lieutenant Watts and Ensign Farrington of His Majesty's Independent Company, and the local citizens led by Mr. Delabare, the colonists were lodged in new barracks. These barracks had been intended for soldiers supporting a new fortification, located three miles from town. Finally, the colonists were able to eat fresh food, rest, relax and spread out after living for two months at sea in cramped quarters.[25] They were now in the New World.

A colonist, Thomas Causton, recorded that many of the company traveled to Beaufort to report that they were "entertained in a very elegant manner and everyone found somebody to entertain them in some shape or other." The Beaufort Town citizens lived in "houses ... all of timber and very few have glass windows or brick chimneys." These people were, according to Causton, "very gallant and generous and seem to live in a plentiful manner."[26]

While the colonists rested, Oglethorpe traveled with Colonel William Bull of South Carolina to select the exact site of the new settlement. Going by canoe through the various sea islands and inlets of the Lowcountry, they came out on the wide expanse of the Savannah River.[27] Heading upriver for 10 miles, Oglethorpe reached a perfect location, as he later described:

> I fixed upon a healthy situation about ten miles from the sea. The river there forms a half moon, along the South side of which the banks are about 40 foot high and upon the top a flat which they call a bluff. The plain high ground extends into the country five or six miles and along the riverside about a mile. Ships that draw twelve foot water can ride within ten yards of the bank. Upon the riverside in the center of the plain, I have laid out a town. Over

against it is an island of very rich land fit for pasturage, which I think should be kept for the Trustees' cattle. The river is pretty wide, the water fresh. And from the quay of the town you see its whole course to the sea with the Island of Tybee, which forms the mouth of the river; and the other way you may see the river for about six miles up into the country. The landscape is very agreeable, the stream being wide and bordered with high woods on both sides.[28]

Oglethorpe was thrilled as he surveyed the high bluff. He looked out at the expanse northward toward Carolina at a beautiful island, rich with pasture land, with trees filling the rest of the landscape. On the southern side on the bluff was an unbroken plain of tall pines, sprinkled by a few oak trees, with gray moss draped from the occasional tree. There were creepers, wild flowers, jasmine and magnolia all around as Oglethorpe declared, "The landscape is very agreeable — the stream being wide, and bordered with high woods on both sides."[29] At the northern end of the bluff they found a trading house and an Indian village known as Yamacraw. Oglethorpe met the Indian chief Tomochichi, as well as a trader, John Musgrove, and his wife, Mary. According to an old treaty with the Creeks, no white settlement was allowed to establish south of the Savannah River without the consent of the Indian nation. Oglethorpe successfully negotiated a temporary treaty through Mary Musgrove, who acted as English interpreter, to obtain an agreement to build a settlement there.[30]

On January 24 Oglethorpe with Bull returned to the colonists at Beaufort Town. He left behind Captain Francis Scott and a contingent of men at the site to await his return with the colonists. On Sunday, four days later, they celebrated their safe voyage by a day of thanksgiving as the Reverend Dr. Herbert delivered a sermon. The local citizens provided a dinner of "four fat hogs, eight turkies, besides fowls, English beef and other provisions, a hogshead of punch, a hogshead of beer, a large quantity of wine, and all was disposed in so regular a manner that no person was drunk nor any disorder happened."

On Tuesday the 30th the colonists boarded a 70-ton sloop, five peraugers (long flat-bottomed boats with a kind of forecastle and a cabin with two masts) and sailed off to the new settlement. They were forced to put in at a place called "Look Out" and spent the night there. The next day they sailed to John's on Trench's Island where they found huts and ate a meal of venison. The next morning they reembarked their vessels and sailed to Oglethorpe's selected site. They landed at their new home, on the southern frontier of British North America, on February 1, 1733.[31] It was to be called Savannah.

2

The Founding of Savannah

"I hope by the Blessing of God we shall be able to go thro' the Undertaking."

In the afternoon of February 1, 1733, Captain Francis Scott and his contingent of armed troops waited in expectation as the five peraugers and sloop sailed up the Savannah River and into view. As Oglethorpe and his settlers approached the landing site, Scott's men fired a welcoming salute from Yamacraw Bluff. The salute was returned and the settlers disembarked. They ascended up the steps that Scott's men had dug into the bluff for them. The voyage was over and Oglethorpe's dream of placing colonists in Georgia was a reality.

As the settlers surveyed the site picked for them, an hour passed before they were greeted by the chief of the Yamacraws, Tomochichi, accompanied by his queen, and Indian trader and interpreter John Musgrove. The Indians were clothed in their finery preceded by "a Man dancing in Antick Postures" using "ratles in his hands" and adorned with a large feather fan. It was a sight to behold as the dancer pranced up to Oglethorpe's tent to meet these curious white colonists. Oglethorpe showed a certain dignity as he approached the natives.

The ceremonial dancing continued for 15 minutes as the Indians "waved his fans over him [Oglethorpe] & Stok'd him on every Side with them." After the dancing stopped, Oglethorpe invited Tomochichi and party into his tent where the chief was seated on his right as John Musgrove was "standing between them." The discussions lasted for a quarter of an hour before the Indians returned upriver to their village.[1]

Before the new Georgia colonists ended their first day at the site of their future settlement, they pitched four large tents and landed their bedding and necessary supplies. The next day, Oglethorpe presented gifts to the Indians, who gratefully received them. The colonists spent the day unloading supplies and organizing the settlement. For the next six days the work of unloading supplies continued using a crane they constructed to get the goods up the 40-foot bluff.

On the seventh day, Oglethorpe ordered the settlers to begin to "dig trenches for fixing palisades" in case of an Indian or Spanish attack. On the next day each family was given "an iron pott, frying pan, and three wooden bowls, a Bible, Common Prayer Book, and Whole Duty of Man." The men started sawing and splitting boards to make "clapp board houses." The families were divided into three groups; one clearing land for planting seed, the second "beginning the palisade," and the third cutting down trees for the town.

On the ninth day each able-bodied person was given "a musket and bayonet, cartridge box and belt" for defense. That same day, Colonel William Bull from Carolina arrived with

Portrait of Chief Tomochichi and his nephew Toonahowi, painted in England in 1734 while the two were visiting the Georgia Trustees there (Hargrett Rare Book and Manuscript Library, University of Georgia Libraries).

"Four Labourers" to help the settlers with construction work. That day Oglethorpe and Bull marked out the town square, the streets and 40 lots for houses. The first house was started that very day, and by the 12th of March there were "two clapboard houses built and three sawed houses framed...." Savannah was slowly taking form.

On the 11th Oglethorpe formed the inhabitants "under arms for the first time." He

His Majestys Colony of Georgia in America

By
George Iones

1 The Ships going up.
2 Mr Oglethorpes Tent.
3 The Crane & Bell.
4 The Tabernacle & Court House.

5 The publick Mill.
6 The House for Strangers.
7 The publick Oven.
8 The Draw Mill.

9 The Lott for the Church.
10 The publick Stores.
11 The Fort.
12 The Parsonage House.

13 The Pallisadoes.
14 The Guard House and
Battery of Cannon.
15 Hutchinsons Island.

divided them into four tithings of ten men each. That evening Peter Gordon set out the first guard and manned the clapboard guardhouse that was located "upon the most convenient part of the Bluff, for commanding the river both wayes."[2]

The town was indeed taking shape as the clapboard houses were going up with quick succession. The checkerboard design of the street plan presented an organized appearance. Streets ran north-south and east-west. Oglethorpe had named the main street for Colonel Bull. Johnson Square was named for the governor of South Carolina, and Drayton Street was named for Mrs. Ann Drayton, who had lent four sawyers to assist the colonists with building. Whitaker, St. Julian and Bryan streets were named for others from South Carolina who provided slaves or their own help for the new town.

While most of the lots were allocated for houses, a trust lot was set aside for Christ Church. Another lot of 10 acres was laid out as the Trustees' Garden, which was to serve as a nursery for trees, vegetables, and vines for the private gardens and orchards of the colonists. As early as 1734, peaches were being grown there. Ultimately some 40,000 white mulberry trees were planted at Savannah. While Charles Town had botanical gardens earlier, Savannah's was the first garden to have a purely public purpose and to be cultivated by a communal labor force.[3]

The town lots were all of uniform size, 20 by 30 yards. The houses were designated to be 24 by 16 feet, with log foundations raised to 30 inches above the ground. From the offices of the Georgia Trust in Palace Court, the old palace yard, at Westminster, London, the effort to clear five 5,000 acres of land as dictated in the plan for Savannah was viewed as being rather simple. They declared that "Half a Dozen strokes of an Ax" at the base of the tree would do it, as the acres of cleared land would suddenly appear. The images the Trustees had of clearing trees were not at all close to reality. The town's site was filled with big, tall pines from 70 to 100 feet tall. When the settlers were assigned to their homes in a ceremony held five months later on July 7, half the town was still covered with trees.

In Savannah, each man received his town lot, a garden plot of five acres and the remaining of his 50 acre maximum in the form of farmland. Deeds to that land were not issued until December 21. As the result of the precision and planning of Oglethorpe and the effort of his workmen, Savannah was indeed the first preplanned city in America. Thomas Causton, a magistrate and storekeeper, wrote that his new home was "beautifully laid out" and was quite pleasing with "an agreeable uniformity."

As men felled trees and built a small fort at the eastern end of the settlement, Oglethorpe selected four big pine trees to be spared from felling so he could pitch his tent. He would call that tent home for almost a year.[4] He also had personally supervised the arrangement of the small battery of cannon, with powder and shot stored in a magazine, all surrounded by 17-foot-high wooden palisades. Military drills had started before the first house had been framed. Within 90 days of the landing, the population of Savannah had grown to 160, with only 70 able to bear arms.[5]

From the very day of the landing at Savannah, Oglethorpe was incredibly busy with the myriad of "necessary things" as he personally directed most activities. The only real comfort he experienced was when he relaxed in his tent under his pines at the top of the bluff. For a man of his station, Oglethorpe was incredibly engaged in the day-to-day life of the colonial experience. He lived as they lived and for that he was called "Father" by many.

Opposite: "His Majesty's Colony of Georgia in America: View of Savannah from the River," drawn by George Jones, 1734 (Hargrett Rare Book and Manuscript Library, University of Georgia Libraries).

Three months after the *Anne* sailed from England, another ship, the *Volant*, was being fitted out to carry all the equipment that had been left behind, including supplies, books and four passengers-two artisans and two apprentices. After 11 weeks, in early March, the *Volant* sailed within sight of Savannah.

On April 6, the Georgia colonists witnessed a most sobering military funeral for Dr. William Cox, the only physician. He was the first of the colonial flock to actually die in Georgia. Tithings were called upon and small arms were fired with the Savannah bell "constantly toling." It was the first, but it would not be the last of such affairs in the coming months as the heat and fever raged among them.[6]

The next ship to visit Savannah was the small, 110-ton *James*, sailed by Captain James Yoakley. In May, Yoakley was given the prize that had been offered for the first ship to unload at Savannah that had not first docked at Charles Town or Port Royal. The *James'* passengers were much-sought-after Italian workers skilled in the propagation of silkworms and the processing of raw silk.

Also in May, and while visiting Charles Town, Oglethorpe wrote the Trustees that some of the prominent Carolina merchants wanted "the Liberty of trading with the Indians in our province." The merchants had offered £1,000 for the trade rights, but Oglethorpe felt that it was worth at least twice that amount. The general idea of giving Carolina official sanction to trade with the Indians was not to the advantage of Georgia. Oglethorpe's vision was that with the superior location and access to Indian country that Georgia afforded, Indian trade would soon make Savannah a busy trading center. He decided to defer the matter until he had an opportunity to resolve it with the Trustees on his visit back home to England.

Oglethorpe had other objections to Carolina and other requests as he reflected upon his first months in Georgia. He became convinced that to achieve his vision of Georgia there must be a total prohibition of Negroes and rum. Acquisition of Negroes would mean that the colonists would soon sink into idleness. It would not be a province of shopkeepers, traders and yeoman farmers as Oglethorpe envisioned. The opportunists and speculators lurking in Charles Town to take advantage of the Georgia colonists was a real potential problem to be averted. If rum were allowed in Georgia, soon it would be used in dealing with the Indians, as well as being harmful to the tranquility of the settlements. The issues of Negroes and rum would be a continual problem in Georgia and with Oglethorpe's dream for some time.[7]

While in Charles Town, Oglethorpe delivered a spirited address to the Carolina Assembly on June 9, speaking of their mutual threats of France, Spain and the Indians and telling of his upcoming early return to England. Before he traveled back to Georgia, the Carolina legislators and their wives gave Oglethorpe a grand dinner and dance where "there was the greatest Appearance of People of Fashion, that has been known upon such an occasion."[8] His visit helped to secure the passage of an act expected to raise £8,000 for Georgia from a fund collected after December 1 by a duty of three pence on each gallon of rum imported into Carolina.

Oglethorpe set out for Savannah on June 10 with serious concerns about his neighbor Carolina, even as he remembered the attention and compliments he had received. To make Georgia the place of his dreams, they must take what was good and proper from Carolina, but not become weak and undisciplined. Unfortunately, and to his dismay, he returned to find some of his people "very mutinous and impatient of Labour and Discipline." They were becoming idle as they worked Negroes and some had even tried to sell the food provided by the Trustees "for a little Rum Punch." To solve these two problems, Oglethorpe sent all the Negroes back to Carolina and forbade the settlers to have rum. This was difficult to enforce since rum could be acquired at the close-by Indian settlement. In an attempt to placate the drinkers, he allowed moderate amounts of wine to be drawn from the Trustees' supply in place of stronger drink.[9]

On July 7 the *Pearl* arrived with two dozen settlers, along with a potash maker, Roger Lacy. The Trustees had agreed to let Lacy bring 20 charity children to serve as indentured servants until age 24 to support the production of silk. For some reason, these children did not later sail with Lacy. Oglethorpe assigned them to establish a settlement at Thunderbolt.

That same day, Oglethorpe brought all the colonists together to witness the implementation of the Trustees' commission to establish a court and appoint local officials. The court appointed three bailiffs, a recorder and a registrar. All civil and criminal matters were to be handled by this body with the consultation of a 12 man jury summoned by the recorder. More officials could be summoned by the magistrates if they saw a need. The expectation was that the judicial body would convene court every six weeks and operate under the English system of petty and grand juries. One unique change was that lawyers were forbidden to operate in Georgia so that the colony would revert to the old ways when each man would plead his own cause in court. But before long, the lawyers entered Georgia and made themselves indispensable.

Though the system of the Georgia courts and officials was established that day, everyone knew where the true power lay. It was in the hands of James Edward Oglethorpe. With little to no experience in English law, it would be many years before the officials were able to master the full control and meet the expectations envisioned by the Trustees. It was Oglethorpe who would make the transition to full appointed rule a problem.[10] Though Oglethorpe held no official position over the colonists, he was the Trustees' de facto governor.

To everyone's surprise, on July 11, the *William and Sarah* arrived at Savannah with 39 Portuguese refugees and three German Jews. The Trustees were ultimately outraged, as they had simply appointed three Jewish men earlier to solicit citizens of funds for Georgia, but certainly not to come to Georgia themselves. These refugees were neither British nor Protestant. Oglethorpe knew how the Trustees would react, but welcomed the Jews with courtesy and openly rejoiced when he found a doctor among them. Now Savannah had Dr. Samuel Nunez to treat the ills of the citizens.

One month later, more ships filled with colonists found there way to Savannah. In August, the *Georgia Pink* arrived with 84 passengers. The ship's hold was filled with various tools and supplies, and "trinkets" the Trustees had intended as gifts worth £20 to the Indians. In September, the *Susannah* brought a few settlers and a silver chalice and paten for the still unbuilt church, donated by a close friend of Oglethorpe, the Reverend Samuel Wesley.

As the first six months and their first spring and summer passed, there was much that Oglethorpe could be thankful for. But there had been some sad losses. The Rev. Dr. Henry Herbert was sick and died at sea a month out on a passage to England aboard the *Baltic Merchant*. The first birth in Georgia colony had come to Mrs. Hanna Close on March 28. The baby girl was appropriately named "Georgia." Mrs. Close received a silver boat and spoon, which had earlier been promised for the first child born in the colony from Carolina planter James Hume. Georgia's father, Henry, died six months after Georgia's birth. Sadly, young Georgia followed her father to the grave two weeks later.

Death was all around them. James Goddard, a 38-year-old carpenter, died in early July, and two weeks later he was followed by his wife. Oglethorpe placed their daughter, Elizabeth Goddard, with wigmaker James Carwell and his wife, Margaret, and nine-year-old John Goddard was bound to gardener Joseph Fitzwalter. Margaret Caswell, age 32, died in September. On July 12, 31-year-old flax and hemp worker William Littell died along with his five-year-old daughter, Mary. In August "five of them dyed within one week." Aside from the first colonial death of Dr. Cox, his wife lost their third child, christened Mary, 10 days after her birth in October. As winter approached and the brutal heat of summer was behind them, the hand of death was slowed.[11]

On December 15, the *Savannah* arrived with 132 settlers, a Dr. William Watkins, and an improvised aristocrat from Ireland, William Wise. Wise had not been very enthusiastic about coming to Georgia, but it was deemed better than starving at home. In expectation of becoming lonely in the new world, Wise had smuggled aboard a woman "of easy virtue." Hearing of Wise's act, the Trustees later ordered him sent back.

Even as death stalked the colony, each arrival of a ship brought new hope as the settlers continued to come forth. As January of 1734 arrived, Oglethorpe conducted a census that revealed there were 437 persons in Georgia "receiving the support of the Trustees." It was not clear if these numbers included all the special arrivals in the province, like the shipload of approximately 40 Irish convicts who arrived in early January as survivors of a fierce storm at sea. Oglethorpe put these men into service as indentured servants at £5 per head to work the communal or widows' farms, or to aid the magistrates. The official Trustee records maintained in London noted that by June 9, 1734, 237 British and 104 foreign Protestant settlers and servants had been sent to the Province of Georgia. The record of land grants showed that there were also 195 adventurers and some 77 of their servants in Georgia.[12]

Determined to pay attention to the protection of the province, during the first year Oglethorpe had established the idea of a ring of fortifications around Savannah, each manned by 10 families. Evidence of execution of this plan was revealed in the January 1734 report to the Trustees which indicated that the 437 persons supported by Georgia were distributed with 259 at Savannah, 22 at Fort Argyle on the Ogeechee, three at Highgate, 39 at Hampstead, 33 at Abercorn, 21 at Tybee and 28 at Thunderbolt. Fort Argyle, the fort proposed by Captain MacPherson of the Rangers, was started in August of 1733 and supplied "with provision, cannon and ammunition." Another fort was set up on the creek at Thunderbolt under the direction of Hetherington and Bishop. Captain Ferguson of the *Carolina* scout boat undertook a similar fort on Skidaway Island.[13]

In an effort to explore the southern boundary of the province, on the morning of January 23 Oglethorpe left Savannah with 16 soldiers and two Indian guides, trailed by a yawl loaded with supplies and ammunition. On the evening of the 28th the force landed at St. Simons Island in a heavy rain. They spent the night under the Spanish moss draped from the live oak trees as the rain poured. The next morning, Oglethorpe decided that a fort should be constructed at St. Simons as protection from the Spanish at St. Augustine. The party then moved up the Ogeechee River to Fort Argyle for a short visit before returning to Savannah.[14]

As the first-year anniversary of settlement approached, the condition of the colony was a mixture of successes and failures. The plan had called for the colonists to be self-sufficient after the first year. This was not achieved for a variety of reasons. For those who were fortunate to be allocated fertile land that required little clearing, they were able to grow potatoes, peas and other vegetables in 1733. For others who received land covered with pine barrens, marshes, or sand, the struggle to grow crops was most difficult. Some of these disappointed settlers made the decision to abandon Georgia in favor of moving to Carolina and Charles Town to seek better opportunity.

To make up for the food shortage, Oglethorpe purchased substantial quantities of rice and other foods for the settlers. During the first year, the Trustees supplied a guaranteed subsistence to each male which turned out to be 312 pounds of beef or pork, 104 pounds of rice, flour and peas or Indian corn; 16 pounds of cheese, 12 pounds of lamp oil, and one pound of spun cotton. Women and children received fractional allowances, and servants received less meat and more rice. As time would tell, a decade later Georgia colonists had still not reached self-sufficiency, as food and staples were shipped from as far away as New York.

On March 23, 1734, Oglethorpe boarded the man-of-war *Aldborough* at Charles Town to sail to England with a most unique person, the noble Chief Tomochichi. The chief had been banished for political reasons from a tribe of the Lower Creeks. This most dignified, tall and vigorous man was 91 years old the day Oglethorpe met him on the site of Savannah. He would always be a noble man of truth, honor, and most supportive of the colonists of Georgia. Oglethorpe had gained a real love for this man, and the idea of presenting this special friend would in itself answer at a glance many questions of the Trustees and the aristocracy.

Oglethorpe decided to delay his departure to England to support the settlement of Salzburger Lutherans. Oglethorpe greeted the group and then "return'd to Georgia to give directions for their Settlemt." Back in September 1733, the Trustees authorized Samuel Urlsperger to gather 300 refugees from Salzburger or Bertoldsgoden to sail to Georgia. The Salzburgers were from the historic valley of the Salzach River in Austria. These Lutherans were a few of the 30,000 persons who left their homes to avoid the persecution of Protestants by the autocratic archbishops of Salzburg.[15]

In November the *Purisburg* picked up its passengers at Rotterdam and later sailed from Dover, England, on January 8 with 73 persons including 47 Salzburgers. The trans–Atlantic voyage ended at Charles Town on March 7. They arrived at Savannah five days later. The Trustees expected these settlers to intermingle and intermarry with the British Georgians, but the Salzburgers had another idea. Led by Baron Georg Philipp Friedrich Von Reck, they balked at having to live in Savannah. They wanted their own settlement in order to maintain their language and customs, as well as find a place as similar to the mountainous home of Salzburg as possible.

In response to these demands, Oglethorpe decided to yield to the Salzburgers. As recorded in Von Reck's *Journal,* Oglethorpe took the settlers up the Savannah River where they picked a spot "21 Miles from the Town of Savannah, and 30 miles from the Sea, where there are Rivers, little Hills, clear Brooks, cool Springs, a fertile Soil, and plenty of Grass." They called the place Ebenezer, meaning a "place of help" or "divine haven."[16]

After the self-imposed delay, Oglethorpe's voyage to England began on May 7, 1734. In company with Chief Tomochichi were leaders of the tribe including Hillispylli, the war chief of the Lower Creeks, and four of his chiefs; a Yuchi chief; his wife, Senauki; Toonahowi, his nephew and adopted son; and their attendants. Upon arrival from the speedy, and near record, month-long voyage, Oglethorpe hosted his Indian guests with the help of his sister Anne from France at his estate at Godalming while he called on the Trustees in London.

On Friday, June 21, Oglethorpe met with 15 of the Trustees at the Palace Court. Aside from other business, a resolution was passed expressing that "thanks be return'd to James Oglethorpe Esqr for the many and great Services he has done the Colony of Georgia." In London, quarters were rented for the Indian guests in Westminster near the Georgia Office. On their first evening in London, the Trustees gave the Indians a "grand entertainment" which was concluded with a bonfire, bells ringing and "other Demonstrations of Joy and Gratitude." On July 3, Tomochichi and party made their formal visit to the Trustees where brief addresses were exchanged of good will.

The state visit with the king was set up for August 1. Tomochichi and his queen were adorned with scarlet outfits trimmed in white rabbit fur with gold lace. Their Indian faces were "variously painted, some half black, others triangular, and others with bearded Arrows instead of Whiskers." They were taken to the court by three of the King's coaches, each drawn by six large horses. At the door to Kensington Palace, they were saluted by the king's bodyguard, as the Duke of Grafton, who was the lord chamberlain to the king, presented them to King George II, seated on his throne. Tomochichi presented His Majesty several eagle feathers—the highest Indian symbol of esteem. It was a grand encounter as the two worlds came together at court, among the speeches of the king and the chief.[17]

The triumphant visit to England was marred only by the death of a warrior chief who died of smallpox. He was buried in St. John's Cemetery at Westminster. He became the first Indian ever buried on English soil. During the visit, the Indian guests toured the sights of London. They were the guests of Dr. William Walker, the Archbishop of Canterbury, at Lambeth. Together they visited Eton College, the Tower of London, Greenwich Hospital and other stately government buildings. Chief Tomochichi was impressed with the riches of the empire.[18]

While in London, Oglethorpe pursued the second objective of his visit, involving silk. Before the Georgia founding process had begun in 1730, the leaders had distorted ideas of the climate in the region. The plan was to have Georgia produce all the silk that England needed. Along with the 50-acre land grants to the colonists of Georgia, they each were granted 100 morus alba, better known as white mulberry trees. In these trees to be tended were to be silkworms from eggs sent by the Trustees on the first voyage of the *Anne*. Oglethorpe's friend Sir Thomas Lombe took his raw silk from Georgia to London and had a quantity of organzine produced. Caroline of Ansbach, the queen of Great Britain, used this silk for the dress she wore on October 30 to the king's birthday party.

The return to England gave Oglethorpe a chance to correct his previous campaign that portrayed Georgia as the promised land. In 1735, he made an effort to reveal that the old image of "the most delightful country of the universe" had been properly described as a place where settlers might have "great Hardships in the Beginning." There would be no housing until the settler cleared land and provided his own shelter. The men would stand guard on an appointed rotation. The summers would be hot with "Flies in Abundance," and even worse the "little red Vermin called Potatoe Lice which in Summer time crawl up the Legs of those that lie in the Woods, and if scratched raise Blisters." For their own health, temperance was necessary as "Sicknesses were dangerous to those who drank distilled Liquors." Though warned of the difficulties, if a family was "industrious," and strong in stamina they could succeed "in a comfortable Way."[19]

Before Oglethorpe sailed back to Georgia, he appealed to Parliament for a defensive force for Georgia. He detailed a plan to establish 18 forts to be manned with 40 soldiers each, plus two new fortified towns. He needed at least £25,800, and though the Parliament had little desire to defend Georgia, they had every reason to support of the rich and thriving colony of South Carolina. In fact, Oglethorpe left with a commitment of £26,000.

With this appropriation, Georgia was to move from the era of philanthropism to that of an agricultural and mercantile colony, and a "military bastion of imperial Britain." During the lifetime of the Trust, Parliament would pump a most significant sum of £401,886 into the struggling little colony of Georgia. Concerned about the exclusive control

Oglethorpe held over the funds, the Trustees directed that a secretary would be selected to accompany him on his second voyage to Georgia. Accordingly, the Trustees chose as the secretary-designate the Rev. Charles Wesley. Traveling with Charles was Wesley's older missionary brother, John.[20]

With rumblings of imminent dispute with Carolina; reported insurrections in Georgia; and complaints about the surveyor of the colony, Noble Jones, and the shopkeeper, Thomas Causton, Oglethorpe needed to return to Georgia as soon as possible. Thus, on September 25, 1735, Oglethorpe gave a farewell dinner for the "Agents of the several British Colonies on the Continent of America" at Pontack's. On the 29th he met with the queen, and finally, at 9 A.M. on October 14, Oglethorpe set out from Westminster for Cowes to join the ship *Symond*.[21]

At Cowes, he discovered the largest party ever to sail to Georgia. Ready to sail on a convoy were the *Prince of Wales*, the *Symond*, and the *London Merchant*, under the escort of the sloop-of-war *Hawk*. With the *Symond* were designated some 123 passengers and a contingent of 100 Highlanders, 100 male servants with 50 wives and children, 40 English males with 60 wives and children, 100 Austrians, in excess of 100 Palatines, 43 Swiss Grisons going as servants and 55 Moravians.

The numerous departure dates just seemed to be meaningless as the postponements continued because of contrary winds. On October 27, Oglethorpe reported that two other vessels at Cowes on the Isle of Wight had passengers that were in good health and "behaved very orderly." On November 19, Oglethorpe wrote, "I hope by the Blessing of God we shall be able to go thro' the Undertaking." After a fever forced him to bed, on December 3 Oglethorpe was frustrated as he avowed, "I had rather have run the danger of my life at sea than have risqued the losing of the season of the year in Georgia and the sickness which may probably happened to the people by lying here. Some are already ill!"[22] As tempers flared aboard ship, Oglethorpe spent 15 shillings to bring fresh water to the voyagers to "wash up the Linnen they had dirted during our stay in Harbour." He also "furnished Flour & Plumbs to make Puddens."[23]

On December 10, Oglethorpe issued a formal complaint to the Admiralty of the delay of Royal Navy captain James Gascoigne in reporting for duty to command the escort. Finally, that same day, after months of delay, Oglethorpe sent his final message, "God be praised we at last have got an Easterly Wind in the morning" and he sailed with a most sickly bunch of fellow voyagers.[24]

Oglethorpe ordered twice-daily prayers with the support of the numerous ministers, his dinner guests Benjamin Ingham of Queen's College at Oxford, Moravians August Gottlieb Spangenberg and Bishop David Nitschmann, and two of the most interesting people ever to visit the early colony of Georgia, John and Charles Wesley. The voyage was unusually rough according to some accounts, but it passed with no serious accidents or events. John Wesley's journal recorded "the Waves of the Sea were mighty and raged horribly. They rose up to the Heavens above, and clave down to Hell beneath."[25]

In transit, the Wesleys were impressed with Oglethorpe's fairness and effectiveness even as the waves promised certain destruction. Ingham wrote of their leader as constantly encouraging the ill while he ate only "salt provisions" so they could "give the fresh to the sick." When the sea became incredibly high, Oglethorpe gave up his dry cabin to the sick while he slept in a hammock. Though of lofty station, Oglethorpe was never one for luxury. He was a man of austere tastes and was comfortable enduring the hardships of his fellow colonists to their delight and appreciation.[26] Now Oglethorpe's second visit to his colonial Georgia was in dynamic motion on the fury of the Atlantic waves.

3

The Spanish and Georgia

"If we do not attack, we shall be attacked."

The colonial expedition sailed into the mouth of the Savannah River on February 5, 1736. Aboard the *Symond*, Oglethorpe decided that the settlers should remain aboard until he could transport them to their new home, Frederica, on St. Simons Island. Before he would deliver them there, he had to visit Savannah to speak with the officials and promulgate new laws from the Trustees, as well as deal with a conflict with the first group of Salzburgers.

Reaching the town, Oglethorpe sent fresh meat and provisions to the settlers.[1] Though they would have to sleep on the ships at night, the settlers landed at 8 A.M. on Friday the 6th at Cockspur Island near Savannah. On landing and ready to begin his work in America, John Wesley recorded, "Mr. Oglethorpe led us to a rising ground where we all kneeled down to give thanks." On a Sunday, a month and a day later, John preached his first sermon in America in Savannah beginning with "the epistle for the day, being the thirteenth of First Corinthians." On March 13, he held his first service inside a church attended by some 20 worshippers.

The Salzburger dispute, which forced a significant delay for Oglethorpe's colonists, was over the poor quality of the ground at the designated place of settlement at Ebenezer. Boltzius, the group's leader, called the soil fit for nothing but "peese and potatoes." Though disappointed in their position, and calling them "ignorant & obstinate," Oglethorpe granted their request to relocate to Red Bluff, at the confluence of the Ebenezer River and the Savannah River. They named the place New Ebenezer and soon turned it into the most prosperous town in Georgia.

Intent on establishing his new fort system and making sure all was prepared for the colonists of the second voyage, Oglethorpe and a small group of the settlers sailed from Savannah, landing at St. Simon Island on February 18, 1736. The next day, Oglethorpe started coordinating the work on the fort that would anchor the new town of Frederica. Oglethorpe laid out the town, and the fort that was to protect it. The ramparts were to be sloped and a moat dug out. He prescribed that temporary huts with palmetto tree fronds would provide shelter until the rest of the settlers arrived.

But Oglethorpe was too busy to stay put. Four days after landing at St. Simons Island, he crossed over the bay to Darien and met with the Highlanders working on Fort Darien. In support of Oglethorpe's plans to provide a real military presence in Georgia, for which he had received the approvals from Parliament and the Trustees during his last visit to

England, troops were being sent to defend Georgia. On the previous October 18, the *Prince of Wales* had sailed from Inverness with Scottish Highlanders under the command of Hugh Mackay. With the landing of these seasoned veterans of European wars at Savannah on January 10, 1736, the colony finally had a real defense. Soon, under the command of Mackay, the Highlanders were sent via ship to the abandoned Fort King George on the Altamaha River. Landing at New Inverness (Darien) on January 19, the Highlanders erected the new fort.

When Oglethorpe arrived at Darien, he found it impressive. The troops were "a most manly appearance with their Plads, broad Swords, Targets & Fire Arms." Hugh Mackay had done an excellent job getting the fort ready. Though Mackay offered "a very good bed" to Oglethorpe, the leader chose to sleep "under a great Tree." The other officers followed Oglethorpe's lead and likewise slept though "the Night was very cold." Before Oglethorpe took his leave from Darien, a body of Rangers arrived from Savannah, having taken a road and establishing a communications route "for Horsemen between the two Towns."[2]

In the evening air of February 25, Oglethorpe returned to the main body of the settlers still living in the Savannah River off Cockspur Island to explain that he was having difficulty securing a ship of sufficient size or a captain willing to sail them to St. Simons. These settlers had been stranded in the Savannah River for three weeks since their first arrival from England. Oglethorpe explained that the only way he could get them to their new home was to have them sail over in small boats, a journey expected to take as many as 14 days. With the risk so high and comforts so low, he said they could elect to settle in Savannah if they desired. He gave the settlers only two hours to decide whether they had enough confidence in Oglethorpe to shuttle them to Frederica safely. The vote was unanimous in favor in following "Father" Oglethorpe.

The flotilla of boats, accompanied by Oglethorpe's scout boat in the rear, set out along the inland waterways to St. Simons Island. The lead boat held all the "strong Beer" as the peraugers sailed slowly in tight formation to the destination. Encountering no problems along the way, the flotilla sailed to St. Simons in only five days. The settlers landed and were reunited with their lead party, and then taken to their temporary huts.

With Fort Darien now ready and garrisoned, Oglethorpe had a certain pride in his second major fort at the mouth of the Altamaha River at St. Simons Island. Though it was only 124 feet square, Fort Frederica was built to protect the southernmost extremity of the colony, as the Georgia Charter defined it, from the Spanish threat.

Arriving at Frederica on March 9, Charles Wesley immediately took up his duties as the secretary to Oglethorpe, as his brother, John, served as the parish minister to the Georgia colonists and pastor to Christ Church in Savannah. On his arrival Charles noted, "Mr. Oglethorpe received me very kindly."[3] But soon Charles would become discouraged as he was only assigned to scribe private letters for Oglethorpe. Almost immediately, Oglethorpe turned against Charles. He forced Charles to sleep on the floor of a hut, and when this arrangement made him desperately ill, Oglethorpe denied his request for a bed. Bewildered, Charles finally discovered that two women had been spreading vicious rumors about him.

Oglethorpe apologized for his behavior and reinstated Charles's privileges, but Charles remained unwell and discouraged. Soon afterward, Oglethorpe ordered Charles to return to England and put down vicious reports that Georgia was in shambles. Charles was only too happy to go. After only five months in Georgia, Charles Wesley sailed away from his troubles in Georgia at the hands of Oglethorpe on July 26. He arrived back in England on December 3, 1736.

On April 18, Oglethorpe made a move that would ultimately prove to be quite serious and most provocative. It would be the definitive end of Oglethorpe's colonizing era in Georgia as he turned his attention and efforts to the Spanish threat. With 40 Yamacraw warriors, a party of Rangers and 30 indentured Highlanders, Oglethorpe, with daring, moved past the borders of Georgia to survey an island south of the one he named for his friend Sir Joseph Jekyll. At the suggestion of young warrior Toonahowi, Oglethorpe named the island Cumberland, for the Duke of Cumberland who had presented the Indian a gold watch.

At the only geographical feature that one could safely call a hill on Cumberland Island, Oglethorpe erected Fort Saint Andrew. The fort, built with dimensions 65 feet deep and twice as wide, was located some 50 miles south of Darien, which made it about one-fourth the way between the Altamaha River and Spanish St. Augustine. Clearly aware that this fort was beyond the domain of Georgia, Oglethorpe was unaware that special envoy Charles Dempsey, at the direction of the British secretary of state, Thomas Pelham-Holles, the Duke of Newcastle, was on a peaceful mission to Florida to settle the disputes over territorial claims with Spain.

From Frederica, Oglethorpe sent Newcastle information on his activities relating to Georgia's charter. He revealed that his friend Tomochichi had claims on the island and area extending to the St. John's River. Oglethorpe wrote that the colony should extend to the tip of a newly discovered small island at St. George's Point as the "farthest part of the dominions of His Majesty on the seacoast of North America." Later he would defend his new boundary claim, declaring that the river of St. John's was actually a southern branch of the Altamaha, which was wholly incorrect as he knew. A map was even forged to support his claim.

With his bold claim, Oglethorpe had doubled the coastline of Georgia. Before long, Oglethorpe had established an outpost, Fort St. George, "within earshot of muskets" from the Spanish on the St. John's River. With no authorization, Oglethorpe began negotiations with Spanish Florida's governor, Francisco de Moral Sanchez. Soon Moral was recalled to Madrid with the anger of the Spanish authorities.

Realizing the serious situation he had placed the British government in, Oglethorpe decided that he must return to England to clear up the boundary issue. In a letter in October he related, "All matters with the Spanish are regulated, and the governor of Augustine contented. Therefore all being safe I shall set out immediately for Europe." With haste, Oglethorpe sailed on Tuesday, November 23, aboard the *Two Brothers*. After a difficult voyage of 70 days, the ship finally arrived on the English coast, where he spent another nine days fogbound. Oglethorpe landed at Ilfercomb, Wales, on January 2, 1737. He was 41 years old.

Oglethorpe had left Georgia in less than ideal straits. While Oglethorpe was focusing on the Spanish threat, many settlers had departed Georgia for greener pastures. Food had become scarce and expensive. Incredibly, rent in Savannah was in some cases greater than in London. Though many Germans and other Europeans had become self-sufficient, many of the colonists had not been as successful in fair Georgia and found themselves poor and in debt. The dream of a utopian society was now a faded memory as Oglethorpe prepared to meet the icy reception he expected back at home.[4]

In four days, Oglethorpe arrived at the Old Palace Yard at Westminster, London. On Friday, the next day, he began a series of important meetings. First, he had an audience with Queen Caroline, where he was encouraged to seek a meeting with His Majesty. He promised to return with "all the latest intelligence concerning His Majesty's southernmost

North American domain." From the palace, Oglethorpe hurried on to see Sir Robert Walpole, the prime minister, at 10 Downing Street. There he pushed for support for Georgia. What Georgia needed was money, which was of course all too common a request from James Edward Oglethorpe. After leaving Walpole, he moved to attend a short session with the Trustees. There he set up a session scheduled for Monday, January 12, to cover the detailed events of his second and quite eventful stay in Georgia.

At the January meeting, with Oglethorpe in attendance, the Trustees decided that the first chief civil administrator and trust secretary of the colony of Georgia would be William Stephens. At the time, Stephens had been working for Colonel Samuel Horsey as his agent in London. His new commission came on April 18, which bound other Georgia officials to "pay due Regard to all and every the Instructions" that he should give. He was directed, among other things, to take a census, report on the behavior of the magistrates, provide an accounting for the cultivation of crops, and to report a status of how often the people attended divine worship. He was also urged to push the other officials to send in their reports. Officially Stephens was simply an agent of the Trustees, tasked to provide reporting.[5]

The appointment of William Stephens should not have been a surprise to Oglethorpe. The founder had always been negligent in corresponding as often as the Trustees expected. Back in March of 1734, James Vernon approached Percival (Earl of Egmont) complaining of "the neglect Mr. Oglethorpe shows in not corresponding with us frequently, and thereby keeping us in great ignorance of his proceedings in Georgia and the state of the Colony there, he not having writ to us since December last, and never once in any full and satisfactory manner, though by all accounts from thence writ occasionally by others he is very indefatigable in the settlement of the Colony." Some 10 days after Vernon's complaint the Trustees' Committee of Correspondence drew up a letter to Oglethorpe noting the situation and asking Oglethorpe to find a suitable person to correspond with the Trustees. Oglethorpe never complied with the request, and though rather delayed in taking action, the die of Stephens' appointment was cast.[6]

Of the newly appointed Secretary Stephens, the Earl of Egmont wrote, "This is highly pleasing to us, he being a Man of cool temper and excellent Sense, and great industry and punctualness, and by him we were sure of having constant information of the State of the Colony concerning which hitherto we had been kept too much in the dark." Stephens, born in 1671, was a native of the Isle of Wight and the son of Sir William Stephens, who had been the island's lieutenant governor. Colonel Stephens had attended Winchester, King's College at Cambridge, and studied law at the Middle Temple, London. In 1697, he married Mary, the daughter of Sir Richard Newdigate of Warwickshire.

In 1702, William Stephens ran for Parliament from Newport, Isle of Wight, and was elected. Under Queen Anne, Stephens served as a staunch Tory and was reelected from his conservative constituency in 1715. In 1722, he lost his support in Newport but was able to regain his seat representing Newtown, also on the Isle of Wight. In Parliament, Stephens held various posts, including the position as commissioner for the victualling-a position that required him to entertain often. With such lavish entertaining, Stephens was financially ruined and lost his seat in Parliament in 1727.

Stephens then took a position with the York Buildings Company, which sold lumber and speculated on lands in Scotland. When that business was reorganized and the assets sold, he lost his job and was pursued from the Highlands to London by swarms of creditors. In 1736, he took a commission from an old friend and an associate from York Buildings Company, Colonel Samuel Horsey, and traveled to South Carolina. There he was to inspect and survey the land grant Horsey had been given on the Carolina side of the Savannah River.

Stephens arrived in Georgia the first time in April 1736 at age 65, and waited for over a month in Savannah while Oglethorpe was tending to affairs in the southern part of the province. When, in late May, Oglethorpe finally arrived, they both exchanged less than friendly greetings. Both had known each other in Parliament and even more importantly, Oglethorpe had little interest in seeing land interests in Carolina go to others as he had aspirations of his own for property. Oglethorpe did advise Stephens on what to look for when he moved upriver to scout the lands.

After six weeks of inspecting the Horsey barony, the exhausted Stephens again met with Oglethorpe before the latter was about to return to England. Stephens noted that Oglethorpe was most critical of the Carolinians because they did not agree with Georgia policy. Oglethorpe explained of the "many Slippery tricks" the leaders in Charles Town pulled on Georgia regarding land matters. During one four- to five-hour diatribe, Oglethorpe discussed the possibility of revenge against the Carolinians. Stephens noted that with "great warmth" Oglethorpe said he "would make some of them repent dearly." Stephens felt the words from the founder were too overheated and he wrote, "Much more pass'd in Conversation, tending the same way, not to be committed to Paper." Stephens returned to England with his assignment completed with the feeling that Oglethorpe was a hotheaded man without an objective view of Carolina.

At his appointment with a six-year term as the Georgia secretary position in April 1737, Stephens decided to take his third son, Thomas, with him. Stephens received a 500-acre land grant, free passage to Georgia, servants to clear his land, and £50 spending money with £50 more upon request. A committee was set up to draw up his instructions, which were sealed on April 27 with "a paper Sign'd of more private instructions to him."[7]

Happy to receive this assignment from Parliament, Stephens sailed on August 10 aboard the *Mary Anne*, reached Charles Town on October 20 and arrived at his new job on Yamacraw Bluff at Savannah on the first of November.[8] From the moment he landed on Georgia soil, he was to be beset with challenges.

Through the hard work of Oglethorpe to calm the waters of discontent, the Parliament voted on March 17 to invest another £20,000 in Georgia. But this was not the only delightful thing to happen for Oglethorpe in 1737. To settle the military administration of the southernmost colony, on June 19 Oglethorpe kissed the hand of King George II and accepted the appointment as "General and Commander in Chief of all and singular his Majesty's Forces employed and to be employed in his Majesty's provinces of South Carolina and Georgia in America; and likewise to be Captain of that Independent Company of Foot doing Duty in his Majesty's said Province of South Carolina." With his new salary of £1,000 per year, which was more than three times what the rents on his estate brought, a man who had never worn the uniform of any branch of the British armed forces had become captain of foot, colonel of a yet-to-be-established regiment, and the general of all the forces in two colonies in America.

In July of 1737 John Wesley, now at age 33, went house to house in Savannah to take a census. The count of the inhabitants was 518 people.[9] It was not the only thing John was involved in at the time. While Oglethorpe was in England working a deal with Parliament and the Trustees on Spain and on Georgia funding, Wesley had fallen in love with one of his Savannah parishioners, Sophy Hopkey. A good-natured girl of 18, "Miss Sophy," as John always called her, was one of his first friends in America. Although he enjoyed spending time with Sophy, he feared that a serious relationship would end his career as a missionary. After much prayer, he painfully resolved not to marry until he had begun his work.

Following this announcement, Sophy, who usually took breakfast and lessons with John, told him she would no longer meet with him alone. He was, however, permitted to visit her at her home. After one such visit, John wrote in his journal: "This was indeed an hour of trial. Her words, her air, her eyes, her every motion and gesture, were full of such softness and sweetness. I know not what might have been the consequence had I then but touched her hand! And how I avoided it I know not. Surely God is over all."

Soon after this visit, John received the shocking news that Sophy had agreed to wed Mr. William Williamson—"if Mr. Wesley had no objection." John wondered at first if she was testing him, but he concluded that if she had given her consent to be married, his chance must have

Portrait of John Wesley (Hargrett Rare Book and Manuscript Library, University of Georgia Libraries).

passed. Though distraught, he offered no objection. Inside, though, John thought he would die of grief and he even made out his will.

Following Sophy's marriage, John threw himself into his work. He tried to be the Williamsons' pastor, but of course it did not work. Five months later, John refused to serve Mrs. Williamson Holy Communion. No doubt jealousy played a role in his decision, though he said he rejected her because he knew of unconfessed sin in her life. Wrath from all over the colony fell upon John's head, and the Williamsons sued for defamation of character. The trial dragged on for months, and finally John told his journal, "I saw clearly the hour was come for leaving this place." John left Savannah with three companions toward Purrysburg, South Carolina, reaching Charles Town on December 2.[10] John left for England 20 days later, and landed at Deal on February 12. His missionary career in America was over.[11]

While Oglethorpe was in London, he had renewed his friendship with Charles Wesley to such an extent that Oglethorpe offered Charles the opportunity to return to Georgia. When John Wesley returned home he presented his largely negative account of the situation in Georgia to the Trustees, as had his brother on his return. The experience of the Wesleys in Georgia was a sad failure for Oglethorpe, the Wesley brothers and Georgia. John's religious ways were too dogmatic and strict to suit a frontier world. He would often hold service at 5 A.M. and seemed to preach to the specific sins of individuals in the congregation. Charles and Oglethorpe just did not get along. But the future would be brighter for the Wesleys. Ultimately John would become known as the founder of the Methodist Church and Charles would come to write hundreds of hymns.[12]

Before Oglethorpe sailed back to Georgia, he invited his colleagues to see his regiment march through Holborn, followed by "a very elegant dinner" at the White Hart Inn. At 2 P.M., Major Cooke led the regiment smartly by the crowd of well-wishers. On May 1, 11 of the Trustees held a farewell dinner for Oglethorpe to the whispers of conversation over the poor state of cash in England.

From Spithead on June 6, 1738, Oglethorpe sent his last correspondence to the secretary of state repeating his old arguments for maintaining a firm stance against Spain in the boundary dispute over Georgia. A month later, Oglethorpe sailed on his third journey to his beloved Georgia he founded. The general sailed aboard the man-of-war *Blandford* with his 42nd Regiment of Foot embarked. Another man-of-war, the *Hector*, sailed as escort to five transport ships filled with new colonists. On September 18, Oglethorpe landed at St. Simons Island, Georgia, for his third visit.[13]

After spending time at St. Simons, Oglethorpe traveled to Savannah on October 10. He waited only seven days before he held a mass meeting with the colonists and "made a pathetick Speech" to the town according to William Stephens.[14] Oglethorpe told his followers, "it cut him to the heart to be obliged to tell them that he had the Trustees' order to shut up the stores." Ignoring the formal role of Stephens, Oglethorpe talked about the debt that the Trustees were in and said that retrenchment was necessary. The contents of the store would have to be applied to the debt.

Oglethorpe returned to Frederica on the 25th after having left behind "a gloomy Prospect ... and many sorrowful Countenances." Stephens was distraught that Oglethorpe would set about to beat down the citizens as he "laid the Whole open." Stephens wrote, "The greatest Part of the Clamour fell to my Share, which indeed gave me great Disquiet." Oglethorpe returned to Savannah on November 11 to "upbraid" the recently dismissed Georgia storekeeper, Thomas Causton. Thomas Jones, the new storekeeper for the colony, had written the general that Causton was "casting aspersions" on his good name in Savannah. Sadly for Stephens, Oglethorpe took no action is helping him resolve any of the pending issues before the people.

The malcontents in Georgia were preparing a formal appeal to the Trustees for resolution of their present conditions. They wanted slave labor and clear titles to their land. The economic problems were starkly obvious to them. Prosperity was not to be had when the expensive and unreliable white labor made profitable deals impossible. Labor was so expensive in Georgia that timber could not be cut and processed "fit for a foreign market but at double the expense of other colonies."

Only a few miles away from "stagnant Savannah" in Carolina, businesses able to use black labor were busy loading ships with timber products as Savannah saw its sea traffic dwindle. Georgia was so unproductive that ships leaving Savannah charged extra high fees because they left the port with their holds empty. Georgia simply had no goods to trade. Competing with Carolina was impossible as a vicious cycle of economic ruin continued, driven by the restrictions laid upon Georgia by the high-minded Trustees and the charter.[15]

Oglethorpe was not totally unsympathetic in these economic matters, but concern over the military situation was laying heavy upon his focus and actions. To the Trustees he reported, "I can see nothing but destruction to the colony unless some assistance be immediately sent us." Oglethorpe now began a self-inflicted campaign of laying his fortune on the line to support the Georgia colonists. Before the impact of Oglethorpe's decision had been realized, he received disturbing news.

As it turned out, some of his regulars from the 42nd Regiment of Foot from Gibraltar were malcontents who expected extra pay for time at sea. After having experienced numerous delays in traveling to Georgia, in November at Fort St. Andrews on Cumberland Island the soldiers engaged in a full mutiny. One of the mutineers fired at their leader, but missed the target and singed Oglethorpe's uniform. Several others tried to fire off a round but failed to achieve their objective. As Captain Hugh Mackay received a flesh wound, Oglethorpe grabbed a musket away from one shooter and threatened to use it as a club if they did not desist. The mutineers broke ranks and dispersed in awe of Oglethorpe. The general proceeded to deliver them back pay out of his own funds. A Carolina leader attributed the mutiny to a soldier with Spanish leanings "who had so much of a Roman Catholic spirit as to harbour an aversion to Protestant heretics."

On the 9th day of December in 1738, a group of 121 freeholders drew up a formal petition to the Trustees for the "Use of Negroes with proper limitations" and to gain a new system of land tenure. The message they sent was clear. Either the Trustees provided greater flexibility to the Georgians, or they would take things in their own hands. Oglethorpe was now asking Parliament for £17,000 to cover a portion of the pressing needs—£8,000 for debts, £5,000 for local colonists and £12,000 for the military.

As the situation with internal strife festered, the negotiations between Britain and Spain at El Pardo were heating up too. The Trustees wanted the British to stand firm on the Georgia boundary issues. In the climate of the day, Oglethorpe's supporters in Parliament gained Walpole's support for a bill to fund the colony for another year. In March of 1739, the Convention of El Pardo had yielded agreement on most of the issues of dispute except for the Georgia question. But the more that Elizabeth Farnese, the greedy and ambitious second wife of Spain's mad King Philip V, took over, the British turned more toward the idea of a war.

Oglethorpe learned the news of Parliament's funding allocation of £20,000 and referred to it in his note to the Trustees, dated July 4, as he provided information on his planned departure for a parlay with the leaders of the key Indian tribes. By this time, Oglethorpe was clear that there would be war with the Spanish very soon. His message to William Bull, the lieutenant governor of South Carolina, noted, "If we do not attack, we shall be attacked."

The Spanish were not the only potential threat Oglethorpe had to confront in Georgia. As the appointed British commissioner of Indian affairs, Oglethorpe agreed to parlay with the Indians at Coweta. This was the principal town of the Lower Creeks, which was located on the Chattahoochee River on the western boundary of present-day Georgia. On the long and difficult 200-mile trip to Coweta, Captain George Dunbar, Ensign John Lemon and 25 handpicked Europeans and Indians accompanied the general. The meeting resulted in Oglethorpe gaining support against the Spanish from the Cherokees, Choctaws, Chickasaws and especially the Creeks. Oglethorpe was also able to gain legal title to vast tracts of Georgia land, and extended the southern border to the St. Johns River. These gains were critical in the coming years in keeping Georgia from being annexed by South Carolina, while securing the ultimate independence of Georgia.

On his return from Coweta by way of Augusta, Oglethorpe received unofficial word of Anglo-Spanish hostilities. When Oglethorpe reached Savannah he found dispatches from England. After the June 15 declaration from King George II that suggested that he should "annoy the Subjects of Spain," Oglethorpe made plans to initiate offensive action against St. Augustine. News of the English declaration of war with Spain brought out the citizens and "the Militia gave three Handsome Vollies with their small Arms ... as it were in Defiance, without the Appearance of any Dread of the Spaniards."[16]

On October 3, Oglethorpe called a meeting of the citizens at the courthouse. Gathered, with the magistrates clothed in their gowns at their benches, Oglethorpe proceeded to explain the present danger of the Spanish, and the support they could expect from the Indian nations. He also hoped they would all see the sails of the British fleet protecting the coastal regions. Savannah residents were asked to be watchful and brave.[17]

Two days later, citizens of Savannah and Oglethorpe were saddened by the death of their exceptional friend and ally Tomochichi. The old chief had lived to age 97. His corpse was brought up the river as Oglethorpe, the magistrates and people of Savannah met it at the water's edge. The body was carried to Perceval Square (now Wright Square) to the funeral ceremony. A gun salute was fired as the great Indian leader was laid to rest in a grave soon to be marked with Georgia granite stone. The London *Gentlemen's Magazine* provided an account of the events: "He desired his Body might be buried amongst the English in the Town of Savannah ... the Pall was supported by the General, Colonel Stephens, Colonel Montaigut, Mr. Carteret, Mr. Lemon, and Mr. Maxwell. It was followed by the Indians and Magistrates and People to the Town.... There was the Respect paid of firing Minute Guns from the Battery all the time during the Burial, and funeral firing with small Arms by the Militia, who were under arms."[18]

It was not long before the war with the Spanish came to Georgia. On November 16, 1739, Oglethorpe wrote from Frederica to the Trustees notifying them that the Spanish had struck first at Amelia Island. Apparently one of the scout boats first "took the alarm" but not before the Spanish party had "surprised two poor sick men [Highlander soldiers], cut off their heads, mangled their bodies most barbarously, and as soon as a party and boat appeared ... they retired with utmost precipitation."[19]

Oglethorpe quickly retaliated as he "pursued them [the Spanish] into Florida, swept the River Saint Mathao, by the Indians called Alata which the Spanish would fain now call Saint John's." He searched the countryside but could find no enemy there. Oglethorpe then detached Lieutenant George Dunbar to attack Spanish forts St. Francis de Pupa and Picolata. Dunbar left with two scout boats to "destroy boats the Spaniards had and to view their forts and attack them if weak." They rowed up the Alata for 12 hours and entered a lake. On the northern side of the lake was Fort St. Francis de Pupa, with Fort Picolata on the southern point, located some 21 miles from St. Augustine. Dunbar landed at night and, to his surprise, was met with gunfire. After three hours of trading musket fire, and with three men wounded, Dunbar returned.

On New Year's Day of 1740, Oglethorpe "set out with a party of the regiment accompanied by Captain Hugh Mackay, Captain Desbrisay, Lieutenant Dunbar, and Ensigns Mace, Mackay, Sutherland and Maxwell and Adjutant Hugh Mackay, the Rangers, Faunee Mico with the Chickasaws, and Captain Gray, the Uchee King with the Ichees and Howitt, Hillispilli and Santouchy with the Creeks, Mr. Mathews, Mr. Jones, one pettiagua, 13 boats and a small privateer sloop" up the Alata River. At daybreak on the 7th, Oglethorpe's Indians attacked and burned Fort Picolata, which had been abandoned by the Spanish.

At 10 A.M. the same day, they landed and attacked Fort St. Francis de Pupa with the Rangers and Indians. Firing was brisk until 3 P.M., and at 5 P.M. the first of Oglethorpe's cannon fired at the fort. The "garrison was very weak, consisting only of a Sergeant, a Corporal, nine soldiers and one Indian," as the governor had vacated earlier with a "commissioned officer and thirty men." After the second cannonball was fired, the Spanish surrendered.[20]

Having taken care of the Spanish forts, Oglethorpe was now determined to carry out a major siege of the heavily fortified Spanish fort at St. Augustine. From former prisoners he learned that the fort was "built of soft stone, with four bastions, the curtain sixty yards in length, the parapet nine foot thick, the rampart twenty foot high, casemated underneath for lodgings and arched over and newly bombproof."[21] The fort contained fifty mounted cannons.

While Oglethorpe was gathering all the troops and Indians he could muster, he received orders from King George II to "make an attempt upon the town and castle of Augustine with what numbers of men" he would raise in "Carolina, at Purrysburg and in Georgia" as well as Indian forces. On May 10, after a rough march on the "River Saint John's," Oglethorpe's force took Fort San Diego, which was located three leagues from St. Augustine. This raid yielded 57 prisoners, "nine small cannons and two larger ones, 70 small arms and a proportional quantity of ammunition...." He also captured two large launches from the Spanish when they attempted a relief operation. Oglethorpe left a force under Dunbar at the fort and moved toward St. Augustine. Before he arrived back in April, the Spanish had been able to evade the British fleet patrolling off Florida and five or six Spanish galleys with 400 soldiers and supplies were able to reach St. Augustine.[22]

A letter found on board the H.M.S. *Hector* described the siege preparations and the arrival of the British fleet under Commodore Pearse:

> May 30th, [1740,] we arrived near St. Augustine. June 1st we were joined by the *Flamborough*, Captain Pearse; the *Phoenix,* Captain Fanshaw; the *Tartar*, Captain Townshend; and the *Squirrel*, Capt. Warren, of twenty guns each; besides the *Spence* Sloop, Captain Laws, and the *Wolf,* Captain Dandridge. On the 2d Colonel Vanderdussen, with three hundred Carolina soldiers, appeared to the north of the town. On the 9th General Oglethorpe came by sea with three hundred soldiers and three hundred Indians from Georgia: on the which they were carried onshore in the men-of-war's boats, under the cover of the small ships' guns. They landed on the Island Eustatia, without opposition, and took the look-out.[23]

With the arrival of the English forces, Spanish governor Manuel de Montiano sent the news to the governor of Cuba at Havana for help. At the Castillo fort, Governor Montiano had 750 soldiers and some 120 sailors who usually manned the galliots (small galley vessels). Oglethorpe had 1,324 men including sailors and Indians.

With the harbor entrance blocked by the British fleet, Colonel William Palmer, a veteran of various Florida campaigns, came in from the north with his company of Highlanders and occupied the abandoned Fort Mose. Oglethorpe landed his men and cannons on each side of the inlet on June 23 and began to build batteries across the bay from the Castillo. Oglethorpe's cannons began the bombardment on the next day. Realizing that Oglethorpe's forces could not easily reinforce each other as they were separated by water, Montiano decided to hit at the weakest point.[24]

At Fort Mose, a village of black runaways located a few miles north of the Castillo, the Spanish struck Palmer's force on the dawn of June 26. In the bloodiest action of Oglethorpe's siege, the Spanish were able to scatter the Highlanders, burn the palisaded fortification and kill Colonel Palmer. Three days later, Captain Norbury wrote "From camp before Saint Augustine" that "General Oglethorpe and all his officers and his regiment are well, and that now we are very busy in bombarding and cannonading the town and castle of Saint Augustine." Though the British forces were within a half-mile of the town and castle "knocking down and burning with our shells part of the town and castle," there was for Oglethorpe constant "enemy fire upon us day and night."[25]

Bombs from mortars and cannonballs filled the sky as the 2,000 townspeople fled to

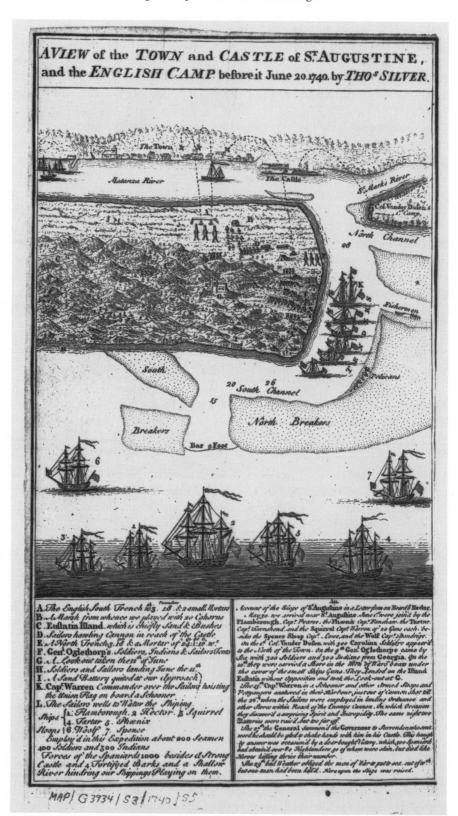

the woods and into the covered way in the Castillo. Oglethorpe continued the shelling for 27 days but the rock of the fort was so unique that it would "give way to cannon ball as though you would stick a knife into cheese." The Spanish cannons of Castillo de San Marcos and the 9-pounders of the fast former Havana galliots held the British back.

Oglethorpe's men battled not only the Spanish, but also the insects, the sun and hunger. Montiano noted on July 6: "My greatest anxiety is provisions. If these do not come, there is not doubt that we shall die in the hands of hunger." On the following day, news arrived that supplies aboard seven vessels had reached the harbor at Mosquito Inlet, located 60 miles down the coast from St. Augustine. Montiano had shallow-draft vessels fight their way behind Anastasia Island, out the Matanzas Inlet, and hugged the coast to get down to the provisions. That same evening, the Spanish returned the same way, but the British blockade of the inlet was gone.[26]

Though the morale of the men was low, Oglethorpe still wanted to press the assault on the Castillo. But on July 16, after having stated his position 11 days earlier that the hurricane season was upon them, Commodore Pearse refused to cooperate with Oglethorpe any further and sailed away with his fleet. Without naval support, and with a resupplied Spanish force in the Castillo, Oglethorpe saw no way to continue the siege. At daybreak on July 17, Oglethorpe's grand military adventure was over. Oglethorpe wrote on the 19th: "I marched with drums beating, colours flying in the day from my camp near the town to a camp three miles distance, where I lay that night. The next day I marched nine miles, where I encamped that night ... I am now encamped on Saint John's River waiting to know what the people of Carolina would desire me farther to do for the safety of the provinces."[27]

Tired and weak from fever, and discouraged over the failure of the siege, Oglethorpe retired to his cottage at St. Simons Island. On the 50 acre grounds around his home and pleasant garden, he recovered his strength while he paced the floor for hours at a time reflecting upon his situation. Taking stock was not an entirely pleasant task. Savannah had shrunk from a peak population of 5,000 citizens to around 500. Because Oglethorpe had removed to Fort Frederica at St. Simons Island, it was now half as large as Savannah. Once, prosperous Darien had dropped as well to some 100 folks. On top of his Georgia condition, he was £15,000 in debt, finding it ever more difficult to retain his seat in Parliament, and hoping to stave off his creditors to retain possession of his Westbrook Manor estate. The general spent 60 days in his seclusion, brooding as the Spanish threat loomed over the heads of all citizens of Georgia and Carolina.[28]

As if Oglethorpe didn't have enough problems, on November 22, settlers in Savannah gathered and issued a letter to the Trustees. They asked in "articles" for:

1st. A free and ample title to our lands, as the rest of His Majesty's colonies have.

2d. The use of Negroes properly limited....

3dly. That any person having a right and title to land here shall have to take the same up where he finds it most convenient....

4thly. That we be released from the excessive quitrent of 20 Shillings for the 100 acres of land, none of the neighboring colonies paying one-sixth so much....

5th. That we may have the liberty of our own Baliffs yearly....

6th. That our Constables and Tythingmen may be under the command of Your Honours and the Magistrates only....

Opposite: **A view of the town and castle of St. Augustine and the English camp before it June 20, 1740, by Thos Silver. Published in** *Gentleman's Magazine,* **July 1740, opposite page 359 (Hargrett Rare Book and Manuscript Library, University of Georgia Libraries).**

That Your Honours may grant our request.... If so, Georgia will yet, we hope, flourish; the town of Savannah that is now deserted, be full of inhabitants; our villages that are now abandoned, quickly be stocked with people; the whole country have cause to rejoice.[29]

Georgia was eating up the funding from London at an unprecedented rate. The colony had already received more money from the treasury than any other colony in British North America. Undeterred by Oglethorpe's pleas, the Parliament cut the 1741 appropriation to Georgia to £10,000. For many leaders in London, Georgia was indeed a "sinking ship."

4

A Georgia Victory and Charter Surrender

"Our deliverance from the Spanish is singular!"

The Court of Savannah was open on November 10, 1740, as William Stephens "Attested upon Oath," and witnessed with the signatures of 24 other prominent leaders "being duly sworn," of the accuracy of a remarkable document entitled "A State of the Province of Georgia." In his testament, which was later published in 1742, Stephens gave a most detailed and accurate account of the entire province as it existed in 1740. He wrote:

The Town of Savannah ... in which are now 142 houses, and good habitable Huts.

The Soil in general, when cleared, is productive of Indian Corn, Rice, Peas, Potatoes, Pumpions, Melons, and many other Kinds of Gourds, in great Quantities; Wheat, Oats, Barley, and other European Grains....

Mulberry Trees and Vines agree exceedingly well with the Soil and Climate, and so does the Annual Cotton....

Cattle, Hogs, Poultry, and Fruit Trees of most Kinds, have increased even beyond Imagination.

Ships of about three hundred Tons can come up to the Town, where the Worm (which is the Plague of the American Seas) does not eat....

The River is navigable for large Boats, as far as the Town of Augusta ... and is 250 Miles distant from Savannah by Water; small Boats can go 300 Miles further, to the Cherokees [in the eastern part of the province].

There is already a considerable Trade in the River; and there is in this Town a Court House, a Gaol [jail], a Store House, a large House for receiving the Indians, a Wharf or Bridge, a Guard House, and some other public Buildings; a public Garden of ten Acres cleared, fenced, and planted with Orange Trees, Mulberry Trees, Vines, some Olives which thrive very well, Peaches, Apples, &c. It must be confessed, that Oranges have not so universally thriven with us, as was expected, by Reason of some severe Blasts by Frost in the Spring....

Notwithstanding the Quantity of Silk, ... has not been great, yet it increases....

Vines likewise of late are greatly increased ... and this Year has produced a considerable Quantity of very fine Grapes, whereof one Planter in particular made a Trial [batch], to see what Kind of Wine they would make, which he put into a large Stone Bottle, and made a Present of it to the General; who upon tasting, said he found it to be something of the Nature of a small French White Wine, with an agreeable Flavor....

Three Miles up the River there is an Indian Town, and at six Miles Distance are several considerable Plantations: At ten Miles Distance are some more, and at fifteen Miles Distance is a little Village, called Abercorn.

Above that [Abercorn], on the Carolina Side, is the Town of Purysburgh, twenty-two Miles from Savannah; and on the Georgia Side, twelve Miles from Purysburgh, is the Town of Ebenezer, which thrives very much; there are very good Houses built for each of the Ministers, and an Orphan House; and they have partly framed Houses, and partly Huts, neatly built, and formed into regular Streets; they have a great deal of Cattle and Corn Ground, so that they sell Provisions at Savannah; for they raise much more than they can continue.

Thirty Miles above Ebenezer, on the Carolina side, lies the Palachocolas Fort: Five Miles above ... lies the Euchee Town (or Mount Pleasant) to which about a hundred Indians belong.... All the Land from Ebenezer to the River Briers belongs to those Indians....

One hundred and forty-four Miles above Mount Pleasant, on the Carolina Side, is Silver Bluff, where there is another Settlement of Euchee Indians: On both Sides of the River are Fields of Corn planted by them.

Thirty Miles above Silver Bluff is New Windsor, formerly known by the Name of Savannah Town, or Moore's Fort, where there are but two or three Families on the Carolina Side, and a small Fort.

Seven Miles above New Windsor, on the Georgia Side, lies the Town of Augusta, just below the Falls; this was laid out by the Trustees Orders in the Year 1735 ... there are several Warehouses thoroughly well furnished with Goods for the Indian Trade, and five large Boats belonging to the different Inhabitants of the Town, which can carry about nine or ten thousand Weight of Deer-Skins each, making four or five Voyages at least in a Year to Charles Town for exporting to England.... This is a very advantageous Trade to England, since it is mostly paid for in Woollen and Iron.

Above this Town [Augusta] to the North-West, the Cherokees live, in the valley of the Appelachin Mountains; they were about five thousand Warriors; but last Year it is computed they lost a thousand, partly by the Small Pox, and partly by too much Rum brought from Carolina.... The Creek Indians live to the Westward of this Town. Their chief Town is the Cowetas, two hundred Miles from Augusta.... The Lower Creeks consist of about a thousand and the Upper Creeks of about seven hundred Warriors, upon the Edge of whole Country, the French Fort of Albemahs lies.... Beyond the Creeks lie the brave Chikesaws, who inhabit near the Mississippi River....

At Augusta there is a handsome Fort, where there is a small Garrison of about twelve or fifteen Men....

This is the Situation of the Settlements upon the River, at the Mouth of which lies the Island of Tybee, with the Light House....

But from Savannah Southward, there are several Plantations (beside the Villages of Hampstead and Highgate).... Besides these Settlements, there are some others of five hundred Acres per Grant from the Trust, which extend as far as the Ogeechy River; upon which the River lies Fort Argyll....

The next is Darian, where the Scots Highlanders are settled; the Buildings are mostly Huts, but tight and warm; and they have a little Fort.... Below the Town of Darian, is the Town of Frederica, where there is a strong Fort, and Store House, many good Buildings in the Town, some of which are Brick; there is a Meadow near adjoining ... of about three hundred and twenty Acres, of which there is good Hay made.... There are some Villages upon the Island of St. Simon's, and some very handsome Houses built by the Officers of the Regiment; and there has been Pot Herbs, Pilse and Fruit, produced upon the Island.... But Corn, Beer, and Meat, they have from elsewhere.

Between this Island and Jekyll Island, is an Inlet of the Sea, called Jekyll Sound, which is a very fine Harbor, and is one of the best Entries the English have to the Southward of Virginia. This is an excellent Station for Ships to Cruize on the Spaniards, it commanding the homeward bound Trade....

To the Southward of Jekyll lies the Island of Cumberland, and the Fort of St. Andrew's, situated upon a fine commanding Ground; and on the S.E of the same Island, is another strong Fort called Fort William, which commands Amelia Sound, and the inland Passage from Augustine. The next Island is Amelia; beyond that is St. John's, one of the Spanish Outguards; and between forty and fifty Miles from that is Augustine.[1]

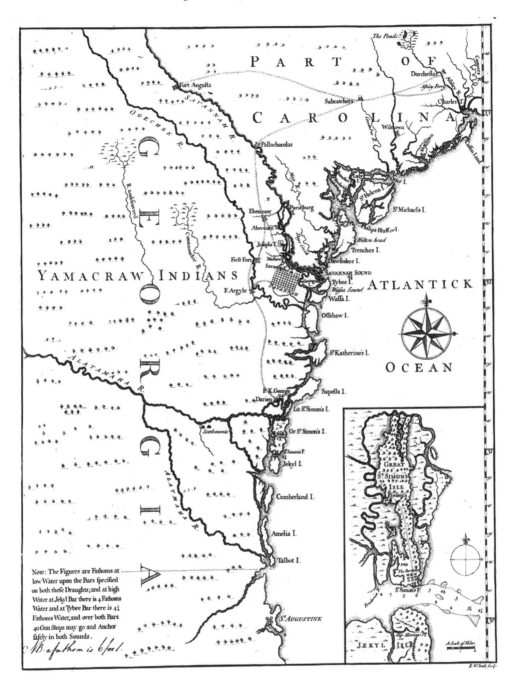

Map of Georgia drawn by Seale, 1741 (Hargrett Rare Book and Manuscript Library, University of Georgia Libraries).

As the December 1740 meeting of the Georgia Board of Trustees in London moved along, James Vernon gave notice to the body of how poorly their orders were being executed in Georgia by Oglethorpe. He reminded them that Oglethorpe was interfering with their mandates and causing mischief, disgrace and expense. He declared that it was indeed time to totally reorganize the government of the province of Georgia, and with an executive wholly independent of Oglethorpe. Vernon's plan suggested that the colony be divided into two counties each with a president and four assistants.

Details of Vernon's proposal were worked out and the Common Council ratified it on April 5, 1741. The two counties were called the County of Savannah and the County of Frederica. The Savannah county would include the town and all settlements on the Savannah and Ogeechee rivers and southward, while that of Frederica would be all the remaining area. The instructions sent to the "new" president of Savannah, William Stephens, were not general in nature but rather spelled out specific duties including "to take care that God Almighty be devoutly and duly honoured and served ... according to the Rites of the Church of England." Keeping records was a given, and definite authority of the control of boats and servants of the trust. The president was to keep "a strict eye" to the observance of the prohibitions against slaves and rum. For the service to the Trustees, the new president would receive a sum not to exceed £300 per year.

The assistants acted as the council to the president, and with any two of them and the president, a quorum was reached. The first assistant presided in the case of the absence of the president. The council was expressly empowered to license public houses for the sale of liquor and ordered to revoke licenses in the case of abuse.

The county system of government was not put into effect at Frederica. Oglethorpe never established it or appointed a suitable person to be president in this southern area of the colony. The de facto executive of the colony was always the founder of and creator of Georgia, Oglethorpe, though he was never named as such. In a report by malcontents to the Trustees, *A True and Historical Narrative of the Colony of Georgia in America*, published in Charles Town in 1741, they declared, "Under the influence of our Perpetual Dictator we have seen something like Aristocracy, Oligarchy, as well as the Triumvirate, Decemvirate and Consular Authority of the famous Republics which have expired many years before us." And the founder and father of Georgia was too concerned about Georgia's continued threat to the South, the Spanish.[2]

The closing sentence summed up the situation according to the malcontents: "By these and many other such Hardships, the poor Inhabitants of *Georgia* are scatter'd over the Face of the Earth; her Plantation a Wild; her Towns a Desert; her Villages in Rubbish; her Improvements a By-Word, and her Liberties a Jest: An Object of Pity to Friends, and of Insult, Contempt and Ridicule to Enemies."[3]

And the Spanish threat was more than real. On May 12, 1741, Oglethorpe informed the Duke of Newcastle that he had sent out Creek Indians in two scout boats to the vicinity of St. Augustine and took a Spanish prisoner. This intelligence revealed that the fort had been newly augmented from Cuba by 800 men, of which 600 were regular troops. They also learned that British admiral Edward Vernon was active in the West Indies, had served up a great victory at Jamaica and was not going to Havana. Vernon was more interested in attacking Santiago. As soon as the governor of Havana discovered Vernon's move, he would logically send his extra troops and galleys to St. Augustine. Oglethorpe alerted Newcastle that, "My private intelligences farther add the Spanish emissaries have been employed to fire the English towns and magazines of North America ... I send Your Grace enclosed their present strength and hope such succours will be sent to us as His Majesty shall think necessary."[4]

From the Spanish waters of the Caribbean, privateers terrorized northward from Georgia to New York. By August 1741, there were more than 30 captured English vessels at St. Augustine. Attacks were reported at several villages in North Carolina and at Carr's property inland from Jekyll Island. From Frederica on June 29 Oglethorpe wrote, "I have wrote very fully to the Ministry to obtain assistance for the defense of this colony, which every day I believe shows the usefulness of...."[5]

In October, secret orders from Madrid arrived at Havana. Those orders directed Cuba's governor to assemble a mighty fleet and invasion force to attack Georgia and Carolina. Just as Oglethorpe appealed to the Trustees and Parliament for more funds, arms, ammunition and naval stores for his command to defend against the Spanish, funds were being cut as the anti-Oglethorpe element in Parliament issued booklets. Likewise, Georgia settlers who had fled to Charles Town had printed contrary views to the conditions in Georgia. Thomas Stephens worked on his views in *The Hard Case of the Distressed People of Georgia.*[6] It was a perilous time for Georgia.

Finally, the long, awaited attack by the Spanish came to reality. Under orders from General Hozcasilas, the governor of Havana sent all his extra troops to St. Augustine to take part in the secret expedition. From St. Augustine the Spanish fleet of 51 vessels sailed for St. Simons, just 90 miles away, with "a land army on board," under the command of General Montiano and Major Antonio Ardondo.

At Fort William with a schooner, Captain Dunbar with 14 guns and some 90 men discovered the first wave of 14 Spanish sails attempting to come in. With the cannons of the fort and the schooner, Dunbar was successful at fighting off the invaders.

The Spanish then moved to Cumberland Sound where Oglethorpe sent Captain Horton with troops and Indians to repel. Joining his men later after fighting his way through, Oglethorpe's men engaged the Spanish with significant success. He recorded, "The enemy in this action suffered so much that the day after they ran out to sea and returned for Saint Augustine and did not join their great fleet 'till after their grenadiers were beat by land."[7]

Oglethorpe then moved the garrison from Fort St. Andrews to reinforce Fort William, as he returned to St. Simons with the schooner. The main Spanish fleet appeared off the bar on June 28, flying the banner of His Most Catholic Majesty, King Philip V of Spain. Oglethorpe took immediately steps to prepare for the imminent attack. He put Captain Thomson's ship into service to defend the harbor, raised another troop of Rangers, and "embargoed all the vessels, taking their men for the service and gave large gifts and promises to the Indians, so that every day we increased in numbers. I gave large rewards to men who distinguished themselves upon any service, freed the servants, brought down the Highland Company and Company of Boatmen, fitted up as far as we had guns."

On the evening of July 5, with "a leading gale and spring tide, 36 sail of Spanish vessels run into the harbour in line of battle." After a spirited four-hour battle, with batteries firing cannons and the invaders' attempts to board the schooners of Captains Thomson and Dunbar, "they [the Spanish fleet] lost abundance of men passed all our batteries and shipping and got out of shot of them towards Frederica." With one guard sloop sunk and one of the batteries destroyed, Oglethorpe held a council of war. With unanimous support, Oglethorpe's officers decided to march to Frederica before the Spanish could get there and to "defend that place, to destroy all the provisions, vessels, artillery &c. at Saint Simon's that they might not fall into the enemy's hands."

In a desperate move, as he faced 36 Spanish vessels loaded with troops, Oglethorpe sent Captain Thomson's ship, the guard sloop and a Spanish "prize" sloop to Charles Town for reinforcements. Oglethorpe's force reached Frederica only to watch the Spanish land. On the 7th, the Rangers discovered the Spanish on the march and heading toward the town. Oglethorpe advanced with a party of Indians and the Highland Company as the regiment followed. He was determined to engage the Spanish in the woods before they reached open ground.

The lead party routed the "first party, took one Captain prisoner and killed another and pursued them two miles to an open meadow or savannah, upon the edge of which I posted three platoons of the regiment and the company of Highland foot so as to be covered by the woods from the enemy, who were obliged to pass through the meadow under our fire." The Spanish force of 100 grenadiers and 200 foot, some Indians and Negroes, under the command of Captain Don Antonio Barba and two other captains, advanced from the Spanish camp into the savannah "with huzzahs and fired with great spirit, but not seeing our men by reason of the woods, none of their shot took place but ours did."

Two miles off, Oglethorpe heard the firing and rode toward the battle. Fearing his forces were being routed as he ran into retreating men, he moved swiftly to the engagement. When he arrived the "fire was done." He discovered that the Spanish had been totally routed by the lone platoon of the regiment under Lieutenant Sutherland and the Highlanders under Lieutenant Charles Mackay. The wounded Captain Barba was taken prisoner and many dead were laying "upon the spot." Having distinguished themselves in the engagement, Oglethorpe promoted Mackay to brigade major and Sergeant Stuart to second ensign.

Oglethorpe then advanced with Captain Demere, Ensign Gibbon and Lieutenant Cadogan with the entire regiment of Rangers and Indians to the "causeway over a march very near the Spanish camp." After camping there for the night, the next morning the Indian scouts advanced to the Spanish camp and found it abandoned to the ruins of the fort. Based on their analysis of the camp before them, they estimated that some 4,000 Spanish had been bivouacked there. Unable to attack such a large force with a frontal attack, Oglethorpe retired back to Frederica to "refresh the soldiers," as he sent out parties of Indians and Rangers to harass the enemy. The fabled Battle of Bloody Marsh was over.

On July 11, three Spanish galleys sailed up the river to the town, but were repelled by the few cannons they had mounted. This was enough to cause the Spanish to retire as Oglethorpe's boats chased them until they reached the protection of the Spanish fleet guns in the sound. Intelligence was gained from the Spanish camp that they had lost four captains and 200 men in the previous action, not counting the men killed at sea and the first engagement.

Though he had been successful so far, Oglethorpe was still severely undermanned relative to the Spanish force before him. He needed to convince the Spanish that he was stronger than he was in troop strength. Oglethorpe came up with a terrific plan. He prevailed upon a prisoner by giving him a large bribe to carry a false letter to a Frenchman who had deserted. The letter, written in French with a text to give the impression that it was from a friend, revealed that he had received money, and that he should make the Spanish believe the English were weak and that they should take their galleys and bring them "under the woods where the hidden batteries were." The letter noted that if he were to aid in this effort, the French deserter would receive double the funds he had already received.

The prisoner with the false letter arrived in the Spanish camp and was immediately brought before General Montiano. He interrogated the new arrival as the deserter Frenchman denied knowing anything about the letter or the prisoner. The ploy worked. Montiano embarked all his troops and moved off to Jekyll Island. He also confined all Frenchmen on board. Montiano departed so fast that the Spanish had left their cannons in place and their dead unburied. The fleet from Cuba, consisting of 20 sail, stood out at sea, with General Montiano and his St. Augustine Squadron in Cumberland Sound.

Oglethorpe, aboard a cutter flying the flag of England with the crosses of St. George and St. Andrew on a field of blue, had a letter delivered to Lieutenant Stuart at Fort William on Cumberland Island with orders to defend himself to the last man. The Spanish discovered Oglethorpe's boats and believing that he had landed Indians that night, "set sail in great haste...." Fifteen small galleys attempted to land near Fort William "but were repulsed by the Rangers." By cannon and small arms, Oglethorpe's force under Lieutenant Alexander Stuart shelled the Spanish vessels for three hours before the Spanish fleet hoisted its sails and moved to the southward. Boats from Fort William chased the fleet to the St. John's River as the Spanish continued on to St. Augustine. The Spanish invasion was ended.[8] It was a grand Georgia victory.

News of the victory soon reached Savannah and Charles Town. The Reverend George Whitefield marveled at the victory. He called it a great deliverance and said it was like one of the mighty rescues described in the Old Testament. Oglethorpe wrote of his "thanks to God for our deliverance," as he received letters of congratulations from the royal governors of New York, New Jersey, Pennsylvania, Maryland, Virginia and North Carolina. The governor of South Carolina did not join in the praise, but the people of Port Royal did, to his dismay.[9] From Savannah, John Dobell wrote to the Trustees declaring, "Our deliverance from the Spanish is singular! And may serve for an argument with the enemies of Georgia that Heaven will uphold and maintain it."[10] The praises would be useful in London for Oglethorpe.

On February 17, 1743, King George II permanently altered the status of Georgia's founder, even as his enemies in Parliament and in the colonies complained. Oglethorpe was promoted to brigadier general in gratitude for "good service in repulsing the Spaniards." This was no colonial commission, but a permanent military rank. Unfortunately for Oglethorpe, Lieutenant Colonel William Cooke, an officer in his Georgia regiment, preferred 19 formal charges against his commander. The most significant charge was that Oglethorpe had habitually defrauded his men "by making them pay for the provisions the Government sent them over gratis." Back during the St. Augustine campaign Cooke had become extremely hostile to Oglethorpe and, by pleading to be in ill health, had received a 12-month leave of absence to return to London.

Portrait of James Oglethorpe (Hargrett Rare Book and Manuscript Library, University of Georgia Libraries).

At the same time Cooke was leveling charges, the lords commissioners of the treasury had received complaints over bills of exchange drawn on the government by Oglethorpe. With a court-martial and the treasury affair hanging over him, Oglethorpe decided he must return to England.

On July 22, 1743, Oglethorpe boarded his vessel for the voyage home. At Frederica, he left Major William Horton in command, and William Stephens was made deputy general of Georgia in Savannah. A handful of well-wishers were on hand to see him off. Among them was Mary Musgrove Matthews, a true friend and admirer of the general. Oglethorpe gave her his diamond finger ring, said to be worth £1,000. As Oglethorpe sailed away from Georgia aboard the aptly named ship *Success*, he reflected upon all that he had accomplished, all that would need to be completed, and all the challenges he faced in England. His third passage home, taking 60 days, would be uncharacteristically "tranquil and pleasant." As the coast was but a line on the western horizon above the quiet sea, it was the last time Brigadier General James Edward Oglethorpe would ever see Georgia. Now, even as the general and Georgia parted, history would join them forever.[11]

Back in April that year, the Trustee's Common Council took steps to resolve the confused problem that Oglethorpe caused by never having established a president of the county of Frederica. The body ordered the bailiffs at Frederica, who had been made assistants pending the appointment of the president, to be designated as local magistrates and subject to the president and assistants of Savannah County. For the first time, Georgia had at least some semblance of a united authority throughout the colony.[12]

Finally, to resolve the question of who would lead the province, on July 11, 1743, the old secretary of 70 years of age, William Stephens, was appointed by the Trustees to be the president of Georgia. Though now the new president of the entire province, Stephens would have little real authority over the province. Laws remained under London's Georgia Trusteeship control. A restructured civil government did appear during Stephens' time in office, as the former magistrates became assistants to the president.

As the decade of the 1740s continued, the citizens of Georgia suffered most severely from the "malady" of economic stagnation. It was during these times that the phrase "poor as a Georgian" became in common use in Carolina. In Savannah, many of the lots in the six wards were still vacant. With the indifference from the Trustees in London, and the repeated disappointments of what few people remained in the founder's town, Savannahians fell into a sort of "grim fatalism" about their situation.

Even the character of immigration to the province changed. During the eight years after Oglethorpe returned to Britain, dramatic changes in the type of settlers coming to Georgia occurred. Only seven small groups of charity colonists, totaling a mere 172 people, sailed to Georgia during that period, while the count of privately funded adventurers and their servants totaled 2,499.[13]

For a few years after the Battle of Bloody Marsh, the town of Frederica on St. Simons Island continued to thrive. The colonists felt a sense of finally being safe and the payroll from the army held the base for economic growth there for trade and labor. A James Papot had worked at Frederica and Savannah after the battle, and had helped build clapboard huts for soldiers and houses for the citizens of Frederica. But four years later at least a hundred huts would go up in flames. Before long, the regiment was disbanded, and two decades later pines, oaks and palmettos would "efface the town."

As the forties closed the people of Georgia tried to see a glimmer of hope in their future. Stepping off the *Loyal Judith* from England, Savannah finally received a competent and trusted Anglican minister in the person of Bartholomew Zouberbuhler. He was a Swiss native, raised in Carolina, and about to provide stable religious support for the next 20 years in colonial Georgia. Soon others like James Habersham, who had formed a partnership in the mid–1740s with the former clerk of the Trust's store, Francis Harris, would have a wharf built and see their import-export business succeed.

Life in Georgia and at Savannah was not without some enjoyments and celebrations. The first horse race recorded in Georgia had taken place on June 26, 1740. William Stephens' journal recorded, "An odd Humour being lately sprung up among some of our People for Horse Racing ... I observed it was promoted by that desperate Crew, whose whole Study and Employment was to disturb the Quiet of the Place and keep the Spirits of the Well meaning in a continual Flutter.... The Race, a little more than a Quarter of a Mile from the Gate of the public Garden, to the Midst of Johnson's Square."[14] There was cricket in Johnson Square on holidays, backgammon, cards and quoits at the taverns in the evenings, and festivals during the King's birthday, at weddings and for a few saints' days.[15] Finally, the year of 1750 was to be one of profound change for both the direction of government and, by late summer, the economy of Georgia.

From the very establishment of the Charter, the Trustees had never allowed the colonial leaders in Georgia to express their opinions in laws or govern themselves. But finally, on March 19, 1750, the Common Council authorized the holding of an assembly in Savannah. The president and the assistants would set the time of the meeting. Representatives were selected based on population. Every village, town or district with at least 10 families could have one representative, while settlements of 30 families had two. Savannah had four deputies, with Ebenezer and Augusta with two each. On December 15, writs for holding elections were issued, setting the assembly session for January 15, 1751.

Sixteen leading men of the province showed up for the Savannah assembly on the scheduled date, representing 11 districts. President Stephens opened the deliberations with a speech. The assembly was curious because the Trustees' Common Council had established by resolution that "The Assembly can only propose, debate, and represent to the Trustees What shall appear to them to be for the Benefit, not only of each particular Settlement, but of the Province in general."

More than for any other reason, the Trustees supported the idea of an assembly as a method to gain better reporting of the activities of the various districts in Georgia. They issued instructions to know the census, with the ages, sexes, and races of the inhabitants. In addition they wanted a statement of the quantity of cultivated land by each colonist, as well as the number of mulberry trees planted on each plantation, with detailed accounts of the culture of wine, silk, indigo and cotton by family. As in the early years, the Trustees continued to have only a blurred view of the conditions in their American colony.

Though not particularly expected, the first assembly experiment in Georgia proved to be a success. After only 15 days of deliberations, the Georgia representatives had developed a list of 11 grievances. They wanted weights and measures established, the court house repaired, regulation of the militia, as well as improvements of the shipping facilities. The final nine days of the assembly session were spent in preparing representations to the Trustees. The representatives even desired that the Charter be renewed as the end was near. There was a fear that South Carolina would annex Georgia, and they felt "they might expect to be treated as persons only fit to guard her frontier...." The representatives expressed the desire to have the power to make bylaws for the colony which would be in effect until disapproved by the Trustees.

Upon receiving the representations of the Georgia Assembly, the Trustees were generally delighted. Most of the requests were granted, except, of course, the request to have the power of legislation. They promised to take prompt action on Assembly requests and scheduled the Georgia body to meet annually.[16]

On August 9, 1750, the Trustees put their seal on an act repealing the antislavery statute enacted at the founding. For every five black slaves brought into Georgia, the owners were required to bring in one black female "who would be taught the winding of silk from cocoons." The Trustees continued to nourish the old and fading dream of major silk production in Georgia.

In Georgia, William Stephens remained in charge as president until September of 1750. On the 26th of that month the *Proceedings of the President and Assistants* recorded that "The Assistants for a long Time past ... [had] been under great difficulties in proceeding in Public Business, occasioned by the President's [William Stephens'] Infirmities, and confused mind; and altho' his name ... [had] always appear'd at the Head of the Board, yet for some time past, he ... [had] been utterly uncapable of any Business, but rather retarded it." The assistants resolved that the situation could not continue any longer, and set out to visit Stephens with their notice in hand.

In their presence, William Stephens "voluntarily declared Himself uncapable of any Public Duty, desiring they would proceed without Him and He would soon retire into the Country, where he should be more at Liberty to mind the more weighty Things of the Future State, not doubting but the Trustees would enable Him to end his few remaining Days without Care and Anxiety...." So at age 80 William Stephens retired to his plantation at Beaulieu, near Savannah. He had led Georgia for 10 years with an "inert hand" at the hands of the London-based Trustee government.

On April 8, 1751, Henry Parker, one of the well-known and key assistants, became the temporary president. Parker had a long history in Georgia. During the first summer, that of 1733, Henry Parker had been appointed constable while under sail to Georgia aboard the *Georgia Pink*. By the end of the first year he was made third magistrate, then second in even less time. The Trustees had learned of Henry in the autumn of 1734 when he and his brother William had been working in the garden lot southwest of Savannah to repay Edward Jenkins for work done for the Parkers. Jenkins's servant noticed that a man named Richard White had escaped. Promptly the Parker brothers helped recapture White and lead him to the town. For his support he and his brother shared £50 with Jenkins for the capture.

The Parker family lived on the corner of Bryan Street and Drayton in a house rented from Widow Cooper. Henry's house at York and Bull Street was rented to his brother William. Within a year Henry Parker had acquired a 500-acre tract of land southeast of the town, which was the northern one-third of an island Noble Jones had named the Isle of Hope. The island resembled to him a horseshoe bend in the Thames River at a place called Stanford le Hope.

The Parker country house on the Isle of Hope, where they spent most of their time, overlooked the river to the south, and was open to the morning sun and the favored south-eastern winds. It was a place of true southern beauty. The fish abounded in the river, shrimp teemed in the creeks, oysters everywhere on the muddy banks. There were schools of porpoises in the channel and brown pelicans diving as the possums and raccoons rustled in the undergrowth. All was grand and natural as were the insects-the deerflies, horseflies, mosquitoes and sand flies.

Henry and Anne Parker had lost their first two sons within a month of landing at Savannah, but a year later Henry William was born to them, followed in the spring of 1736 by a daughter. The move up the ladder had made Henry a protégé of Thomas Causton, the first magistrate and storekeeper of the Trust Store. Though Parker would eventually develop a problem with the evil rum, he was a solid member of the leadership. After only a month in Savannah, William Stephens called Henry Parker "an honest, plain, well-meaning Man, and one who I apprehended had as good a Share of Common Understanding as most of his Neighbors."[17]

A packet arrived from the Trustees late in October naming James Habersham as secretary for the Trustees' affairs, Patrick Graham was the new agent to distribute His Majesty's presents to the Indians, and Noble Jones was named an assistant. Subsequently, Parker received the formal title of president.[18]

Henry Parker died on July 6, 1752. Upon Parker's death, Patrick Graham of Augusta succeeded him. On the following April of 1753, the population of the Province of Georgia was 2,381 whites and 1,066 blacks.[19] In that same year, the retired William Stephens died at age 81, leaving his estate to his youngest son, Newdigate.[20]

Even before the representations of the first Georgia Assembly were received in London, the Trustees were in negotiations with the Crown for surrender of their Charter. The warm words of the Assembly could not counter the many harsh addresses of the malcontents or ease the difficulty of funding Oglethorpe's dream. In June of 1753, the Trustees placed advertisements in the *London Gazette* notifying the public that land in Georgia was now being granted "with free inheritance," overturning those restrictions that had long suppressed the natural immigration to the fair colony. As a three-man committee of the Trustees surveyed the financial condition of the colony, they found that they faced continued expenses "without any Fund to answer them, except the Money due from Gen Oglethorpe to the Trust." They gave instructions to the accountant to bill Oglethorpe for "One thousand four hundred and twelve Pounds and two pence half Penny."

Oglethorpe took the bill rather calmly and informed Harman Verelst that according to his last account of expenses he submitted to the Trustees, they owed him funds. The general was actually holding another account of more expenses the Trustees owed. Over a two-month period, Oglethorpe and the Trustees could not reach an agreement.

Meanwhile, in November, the Trustees, led by the Earl of Shaftesbury, wrote a document to be presented to the Privy Council declaring their readiness "for the service of the Crown, to surrender their Trust for granting the Lands" in the colony of Georgia. They did stress the concern that Georgia "be confirmed a separate and independent Province." Members of the Privy Council reviewed the document and presented it to the solicitor general for his legal opinion. While the surrender of the charter was pending, Parliament granted Georgia leaders some £4,000 to settle outstanding obligations.

On May 6, 1752, the papers, books and the seal of the Georgia Corporation were placed in safekeeping. A month later, on June 25th, and a full year before the expected expiration, Georgia was formally established as the royal province of Georgia. The Georgia Trustees surrendered the Charter of Georgia to the crown in a meeting of only four of the 21 members in attendance. The experiment was over.[21]

On the date of the expiration of the Georgia Charter, a proclamation was issued by the Lords Justices directing that all persons vested in any office or places of authority, "ecclesiastical, civil or military," in His Majesty's colony of Georgia should continue therein until His Majesty's pleasure should be further made known. This action was quite appropriate, as the first royal governor did not appear in Georgia to set up the new government until October 29, 1754.

As another sign of change for the citizens of colonial Georgia, in 1752 Britain abandoned the Julian calendar for the Gregorian one. Georgians went to bed on the 2nd of September and woke up on the 14th.[22]

Until the royal governor appeared on December 19, 1752, the Board of Trade appointed Benjamin Martyn, the former secretary to the Trustees, to be responsible as the agent for their Georgia affairs in England. As agent he kept the board informed on all activities in the colony, and administered the Parliamentary grants.

After long deliberations, the Lords of the Council finally recommended that Georgia should be set up as a royal province. After the approval of the king, Georgia, as a royal province, was entitled to a great seal. Thus, on June 21, 1754, the king ordered the dies for the seal to be made of silver and engraved with the coat of arms of the new province. The front of the new Georgia seal shows a female figure, representing the young province of Georgia, kneeling before the king in token of her submission, and presenting him with a skein of silk, while the motto beneath, "Hine laudem sperate coloni," meaning "Hence hope for praise, O colonists!" which notifies the colonists that the king still expected them to supply him with silk. The Latin words around the circumference mean, "The seal of our Province of Georgia in America." On the other side of the seal is the coat of arms of King George II.[23]

5

The Royal Period Begins

"As long as the Sun shall shine and the River run into the Sea."

On October 29, 1754, the 41-year-old naval officer and new royal governor of Georgia, Captain John Reynolds, stepped off a barge that had brought him up the Savannah River from Cockspur Island to this little town now in decay. Signs of the state of the town were everywhere. The Christ Church was in "a ruinous state," the courthouse was in need of repair, and the rotted log foundation of the Council House had only recently been replaced by a stone cellar. Reynolds noted that there were in Savannah "about a hundred and fifty Houses, all ones, very small, and mostly very old."

The long-awaited event of Reynolds' arrival was met with a festive atmosphere as the "bells jangled, musketfire split the sky and sputtered through the evening, and bonfires glowed like the hopes of the revelers." Savannahians of the "lower Class of People" were so overjoyed that "being unprovided with materials that they commonly use in testifying their joy on public Occasions, and unwilling to lose their Share of Rejoicing" the guardhouse was set on fire which nearly torched the old Council House before Reynolds had used it.

John Reynolds was born in England in about 1700. He entered the Royal Navy at an early age, and rose through successive ranks. At the time Reynolds arrived, the local board consisted of Patrick Graham as president, with James Habersham, Noble Jones, Pickering Robinson and Francis Harris as the assistants. To maintain some type of continuity in government, the president and assistants became Governor Reynolds' Council to advise him.[1]

Less than a week after his arrival at Savannah, His Excellency called his council together at Council House to discuss the decrepit state of the building. During the session a stack of chimneys at one end of the house gave way and took the wall with it. Reynolds and the council hurried out of the place to safety and reconvened in a shed behind the courthouse. The council found suitable temporary spaces in a large, two-year-old vacant building located across the street from the silk filature. The governor promptly ordered Councilors Noble Jones, James Habersham and Jonathan Bryan to have the building fitted out for offices.[2]

The place Governor Reynolds had relocated to was indeed a rather forlorn and unimpressive area. The Savannah of 1754 was desolate looking. The population had fallen to only a few hundred citizens who lived in frame houses, surrounded by pine forest on three sides, with no defensive fortifications or walls. The villages of Acton, Abercorn and Vernonburgh nearby were sparse. On the coast on St. Simons Island was Frederica, which was nearly deserted. At Darien were some Scottish Highlanders, and up the coast was Sunbury with the South Carolina Congregationalists. A hundred miles up the Savannah River was the Indian trading post town of Augusta. There were only some 2,381 whites and around 1,000 blacks in the colony at that time. And Governor Reynolds controlled a rather small area of 1,800 square miles along the coast and up the Savannah.[3]

The first "royal" Georgia provincial assembly was scheduled to meet in January 1755 in Savannah as the legislative adventure began. Though Reynolds never expected to have a problem exerting his authority, he was soon to meet his first challenge from a man named Edmund Gray of Augusta. Gray, a political adventurer, set about in the first House of

Captain John Reynolds, first Royal Governor of Georgia (National Maritime Museum, London).

Assembly election campaign to see that his followers gained seats in the new government. Gray had come from Virginia in 1750 and once established he was able to parcel out lands from the public domain to his Virginia friends. Soon he had gained the reputation as the leader of the opposition to the interim provincial administration.

Being a gifted speaker and somewhat radical dreamer, Gray appealed to many of the people. Creating an air of tension and bitterness in the campaign, Gray soon aroused the fear of the freeholders that the royal government would threaten their liberty. He tried to have four of his supporters elected to the assembly. As it turned out only one of them was elected. His opposition declared that they could now keep Gray and his "restless Children within proper Bounds." But Gray fought back by petitioning for the elections of his opposition candidates to be overturned in favor of his defeated supporters, William Francis and Samuel Marcer. He called the election faulty because of the "illicit and partial Practices of the returning Officer" at Savannah.

The controversy continued until January 27 when Gray and Watson were expelled from the Assembly. Gray and his Virginia friends then traveled southward and crossed the Altamaha River, where no government could reach them. While this problem had been resolved for the time being, it was but the first bellwether of things to come under the Reynolds administration.[4]

Aside from the problems created by Gray, Reynolds ran into another conflict which served to set the tone for his entire approach to his office. While Parliament was working to appoint the first Georgia royal governor, the senior councilors of the Governor's Council, Patrick Graham, James Habersham and Noble Jones, were in fact governing the province in the governor's absence. The role of the council was to give the governor their "advice and consent" to various actions of the government.

While the legacy of the council function in many of the other North American colonies had been rather useful and mostly successful, Reynolds had no use for their advice. Reynolds considered any disagreements as personal affronts to him. Criticism was something he could not deal with. Frustrated by one of his many arguments with his council, he burst out exclaiming, "I expect that no Member of this Board will presume again to tell me in Council...." For Reynolds, the council effectively gave him "no Power to determine in anything without their concurrence."[5]

Finding no redeeming value in his council, Governor Reynolds centered all his consulting attention and respect with an old friend and naval associate, William Little. In the summer of 1755, Reynolds appointed Little, his former 20-year shipmate and surgeon, and now private secretary, as speaker of the assembly. Little saw to it that only men who were obedient to Reynolds were elected. Reynolds conferred seven royal appointments on Little, including commissioner of Indian affairs, and clerk of both the general court and the House of Assembly. One of the councilors laid the facts out as he noted, "the Inability of Mr. Reynolds, the Governor of Georgia, conferd, in a few months after his arrival there, the whole Administration of Affairs on Wm Little...." Not surprisingly, soon Little was so unpopular that a grand jury ruled that he was "a public nuisance."

From the first session of the General Assembly, William Little, with great confidence in his power, took charge and exerted his influence in both houses. He often spoke in the name of the governor, and withheld bills that had been passed from the governor feeling they were of "Insignificancy and Non-Importance." The arrogance, rudeness, and aloofness expressed by Little in his day-to-day activities in these various prominent positions he held in the colonial government, coupled with Reynolds' abandonment of support of the prominent community and business leaders exemplified by his council, doomed his administration from the beginning.[6]

In September of 1755, the council members approached Reynolds detailing a number of serious charges against Little. They demanded that Little be "stripped of his offices" and removed from the council. The charges explained his dishonest behavior and interference in all departments of the government, as well as misconduct in extortion of outrageous fees and withholding two bills that had been passed by the assembly from the governor.

Reynolds tried to ignore the charges and let Little put his reply to the charges in the minutes of the proceeding. Only after the council declared their readiness to prove the charges "in the most Formal Manner," did Reynolds yield. In the fall he created a special court, but made himself the judge and jury of Little's fate. Reynolds was "clearly of opinion to acquit Mr. Little of every charge," but "in order to satisfy his Accusers & the whole Country" he did remove Little from two of his seven offices for taking bribes. The council was incensed and from this point forward, all communications between them and the governor were tense and "curt."

In late November, Reynolds traveled to Augusta to meet with the chiefs of the Creeks. Reynolds planned to present gifts to the Indians and act as His Majesty's representative to renew pledges of friendship. The governor invited two less hostile members of the council, the colonial secretary, James Habersham, and, of course, William Little, the designated commissioner of Indian affairs. After waiting for 10 days for the chiefs to assemble, Reynolds departed in a huff and left Little to do the honors. The conference was not the success the colonists had wanted. Some of the Indians were less than impressed with Little, and felt snubbed by being received by less than the direct representative of the king.

Preferring to wait until Little returned, Reynolds deferred the planned January opening of the General Assembly until February 2, 1756. On that day, Reynolds opened the session with an address praising the work of the House the previous year. Since the House had not been in session during the fall disputes between the governor and the council, Reynolds hoped to keep the quarrel out of the proceedings. When the assertion came to the floor on the 3rd that Little had withheld two bills from the governor, the House took no action to answer the council.

The controversy would not go away. Another problem developed on the 4th. Since only 14 of the 19 seats in the assembly had been filled by that date, Charles Watson and Edward Barnard, who were Gary's supporters expelled in the previous session, were elected on writs which Reynolds had issued during the adjournment. An issue arose as to whether Reynolds had acted properly in issuing writs without the request of the House. Before the committee of privileges and elections could file its report, a message arrived at the council stating that there would be no business conducted until the issue of the lost bills was resolved.

At 3 P.M., when the House opened the afternoon session to work on the council's request, Reynolds immediately adjourned the meeting without explanation until February 12. On that day, the governor opened the session by berating the members about their refusal to seat Watson and Barnard. The controversial session continued until 4 P.M. as the House completed a response to the council's message. On the 19th, Reynolds "castigated" the assemblymen for refusing to confirm the election of Watson and Barnard, and then dissolved the General Assembly.

While Reynolds maintained that he broke with the assembly because it refused to seat valid elected members, the assembly held to its belief that he had dissolved the session to protect Little from being investigated. Regardless, Reynolds now found himself in quite a dilemma. He was sure now that the assembly would not approve any of the tax provisions, even as the treasury was empty in the spring of 1756. And he also feared that the council would demand his recall.

His fears were indeed well founded. In April, Jonathan Bryan, a council member and the largest landholder in Georgia, wrote Lord Halifax declaring the "Declining State" of the colony and asking him to gain the particulars from Alexander Kellett, the provost marshal and councilor, who had sailed to London that spring. In London in July, at the request of "most of the Councillors, representatives, Public Officers, & Planters of Substance & Character" in the colony, Kellett presented to the Commissioners of Trade and Plantations a memorial with a detailed account of the activities of Reynolds and Little in Georgia. On July 29, 1756, the board recommended that Reynolds be called back to answer the charges in England and that a lieutenant governor be sent to the province.

Reynolds continued to show his poor character after news of his recall. At the convening of the new House of Assembly on November 1, he opened with a blatant plea for popular support in an attempt to embarrass the new administration. He asked the assembly to build the public treasury balances by reenacting the old inadequate tax by explaining it of being "so Easy that Scarce an Individual felt the Weight of it."

As for Little, he again proved himself to be a great campaign artist as he was elected to the assembly, helped to get four of Gray's supporters elected, and got himself reelected as the speaker. Little even pushed through a resolution exonerating completely the wrongdoings of Gray's factor as he accused the council of "Bad and Sinister design" in fighting with the governor on the election controversy.

Before the Christmas recess of 1756, Little appointed a committee to report on the "State of the Province" which he hoped would shine a more favorable light on Reynolds' administration to the Board of Trade. Unfortunately for Little, the council, and particularly James Habersham, would not release the official correspondence. The report, which was adopted by the House, laid the blame for the deplorable condition of the province on the policies of the previous administrations before Reynolds' arrival.[7]

In his closing months in Georgia, Reynolds abdicated his power as the chief executive and let Little and the House audit the public accounts and disburse funds. John Reynolds sailed away from Georgia in February of 1757 aboard the *Charming Martha*, but en route home to London his ship was taken by a French privateer. When he finally did reach England on July 7, the Board of Trade suggested that he resign his post and return to sea.[8]

Reynolds' legacy as a colonial administrator was indeed an exercise in self-destruction, as he alienated the council and many in the House of Assembly. When he should have been working to solve the real challenges in the province, he dissolved into a world of factional politics and dispute. As his unpopularity spread during his administration, Reynolds even tried to have the capital moved from Savannah to a new town, Hardwicke, he planned on a bluff on the south side of the Ogeechee River. Though he pushed for the towns' development by forcing his friends to agree to buy 27 lots, the town was never built. Reynolds attempted to have Georgia provide military support in the form of regiments and forts to the British as requested by the Parliament, but the Assembly pleaded that there were no funds for such expenditures for a war that did not really touch their borders.

During his short two years in Savannah, Reynolds had displayed incredible greed as he pleaded for a pay raise and acquired land. After only three months in the province, he asked the council to approve the acquisition of 10 acres at the Trust's garden east of town. They complied and the next day they also approved his application for 2,500 acres south of the Ogeechee River. By June of 1755 he had also acquired land from three former owners on Hutchinson's Island across the river from the town of Savannah. Incredibly, by the time Reynolds sailed away from Georgia, he was at the point of bankruptcy.[9]

On April 21, 1758, just four days after the Board of Trade had rejected Reynolds' appeal to retain his position, Lord Halifax asked the Privy Council to approve Henry Ellis as the governor of Georgia. With a commission drawn up on May 8, and the king's signature received on June 16, Henry Ellis became the captain general and second royal governor in chief of the province of Georgia.[10]

In stark contrast to the administration of Captain John Reynolds, Ellis was a gentleman and a scholar who was able to unite the various disparate groups of citizens to meet the challenges of the times. Using his unique personal qualities, social skills and analytical methodology, he was able to guide the province with excellent results. In the three years of his governorship, Georgia doubled in population and in wealth.

Henry Ellis was born to landed gentry in the town and county of Monaghan, Ireland, in 1721. He attended the Church of Ireland parish school across the county at Carrickmac where he received a classic training that included religion, Latin, Greek, Hebrew, oratory, poetry, arithmetic, geography, surveying, writing, antiquaries and "virtue." Though it was a quaint little village to grow up in, Ellis was interested in a more exciting life. At age 20 he went to sea and visited equatorial Africa and the West Indies. After gaining considerable experience at the various duties aboard ship, in 1746 Ellis was offered command of a ship about to sail to search for the Northwest Passage to the Pacific and the Orient. He declined to command one of the two ships in favor of taking a more interesting role as the general scientist.[11] He charted waterways, recorded temperatures, measured tides and salinity, gathered minerals and various "kinds of natural Curiosities."

After attempting to discover the Northwest Passage fruitlessly for a year, he returned to England and published such an intriguing narrative of the voyage that he was elected as a Fellow of the Royal Society and became a deputy commissary general. One of his publications, *Voyages made to Hudson's Bay in 1746-47 by the Dobbs Galley and the California to discover a Northwest Passage*, was presented in 1748 and another, *Considerations Relating to the Northwest Passage*, in 1750. With the considerable influence of the Earl of Halifax, Ellis received the appointment as the royal governor of Georgia on August 3, 1756. After landing at Charles Town on January 27 to the honors of Carolina officials, Ellis spent two weeks conferring with South Carolina governor William H. Lyttleton and Colonel Henry Bouquet, who was the commander of the king's forces in southern America. Together they worked out mail delivery problems and set up a mode of diplomacy that would be used in the coming years between these colonial neighbors. On February 16, 1757, Henry Ellis landed at Savannah.[12]

The new 36-year-old royal governor of Georgia was greeted from the bluff by "loud Huzza's," and "tumultuous demonstrations of joy" as the crackling of bonfires burning William Little in effigy welcomed the amused Ellis. Ellis set out to change the style of government in Savannah. In contrast to Reynolds, Ellis looked at the council as his ally in the politics of the province. He noted their strengths and soon delegated responsibilities to them. He also adjourned the House of Assembly until Reynolds and Little had departed Georgia. Fighting off remaining control of the general courts by those sympathetic to Reynolds, Ellis increased the number of seats from three to five and, thus, gained control on the bench without having to remove anyone.[13]

While he took quick action from the beginning, Ellis complained that before Reynolds had departed he had seen to it that "every publick Office that either existed or were likely to be established, were filled with his Creatures."[14] But Ellis was a master at negotiating for results. Though Reynolds had given away the control of the public accounts to the Assembly, Ellis was able to convince the members that the province was in such a credit crisis that he needed to restore economic credibility by calling in all debts for immediate payment. To solve another obstacle, Ellis agreed to pay for the troop of Rangers out of his own funds rather than disband them. Though Reynolds had formed the force, he had not gained any funding to support them.

When the assembly came back into session on June 16th, Ellis was to learn of a plot left by Little. When Little had departed Georgia in late May 1757, he had left a letter with a local planter, Patrick Mackay. This letter was intended for the assembly and gave them instructions to maintain opposition to the council and new governor at all costs. The plan was to get Mackay into the speaker's seat and then head a junta to block all programs and measures advocated by Ellis.

Ellis moved immediately by announcing that Mackay had "lost the election" and has "retired with disgust and disappointment to his plantation." With the defeat of Mackay, all opposition to Ellis disappeared for the remainder of his administration. Proudly Ellis noted of the first session that nothing "that I proposed to them that was not done, and in the very way I would have it...." Without much modesty and with an air of definite scientific clarity, Ellis summed up his first spring in Georgia, "By address, by bold, but honest arts, & by doing my duty in a way unusual here, I have at length been able to change the temper of my operations to my wishes."[15]

Ellis worked with the assembly and his council to solve the three key challenges before the province: the threat of Indian attack, the scarcity of settlers and the lack of real wealth. They worked together to direct the focus of their defense efforts away from road repair to building forts and defensive works around Savannah. In August and September of 1757, men worked to construct a palisade around the town of Savannah, built a log fort north of Augusta, and three others south of Savannah.[16] Ellis also was able to gain regular troops and in the autumn of his first year in office, the Virginia Regiment of Blues arrived in Savannah.

To provide encouragement to potential settlers, he proposed protection from debts for seven years if they came to Georgia. To reinforce the values of the paper money, Ellis allowed the currency to be accepted by the General Loan Office at face value for public debts. Five months after assuming office, he signed a new bill to print additional paper money for the province.

Ellis also worked for the remainder of his administration to strengthen relations with the Indian nations. Though the chiefs were reluctant to come to Savannah because of their past treatment at Augusta at the hands of Reynolds, Ellis was able to convince them to visit him there. As they gathered at the Altamaha River on the 25th of October in 1757, Ellis sent Captain John Milledge and his force of Rangers to escort the Indians to Fort Argyle on the Ogeechee and on to the capital.

The governor rode out to meet the delegation in a clearing a mile south of the town. Flanked by militia under Noble Wimberly Jones on both sides of the trail, Ellis ushered the Indians through the streets, past the Governor's House and on to the Council House as cannon and musket volleys were fired in salute. After various cordial addresses of mutual friendship were read aloud, Ellis read "A Letter from the great King George to his beloved Children of the Creek Nations." The treaty was affirmed as the chiefs pledged that "the Present Treaty of Peace and Alliance shall remain firm and inviolable as long as the Sun shall shine and the River run into the Sea."[17]

By the fall of 1759, Ellis had become rather unhappy as he suffered in the "intense heats" of the Georgia summers. The heat was more than he could bear. Though he spent every weekend at his "House upon the salt water 12 miles out of town," he could not find relief. Ellis admitted to South Carolina governor Lyttelton, "My judgment has been at variance with my ambition the greatest part of my life, but ill health, subsiding passions and a proper experience give me hope that the former will at last predominate." Convinced that he had to leave Savannah, he petitioned London for a leave of absence. His request was granted and soon the new lieutenant governor, James Wright, was at sea heading to North America.

On the occasion of the arrival of new lieutenant governor, Governor Ellis greeted him and deferred his departure for several weeks to allow Wright to settle into his new job. Ellis reported to the Board of Trade that he was "much pleased" with Wright and he noted him "to be a very capable & worthy man."

The last letter Henry Ellis ever wrote from Georgia to the Board of Trade presented a rather bitter tone at the lack of support of the Georgia frontier by the British government:

> Meanwhile, I cannot help expressing my surprise that his Majestys Southern Provinces should be suffered so long to continue exposed as they are, considering the vicinity, dispositions, & power of the French, and the Savage Nations connected with them, in this Quarter. Surely my Lords 'tis disgraceful to us that whilst our Arms are every where prevailing over the Forces of the Most formidable state in Europe, a few Tribes of barbarians, are murdering the Kings Subjects, and ravaging his Provinces in America, with impunity. From my soul I wish such inattention may not be productive of the most mischievous consequences.

At his farewell address to the Georgia upper house, they thanked him for his efforts to avoid war and asked him to inform the ministry of the continued dangers that still existed in Georgia. With a sense of duty, Ellis decided to first visit New York before heading to England. There he talked with General Amherst about the need for additional troops for Georgia. Later, in January 1761 from New York, Ellis wrote to Wright that Amherst had agreed to send troops under Grant to protect the exposed province of Georgia in addition to South Carolina. On January 6, Grant did indeed arrive in Charles Town Harbor with 1,200 men. The second royal governor of Georgia, Henry Ellis, sailed away from Savannah aboard the small vessel *Bachelor* on November 2, 1760, never to return.[18]

In Charles Town they saluted his arrival with the great guns at Granville Bastion and at the harbor entrance at Fort Johnson. Though Ellis departed in a rather depressed mood, the legacy of his achievements was everywhere throughout the province. In three years he had gained firm control of the lower House of Assembly as all parts of the government worked in unprecedented harmony. He had prevented the potential catastrophe of an all-out Indian war while he organized the establishment of defensive forts and works.[19]

Ellis's Savannah of 1760 was a far cry from that of its origins. The population had grown from 4,500 white persons in 1755 to 7,000 in 1760.[20] Now Savannah had some 200 homes, some made of brick, many with brick foundations, and the remaining of wood. The town had come into its own as a port, as the wharves were crowded with "barrels of rice, beef, and pork: pitch, tar, and turpentine," as well as skins, stacks of staves, and shingles, pine and cypress and oak lumber. The trade and production had doubled as goods flowed from England and other friendly ports, including shoes, Queensware plates, pewter dishes, candles, bowls, castile soap, tobacco, coffee, tea, muscovado sugar, Jamaican rum, Philadelphia double beer, wine, and Madeira, flour, cheese, apples, potatoes, split peas, walnuts, almonds, figs, olives, raisins, currants, capers and spices, herring and mackerel and anchovies.[21]

Ellis had gained not only the respect of the British Board of Trade, but he had restored the royal governorship as the citizens had gained a real affection for this unique man. Henry Ellis was a man who believed that what was best for the province of Georgia and its people was also good for his king and country. Now the reins had been turned over to Sir James Wright, a man who would come to govern over Georgia for more than 15 years.[22]

6

The Wright Era and Patriot Crisis

"[T]his Province is not without some violent Republican Spirits
... still fix't in their strange mistaken Ideas of Liberty."

James Wright's ship dropped anchor at Charles Town on Sunday afternoon on September 7, 1760. Sadly his first act was to set about his unhappy task of arranging the burial of his child who had died at sea. Wright, with his wife and surviving children, spent a month in South Carolina visiting friends before sailing to Savannah.

The leaders of the colony were pleased to see that a man of Wright's stature had been selected to watch over Georgia. On November 3, the day after Ellis departed Georgia for New York, Wright addressed the assembly. As evidence of this respect for Wright, the assembly spoke of Wright's "Integrity and Uprightness joyned with solid sense and sound Judgement."[1]

James Wright was born in London in 1716, the son of a widow Pitts and Robert Wright, a native of Sedgefield in Durham, England. He went to South Carolina in about 1730 when his father became the chief justice of that colony. He returned to England in 1741 and studied the law at London's Gray's Inn. After being called to the bar there, he returned to practice law in Charles Town, holding various court offices. From 1742 to 1757 he served as the attorney general. The next three years were taken up as he represented the colony of South Carolina as its agent in London. On May 13, 1760, James was named as the lieutenant governor of Georgia by royal appointment.[2]

Wright went to Georgia with as a true servant of the king, but came to identify himself with the province of Georgia and its people. Though he was certain to have missed the sophisticated society of Charles Town now that he resided in the mere village of Savannah, he soon took up its cause. In an act of identifying himself with his new home, soon after his arrival he began acquiring land in Georgia. By the end of the colonial period, Wright held 25,578 acres managed by 523 slaves. His crops yielded 2,000 to 3,000 barrels of rice annually, which made him the wealthiest man in Georgia.

Though as governor he had opportunity to abuse legal procedures for land acquisition, Wright always obtained his land by legal means. Almost surprisingly, he maintained a conservative approach to granting lands in such a way as to reduce speculation. He understood that Georgia needed more population and, therefore, more landowners, not fewer planters holding large plantations, which would suppress population growth.[3]

James Wright was to quickly reveal his professional and steady approach to governing Georgia. He easily moved into Ellis's place without taking any steps to radically change the policies previously established. Ellis had felt he had left the province "in full as good a situation, as could reasonably be expected," but did warn Wright that they were "still on a very ticklish footing" with the Creek Indians, especially after the murders of some traders. Wright became convinced that a war with the Creeks must be avoided at all costs.

As the Indian headmen began to wander into Savannah in early November, Wright held talks with each band and insisted that they must uphold their treaty requirements and take responsibility to punish the few hotheaded warriors who committed the terrible acts. Wright spoke sternly to the Creeks as he recounted the results of Cherokee acts against South Carolina.

Portrait of Sir James Wright, third Royal Governor of Georgia (Georgia Historical Society). Painted by Andrea Soldi, n.d.

By the spring of 1761, Wright convinced the settlers to return to the frontier and resume their trading work, as he was convincing the assembly to cut expenditures for defense in favor of economic development. To Wright's dismay as he went into a panic, in June a gang of Creeks murdered a settler on the northern frontier. Two months later, Creek envoys came to Savannah to explain that the incident was a private quarrel between the white man and Indians, and the white man had been at fault.

Wright came to be convinced that most of the problems with the Indians were caused by white traders known to be the "very worst & most abandoned Set of Men." To solve the problem, Wright handed out only a limited number of licenses to a selected dozen or so traders and firms that would handle trade with the Upper and the Lower Creeks. Traders soon returned to their towns and by November Wright would tell the assembly that the Creeks last appeared "disposed to Continue in Friendship" with the province.

With the Indian threat out of the way, Wright was now free to push to divert public funds to build a fort on the lower Savannah for promotion of trade. He called on the engineer John Gerard William De Brahm to draw up plans for a fort on Cockspur Island between Tybee Island and Savannah. The council approved the plan, and in the fall the assembly granted funding for a full fort. Wright's new Fort George seemed even more vital when rumors arrived on May 25, 1762, that Spain was coming into the war on the side of the

French. That prompted Wright to place a detachment of Rangers on Cockspur Island. As it turned out, Georgia's only part in the war involved repeated attempts by officials to deter the merchants from trading with the Spanish in Florida.

In the spring of 1763 news came that the Treaty of Paris had been signed, ending the French and Indian War. Now France and Spain were withdrawing from the New World. This immediately put the Indian nations on the defensive because without France or Spain to play the colonists against, they had lost their leverage. Certainly Indian anxiety over the potential of English frontier expansion was now a real fear. On the first of June, Wright received directions from Earl Egremont to join with the superintendent of Indian affairs, Captain John Stuart, in calling a general Indian congress.

On October 20, Wright set out from Savannah under ceremonial escort to Augusta. He arrived five days later in time to witness the arrival of governors Arthur Dobbs, Thomas Boone and Francis Fauquier in the strange environs of Augusta, Georgia. Wright opened the congress on Saturday, November 5, to a body of 700 to 800 Chickasaw, Choctaw, Cherokee, Catawba, and Creeks. After three days of negotiations, a treaty was signed by the Indians and the governors affirming their pledges and friendship. In return for forgiveness of past sins, the Creeks ceded a large tract of land to Georgia.

The congress was considered a real success, but it was marred later on the next New Year's Day when a party of Creeks murdered 14 people at Long Creek settlement in the South Carolina Upcountry. The congress had enraged a group of "irreconcilables" among the tribesmen against the whites. Eventually Governor Boone was satisfied with the restitution they received from the Creeks in this unfortunate affair. After this event, a quiet calm seemed to come over the Creek nation. A new milestone in the life of Georgia settlers had finally come. For the first time a white man could move across the Savannah River to live without fear of an Indian raid. Soon James Habersham would write to those in England explaining that the danger of Indian attack was about as likely in Georgia as in London. Though there were some Indian issues for the next 50 years, never again would the threat of Indian attack be a dominant theme that would threaten their survival.

A new situation was about to change Georgia forever. Without thoughts of attacks from Indians, the Spanish or the French, the colonists were finally free to turn their attention to trade and the economy. The people's assembly worked with Wright on numerous bills. To aid navigation they approved steps to clear streams, to maintain the lighthouse at Tybee Island, and to hire harbor pilots for Sunbury and Savannah. They passed measures to require inspection of pork, beef, rice, indigo and lumber products. Tax measures were also established to promote shipping from the two Georgia ports, as well as applying a new tax on fur trading between Augusta and Charles Town. The fur tax funds were used to pay for Fort George on Cockspur Island, which now served to provide added protection to shipping and aid in the enforcement of trade laws. Georgia even sent its own agent to represent the province in London. Trade increased so much that the exports in 1764 were equal in volume and value as that of the four-year period between 1756 and 1760. The economy of Georgia was indeed growing as never before.[4]

About the time when Savannah learned that the Treaty of Paris was signed in 1763, South Carolina royal governor Thomas Boone made it known that he would grant land in the area between the Altamaha River and the St. Johns River in Florida. Wright notified the assembly of Boone's intentions. Both Georgia houses quickly agreed to instruct their colonial agent, William Knox, to spare no pains to secure the disapproval of Boone's claims to the lower Georgia area. Councilor Grey Elliott rode to Charles Town to protest the land grab. Boone refused to allow the caveat to be recorded by the colonial secretary and immediately issued warrants of survey for 343,000 of the 400,000 acres of Altamaha lands. The actual number of grants registered was 56 for approximately 90,000 acres.

Boone's claim to the land was based on the fact that Georgia's charter did not extend below the Altamaha River, the renowned issue from the old days during the Oglethorpe era with the Spanish. Wright appealed to the Board of Trade that the area would stop the flow of settlers to Georgia. He also declared that it was unfair that the people of Georgia, who had "borne the brunt & fatigue of settling a new Colony" and had "encounter'd and struggled with innumerable difficulties & hardships," must sit by and see it taken away by strangers. The Board of Trade agreed with Wright and in early 1764 they notified him that the Altamaha lands would be annexed to Georgia.

As the years passed, the leaders of the colony continued to have great confidence in Governor Wright and his actions in support of Georgia. On every occasion the assembly and Wright congratulated themselves on the "great Unanimity" and "general Harmony" between them. While traveling in Georgia in September of 1765, John Bartram wrote in his diary that James Wright was "universally respected by all the inhabitants they can hardly say enough in his praise." But five months later some of these very inhabitants in Georgia would turn on their great leader as the first crisis of the American Revolution was upon them.[5]

The crisis that would change forever the relationship of Governor Wright to his people arose over the Stamp Act controversy. Though he had the interest of the colonists of Georgia in mind, he was still the devoted servant of King George III and the British Parliament. The first official reaction in Georgia came in the form of a letter from the Committee of Correspondence to the colonial agent in London, William Knox, dated April 5, 1765. Knox was not only the colony's agent, but he was also the provost marshal, a former Georgia citizen, a plantation owner, and a friend to Wright and James Habersham.

During the summer and early fall, news spread into Georgia as the fever of opposition to the Stamp Act grew. The first significant controversy surfaced in August when the text of Knox's pamphlet, *The Claim of the Colonies to an Exemption from Internal Taxes by Authority of Parliament Examined*, appeared in the *Georgia Gazette*. The pamphlet defended the right of Parliament to tax the colonies. Though indicating that the tax was "as equal as any, that could be generally imposed on the Colonys," the committee felt it was a "dangerous precedent."

Knox had been cool to the instructions given to him from the Georgia Commons House of the Assembly to raise objection to the Stamp Act, and had decided to publish his infamous pamphlet. For his actions Knox was fired as the Georgia agent and the Commons House voted Charles Garth, the South Carolina agent, to represent Georgia. Problems developed in the Upper House of the Georgia Assembly with the Garth approval, but the motion was carried even though Garth's voucher for payment was not honored.

On Friday, October 25, which happened to be the anniversary of King George III's accession, a demonstration occurred in Savannah in opposition to the Stamp Act. After the usual ceremonies, which brought crowds to the fair town, the locals, sailors and other patriots showed their allegiance as they carried effigies of the stamp distributor through the streets of Savannah. The effigy was "hanged and burnt, amidst the acclamations of a great concourse of people of all ranks and denominations." The same actions occurred on Guy Fawkes Day in November.[6]

With the Stamp Act's effective date of November 1 approaching, the Sons of Liberty met at MacHenry's Tavern in Savannah to proclaim that if the stamp distributor appeared in Georgia, they would threaten him of the peril of his office. On the actual effective date

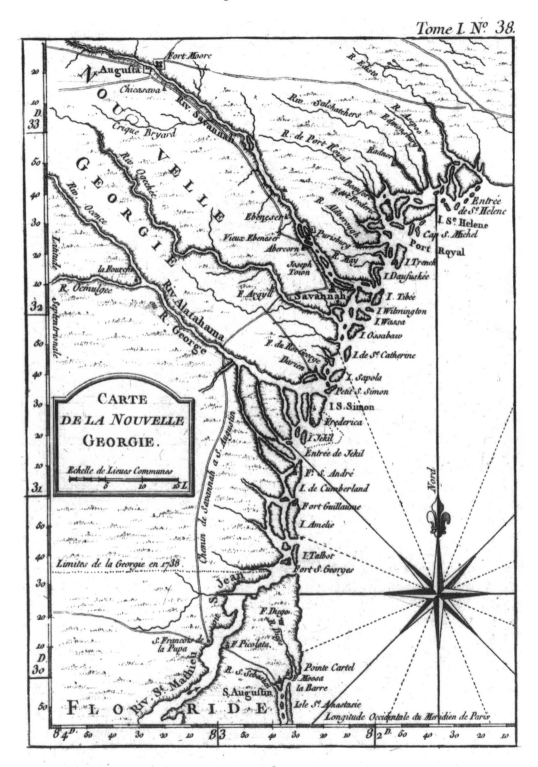

Carte de la Nouvelle Georgie, drawn by Bellin, 1764 (Hargrett Rare Book and Manuscript Library, University of Georgia Libraries).

there were no stamps in Georgia, no stamp distributor or even a copy of the Stamp Act itself. With no stamps, Governor Wright and his council decided to close the courts and land office while they allowed ships to clear customs with "endorsements" on their papers.

Wright finally received a copy of the act in late November "in a Private way" and he took the oaths as specified. On December 4, the Port of Savannah was closed, and the following day stamps arrived at Fort Halifax in Georgia aboard the British man-of-war H.M.S. *Speedwell*, commanded by Captain Fanshaw.[7] The stamp paper was brought ashore the next day without incident, and stored at the commissary at the warehouse used for Indian presents. With around 60 vessels in the harbor, and with many of them ready to sail, there was still no stamp distributor to process the required paperwork. Since it was time to begin to receive the new rice harvests in town, merchants were frantic to be allowed to sail before it rotted in the ships' holds.

Wright and the council met on December 16 to appoint a temporary stamp agent, but the proposal was voted down five to four. Two days later they reversed themselves and approved an agent *pro tem*. Merchants, who were now reluctantly in favor of the Stamp Act to save their rice, cheered the passage. The ships sailed as the duty was paid.[8]

At about 3 o'clock on Thursday afternoon of January 2, 1766, Captains Milledge and Powell of the Rangers informed Governor Wright that a crowd of 200 had already gathered to protest the Stamp Act. Though 56 Rangers and eight officers guarded the stamps, Wright was afraid that the stamps would be destroyed. He took personal charge of the Rangers and confronted the crowd with musket in hand at his gate. Wright was asked if he had any intention to appoint a temporary stamp distributor. In response he asked if theirs was "the manner to wait upon the governor" and said he would indeed carry out his orders from the king. The crowd then disbanded for the time being.

Wright and his Rangers moved the stamps from the storeroom at Fort Halifax on the outskirts of the town to a safe guardhouse in the center of Savannah. Another 40 guards were placed around his home. The stamps were safely moved by 5:00 P.M. to the guardhouse. The Rangers guarded the stamps while a local volunteer patrol made up of sailors, clerks and merchants kept watch over the stamps. The governor was so concerned that he spent several nights fully clothed and ready for action during the standoff.[9]

On the next day, the Georgia stamp distributor, the only non–American stamp distributor, Englishman George Angus, arrived at Tybee Island. He was quietly brought at noon on Saturday, January 4, to Wright's home without incident, where he began to distribute stamped papers to the custom officials. On the 7th, the Port of Savannah was reopened with vessels receiving clearance using Stamp Act paper. These were the only stamps actually used in all the thirteen colonies.[10]

After this initial use of the paper to clear the vessels from the port, there was a general agreement that no more stamps would be used until the issue of a potential repeal of the Stamp Act was known. The stamp distributor, Angus, soon found it difficult to stay in the town after hearing that as many as 600 men were approaching Savannah to seize the stamps.[11] Angus headed "into the country to avoid the resentment of the people." He later returned for a short visit to Savannah in late March, but then he disappeared from Georgia history forever, never to be heard of again.

In a letter to the British Board of Trade, dated January 15, Wright wrote the following about the threat of patriot actions in Georgia:

My Lords
    The beginning of last Month I did my Self the Honor of writing your Lordships two letters which I sent to Charles Town in South Carolina to go by the Grenville Packet, in which

I acquainted your Lordships of the Perplexed Situation I was then in, with Respect to the Stamp Duty, and in the last Mentioned that the Papers &c were brought here by His Majesties Ship *Speedwell*, and had been Landed & Lodged in the Kings Store in Fort Halifax under the Care of the Commissary without any appearance of Mob or Tumult, but that I had great reason to apprehend there was a design, when the distributor Should arrive to Compell him to resign or Promise not to act, as had been done in every other Colony to the Northward of this. I also acquainted your Lordships that I had been Informed Several Persons here, had signed an association to Oppose & Prevent the distribution of the Stamp't Papers, but that I Could not come at Such Proof as was Necessary to Support any Legal Proceedings against them. All which I now Confirm & beg Leave to Refer your Lordships to those Letters. The Military force in this Province my Lords is two Troops of Rangers Consisting in the whole of 120 Effective Men, which occupy 5 Forts or Posts, in different Parts of the Province, also 30 of the Royal Americans, 20 at Fort Augusta 150 Miles from hence, & 10 at Frederica about the Same distance. And on the 1st appearance of Faction & Sedition I ordered in Some of the Rangers from each Post & made up the Number here at Savannah 56 Privates & 8 officers and with which & the assistance of Such Gent as were of a Right Way of thinking I have been able in a great Measure to Support His Majesties Authority. but my Lords I think it my Indispensable Duty to give your Lordships a Short detail of Some things that have happened here relative to the Stamp Duty affair. Since I had the Honor to write last on Thursday, the 2nd instant about 3 o'clock in the afternoon I received intelligence by the two Captains of Rangers, Milledge & Powell, that the Liberty Boys, as they call themselves, had assembled together to the Number of about 200 & were gathering fast and that Some of them had declared they were determined to go to the Fort & break open the Store & take out & destroy the Stamp't Papers &c. Upon which I immediately ordered them to get their Men together and armed myself & went to the guard House. And having got together to the Number of about 54 Marched to the Fort & had the Papers taken out of the Store & Carried in a Cart to the guard House Escorted by the above Number of Rangers. This was done my Lords between 4 & 5 o'clock in the afternoon and without any disturbance or opposition tho there was at that time at Least 200 assembled together.

But my Lords appearances & threats were Such that I have not had less than 40 Men on duty every Night Since that to Protect the [stamped] Papers, or I am Confident they would have been destroyed, and for the 1st four nights I had not my Cloathes off. I had my Lords used Such Precaution as I was Sure to be first Informed of the Arrival of Mr. Angus the distributor [of stamped papers] for this Province, & had notice of its accordingly on friday the 3rd inst about one oclock, when I immediately Sent the Scout Boat to Tybee with an Officer & a party of Men to Protect Mr. Angus & Suffer no Body to Speak to him, but Conduct him Safely to my House, which was done the next day about noon, & that afternoon he took the State Oaths & Oath of Office, & is still at my House, as no other Could Protect him. And I have had the Papers distributed & Lodged in all the different Offices relative to the Shipping & Opening our Ports, but understand my Lords that the People in General are determined not to apply for any other Papers untill His Majesties Pleasure is known on the Petitions Sent from the Colonies. However my Lords I Presume in a very Short time Necessity will oblige them to apply for other Papers.

Notwithstanding my Lords I have been so far Successfull in Supporting His Majesties Authority in this Case. Yet my Lords I must not Conceal from His Majesty, that Several Public Insults have been offered, & abuses Committed, and that I have very nearly seen the Power & Authority His Most Sacred Majesty has been graciously Pleased to Vest in me, wrested out of my Hands, a Matter my Lords too Cutting for a good Subject & Servant to Bear. No Pains my Lords has been Spared in the Northern Colonies to Spirit up and inflame the People here, and a Spirit of Faction & Sedition has been Stirred up throughout this Province, and Partys of armed Men actually assembled themselves together, and were Preparing to do so in different Parts, but my Lords on my Sending Expresses with Letters to many of the Most Sensible & Dispassionate People. I had the Satisfaction to find that my Weight & Credit was Sufficient to Check & Prevent all Commotions & disturbances in the Country, & every thing is at Present Easy & quiet, & I hope Peace & Confidence will be Restored in general. Thus your Lordships will See the Situation I am in, and I Trust my Lords that Effectual Means will be taken to Support his Majesties Authority from Future

Insults, & to Prevent Mobs from daring to attempt to Obstruct the due Course of Law & Civil Power from taking Effect which has been too much the Case upon this Occasion.

The People in general my Lords I think not ill disposed, but have been Misled & Influenced to a degree of Madness, by the Seditious & Rebellious acts & Publications in the other Colonies. And I humbly hope the whole Province will not suffer in your Lordships Opinion for the Rashness of Some. At the Same time my Lords it Seems very Clear that the Executive Part of Government requires Some further degree of Strength & Support.

My Mode of Correspondence being in this Case (as I Conceive) Confined to your Lordships, I have not wrote to Mr. Secretary Conway. I have my Lords Exerted every means in my Power for His Majesties Service on this Occasion, & hope no further disturbances will happen.

P.S. That your Lordships may See a Specimen of the Rebellious Spirit in this Part of the World. I have Liberty to Inclose the last Paper Published in Charles Town So. Carolina.[12]

As more January rumors surfaced of hundreds of patriots heading from the backcountry to Savannah to prevent stamp sales reached the governor, he decided to have his Rangers move the stamps to Fort George. The threatened "invasion" scheduled for January 31 did not take place, but the rumors continued. One such rumor indicated that the governor was to be shot if he did not comply with the desires of the Sons of Liberty. Others said those who had supported the governor were in danger. Even James Habersham was warned not to be at home for several nights.

When the *Speedwell* arrived on February 2, Wright ordered the stamps loaded aboard the ship and removed from the current repository at Fort George. The stamps were to leave the colony immediately. The rumored backcountry people arrived late in Savannah with guns, drums and flags flying on February 4. The backcountry group now faced Wright's Rangers, 20 armed sailors from the *Speedwell* and some 100 supporters. The patriots reluctantly dispersed, disappointed that the other promised 400 to 500 South Carolina supporters had not arrived.

Governor Wright blamed the events surrounding the conflict in Savannah during the Stamp Act on the Sons of Liberty from Charles Town. In fact, Wright blamed most of the ills in Savannah on that neighboring city. The membership rolls of the Georgia Sons of Liberty were never documented, and none of the men were ever identified by the governor or by those who wrote of the events. Another problem in determining the identities of the patriot leaders during this period occurred because the colony's only newspaper, the *Georgia Gazette*, ceased publication when the Stamp Act went into effect because stamps were required for the newspaper. The newspaper did not resume publishing until May 21, 1766, with word of a repeal.[13]

The ordeal of the Stamp Act in 1765 and 1766 served as a turning point for James Wright. He came out of the experience a rather stronger person, with a more "distinct personality." He was somewhat disillusioned with the wisdom of the British government and with the citizens of Georgia. Until this time, the colonial leaders had been trusted partners with the British governors in all affairs of the government. Now they would be either his allies or his adversaries as conflict between Britain and Georgia festered.

One week after the repeal of the Stamp Act, Wright wrote the following:

[A]fter the People in a Country have been inflamed to the highest degree ... its not to be supposed or expected that all Heats & Party Spirit can subside at once. Time & prudent Conduct can only effect that, and this Province is not without some violent Republican Spirits, full of rancour against the Government & Parliament, and still fix't in their strange mistaken Ideas of Liberty....[14]

For the next decade, James Wright would find conflict with the Georgia government and the Sons of Liberty. Wright called the assembly back in to session in November 1766 uncertain of how they would react to past events. He was comforted when the body went about its usual business until the Christmas recess. In the middle of January 1767, the beginnings of another conflict were in the wind. Wright received a letter from Captain Ralph Phillips of the king's detachment of troops in Georgia, asking for action on the provisions outlined in the Quartering Act.

The Quartering Act had been passed in 1765 along with other of the Intolerable Acts and was designed to make the colonists contribute to the garrisoning of British troops in America. Wright asked in a tactfully worded request to the assembly to comply with the act. The House referred the governor's request to a committee where it remained with no action taken. Forcing some response, on February 18, Wright received his answer as the assembly indicated it would not grant the request since to approve it would be a betrayal of trust and would set another dangerous precedent. Wright was only left to report the situation to London in disgust.

This legislative event ushered in the initial appearance of the Liberty Party, which would be a persistent political faction for the remainder of Wright's days in Georgia. Wright's problems between 1767 and 1774 with the revolutionaries in Georgia were not unlike the experiences of the other colonial royal governors. The Liberty Party and the Sons of Liberty were soon to be made up of the established men in the colony. William Ewen, who later became the first president of the provincial Council of Safety, was one such Liberty leader. He was supported by men like Noble Wimberly Jones, Archibald Bulloch, Joseph Clay, Joseph Gibbons, John Smith, and Robert Baillie. Baillie and Alexander Wylly were initial supporters of the patriot cause in the 1760s, but in the end they would be among the loyalists.

By the summer of 1767, Wright was totally frustrated with the antics of the House of Assembly. He wrote after the legislative adjournment that "acts of the British Parliament will I fear for the Future, have very little weight in America." In the fall, Wright called the legislature together and demanded that the assembly comply with the terms of the Quartering Act in the name of the king. Strangely the House submitted to the demand, promising to supply funds for supplies and pay to support the troops on Cockspur Island. After congratulating the House of Assembly, he adjourned them, hoping the raging "fever" of conflict would somehow subside.

That next January, Wright reconvened the legislature. Unfortunately for Wright, the assembly was now back to its rebellious ways again, as it drew up an address to the governor. The address blamed Wright for all the legislative ills of the province of late. Apparently the new Liberty Party tactic was to abandon the challenges to the constitutional rights of the royal governor or the laws of Parliament, but to attack Wright directly.

On February 2, Wright delivered his formal response to the address in an angry lecture to the assembly. With uncharacteristic sarcasm and recriminations, he "castigated" the assemblymen for their disobedience of the Quartering Act, for trying to curtail the powers of the council, and for their "Mock Agent" Garth, who Wright said would not be received by any official in London. He concluded his speech with a harsh command to "forthwith" comply with the king's orders to implement the Quartering Act.

With Garth unrecognized in London, and with an "absolute necessary to appoint an Agent," the patriots recommended Benjamin Franklin as Georgia's agent. With satisfaction, Wright stood before the assembly on April 11th and dissolved it at the request of the House. On paper, Wright had won the first stage of the continuing struggle. This was not to hold.[15]

On the day he dissolved the Georgia Assembly, Wright ordered writs for forming a new legislature. The elections, which began in Savannah, were to be the key elections before the Revolution came to Georgia. The Liberty folks got a great start in Savannah on April 23 at the Union Society meeting. They began a major campaign in a bid to control, as they declared, that all the interests of the colonists in Georgia would be lost if the British suppressed their liberties.

The polls revealed an overwhelming victory for the Liberty Party as it gained 18 of the 25 representatives to the House. Those avowed patriots who were elected included none other than Noble Wimberly Jones, Archibald Bulloch, William Ewen, William Young, Edward Telfair and John Smith. The election made it clear that the Georgia Commons House of Assembly viewed the government as the champions for the colonists against the actions of the governor and his council to further the interests of Britain at the expense of the colony.

Portrait of Archibald Bulloch (Hargrett Rare Book and Manuscript Library, University of Georgia Libraries).

The legislative session began on November 15, 1768, with "the greatest harmony possible between the three Branches of the Legislature." But trouble was brewing. Opposition was rising over the Townshend Acts, and as the subsequent circular letters from the General Court of Massachusetts and the House of Burgesses in Virginia reached Georgia, Wright warned the assembly at the opening that he would dissolve them if they took any notice or action as a result of the rebellious circular letters.

On the day before Christmas, at 1:00 P.M., Noble Wimberly Jones requested Wright to give his approval to the bills already passed and to adjourn the session until January 9. Since the bills would be ready for his signature at 6:00 P.M., Wright invited the assembly to come to his council chamber. At 5:00 P.M., the House approved an address to the king which was similar in tone to the two infamous circular letters. When Wright came into the council chamber at six o'clock the clerk rushed up to tell him what was happening down on the assembly floor. Even though the House had passed the king's address, he decided to assent to the bills, criticized the talk of duties for trade in favor of duties for revenue as being a "Distinction without a Difference," and dissolved the assembly.

The next session met at Savannah with some reduction of tensions at the expectation of repeal of the Townshend Acts. To the list of patriot supporters elected to the assembly was added the names of Button Gwinnett, Samuel Elbert and Benjamin Andrew. Wright was satisfied with the work of the session, and it was dissolved in May 1770.

When the assembly again was called together the next fall, Wright was expecting little trouble. Conflict arose over the writs for the election for representatives of four southern parishes. The assembly refused to pass a tax bill until elections were held. Wright issued the writs the day after the House made its threat, but the House decided to seize upon the pretext and attacked the governor. The next day, Wright dissolved the assembly and in a few days ordered new elections.

The next session began the next April and unanimously elected Jones as the speaker. Wright rejected the radical Jones' election and replaced him with Archibald Bulloch. The assembly adopted a resolution declaring Wright's rejection as "a high Breach of the Priviledge of the House." Wright, on the third day of the session, promptly dissolved the assembly. Shortly after, Wright sailed for a visit back to England. He would be absent for nearly two years. As president of the council, James Habersham took over the government of the colony in Wright's absence. Habersham opened the next assembly on April 21, 1772, but dissolved it on the third day when the House attempted to reelect Jones to the speaker position. For Georgia government, there was only stalemate.[16]

7

Georgia Heads to Revolution

"And to be Plain my Lord I see Nothing but a Prospect of a General Rebellion."

In February of 1773, Wright returned to Georgia with tangible proof that he had the support of the king and his ministers. He had been made a baronet and would soon sit on the Board of Trade. Wright was met and welcomed at the landing by a committee of the assembly. To the delight of the assembly members, in May, with the support of the Indian agent, John Stuart, Wright met with the five major southern Indian nations in Augusta and gained the 1.6 million acres between Savannah and the Ogeechee, and 500,000 acres between the Ogeechee and the Altamaha from the Creeks.[1]

While Wright was negotiating with the Indians, the period of stalemated calm in the British colonies came to an end. On May 10, 1773, the Parliament passed a bill, the East India Company Act, to allow the failing British East India Company to ship surplus tea to the colonies without paying the regular English export duty.

Later in Boston on Sunday, November 28, 1773, the first of four tea ships, *Dartmouth*, arrived and tied up at Griffin's Wharf. Immediately the patriot Committee of Correspondence placed an armed guard at the dock to prevent any tea from being unloaded. The next day a meeting, attended by a crowd of some 5,000 citizens, was held during which it was resolved that "the tea should be returned to the place whence it came." Governor Hutchinson ordered the citizens to disperse, but received only jeers and hissing.

Several weeks later there were now three tea ships under guard at the wharf, the fourth scheduled British tea ship, *William*, having run aground off Cape Cod. As thousands of patriot citizens gathered in the Old South Church, the governor refused to have the tea ships ordered out of the harbor, as he retired to his country estate in Milton. A tea consignee was sent to Milton to see if the governor would change his mind, but it was not to be. The news was revealed to the Old South group, which prompted Samuel Adams to rise from his seat and exclaim, "This meeting can do nothing more to save the country." The cheers went up: "Boston Harbor a Teapot tonight"; "Hurrah for Griffin's Wharf"; "The Mohawks are Come."[2]

On December 16, a group of locals, thinly disguised as Mohawk Indians, with blackened faces and blankets hiding their clothing, boarded the three ships—*Dartmouth, Eleanor* and *Beaver*—and threw 342 chests of tea worth £15,000 into Boston Harbor.[3] This incident, well known as the Boston Tea Party, was to bring about a major crisis within the British colonies. The day after the dumping, Admiral Montagu remarked to the local citizens, "Well, boys, you have had a fine pleasant evening for your Indian caper, haven't you. But mind, you have got to pay the fiddler yet!"[4] Because of the Boston Tea Party, as time would ultimately reveal, not a single chest of tea was sold in America.[5]

While many called for blood to be shed in response, on March 25, 1774, the British House of Commons passed the Boston Port Act by overwhelming majority to deal with the "Boston mutineers." This act closed the Port of Boston to all shipping until the British East India Company had been compensated for the losses incurred by the Tea Party mob and when the crown had been given evidence of their good intentions. The English rejoiced as King George III declared that England was now united.

On May 6, the Parliament passed another bill aimed at continuing to punish the patriots of Boston, the Administration of Justice Act. This act allowed royal officials accused of a capital offense in the performance of their official duties to be tried in another colony or in Britain. The British ministers were not finished as they passed the Massachusetts Government Act, which called for the provincial council to be appointive, as in other colonies, rather than elective. This act gave the royal governor more power to appoint or dismiss officers, judges or sheriffs at will.

News of the Boston Port Act reached Boston on May 11. The Committee of Correspondence went into quick action in sending out a circular letter to the neighboring towns calling for a meeting to be held at Faneuil Hall. The Boston Town Meeting met and the patriotic declarations were expressed with passion.[6] As the effects of the Coercive Acts took full force in Boston, the Massachusetts legislature in June called, via circular letter to the other colonies, for a "general congress of the colonies to bring about united action in the emergency" which was to be held in Philadelphia. The first meeting of the Continental Congress was about to make history.

On July 20, a notice signed by Noble Wimberly Jones, Archibald Bulloch, John Houstoun and George Walton appeared in the *Georgia Gazette* inviting fellow Georgians to meet at the Vendue House in Savannah on the 27th to consider the Philadelphia congress requested by the Massachusetts legislature. In the meeting, various letters and resolutions from the other colonies were considered. A committee was assigned to draft resolutions to be formally considered in a second meeting planned for August 10 in Savannah.

The resolutions derived at Tondee's Tavern in Savannah on August 10, 1774, were as follows:

> Resolved, nemine contradicente, That his Majesty's subjects in America owe the same allegiance, and are entitled to the same rights, privileges, and immunities with their fellow subjects in Great Britain.
>
> Resolved, nemine contradicente, That as protection and allegiance are reciprocal, and under the British Constitution, correlative terms, his Majesty's subjects in America have a clear and indisputable right, as well from the general laws of mankind, as from the ancient and established customs of the land so often recognized, to petition the Throne upon every emergency.
>
> Resolved, nemine contradicente, That an Act of Parliament lately passed, for blockading the port and harbour of Boston, is contrary to our idea of the British Constitution: First, for that in effect deprives good and lawful men of the use of their property without judgment of their peers; and secondly, for that it is in nature of an ex post facto law, and indiscriminately blends as objects of punishment the innocent with the guilty; neither do we conceive the same justified upon a principle of necessity, for that numerous instances evince that the laws and executive power of Boston have made sufficient provision for the punishment of all offenders against persons and property.
>
> Resolved, nemine contradicente, That the Act for abolishing the Charter of Massachusetts Bay tends to the subversion of American rights; for besides those general liberties, the original settlers brought over with them as their birthright, particular immunities granted by

each charter, as an inducement and means of settling the Province; and we apprehend the said Charter cannot be dissolved but by a voluntary surrender of the people, representatively declared.

Resolved, nemine contradicente, That we apprehend the Parliament of Great Britain hath not, nor ever had, any right to tax his Majesty's American subjects; for it is evident beyond contradiction, the constitution admits of no taxation without representation; that they are coeval and inseparable; and every demand for the support of government should be by requisition made to the several houses of representatives.

Resolved, nemine contradicente, That it is contrary to natural justice and the established law of the land, to transport any person to Great Britain or elsewhere, to be tried under indictment for a crime committed in any of the colonies, as the party prosecuted would there be deprived of the privilege of trial by his peers from the vicinage, the Injured perhaps prevented from legal reparation, and both lose the full benefit of their witnesses.

Resolved, nemine contradicente, That we concur with our sister colonies in every constitutional measure to obtain redress of American grievances, and will by every lawful means in our power, maintain those inestimable blessings for which we are indebted to God and the Constitution of our country-a Constitution founded upon reason and justice, and the indelible rights of mankind.

Resolved, nemine contradicente, That the Committee appointed by the meeting of the inhabitants of this Province, on Wednesday, the 27th of July last, together with the deputies who have appeared here on this day from the different parishes, by a General Committee to act; and that any eleven or more of them shall have full power to correspond with the Committees of the several Provinces upon the continent; and that copies of these resolutions, as well as all other proceedings, be transmitted without delay to the Committees of Correspondence in the respective Provinces.[7]

Governor Wright immediately issued a proclamation condemning the upcoming session to no avail. The August session was attended by 21 representatives from the parishes in the same number as the Commons House of Assembly. The delegates adopted a number of resolutions, including condemnations of the Boston Port Act, the abolition of the Massachusetts Charter, the attempts to tax the colonies, and moving trials to England. They also expressed support for the redress of grievances for actions by the British in their sister colonies and affirmed their right to petition the crown for historic British rights, privileges and immunities. Even though there was considerable support for sending delegates to the first Continental Congress, it was ultimately agreed that no delegates would be sent because the colony was too divided.[8]

Wright, now deeply disturbed by the patriot actions, came to some small degree of cheer in the fall of 1774 when resolutions from dissenters began to arrive in heavy numbers. Some 500 to 600 people of the province had been willing to put their signatures on public record as opposing the patriot resolutions of August. Wright had come to believe that "the Sense of the People" in general was against strong support of Boston.

Wright's cheer was shortlived when on November 23 the Liberty group published a copy of the nonimportation agreement adopted at the Continental Congress, and urged all "Freeholders, Merchants, and other Inhabitants" to send delegates to Savannah on January 15, 1775, to vote on joining the association. On the day the delegates gathered, Wright called the legislature into session. He opened the session with perhaps his best speech ever, as he made a persuasive plea to the elected leaders of Georgia not to "be led away by the voices and opinions of men of over-heated ideas." He asked them to "consider coolly and sensibly the terrible consequences" of what they were doing, and reminded them that "where there is no law there can be no liberty."

The Savannah congress was a disappointment to the patriots, as only five of the 12 parishes sent delegates. They did adopt the recommendations of the association, but put the date back for putting them into effect. The Sons of Liberty had failed to arouse the trade ban, as most of the Savannah merchants opposed it outright and the colony's planters seemed unenthusiastic. As both the assembly and delegates to the congress left Savannah, the people of Georgia were left to "fluctuate between liberty and convenience."

Wright had been so successful at applying pressure to bear that on April 6, Jones, Bulloch and Houstoun had notified John Hancock that they would not be in attendance at the upcoming Second Continental Congress with so much sentiment against the congress in Georgia. Wright had been so proud of the "great Decency and Respect" shown to him by the Georgia citizens during the calm spring of 1775. Only the radicals in neighboring South Carolina had shaken the peace with their threats of trade bans with Georgia.

The peace was shattered on May 10 when news of the fighting at Lexington and Concord came to Savannah. The next day, the Liberty boys headed by Jones, Joseph Habersham and Edward Telfair broke into the public powder magazine and took 500 pounds of gunpowder. Back on May 2, Wright had written that he was "very hopeful that no Unlawful Restraint on Trade, or Violence will be Attempted in this Province." Three weeks later he wrote, "And to be Plain my Lord I see Nothing but a Prospect of a General Rebellion." By August, his royal government had all but disappeared in all but name.[9]

On June 21, a call went out to the inhabitants of Savannah, Georgia, to meet the following day at 10 A.M. at the Liberty Pole for the purpose of selecting a committee to form a union with the other colonies in the cause of liberty. The first act of the session was to establish a Council of Safety with 15 leading members of the colony, and a secretary. The council was instructed to correspond with other councils of safety, the Continental Congress and other committees in Georgia. A number of resolutions were considered at this meeting, including one providing that Georgia would not become an asylum for those who were escaping censure in other colonies. One young man named Hopkins spoke openly against this measure. He was later arrested, tarred and feathered and was displayed on a cart through the streets of Savannah for four to five hours. After the meeting, the union flag was hoisted up the Liberty Pole and two cannons were posted at its base. The council then adjourned and many retired to Tondee's Tavern for dinner, where 13 toasts of patriotic salute for the 13 American colonies were delivered, each followed by cannon fire.[10]

On July 4, the Second Provincial Congress of Georgia met at Tondee's Tavern in Savannah with delegates from all but two of the parishes. The first item on the agenda was essentially a sermon by the Reverend John Zubly on "The Law of Liberty." Then, the congress passed a petition to the king, followed by a variety of resolutions stating the rights of Americans, using much of the same language as presented by the other colonial bodies.

The Georgia Provincial Congress adopted the Continental Association and elected delegates to the Second Continental Congress already meeting in Philadelphia-Archibald Bulloch, Dr. Lyman Hall, John Houstoun, Noble W. Jones and the Reverend John J. Zubly. The congress also issued £10,000 in certificates for expenses, and formed the Council of Safety to serve as the executive body when the congress was not in session. The congress adjourned on July 17, having finally taken Georgia fully down a new path toward independence. The Georgia delegates Bulloch, Houstoun and Zubly attended their first meeting with the Second Continental Congress on September 5, along with Dr. Lyman Hall, who was already in attendance representing Georgia's St. John's Parish.[11]

On July 5, a dispatch from Whitehall from the Earl of Dartmouth informed Wright "advices received from every quarter contain evidences of an intention in all the Colonies to the northward to take up arms against the government of this Kingdom." He continued with:

[I]t is the King's firm resolution that the most vigorous efforts should be made both by sea and land to reduce his rebellious subjects to obedience; and the proper measures are now pursuing not only for augmenting the army under General Gage, but also for making such addition to our Naval strength in North America as may enable Admiral Graves to make such a disposition of his fleet as that besides the Squadron necessary for the New England station there may be separate squadrons at New York, within the Bay of Delaware, in Chesapeake Bay, and upon the coast of Carolina.[12]

At the request of Governor Wright, Savannah loyalist John Hopkins wrote the following affidavit on July 29, 1775. On that same day, Wright drafted a letter to Lord Dartmouth describing the loss of royal authority in Savannah and included this document. Hopkins had been tarred and feathered five days earlier by activitist patriots.

About 9 of the clock in the evening of the 24 instant as I was sitting at supper with my family there came to my house a number of persons (some were in disguise) and opened the door. Joseph Reynolds of Savannah, bricklayer, Captain McCluer and Captain Bunner, at present of Savannah, mariners, laid hold of me, without saying anything to me. As soon as the aforesaid people laid hold of me, a great number rushed in and hurried me out of my house and led me to the outside of the town. They consulted to tar and feather me, but the majority resolved to carry me to a more public place. Accordingly they led me into the middle of the square near the dial in Savannah and stripped me of my jacket and shirt and with great reluctance left the rest of my apparel on me and then they proceeded to tar and feather me and immediately put me into a cart and carted me up and down the streets of Savannah for upwards of three hours in the above condition.

During the time they carted me to the Liberty Tree and there swore they would hang me. Bunner said he was rather fat but he would go up the tree and hang me. Bunner further said that unless I would drink "Damnation to all Tories and success to American Liberty!" I should be hung immediately, which request I was obliged to comply with. They continued to abuse me, gave me a great deal of ill language and upbraided me with my conduct. Some one or other said that if they could lay hold of the parson they would put him along side of me in the cart. I also heard said in the mob that Mr. Smith should be next and that they intended to continue on until they had tarred and feathered all the Tories, or words to that affect.

I saw in the aforesaid mob, together with the persons aforementioned, Thomas Lee, carpenter, John Spencer, carpenter, Alexander Phoenix, merchant, Ambrose Wright, planter, Samuel Wells, mariner, Francis Arthur of Savannah, surveyor, Oliver Bowen, merchant, John McCluer and Captain McCluer, Joseph Habersham and Francis Harris, gentlemen, Quintin Pooler, merchant, Captain Hawkins, mariner, and Thomas Hamilton, butcher, and several others that I cannot recollect. Between the hours of 12 and 1 of the clock they discharged me at the vendue house with orders "to beg all American pardon.[13]

Helpless, Wright watched for six months as the Revolution continued to undermine the royal government of the province. He lost the militia in July, and the courts in December. To Dartmouth Wright wrote: "The Powers of Government are wrested out of my Hands ... Law & Government are nearly if not quite annihilated." The end was near.[14]

It was January 12, 1776, as British captain Barclay looked out across the channel from the deck of his man-of-war, H.M.S. *Scarborough,* at the little island of Tybee. In company with another man-of-war and a transport, he had sailed from Boston with a detachment of royal troops under the command of Majors Maitland and Grant. With their arrival now, they were at anchor at the entrance to the Savannah River, with the town of Savannah only some 15 miles upriver. Captain Barclay's thoughts turned to their need to gain supplies as well as to meet with the third and longtime royal governor of the province of Georgia, Sir James Wright.

Within a few hours the news of the arrival of the British ships was reported to the Council of Safety at Savannah. As the days went by and the council members reflected on their best move, the air of danger and imminent conflict with the British forces off Tybee was the subject of much deliberation. After six days, the fears of the Council overtook them and the body voted the following:

> [T]hat the persons of his excellency Sir James Wright, Bart, and of John Mullryne, Joseph Tattnall, and Anthony Stokes, Esqrs., be forthwith arrested and secured, and that all non-associates be disarmed except those who will give their parole assuring that they will not aid, assist or comfort any of the persons on board his Majesty's ships of war, or take any of the persons on board his Majesty's ships of war, or take up arms against America in the present unhappy dispute.[15]

Realizing that he was the best man to arrest the governor, the 25-year-old Major Joseph Habersham volunteered, "to secure the person of the governor." With a party of his selection, Habersham proceeded to the residence of Wright, who was in conference with his council. With determination and personal courage, Habersham passed the sentinel at the door and moved into the hall and over to the governor. With what could have been perceived as a show of friendship, Habersham turned to Wright, with the council peering on with some curiosity, and placed his hand on Wright's shoulder as he exclaimed, "Sir James, you are my prisoner."

With looks of astonishment on their faces, Wright's council promptly fled from his house. Habersham then sat down with the now indignant Wright and explained the situation to him. Soon Wright gave Habersham his "solemn promise ... neither to depart from Savannah nor to hold any correspondence with the officers and soldiers on the ships lying in Tybee Roads." A guard was placed in front of his house to keep watch on his movements and to "prohibit all intercourse with members of the council, Crown officers, or persons deemed inimical to the cause of America."

Confinement to his mansion became ever more distressing to Wright as the days went by. In addition to being generally harassed, Wright had endured shots being fired into his dwelling. Unable to communicate with the British force just downriver and fearing for his life, Wright escaped from out the back of his mansion on the night of February 11. He fled to the river and moved to Bonaventure Plantation, the home of his friend John Mullryne. There a boat and crew were waiting as they conveyed Wright through Tybee Creek to Captain Barclay's *Scarborough* "at three o'clock on the morning of the 12th."[16]

On the 13th, Wright sat down at his desk in his cabin aboard the *Scarborough* and penned a letter of complaint to James Mackay and the other members of his council remaining in Savannah. It explained that he had indeed tried for "upward of three weeks to prevail" on the rebels' ruling body that "the commanders of his Majesty's ships here might obtain assurances that they might come to town and have free intercourse with" him. Also on Tuesday the 6th he asked, "that the King's ships might be supplied with provisions" but had not received any answer. Wright continued that since he was unable to communicate with his officers and "for these reasons and many others which you were made acquainted with and approved of" he determined that his best action was to come to the British ships off Tybee. Wright wrote:

> And after having examined and duly weighed and considered my several letters from England, and General Howe at Boston, and after having had a conversation with his Majesty's Officers here, I have the great satisfaction to be able to affirm from the best authority that the forces now here will not commit any hostilities against this Province, though fully sufficient to reduce and overcome every opposition that could be attempted to be made: and that nothing is meant or wanted but a friendly intercourse and a supply of fresh provisions. This his Majesty's officers have an undoubted right to expect, and what they insist upon: and this I not only solemnly require in his Majesty's name but also, as

(probably) the best friend the people of Georgia have, advise them without the least hesitation to comply with, or it may not be in my power to insure them the continuance of the peace and quietude they now have, if it may be called so.

His Majesty has been graciously pleased to grant me leave to return to England, and my regard for the Province and people is such that I cannot avoid exhorting the people to save themselves and their posterity from that total ruin and destruction which, although they may not, yet I most clearly see at the threshold of their doors: and I cannot leave them without again warning them in the most earnest and friendly manner, to desist from their present plans and resolution. It is still in their power: and if they will enable me to do it, I will, (as far as I can) engage to give and endeavour to obtain for them full pardon and forgiveness for all past crimes and offenses: and this I conjure you to consider well and most seriously of, before it's too late. But let things happen as they may, be it remembered that I this day in the King's name offer the people of Georgia the Olive branch, that most desirable object and inestimable blessing, the return of peace to them and their posterity.

Captain Barclay has desired me to notify that he is willing and ready to give every assistance in his power to the captains of all such merchant ships as may be legally cleared out to enable them proceed on their respective voyages....

This letter, which I consider as of the utmost consequence and importance to the whole people of Georgia, I must desire you will be pleased to communicate to the Assembly, if sitting, and if not, to those who are called the Council of Safety, and especially to the inhabitants of the town and Province in general, and acquaint them that I shall expect their full and clear answer to every part of it in a reasonable time.[17]

Out of a sense of courtesy for the long-time royal governor of Georgia, the newly elected president of the Provincial Congress, Archibald Bulloch, responded to Wright's letter. Wright's warnings were disregarded.

Portrait of General Lachlan McIntosh (Hargrett Rare Book and Manuscript Library, University of Georgia Libraries).

On February 16, Colonel Lachlan McIntosh, the selected commander of the Georgia Continental Army forces, noted that the British vessels off Tybee Island included five men-of-war-the *Syren*, the *Scarborough*, the *Raven*, the *Tamer*, and the *Cherokee*-a few tenders and two large transports. McIntosh declared that the "Province has declared itself in a state of alarm...."[18]

Captain Barclay was frustrated with the continued lack of cooperation shown by the rebels in supplying his small fleet with food. He was determined to remedy that situation as best he could. With negotiations failed, on the last day of February, Barclay directed the *Scarborough* (20 guns), the *Tamer* (16 guns), the *Cherokee* (10 guns) and the *Hutchinbrook* schooner (8 guns) into Five-Fathom Hole off Tybee Island. Accompanying the ships aboard two transports were between 250-300 British light infantry and marines under Major Grant. Captain Barclay's intended rebel prizes were 11 merchant ships loaded with rice and ready for sea then lying at the Savannah wharves.

The local rice merchants had been

unable to export their rice by previous order of the Continental Congress, but on March 1 those regulations had expired. Only the presence of the British ships off Tybee Island now blocked their putting to sea. Knowing that many of the merchants were motivated to have their rice transports sail as soon as possible, and realizing that the old restrictions had expired, President William Ewen and his Savannah Council of Safety passed the following resolution on March 1:

> Resolved that no ships loaded with rice, or any other article of produce, in this Province, shall be permitted to sail without leave of the Council of Safety or next Congress, except such vessels as are or shall be permitted to sail for the purpose of procuring the necessary means of defence.

After taking soundings of the Back River opposite Hutchinson's Island, the two British transports were able to pass up the Savannah River. One vessel anchored in front of the town and while the other ship tried to "round the upper end of the island so as to attack from above...." That vessel ran aground opposite Rae's Hall and remained disabled. With dispatch, Major Joseph Habersham, with his riflemen, fired on the troops aboard the disabled vessel and drove the British off the decks. Without boats to support a patriot boarding of the transport, Habersham and his men could only look on as the tide rose. At high tide the vessel was able to liberate itself off the bank, and it moved away and out of harm's way.

Undeterred by the late action of the patriots, Majors Maitland and Grant, on the night of March 2, landed their several hundred troops from the Back River and marched across Hutchinson's Island. At 4 A.M. on the 3rd, they took possession of the rice-laden transports opposite Savannah. It was 9 A.M. before the patriot militia discovered the British maneuver. The British action was successful because of extra silence maintained by the British troops, and some collusion on the part of the captains of the merchantmen in surrendering their ships.

The first intelligence regarding the taking of the rice ships came from two sailors from one of the vessels. Having come ashore with the excuse of obtaining their clothing, they reported that Captain Rice had boarded their ship to explain the order issued by the Council of Safety requiring all ships to stand down when he was forcibly detained.

Reacting to the news, Colonel McIntosh at once proceeded with 300 men to Yamacraw Bluff where a breastwork was hastily thrown up. Three 4-pounders bearing at the captured shipping were posted at the breastwork. Under a flag of truce, patriot lieutenant Daniel Roberts of the St. John's Rangers and Captain Raymond Demerè of St. Andrew's Parish rowed over to the vessel now under the control of Captain Barclay and Major Grant to demand the release of the ships. As they boarded the vessel they were immediately arrested and held as prisoners.

After half an hour elapsed without the return of the patriot party, the vessel was hailed through a bullhorn to release Rice, Roberts and Demerè. Receiving only insults from the British, two cannon were fired at the vessel. The British answered the volley saying they should send two men "in whom they most confided and the British commander would meet with them." Captain Screven of the St. John's Rangers and Captain Baker of the St. John's Riflemen were detailed, along with 12 Rangers. They rowed out to a point directly under the stern of the vessel and demanded the return of the officers and Rice. After receiving an insult, Captain Baker fired his rifle at someone on board. This was answered by a discharge of small arms and swivels from the vessel. One patriot Ranger was wounded and the boat almost sunk as Screven and Baker retired out of range.

The shore battery now opened fire at all the captured vessels, which was maintained for four hours' duration. After convening, the Council of Safety directed that the ships be set on fire. Volunteers for the firings were Captain Bowen, John Morel, Lieutenant James Jackson, Thomas Hamilton and James Bryan. They set on fire the *Inverness*, formally commanded by Captain McGillivray, which was loaded with rice and deerskins. Afire, it was set adrift in the river.

Confusion reined as the British troops got ashore on the marsh while the patriot riflemen and field pieces, loaded with grapeshot, fired at them. Some of the vessels got up the river under the cover of the armed schooner, while others caught fire. As the night closed in, the resulting flames from the vessels of Savannah exhibited quite a brilliant scene. Two of the merchant ships under Captains Inglis and Wardell were recaptured and, having not been set a fire, were under the control of Captain Screven as they were moved into a local wharf. The British troops aboard these two vessels were allowed to write a letter to Captain Barclay that evening requesting an exchange for patriot prisoners. Barclay refused the exchange.

Responding to a previous request for assistance, the South Carolina Council of Safety sent 150 volunteers from Charles Town and 350 from the county militia under the command of Colonel Stephen Bull. These forces arrived at the most opportune time to assist in dislodging the British. Soon three merchant vessels were burned, "six were dismantled, and two escaped to sea." Before the British had all returned to their previous station off Tybee Island, they sent a detachment of marines ashore at Skidoway Island. A company of militia commanded by Lieutenant Hext drove off this detachment. Elsewhere, at Cockspur Island a skirmish ensued, resulting in the deaths of patriot lieutenants Oates and Laroach.

The infamous "rice engagement" was essentially a failure for the British, though Governor Wright chose to frame it in a different light. He wrote Lord Dartmouth on March 10 that the expedition returned "with 14 or 15 merchant ships and vessels of one sort or another having on board about 1600 barrels of rice." He also incorrectly reported that the British troops sustained no loss and that only four sailors were wounded. After the affair, there were eight vessels off the Savannah wharfs that had not been previously set on fire or captured.

To prevent any further chance of these vessels sailing, the Council of Safety ordered the rigging brought ashore, as well as the riggers "unhung." Lieutenant Colonel Stirk, with 40 troops from the Georgia Militia, ensured the compliance of these orders.

With Rice, Roberts and Demerè still being held as prisoners by the British, the Georgia authorities took retaliatory action by arresting James Edward Powell, Anthony Stokes, Josiah Tattnall, John Mullryne and other members of the king's council remaining at Savannah. After negotiations, the patriot prisoners were released under conditions that the king's council members be set free and allowed to stay under parole conditions or leave with their personal apparel and provisions aboard the British ships off Tybee.

With the passing of the British expedition up to Savannah, the patriot Council of Safety was determined to sever all relationships with the British fleet off Tybee. Accordingly, on the 25th of March, a patriot expedition of some 150 men, consisting of riflemen, light infantry, volunteers, and several Creek Indians, led by Archibald Bulloch, moved to Tybee Island. The purpose of the expedition was to stop the British fleet officers and troops from going ashore at Tybee and utilizing the houses "for their comfort and enjoyment." Bulloch's force burned every house on Tybee Island except one used by a sick woman and several children. The British suffered the death of two marines and a Tory, with a marine and several Tories captured. Though the British armed sloop *Cherokee* sailed up to provide support with cannon fire, the patriots sustained no injuries.

With the danger of immediate attack now passed, the previous day Colonel Bull had collected his South Carolina forces and departed back to Charles Town. The protection of Savannah was now passed to Colonel Lachlan McIntosh and his Georgia battalion of 236 named militia, of which only around 100 were actually present for duty. The province was thinly defended with 60 men along the Florida border preventing cattle stealing, and a like group of cavalry on the western frontier guarding against invasion from Indians.[19]

With circumstances off Tybee Island restricted, and having received communications from General Howe and Sir Henry Clinton that no military operations were planned for the province of Georgia, in late March Sir James Wright sailed away to Halifax, arriving on April 21, 1776. Soon he was on his way to London on his leave of absence. The administration of the last British royal governor of the province of Georgia was now ended.[20] The royal period in Georgia was at an end.

8

A Frontier War in Georgia

*"If I am ever to depend upon operations I have no right to guide,
and men I have no right to command, I shall deem it then ...
one of the most unfortunate accidents of my life."*

It was a desperate affair as Georgia president Archibald Bulloch from Savannah wrote to Major General Charles Lee, the commander of the Southern Department of the Continental Army, in Charles Town alerting him to the situation in the province of Georgia. It was July 3, 1776. He explained to Lee his "helpless situation-The Importance of this Colony to the American cause is very great & therefore I'm persuaded we shall claim part of your attention-Your presence here would give a most happy & favorable Complexion to our affairs-The Post-Boy is waiting & I can only wish that the Lord of Hosts, the God of Armies may be your guide & protection."

To Congress Lee forwarded a letter presented at the conference he held with the "Georgia Deputies." The Georgia patriot leaders presented a rather grim view of threats to their fair province. Lee noted that even though they had "great Plenty of Provision-numerous stocks of Cattle ... upwards of 30,000 of Head of black Cattle in the Province ... excellent Inlets-Harbours and Rivers (perhaps equal to any upon the Continent)" and the "firm attachment of its Inhabitants to the American cause," they had "To the East ... the Ravages of British Cruizers ... their Negroes are daily inveigled & carried away from their Plantations.... To the South they have the Province of East Florida-the Inhabitants and Soldiery in which must of Necessity make Inroads upon Georgia for the Article of Provision with which they have been chiefly supplied.... Accounts of their being at time upward of 1000 British Troops in St. Augustine.... To the West ... are the most numerous tribes of Indians now in North America-to wit the Creeks, Cherokees, Choctaws and a number of small Tribes, in whole at least 15,000 Gun-Men-All these Nations have been much tampered with ... we consider their natural Principle of Infidelity and how much more able our Enemies are to purchase their Friendship by presents.... Add to all these considerations the vast Number of Negroes we have, perhaps of themselves Sufficient to subdue us...."

Lee noted that with all these "Circumstances" upon the Georgia people, the leaders requested "Measures be immediately taken for the Defence and Security of that Province." The specific requests included funding for regiments of Continental Army troops, fortifications and "Guard Boats," and that the Indians be paid for their "good offices," for those that supported the Americans.[1]

The British indeed represented a threat from their advanced post on the St. Mary's River and from St. Augustine, Florida. In July, Jonathan Bryan arrived in Charles Town to alert General Lee of the potential of taking St. Augustine in East Florida. Byran noted that "there were but a very few men in that garrison." The British had continually sent raiding parties with regular troops, loyalists and Seminole Indians to the Georgia frontier. During these incursions the attackers would often take cattle, carry off slaves and kill frontier citizens. The British also were actively engaged in persuading the Creek Indian nation to send their savage warriors to attack Georgia. Now Georgia leaders begged Lee to come to their aid to deal with the British of Florida. They pleaded for an attack on St. Augustine.[2]

General Lee could not ignore the calls as he made plans to undertake just such an expedition to East Florida. In his mind an expedition would give "security to Georgia, occasion infinite distress to the Garrison of St Augustine, but above all, make a salutary impression on the minds of the Creeks."[3] But it was no small order. He faced many challenges getting adequate troops, supplies and wagons to undertake such an expedition.

Not everyone shared Lee's enthusiasm. General Robert Howe was skeptical of the new expedition for he felt the objectives "can not be very important." General Armstrong, who was laid up with sickness from the excessive heat, was not impressed with the upcoming deployment either. He had withdrawn his name from consideration for command of the expedition as he praised Howe as "a genius among our American best." This was a curious honor from Armstrong as he noted Howe's social graces. He wrote "Howe has a thousand qualifications for this meridian ... and he is able to wash off all the dryness incidental as it was, with half a dozen of Madeira, or a single dance with the ladies will shake it off as we do the dust from our feet."

Lee marched out of Charles Town on August 7 with 1,500 men carrying no artillery or even a medicine chest to join the militia stationed in the vicinity of Port Royal. Moultrie felt the season was too inclement to proceed, but Howe, Lee and Moultrie headed out anyway. General James Moore was left in command of Charles Town in Lee's absence. On their arrival at Port Royal that same day, they discovered several British transports loaded with sick soldiers. Lee agreed to allow the infirm British to recuperate on shore. When the British finally sailed away, Howe was left in the area to straighten the "Damnable Hobble" of the "Hotch Potch Camp" stationed there.

Lee continued to move toward Savannah, followed by Howe's regulars on the 8th. Lee moved to Colonel Bull's home outside Beaufort and wrote John Rutledge, the president of South Carolina, on the 10th that Port Royal "has so many natural advantages for defence that few works will be necessary to put it hors d'insult." Lee had given orders to improve "the Fort and the lines on the narrows." He directed that the chief engineer, Baron de Brahm, would proceed after he laid out the "Redoubts and fleches" on Sullivan's Island to survey Port Royal and St. Helena Island.[4]

While Lee's force was on the way to Savannah, on Thursday, August 8, a special messenger arrived in Savannah with correspondence from the distinguished president of the Continental Congress, John Hancock. Two days later, on Saturday, the Declaration of Independence was read aloud at Peter Tondee's Tavern to the Council of Safety by Georgia president Bulloch. Clearly visible on the document were the signatures of the Georgia representatives Button Gwinnett, George Walton and Lyman Hall. They had signed the Declaration in Philadelphia. Bulloch then moved outside and delivered the words of the Declaration to the assembled public. The throngs demanded that it be read yet again. This time the president moved under the liberty pole at Johnson Square. Later in the afternoon he read the famous document at the location of the first Oglethorpe landing at the Founding. The air was filled with cheers and cannon fire.[5] It was a new day for Georgia and American patriots everywhere.

That evening Bulloch, his council, Colonel Lachlan McIntosh, other gentlemen and the militia dined under the cedar trees as they drank and toasted the United States of America. In a town lit up with excitement, it was not long before muffled drums and fifes were heard as the citizens witnessed the mock funeral procession and burial of King George III. The king in parody committed "his political existence to the ground ... in such and certain hope that he will never obtain a resurrection to rule over the United States of America." Messengers were sent to the backcountry as the glorious word spread throughout Georgia of a new independence.[6]

In support of the expedition, a detachment of troops from South Carolina was sent off on August 11 to Savannah, Georgia, along with two field cannons. Meanwhile, Lee asked Moultrie if he would take command of the expedition, even though his brother was there as governor. Moultrie responded that he had no reservations about taking on the expedition except that he needed 800 men and proper supplies. The colonel made a list and Lee forwarded the list to Augusta to be filled.

Lee moved southward from Beaufort to Purisburg. From there he wrote General Armstrong to forward the 147 sick men from Colonel Muhlenberg's Regiment to Williamsburg when they recovered. Lee and Howe then traveled from Purisburg to Savannah, arriving on August 17 after having left behind a number of smaller detachments of North Carolina troops stationed at the various small communities along the way.[7]

Engraved for Murray's History of the American War.

GENERAL HOWE.

Printed for T. Robson, Newcastle upon Tyne.

Portrait of General Robert Howe, taken from **Dead Towns of Georgia**, C.C. Jones, Jr., Vol. I, opposite page 130 (Hargrett Rare Book and Manuscript Library, University of Georgia Libraries).

At Savannah, Lee consulted with the local Georgia patriot leaders. Unfortunately they had little to give in the way of resources for the proposed expedition southward. Lee complained when he wrote, "I shou'd not be surpris'd if they were to propose mounting a body of mermaids on alligators...." With feeble support from Georgia, Lee was convinced that it was impossible to supply and recruit sufficient men to carry out a meaningful attack on St. Augustine. When he learned that the British outpost on the St. Mary's River had been evacuated, he decided to downsize and send a raiding party. To provide better protection of Georgia, Lee proposed that a cavalry should be raised, several small frontier forts be built, and that armed patrols on the rivers be established.[8]

The troop situation in Savannah and in the surrounding towns and villages grew worse. In Sunbury, they were losing 14 to 15 men each day to disease. General Howe came to regard the situation as "a fatiguing, pointless expedition." The troops watched as the supplies dwindled. Rations usually consisted only of rice. To get wood, troops would pull down entire houses. As the discontent festered, discipline decayed. Those who violated orders were sentenced to specific days in "the Black Hole" on a diet of "Rice and Water." Because some South Carolinians charged outrageous prices for necessities, Lee predicted any future British attack that occurred upon Charles Town would be such "a dangerous repugnance" among the Virginia and North Carolina troops it was unlikely that these men would come to South Carolina's aid. It was a deplorable situation for the patriot cause.[9]

Lee assessed the condition of his planned expedition on August 27 in the best terms he could, but all was rather dismal. The enemy had abandoned their post at the St. Mary's River, but had taken with them "all the stock and slaves" across the St. John's River. Patriot forces in Savannah had no cannon, no ammunition, insufficient troops, no boats, few wagons or any "means of transportation to undertake the siege of St. Augustine." Lee had at Savannah Colonel Lachlan McIntosh's Continental Battalion made up of three officers, 23 privates and 2,500 militia with varying levels of inexperience. His other military forces had been sent to engage the Creeks and Cherokees.[10]

Unknown to Lee, John Hancock had sent a letter southward to Lee from Philadelphia on August 8 with news that would change the command situation substantially in the Southern Department. Hancock disclosed that Congress had received notice, dated August 7 at one o'clock P.M., from General Washington that Clinton's force of 3,000 men arrived at New York, with the Sunday landing of Hessian and Highlander troops on Staten Island from 13 transports. With the remaining 12,000 troops of Lord Howe's fleet expected to arrive shortly from Newfoundland, it was clear that an all-out attack from British forces gathering at New York was imminent. Hancock's letter covered the change in command.

> In this situation of our affairs the Congress being of the opinion your services in the Middle Department will be necessary, I have it in Command to direct, that you repair as soon as possible to the City of Philadelphia there to receive such Orders as they may think proper to give you. The attack at New York being hourly expected, and the Event of it uncertain, I am to request you will use the greatest Expedition on the Way.[11]

Around the 5th of September, as Generals Moultrie and Howe with Colonel McIntosh were preparing for the expedition to St. Augustine at Savannah, an express rider came in for General Lee. That was the end of the planned expedition to St. Augustine. Lee departed in two days from Savannah and arrived on the 8th in Charles Town. Lee's command of the Southern Department was ended on September 9, 1776, when Lee issued his last orders in South Carolina.[12]

Work on organizing the Georgia patriot government continued as President Bulloch called for a constitutional convention to assemble in Savannah on the first Tuesday in October. Carefully selected patriot delegates from each of the parishes gathered to begin the process of creating a new government. The name of the group was changed from the Provincial Congress to the Assembly. A new Georgia state constitution was completed and presented on February 5, 1777, before the body. The key elements of the 63-article constitution called for the government to be organized with executive, legislative and judiciary branches. To vote for the members of the legislature, one had to be male, a Protestant, at least 21 years old, white, own at least 250 acres or possessions worth £250, and have lived in the state for at least 12 months. Parishes were abolished and counties were defined. State-supported schools were to be erected in each county. The constitution granted freedom of religion, freedom of the press and trial by jury.[13]

Suddenly, on February 12, President Archibald Bulloch died. As Georgia was overwhelmed with grief, on March 4 Button Gwinnett was sworn in as the acting president until a duly elected governor under the new constitution could be elected. Gwinnett had been born in Down Hatherly, Gloucestershire, England, in 1735 as the son of a Welsh clergyman and an English mother. His parents raised him well and provided him with a good education according to their moderate circumstances. As a young adult, Gwinnett became a merchant in the city of Bristol, married when he was 22 and then emigrated to Charles Town, South Carolina, in the early 1760s.

Gwinnett stayed in Charles Town for about two years and then moved to Savannah in 1765 where he established himself as a general trader. Five years later, after selling all his merchandise, he purchased a large tract of land on St. Catherine's Island in St. John Parish, Georgia, where he devoted himself extensively to agricultural pursuits as a plantation owner. In 1769, he was elected to the Commons and soon distinguished himself for all his absences. In 1773, Gwinnett ran into financial difficulties and had to put his plantation and much of his estate up for sale. Before 1775, Gwinnett had no political aspirations but his subsequent enthusiasm for maintaining colonial rights attracted the attention of his fellow citizens. At the meeting of the provincial assembly in Savannah on January 20, 1776, he was appointed as a representative to the Continental Congress.[14]

About the time the Georgia Constitution was in place, serious events developed on Georgia's southern boundary. Loyalists, runaway slaves and hostile Indians organized into the Florida Rangers and conducted guerrilla attacks on southern Georgia settlements. On February 18, 1777, Captain Richard Winn surrendered Fort McIntosh, a small stockade fort on the Satilla River (between the Altamaha and St. Mary's River), and his garrison of 50 troops to the Florida Rangers.[15] Georgia militia captain John Baker, with 70 mounted volunteer militiamen from St. John Parish, moved to the St. Mary's River to surprise a fort held by the Rangers. Baker was forced to retreat with the discovery of an English ship supporting the fort.[16]

When General Robert Howe was notified of the loss of the fort and the recent raids on the Georgia border, he ordered Continental troops under Colonels Thomas Sumter and Isaac Motte with instructions for Lt. Colonel Francis Marion to proceed immediately by water to Savannah. In March, General Howe conferred with acting president Gwinnett and his council. The Georgia light horse regiment refused the duty. With many of the disaffected in the upcountry not to be trusted, that left Brigadier General Lachlan's First Georgia Battalion of Continentals as the only force ready for action with some 400 men.[17]

President Gwinnett now saw his golden opportunity to command a military operation over the head of Lachlan. He and his council were convinced that with proper help they could stop the Florida Rangers and capture St. Augustine. Howe clashed with Gwinnett from the time he first met the man. He had significant respect for his fellow Continental officer, Lachlan McIntosh, having described him as "an active, vigilant, and spirited officer." But Howe was not as convinced of the practicality of an expedition to Florida and refused to send any troops from South Carolina to Florida, though he did send a battalion to Sunbury. He felt that there were too few troops, few supplies, and it was the wrong time of the year to undertake such an operation. In addition he complained of the desire of Gwinnett and his state officials to dictate the expedition. Howe called it quits and returned to Charles Town, complaining of his "fatiguing, fruitless, expedition to Georgia."[18] Gwinnett complained in writing of Howe's action noting that, "He came, he saw, and left us in a low Estate."[19]

But Gwinnett would not give up. He called out the militia, seven armed galleys of the Georgia Navy and brushed McIntosh aside as he planned to lead the expedition. It was not until March 27 that the council finally requested McIntosh's assistance. McIntosh noted that their action was only prompted because they needed his Continental force since they had only around 200 militia so far. By this time, Florida governor Tonyn asked Indian superintendent Stuart to call out the Creeks and the Cherokees to attack the Georgia frontier yet again.

The state expedition to Florida set out from Savannah in early April. By the time they had reached Sunbury in the middle of the month, conflict between Gwinnett and McIntosh flared up again over who was in charge of the military force. Their cooperation waned. On the advice of the council, both men returned to Savannah as Colonel Samuel Elbert, now the ranking Continental officer, took over the expedition. Elbert moved out on May 1 by boat with 400 Georgia Continentals from Sunbury and proceeded toward the St. Johns River, while Colonel John Baker with his 200 mounted militia headed overland to rendezvous with Elbert.

Progress of the water-born Continentals was slow as the militia reached the St. Johns first. St. Augustine was alerted to the patriot expedition as usual, and the British sent loyalist colonel Thomas Brown with his Florida Rangers and Major Mark Prevost with a detachment of British Regulars to engage. Colonel Baker's militia arrived at Sawpit Bluff, south of the Nassau River, with Elbert nowhere to be seen. After several small encounters with the Rangers and Indians, Baker moved his force inland to avoid the enemy. After his men bivouacked on May 17 at Thomas Creek, Baker was attacked by a vastly superior force of Rangers, British Regulars and Indians. The patriots suffered three killed, nine wounded and 31 men taken prisoner as they withdrew in defeat. Many of the wounded died in the hands of the enemy.[20]

Florida authorities monitored the slow progress of Elbert's flotilla southward as his expedition began to fall apart. The men were hot, tired, short of supplies and getting sick. To add to their misery, the boats could not get through the Amelia Narrows just below the St. Mary's River. As Elbert sized up the condition of his troops and his expectation that the Spanish were fully apprised of his activities, he abandoned the second expedition to Florida on May 26. On June 15, the beleaguered troops arrived back in Savannah with nothing to show for their actions except some 1,000 head of cattle they had collected.

The failed expedition was the signal for the Florida Rangers to begin their raids into Georgia again. Tonyn reported that they were soon within five miles of Savannah, and had actually gone through Augusta. These raiding parties of around 150 were generally able to move at will away from Savannah as patriot citizens were left to live in fear.[21]

On the governmental front, on May 1, 1777, the Georgia Assembly met to elect the successor to Governor Bulloch. Acting president and candidate for the permanent post, Button Gwinnett, was not elected, as they selected John Adam Treutlen. Discouraged by the election results and his failed expedition to Florida, Gwinnett became depressed. To add to his misery, in the May 15 session of the Georgia Assembly, Gwinnett and Lachlan McIntosh were called to answer for their actions in the failed Florida operation. Gwinnett was convincing in his explanations before the body and was released from any blame. McIntosh was outraged and lost his temper, calling Gwinnett "a Scoundrell & lying Rascal." The assembly made no comment on the rude statement. Encouraged by his friends, Gwinnett felt like the injured party, having had his honor challenged. Gwinnett sent his second, physician and assembly member George Wells of Augusta, to present McIntosh with a letter requesting a duel for the next morning before sunrise. McIntosh accepted the duel even though he said it was rather early for him. McIntosh chose Major James Habersham as his second. They agreed to meet with pistols at the meadow at Sir James Wright's estate near Thunderbolt.

The conflict between these two men had actually begun the previous summer. Button Gwinnett's animosity towards Lachlan McIntosh had begun back in the summer of 1776. After signing the Declaration of Independence at Philadelphia on August 2, Gwinnett rode the 800 miles to Savannah with instructions from the Continental Congress for raising an army in Georgia. Gwinnett saw himself as a military leader, but on arrival he was disappointed to learn that the Provincial Congress had selected Colonel Lachlan McIntosh to be the new brigadier general of the Georgia Continentals. From that day on, Gwinnett considered McIntosh to be his rival and personal enemy.

For McIntosh, his conflict with Gwinnett was fostered by the competition over the Continental leadership and a most curious event that occurred during Gwinnett's short period as the acting president of Georgia. Gwinnett had received a letter from John Hancock, the president of the Continental Congress, accusing Lachlan's brother and member of the assembly, George McIntosh, of treason for helping William Panton to buy rice for the British forces in Florida. Since the assembly was not in session at the time the letter arrived, Gwinnett ordered George to be arrested and brought to Savannah. George McIntosh was indeed delivered to the provost marshal at Savannah and put in irons. George's friends proposed a bail of £50,000 but Gwinnett refused. Thankfully for George, when Gwinnett traveled to Sunbury, the assembly released George on £2,000 bail. For the McIntosh family, this assertion against George was a dishonor. The McIntosh family had arrived in Georgia as poor refugees, but had raised themselves up to become wealthy as they led the plantation life near Darien.[22]

Portrait of Button Gwinnet (Hargrett Rare Book and Manuscript Library, University of Georgia Libraries).

On the morning of May 16, at sunrise, McIntosh and Habersham arrived at Wright meadow. Fifteen minutes later, Gwinnett and Wells came up to the designated place. After the seconds examined the pistols, and the ground was chosen, Gwinnett yielded to McIntosh on the question of the separation distance for the duel. The general proposed eight to ten feet, but Habersham protested. At only twelve feet apart both men faced each other and on the proper word, both men fired. McIntosh was shot in the thigh, but remained standing. Gwinnett fell with his leg fractured above the knee. McIntosh questioned whether Gwinnett wanted another shot. Though Gwinnett replied "yes," both seconds interceded. Both men declared each other to be gentlemen and they shook hands, and departed the meadow. The duel was ended.[23] But the controversy was not over.

Though both wounds by modern standards were not particularly serious, Gwinnett's wound became gangrenous in the heat of the Georgia summer, and he died on the 27th of May at age 45. Though both McIntosh and Mrs. Gwinnett agreed that the death was due to the "unskillfulness of his doctor," Dr. Lyman Hall, Joseph Wood and others of prominence declared that General McIntosh was guilty of murder. Charged with murder, McIntosh was acquitted of the charge. But after Governor Treutlen produced a petition signed by 574 people demanding that McIntosh leave Georgia, George Walton and Henry Laurens arranged a transfer for General McIntosh to General George Washington's service at Valley Forge, Pennsylvania. On August 6, McIntosh was ordered to report to Washington.[24]

Later George McIntosh was arrested by Governor Treutlen and he had him sent to Philadelphia to be tried for treason by the Continental Congress. George escaped and made his way to the McIntosh plantation on the Georgia coast and hid in the swamp. George's friends convinced him to return to Philadelphia for trial. He did stand trial and was acquitted for lack of evidence. He then returned to Georgia and supported the patriot effort.[25]

As General Lachlan McIntosh left Georgia on October 10, 1777, for his duty in the north, Colonel Samuel Elbert was selected to lead the Georgia Continental Army brigade. When Elbert's Continentals had returned from the failed expedition in June, the men were deployed in healthier surrounding as frontier guards. Despite Colonel Elbert's effort to improve the situation for the men, the garrison and guard duty proved to be disagreeable as the troops deserted or showed poor discipline for the rest of the year.

The year of 1777 had been a difficult one for Georgia. In addition to problems on the Florida border, there were serious issues with military recruiting, finance and supplies. To fill the ranks of the Georgia Second and Third Continental battalions, recruiting efforts moved into North Carolina and Virginia, and for the Fourth Battalion the work extended to Pennsylvania. Against the wishes of the Continental Congress, the Georgia Assembly even sent blank commissions to their agent in France to attempt to find qualified engineers and artillery officers.

From the moment Major General Charles Lee departed the South in September 1776, thereby giving up his command of the Southern Department of the Continental Army, the command of this critical military force began to gravitate toward Brigadier General Robert Howe of North Carolina. First, the command was assumed by Brigadier General John Armstrong as the ranking Continental officer in the South. That left other brigadiers like James Moore, who was defending North Carolina in the Cape Fear area; Andrew Lewis, in command in Virginia; and Robert Howe in Georgia. When Armstrong heard that Howe was returning to Charles Town in September 1776, he departed for the north, complaining that he was in poor health and was having difficulty dealing with the southern climate.

After Armstrong, the command of the Southern Department reverted to James Moore. This son of the founder of Brunswick Town, North Carolina, took command in Charles Town in keeping with congressional orders. Moore retained the command until February 1777, when he was ordered to support Washington in the north with his North Carolina regiments. Because of the lack of supplies, Moore's departure was delayed in Wilmington where he became sick with "gout of the stomach" or as some others recorded, from the aftereffects of malaria.[26] James Moore died on April 9. As the next ranking officer in the South, Robert Howe, a cousin of Moore, immediately assumed the duties as the commander of the Southern Department. Now Major General Robert Howe was to play a major role in the direction of patriot military events for Georgia.[27]

Back in 1732, while Oglethorpe was busy preparing his colonists on the Thames River at Deptford for the voyage to build Savannah, a Robert Howe was born at Howe's Point Plantation on New Topsail Sound in North Carolina. Located opposite Barren Inlet, in the Cape Fear region of the Atlantic coast, and to the northeast of the future town of Wilmington, young Robert's parents, the wealthy Cape Fear planter Job Howe and Martha Jones Howe, looked upon their young son with affection as they reflected in what his future would hold.

Young Robert's start in life was better than most of his day and in this region. Robert's family heritage in Carolina and the Cape Fear area was reflective of the more distinguished plantation settlers of the Cape Fear valley. Little detailed information is known of Robert Howe's youth. He had a love for Shakespeare and other English writers, spoke fluent English, and carried an "air of breeding and confidence" that became part of his demeanor. His handwriting was for all practical purposes illegible. Young Robert married the daughter of Thomas Grange of Bladen County, Sarah Grange, around 1751, and they settled on Grange-owned property where Beaver Dam and Waymans Creeks flow into Cape Fear. In 1754, Robert became a captain in the local Bladen County militia. Two years later, he became the justice of the peace, and in the spring of 1760, he was elected to the North Carolina General Assembly as the representative from Bladen County. He attended every session of the assembly, almost unbroken, until 1775.

In 1764, Robert Howe and family moved away from Bladen County to Old Town Creek below Brunswick Town where he had purchased several plantations. In 1770, Robert purchased Kendal Plantation on the Cape Fear River adjoining Orton Plantation. Kendal, containing 400 acres, with some 180 acres of excellent rice-field marshes, was a part of the original 1726 grant to Roger Moore and would be Robert Howe's residence for the remainder of his life.

Over the years, Robert Howe turned out not be as successful a planter and businessman as he hoped. In 1754, he had received slaves from his grandmother, and in 1759 he had inherited a 1,000-acre plantation opposite Mount Misery. While he had acquired his Old Town Creek properties, by 1766 Robert was mortgaging or selling his land. He even had to mortgage his Kendal Plantation for £214 3s 5d. Many had their views of what led to Robert's financial woes, but perhaps Royal Governor Josiah Martin said it best when he noted that Robert "had inherited a good fortune but had wrecked it."

Robert's personal life also had its problems over the years. Robert was apparently quite notorious for his female conquests. Probably for this reason, he legally separated from his wife, Sarah, in 1772. With their children, Sarah moved to another place in Brunswick County, and remained separated to her death in 1804.

Robert, called Bob by his associates, was portrayed as a man with "charm, sophistication, and imagination." He was known to be rather impressive at social gatherings, loved to dance, and was once characterized as having "that general polite gallantry, which every man of good breeding ought to have." Robert's character elicited some negative impressions, especially in his personal and romantic exploits. A visitor to the Cape Fear area in 1774 wrote, "he is deemed a horrid animal, a sort of womaneater that devours every thing that comes in his way ... no woman can withstand him." Though Robert Howe had his flaws, he was eventually to play a major role in the history of Savannah and Georgia in the American Revolution.[28]

On September 1, 1775, Howe was given command of the Second North Carolina Regiment assigned to the northern part of the province that extended from the Albemarle region to the Virginia border. The following November, his regiment was taken over by the Continental Congress and became part of the Continental Army. That same fall, Howe agreed to supported Colonel William Woodford's Virginia forces against the fallen royal governor of Virginia, Lord Dunmore, in the Norfolk area. When Lee had taken on the command role over the Southern Department, Howe had been selected as one of the six brigadier generals over a Continental regiment by the Continental Congress. Howe then joined Lee and moved into North Carolina and supported the patriot victory at the Battle of Sullivan's Island in late June 1776 off Charles Town.[29]

Meanwhile, on January 10, 1778, the Georgia Assembly elected John Houstoun as governor. Houstoun, the wealthy, well-educated 30-year-old son of Sir Patrick Houstoun, had been a member of the executive council, and was known for his unimpeachable character.[30] On the 28th, the assembly passed a resolution calling for General Howe to undertake an expedition to East Florida to "annoy" the enemy. That same day, Howe had sent the new governor a letter presenting his recommendations for additional defensive needs for Georgia. Howe felt that the discontent and pro-loyalist leanings were as a result of the poor economic conditions of the Georgia residents rather than their political slant. Howe wrote, "The common people seldom speculate or refine upon any subject and therefore embrace Political opinions as matters of faith rather than as matters of Judgement."

To Howe, the survival of Georgia was primarily dependent on trade. He said trade would create credit, establish a basis for the currency exchange and provide an abundance of goods for the citizens. Howe noted that Savannah and Sunbury should be fortified as the primary trade ports to protect shipping. Forts should be maintained on Tybee and Cockspur islands for Savannah's protection, just as St. Catherines and Cedar Hammock islands would safeguard Sunbury. He also called for fortifications up to the frontier between the St. Johns and the St. Mary's rivers. Howe even proposed that the state create an insurance office to protect shippers from loss. Howe sent several letters addressing various military matters as he underscored the need for the state to defend itself, provide hospitals, clothing, food, barracks and logistical support to the Continental establishment. Over time Howe, would acknowledge that Georgia had undertaken little or no action in these matters.

Governor Houstoun and the Georgia Assembly took great offense to Howe's letters as "containing things which belong only to the civil authority & which are without his line of military duty." The state leaders would not be "dictated to" and they only awaited what plan he had for another expedition to East Florida. Howe did call a council of war with his Continental officers to discuss the feasibility of such an operation. His officers were of the opinion that there was no military object short of St. Augustine that was worth the effort, and that since the state and the army lacked sufficient troops, supplies and equipment, it was out of the question. Echoing Howe's previous recommendation, they suggested the best course of action was to build a strong fortification on Satilla Bluff, south of the Altamaha River, and permanently garrison it with a full battalion to control the border.

The Georgia Assembly attacked Howe's Continental council of war as being too much under the thumb of Howe to be independent in thinking. They demanded that another council of war be called with Governor Houstoun being given full voting rights. Howe rejected that request as being an unprecedented move for a civil authority. The debate degenerated into charges and countercharges and finally was appealed to the Continental Congress. Howe, who was not at his best as the spring came along with a "contagious sore throat and very dangerous fever," was unable to convince Houstoun or the assembly that the state's defenses were weak and the expedition was inappropriate until they were better supplied.

Howe complained to the Continental Congress of his Georgia problems:

> They spent a number of weeks in Assembly without one thought of Defence, almost wholly employed upon a Confiscation Act of which ... the people are now in a state of confusion and dispute. What with an exhausted Treasury, with such arrears of pay due the Soldiers so that they were almost in a state of mutiny, most of the men so naked that it was indecent to parade them, with not three days provisions for the Army ... in short tho' destitute of almost every military requisite they were for impelling the Army to undertake an Expedition into and against East Florida.[31]

As Howe noted, the Georgia Executive Council authorized any person who raised 15 or more volunteers to plunder at will in East Florida under a commission from Georgia. All Georgians who would settle for three months on the lands between the St. Mary's and St. Johns rivers would be given a grant of 500 acres in the region. This approach yielded no results, as Howe expected.[32]

Meanwhile, Governor Tonyn, the Florida Rangers and the British Regulars were not idle. In February, Tonyn sent German emissaries out to attempt to influence the Germans in Georgia to desert the Georgia militia and come to East Florida. Meanwhile, the Continental Congress debated a resolution that would send either Howe or Colonel Elbert to undertake the East Florida Expedition. Though the measure was tabled, the resolution left no doubt that some action was expected. Although he was quite ill, Howe began to take steps to engage in some type of expedition. He issued instructions to his officers to equip their men for the eventual march as best they could.

On March 12, 1778, Lt. Colonel Thomas Brown with 100 of his Florida Rangers and 10 Indians moved through the swamps, swam a quarter of a mile across the Altamaha River at night, and attacked Fort Howe (formerly Fort Barrington) at daybreak. Brown's force took the fort, killed two patriots, wounded four others, and gained 23 prisoners. Brown lost one man killed. This and other raids into Georgia by the British and loyalist supporters was ample evidence in Houstoun's mind that Georgia had to take action.

To add to patriot worries, in mid–April a band of some 400–500 disaffected people, called Scopholites or Scoffellites after their leader, Colonel Scophol, marched southward from the backcountry of South Carolina and Georgia to join Governor Tonyn and other loyalists at St. Augustine. They crossed the Savannah River below Augusta, plundering as they went. At the same time, another group of loyalists and Indians from West Florida was reported as British regulars in company with loyalists headed northward from St. Augustine.

Howe realized the danger posed by the possible juncture of the Scopholites with the East Floridians. On April 6, Howe ordered Colonel Elbert to march with all possible speed to intercept the insurgents if possible. Since Elbert had no mounted cavalry, his troops were unable to make contact with the Scopholites and they passed untouched into East Florida. Howe's requests for mounted cavalry had always been ignored by the Continental Congress as in this situation. Howe lamented, "they laugh at foot soldiers with scorn. Only cavalry troops can stop them."[33]

On April 18, Colonel Elbert and his 300 Continentals aboard the galleys *Lee, Washington* and *Bulloch* arrived at Frederica on St. Simons Island where the British brigantine *Hinchinbrook*, the sloop *Rebecca* and another brig were moored. Elbert retook the town, taking five prisoners from the *Hinchinbrook* who were onshore. The next morning, the patriot galleys attacked the ships with success. Captain Alexander Ellis of the *Hinchinbrook* was drowned, while Captain John Mowbray and the crew of the *Rebecca* fled. Elbert was fortunate; with the captured gear aboard the *Rebecca* were 300 uniforms that had been taken originally from Charles C. Pinckney's South Carolina Continentals off Charles Town. The loss of these two British ships lessened somewhat the threat to patriot Georgia.

By early May, Howe was ready to start the southern expedition as he defined it. For Howe, this meant that he intended only to chase the British and loyalists across the St. Johns River and to secure to the St. Mary's River against "the Predatory War." Reports from spies and deserters came in to Howe reporting that in that area the British had 1,400 Regulars, 200 manumitted Creeks, 400 Florida scouts, 400 insurgents and 100 renegade Indians established in posts. All were well armed and mounted. To meet such a threat, Howe ordered an additional 300 troops from the South Carolina Continentals. South Carolina called up 1,100 men but only sent Howe half that number for Georgia.

Howe planned to join with Colonel Elbert's force and proceed to the southern border. He wrote, "As soon as I form a junction with him if the foe does not advance, I shall most probably seek them and endeavor to dislodge them from the Post which they ought not be suffered to possess." On May 9, Howe and his army arrived at Fort Howe on the north side of the Altamaha River. His force consisted of 600 from the South Carolina brigade under the command of Colonel Charles Cotsworth Pinckney and Colonel Elbert's Georgia brigade of 500 men. Artillery units from the two states had formed under Major Roman de Lisle. In addition to this force, Howe expected to soon be joined by 1,000 South Carolina militia under Colonel Andrew Williamson, and 1,300 Georgia militia under Governor Houstoun. With a force of over 3,000 men, Howe had great expectations for a successful campaign.[34]

In the summer heat of south Georgia, Howe's forces lingered at Fort Howe as Pinckney and Elbert reconnoitered locations across the river for the army's next move. An Engineer, Captain John Christian Senf, surveyed the terrain for sites to construct roads through the swamp that bordered the southern banks of the Altamaha River. The men lived on two meals a day of mostly boiled rice, beefsteaks and water or coffee. Howe provided rum for the troops to counter the boredom and generally unhealthy climate. Desertions were getting fairly common. Various punishments were handed out to deserters including whippings, hangings or being shot.

Delayed by the late arrival of a South Carolina galley and a provision boat bearing ammunition and supplies, on May 27 Howe's Continental Army finally moved across the Altamaha River and took up camp at Reid's Bluff, located three miles below the fort. Colonel Pinckney wrote "the reasonable and candid gentry of this state are throwing a thousand reflections on the general and the army, for not marching to attack the enemy, and storm lines, without Provisions and without ammunition." Howe sought an army moving to fight prepared with arms, ammunition, wagons and food. He had requested that 300 slave "pioneers" be sent from Georgia plantations to support road building through the dense terrain. The assembly voted Howe only 200 slaves and actually only 56 showed up on schedule. These men dug wells for drinking water, as well as latrines and fortifications.

The Georgia government was uncooperative with Howe to the point of causing Howe's men to suffer needlessly. Governor Houstoun had diverted 200 barrels of rice that belonged to the Continental Army to his Georgia Militia. He also seized cattle, which restricted the meat intake of the Continentals, and impressed Continental horses, leaving Howe's deputy quartermaster general unable to deliver clothing and stores to the troops. General William Moultrie wrote, "The governor seems to be taking the bread out of your mouths. I heartily wish you all success, and a great many laurels; though you have but a barren field to gather them from."

The days simmered as time moved on, with Howe's army stationary, with no signs of Williamson's force from South Carolina or Houstoun's Georgia Militia. By June 7, Howe was indeed frustrated as he waited, "Puzzled, perplexed, disappointed, and the devil and all ... I have but advanced to this post having been for several weeks waiting the arrival of the militia...." Howe sent Colonel Elbert and his Georgia brigade forward to the Satilla River, some 50 miles ahead. On June 14, Howe's main army moved some five miles to Spring Branch and rested the first night.

At that same time, Houstoun was just leaving Sunbury. Houstoun's messenger arrived at Howe's position requesting a meeting with Howe back at Reid's Bluff. That meeting between Howe and Houstoun did occur and it yielded a promise from Houstoun that the militia would march in three or four days to meet up with the Continentals. Meanwhile, Howe's Continentals moved on the 16th and 17th eight miles and camped the second night at a branch of the Little Satilla River. As the army pushed forward, a scouting party made up of the light infantry, commanded by Lt. Colonel Francis Henry Harris, with the mounted volunteers under Colonel James Habersham skirmished with a detachment of the Florida Rangers. The patriots won the engagement as the Rangers lost one man as prisoner, eight horses, five saddles, bridles and blankets.

The patriot army moved out on June 18 at 4 A.M. and had moved by noon some 12 miles. The next day the main army formed up with Colonel Elbert's brigade at Cowford on the Great Satilla River, in striking distance of Fort Tonyn on the St. Mary's River. Commodore Oliver Bowen arrived at Wright's Landing on the St. Mary's and communications were established with Howe for combined operations. Bowen, who had been commissioned a captain in the Continental Battalion formed in February 1776, had been elected by the assembly in January 1777 as the commodore of Georgia's naval assets. The ships had been taken over by the Continental establishment, yet the state still maintained some control over the force consisting of five galleys, eight row galleys and two sloops by the spring of 1777.[35]

On June 22, 1778, the Georgia Militia was near Sunbury, but Colonel Williamson's South Carolina Militia was only nine miles below Savannah. From Charles Town, Moultrie commented on the lack of coordination of the American forces, "If this be the case, for God's sake! When will you all join: if you still continue moving from each other nothing but Augustine Castle can bring you up."

On June 23, the Continentals moved across the Satilla in a large raft of dead pine trees to camp at the old field at Cantey's place. The next morning, the army marched the 12 miles to the St. Mary's River and settled in for an upcoming engagement with the British and loyalists. On the 28, Houstoun's force finally made camp only a few miles from the Continentals. The previous day, the governor had refused to dispatch Major John Maker's Light Horse to assist the Continentals. He also had Major Wilder arrested for marching from the Altamaha to the Satilla without orders. It was an omen of things to come.

The expected conference between the leaders finally took place, but it was a sad affair. Young 30-year-old Houstoun, who had no military experience, refused to place his Georgia militia under the command of Howe. Howe was unquestionably the senior military leader in attendance and as the commander of the Southern Department had clear right to assume command of the joint forces. At this meeting, Houstoun's flawed decision made any chance for a successful expedition and victory over the enemy an improbability. Tempers expectedly flared as an "altercation arose respecting the sole command." Howe demanded that Houstoun declare whether he planned to march his militia against Fort Tonyn or to attack the British commander, Major Mark Prevost, whose force was located some 15 to 20 miles away down the road toward St. Augustine. The governor chose the latter.

On June 29, Howe's Continentals moved on to Fort Tonyn, which had been abandoned and burned. In the meantime, Thomas Brown's Rangers camped at nearby Cabbage Swamp, ready to attack the patriot forces. Reconsidering his inferior strength, Brown's Rangers set out to join Major Prevost at Alligator Creek Bridge. Meanwhile, Houstoun dispatched a unit of his militia, led by Brigadier General James Screven, to reconnoiter the enemy force at Alligator Creek. As the force approached Prevost's position, the militia attacked the pickets at the bridge as an engagement ensued. During the attack, Colonel Elijah Clarke of Georgia was seriously wounded in the thigh as he led the attack of the British flank. Unfortunately for the militia, Brown's Rangers closed on the American flank and the Georgia Militia had to retire with 14 killed and several wounded. The Americans were unable to remove all their casualties, as the enemy found the body of an ensign and a black patriot on the field.

In the early morning of July 1, Governor Houstoun asked Howe to advance against the enemy without delay in cooperation with him. Howe agreed to move if the governor would provide a quantity of rice for the Continental troops until a supply ship arrived. Houstoun immediately changed his mind, withdrew militia support and indicated that he did not have adequate supplies to help the Continentals, though only five days earlier he had boasted that he had ample provisions.

On the 8th, Colonel Williamson's South Carolinians arrived to complete the full contingent of expedition forces. A conference was soon held with leaders Howe, Houstoun, Williamson and Bowen. A cruel reality settled in as the command situation turned into a "Chaos of Command," as Howe explained. Howe was adamant that he was senior commander as the commander of the Continental Army of the South. Houstoun would not relinquish the command of the Georgia Militia to Howe. Williamson refused to yield command to anyone but himself. Curiously, Commodore Bowen said that in all naval matters he must remain supreme. Howe lamented, "if I am ever to depend upon operations I have no right to guide, and men I have no right to command, I shall deem it then, as now I do, one of the most unfortunate accidents of my life." The expedition had come to a halt.[36]

For Howe it was a grand mess. His troops had endured weeks of exposure in the sun with the insects of the swamp. Less than 400 Continentals were fit for duty. The 550 men of the Georgia Militia had fared a little better. The Continentals also continued to be without an adequate number of horses and pioneers to help support the movements of the army. Horses used for scouting and light duties were dying at an alarming rate. One officer wrote, "we have now with great toil and difficulty thro' parching Lands and uncultivated wilds, frequently in the Meridian heat, Marched 300 Miles to this Place, and the rewards of our trouble has been [sic] to find a half demolished Stockade Fort, a few Cloaths, Blankets, and trifling Necessaries."

The independent commands could not even agree on the objective of the expedition. Houstoun wanted the three armies to cross the St. Johns River and move independently to St. Augustine. Colonel Williamson recommended that they move to the St. Johns to clear the British, but not to proceed further. Howe felt the expedition had already accomplished its mission to clear the area. Continental scouts reported that the British had retreated to the St. Johns to avoid the Americans.

On July 11, the Continentals held a council meeting at Fort Tonyn to consider their situation. Those in attendance, which consisted of all officers over the rank of captain, unanimously voted that they had accomplished their mission to clear the British and loyalists out of the Georgia frontier. They agreed that the prospects of success in proceed-ing into East Florida were slim due to the lack of a unified command and the poor condi-tion of the men. The group recommended that they move northward immediately.

Howe tried to call a meeting with Houstoun and Williamson with the usual problems. Colonel Williamson refused to enter the Continental camp until Howe sent Captain Dray-ton to demand his appearance at his headquarters. Houstoun sent an aide to find out what Howe planned. Howe refused to reveal his plans until the governor reported his. After a day waiting for Houstoun's information, Howe decided to prepare to depart. After burn-ing the fleches and fort, Howe and his Continentals marched out of the camp on July 14. One hundred twenty men would return via land, while Colonels Elbert and Pinckney marched to Wright's Landing for travel by boat to Savannah. Howe, with the land force and leaders Colonel Nicholas Everleigh, Major Thomas Pinckney, Captain Roger P. Sanders and Captain Drayton, arrived at Charles Town on July 30.

The failed Florida Expedition of 1778 was a disaster for Howe's reputation, though he was just another officer caught up in the command problem that faced all Continental com-manders in the South. With Georgia's governor Houstoun and Williamson's South Car-olina Militia refusing to yield to the authority of the Continental commander, the expedition was doomed from the beginning. Howe's letters to the Continental Congress provided a vastly different account of the expedition, as did those from Houstoun. Houstoun expressed surprise that Howe retreated from Fort Tonyn, and noted, "The particular reason which induced this measure I am unacquainted with ... I am happy in being able to say that a more unpopular manuaver [sic] never was attempted than this among all ranks and orders of the militia who were present and saw for themselves." Houstoun contended that he had 2,000 "hearty determined" troops ready to sweep the British and loyalist forces from the Castle at St. Augustine. The governor also had objections with Commodore Bowen's actions during the expedition, and had him suspended for failing to take orders from him. The captains of the vessels were directed to take orders from the executive council.

Though Houstoun's information was inaccurate, Howe was unable to convince the Continental Congress that he did not have 1,600 men, including the militias, under his command for the expedition. It seemed that no facts would overcome a destiny of failure for Howe. Unfortunately, the Florida Expedition was Howe's failure for all of history to come.[37]

9

The Fall of Savannah

"It is the King's intentions that an attack
should be made upon the Southern Colonies."

In New York, Sir Henry Clinton, the new British commander-in-chief in America, opened his letter with care. It was marked "Most Secret" and the date on the correspondence was March 8, 1778. It was signed by Lord George Germain, the British secretary of state, and it notified Clinton of his formal appointment with assurances that he would receive an army equal to that commanded by his predecessor, General William Howe, whose resignation had been accepted on February 4.

With special attention, Clinton read his orders for military offensive operations that would be prosecuted "upon a different plan from that which it has hitherto been carried on." While he was instructed to attack shipping and rebel ports from New York to Nova Scotia, the orders specified that "it is the King's intentions that an attack should be made upon the Southern Colonies, with a view to the conquest and possession of Georgia and South Carolina." The attack was detailed to be by way of Georgia, carried out by a detachment of 2,000 troops sailing from New York to capture Savannah, with the assistance of General Augustine Prevost's forces marching up from St. Augustine.[1] The directions went on to reveal the overall objective of the operations in the South:

> The conquest of these provinces is considered by the King as an object of great importance in the scale of the war, as their possession might be easily maintained, and thereby a very valuable branch of commerce would be restored to this country and the rebels deprived of a principal resource for the support of their foreign credit, and of paying for considerable part of their remittances to Europe.... Should the success we may reasonably hope for attend these enterprises, it might not be too much to expect that all America to the south of the Susquehannah would return to their allegiance, and in the case of so happy an event, the northern provinces might be left to their own feelings and distress to bring them back to their duty, and the operations against them confined to the cutting off all their supplies and blocking up their ports.[2]

This new and what was a second attempt at a British southern strategy was now promulgated as failed operations in the North had sent the British government into disarray. The disastrous news of Lieutenant General John Burgoyne's surrender of his entire army to patriot General Horatio Gates at Saratoga had reached London back on the previous December 2. As King George III noted, now the British would have to "act only on the defensive in America," Parliament returned from its six-week Christmas break to debate the merits of the war effort in the colonies and the very leadership of the ministry. Christain D'Oyley, the undersecretary of the American Department, resigned his post almost immediately and Lord Bathurst, the lord chancellor, announced his retirement from Parliament on February 16. After calls for the resignations of Germain, and even Lord North, subsided, the ministry survived as the new British military strategy shifted focus to the South, where it was hoped the presence of British Regulars would yield overwhelming loyalist support.[3]

Even greater and more depressing news was soon to reach London. On March 13, 1778, the French ambassador to Britain, the Marquis de Noailles, received instructions to present some important news to the English minister. So it was that at 4 P.M. that day Noailles stood before Lord Weymouth announcing a treaty between France and the American colonies. The treaty had actually been signed by Louis XVI back on February 6 and outlined French recognition of the United States and a defensive alliance between the two countries.

According to Noailles, Lord Weymouth was so shocked by the treaty he was almost moved to tears. The English minister said he could make no reply until the King was notified. The next day a courier rushed to France with word to Lord Stormont that he had been recalled. Stormont departed Paris on March 16. Noailles was also recalled home from London.

Reaction to the treaty took the form of conflict when at 6:00 P.M. on June 17 an English frigate, *Arethusa*, and a sloop opened fire on the French frigate *La Belle Poule* off Brest.[4] The engagement lasted until almost midnight. Forty men were killed in the battle before the ships finally departed in the darkness. The war had begun.[5]

In support of the American cause, on April 13 a French fleet sailed from Toulon with "one 90-gun ship, one of 80 guns, six of 74, three of 64 and one of 50." Aboard the flagship man-of-war *Languedoc* was the commander, Admiral Charles-Henri, Compte d'Estaing, with Gerard, the new minister plenipotentiary of France to the American Congress, and the American ambassador to France, Silas Dean.[6]

The fleet commander, Admiral Charles Hector Theodat D'Estaing, belonged to a family with a long heritage going back to the king of the Visigoths in the eighth century. D'Estaing was born in Auvergne, France, at the Chateau Ravel in 1729. At age sixteen he entered the Mousquetaires and by 1748 he had been promoted to regimental (Rouerhue) colonel. He became a brigadier at age twenty-six and in 1757 served in the fleet of the Count d'Ach. Soon he entered the East Indian Squadron of Count Lally. In 1759 he was taken prisoner by the British at Madras and was paroled. Violating his parole in 1760 by leading naval operations near L'Orient, he was again captured and sent to prison at Portsmouth, England.[7]

D'Estaing became a lieutenant general in the French Navy in 1763, and by 1777 had moved up to vice admiral. Now, at age 50, the count was given command of the fleet bound for America. The selection of D'Estaing to command the fleet was evidence that the generals and admirals whom Louis XVI sent over to America were, for the most part, men of mature years. Lafayette seemed to be the only such officer who still retained the enthusiasm of youth and its readiness to take great chances. D'Estaing would show in this expedition a deliberation and prudence in keeping with his years, but it was not calculated to secure brilliant results.

Out of port at Toulon, D'Estaing's fleet soon ran into bad weather. It took 35 days at sail in the Mediterranean to finally reach the Atlantic Ocean at the Straits of Gibraltar. In the Atlantic on May 20 D'Estaing opened his sealed orders and read them aloud. They directed him to head to Boston.[8]

Meanwhile, in the aftermath of the failed Florida Expedition, Major General Robert

Howe languished on his return to Charles Town from July 30, unaware of the true mood of the patriot leaders in Philadelphia. Sadly for Howe, on September 25 the Continental Congress took action that would soon embarrass and essentially wreck his career. The august body decided to replace Howe as the commander of the Southern Department with Major General Benjamin Lincoln. With so much bad press over the events in Georgia reaching Philadelphia from all sides, the news should have come to no surprise to Howe. But it was. Howe learned the discouraging news on October 9 as he lamented, "Have I not sacrificed my Fortune & Peace to the service of my Country! Have I not by the most unwearied diligence & with a Zeal which at least has some merit attended to the duties of my station & by my every effort endeavored to do my Duty! And shall I, after being kept against my wish from the Scene of immediate Action, be recalled at that moment when this Country is likely to become the Scene of it — How Sir have I deserved this disgrace?"

Howe pleaded with his friend Henry Laurens, the president of the Continental Congress, to use his influence to have his orders rescinded.[9] Though Howe had friends in Congress, there was no hope for him. General Lincoln was soon to learn that the challenge of the Southern Department command was mostly full of opportunities for failure, with little hope of any real success. Lincoln, who learned of the appointment on October 3 at Quaker Hill in the state of New York, left camp on October 8 toward Philadelphia to spend a week dining with members of Congress as he became acquainted with the military situation in the South. Having missed Washington on a short visit on his way southward, Lincoln wrote Washington that he was most displeased with the assignment: "I wish the Congress had fixed their minds on some other officer for the Southern department."

Lincoln, still recovering from a serious ankle wound received in battle, got a letter from his Albany surgeon and friend, Dr. Browne, on his appointment noting, "I am sensible you are acquainted with the difficulties of the command and the dangers to which you expose your health in the climate to which you are going." Browne's medical advice continued with, "the seat of the action is a low marshy country, abounding with pond of stagnant water from which exhales a fetid, putrid vapour," that you are never to "expose your person to the night; nor without the greatest necessity ride out in the morning before the sun has dispelled these noxious vapours."[10]

Back on January 25, 1733, the same day Oglethorpe's Georgia colonists were safely bivouacked at Beaufort Town, South Carolina, preparing for the final segment of their trip to Savannah, Benjamin Lincoln was born in the quaint village of Hingham, Massachusetts. This sixth child and the first son of Colonel Benjamin Lincoln and Elizabeth Thaxter Lincoln was to be another man destined to play a memorable role in Savannah's history. Benjamin was to begin a life immersed in a world of order and expectation as a small-town New England aristocrat, where the bonds of kinship and service to the community and nation were to provide the security and solid foundation for all he would encounter as the future unfolded.

Benjamin's family legacy in the British North American colonies began in August of 1638. It was in that month that Thomas Lincoln, a cooper, and his wife, Annis Lane, arrived in the colony of Massachusetts Bay. They were Puritans from Hingham in Norfolk, England. Like many others of their sect, they had immigrated to establish a godly community where the church would be the center of their lives. Thomas prospered in the new settlement where he had begun "transporting Timber, plank and mast for shipping to the Town of Boston, as also Ceder and Pine-Board to supply the wants of other Townes."

Benjamin's distinguished father, Colonel Lincoln, served in the Governor's Council, as a longtime Hingham officeholder, as the crown's justice of the peace and representative of the Massachusetts General Court. As a fourth generation Lincoln, Benjamin had to carry on the family tradition of the Lincoln men for all his life. His responsibilities were not only for himself alone as he moved through life, but were also for all that his ancestors in the New World had built for him in wealth, social status and unquestionable service to Hingham and the province.[11]

Portrait of General Benjamin Lincoln (1733–1810), by Charles Willson Peale, from life, circa 1781–1783. Oil on canvas, 22" × 19" (55.9 × 48.2 cm). Independence NHP, INDE 14097 (Library of Congress).

Benjamin spent his youth under the supervisor of his father, working on Colonel Lincoln's farm with the usual chores of plowing, planting, hoeing corn and harvesting. Benjamin received what would be a basic education in Hingham. The blue-eyed youth grew into a man of average height, around five feet nine inches tall, but with "so uncommonly broad person, as to seem to be of less statue than he was." Though he was a strong young man, he had a speech impediment and suffered his entire life with narcolepsy—a condition in which a person falls asleep for brief periods. One of his friends wrote that "in the midst of conversation, at table, and when driving himself in a chaise, he would fall into a sound sleep." Benjamin would at times in his life be criticized for his sleeping episodes, but his friends and usual associates came to accept his problem.

In 1754, Benjamin continued the civic legacy of public service by becoming the town constable. The next year he was appointed as adjutant in his father's militia regiment, the Third Suffolk. Benjamin continued on and held various positions in his community and with the local militia. As the events of the Stamp Act and other British acts were revealed to the people of Hingham, Benjamin found himself engaged deeply in the patriot movement in Massachusetts. In May 1772, he was elected to serve as the representative to the General Court. That same year he was appointed lieutenant colonel of the Second Suffolk Regiment. His varied duties and endless responsibilities at this time in his life induced him to acquire his first slave, a man named Cato. Though he would own several more slaves during his lifetime, later in life, as he saw the type of slavery practiced in South Carolina and Georgia, Lincoln would declare slavery as an "unjustified and wicked practice."

In 1774, Lincoln was elected as the chairman of the Hingham Committee of Correspondence. He was reelected to the General Court in September 1774 just as the British royal governor, General Thomas Gage, dissolved the Salem assembly, and unknowingly created a new Provincial Congress of patriot leaders. Lincoln was elected as secretary of the congress and served in this permanent position reorganizing and supplying the militia.

As the incredible events at Lexington and Concord occurred on April 19, 1775, the Second Suffolk Regiment hurried off to support the patriots of Boston. Lincoln was chosen as muster master of militia at Watertown, and became a member of the new Committee of Safety. In July, he was elected to the House of Representative of Massachusetts and served as a councilor. At age 42, Benjamin Lincoln had achieved all his father had achieved as he gave up his Hingham duties to work on provincial affairs. This was just the beginning.

On January 30, 1776, Lincoln was appointed by the General Court as a brigadier general for the Suffolk County militia and soon was promoted to major general. About the time he settled into his new position, the British evacuated Boston on March 17. As Lincoln helped plan operations and defenses in New England, his stature as a military leader grew. When James Warren declined the role, Lincoln was selected to lead the state's force of 5,000 militia to support the Continental Army with Washington around New York. It was Lincoln's first command, and one that would only strengthen his reputation with the patriot establishment.

Lincoln served with Washington in operations around New York and for his loyal leadership, Congress appointed him to major general in the Continental Army on February 14, 1777. Working with General Horatio Gates, Lincoln's right ankle was shattered by a musket ball at Fort Edward. He returned to duty at White Plains in August 1778 and by September 25 he was selected for his first independent command, the Southern Department.

In as optimistic a mood as he could muster, Lincoln departed Philadelphia on October 24 carrying his formal commission and letters of introduction to the southern leaders. In transit he had a carriage accident in Virginia, hurting his knee, which forced a two-day layover. He then spent a week in Williamsburg, staying with Colonel Carter Braxton, while dining out with the elite society which included Governor Patrick Henry. After crossing the James River, on his way toward Charles Town, he traveled some 30 to 40 miles per day, making farmer-like observations of the local natural environment and crops as he went.[12]

Back on October 13 when Lincoln was being briefed by leaders of Congress in Philadelphia, Moses Kirkland, the British deputy Indian superintendent for the Southern Department, then in New York, and General Augustine Prevost, the British commander in St. Augustine, submitted a proposal to Sir Henry Clinton. This proposal advised Clinton that the expedition against Georgia should occur in the winter because of the climate in the South and to utilize troops available from northern operations. As outlined in Germain's orders, Prevost's force from East Florida would join with an invasion force, which would sail from New York to Georgia.[13]

Augustine Prevost had been born in Geneva, Switzerland, in 1723. His earliest military service had been with the Royal American Regiment (later the King's Royal Rifle Corps) in North America, where he had served as a major. Supporting the Seven Years War, on September 13, 1759, he suffered a serious wound in the Battle of Quebec on the Plains of Abraham. In 1761, he was promoted to lieutenant colonel and served at the outbreak of the American Revolution as the British Army commander of East Florida.[14]

In New York, the Georgia Expedition assembled British, German and loyalist troops under the command of Lieutenant Colonel Archibald Campbell of the Highland Scots 71st Regiment of Foot. There were two battalions of the 71st Regiment, the Wessenbach and Woellwarth regiments of Hessians infantry, two battalions of the North and South Carolina Provincials (loyalists) and a fine provincial regiment of the New York Volunteers of

Ireland, formed in Philadelphia by Lieutenant Colonel Lord Rawdon, and made up of deserters of Washington's army.[15] Also in company was a detachment of the Royal Artillery. Colonel John Hamilton, a wealthy southern planter, commanded the North Carolina loyalists, while the South Carolina group was under Colonel Alexander Innes, a former secretary to Lord William Campbell, the former royal governor of South Carolina. The total force of some 3,500 troops would proceed via transport to Georgia aboard Commodore Hyde Parker's fleet.[16]

Lieutenant Colonel Archibald Campbell, the man designated to lead the attack on Georgia, was born at Dunderaive Castle near Inveraray, Scotland, on August, 21, 1739. He was the second son of James Campbell, a distant relation of the dukes of Argyll, and Elizabeth Campbell. His father was a lawyer at Inveraray, and was also involved in the timber trade. His mother was the daughter of James Fisher of Durren, a merchant who periodically served as the Provost of Inveraray. Both of Archibald's parents were ambitious, and with the backing of their kinsman, the third duke of Argyll, in 1751 they opened a successful spinning school at Inveraray. The spinning school's success brought his parents national recognition in Scotland. It also earned the couple the third duke's trust and gratitude, a fact reflected in James Campbell's appointment as the duke's chamberlain, and in his appointment as the commissary for the Western Isles.

James Campbell's important role in the administration of the third duke's estate brought his family into close contact with the duke. Young Archibald Campbell, or "Archy" as he was called by the family, became one of the duke's favorites. Growing up in the town of Inveraray, it was not too long before the 3rd Duke recognized Campbell's ability and talents. In this respect, the third duke commissioned Campbell to produce a landscape plan of the Argyll estate, which he completed in 1757 at age 18, just before he joined the army.

Campbell studied at Glasgow and Edinburgh universities "where he greatly distinguished himself by his proficiency in the various branches of erudition to which he directed his attention." Having made his mark at these universities, he next attended the Royal (Military) Academy at Woolwich. There he again enjoyed considerable academic success, and subsequently joined the British army as an engineer. With the outbreak of the Seven Years War, he participated in three raids on the French coast during 1757, and is reported to have "proved himself an able and gallant officer." He also served in the expeditions to capture Guadeloupe, Dominique, Martinique and St. Lucia and Grenada. As the war escalated, Campbell was sent to North America where he served as a captain with Fraser's Highlanders until he was seriously wounded during the capture of Quebec in 1759.[17]

At the end of the Seven Years War, Fraser's Highlanders were disbanded, leaving Campbell to find another posting. Recognized as a talented engineer, Campbell was approached by the Venetians to join them as their army's chief engineer. Campbell declined the offer and decided to go to India instead to serve with the 29th Regiment of Foot, and later with the 42nd Highlanders (the Black Watch). In India, Campbell quickly proved himself to be a quite capable and energetic officer, and one ready to move up to higher rank.

On February 5, 1768, the East India Company appointed him as their chief engineer in Bengal, after having received "ample testimonials" about his skills as an engineer. The 29-year-old engineer quickly impressed his new employers. His design for the defenses of Fort George was much admired and soon earned him rave reviews. After catching the attention of the East India Company's Court of Directors by saving his employers significant funds during the construction of Fort George, Campbell was promoted in just over six months to the rank of lieutenant colonel.

Service in India earned Archibald Campbell considerable recognition, but the rigors of serving in that country's harsh climate took its toll on his health. In December 1772, he was forced to resign due to his rapidly declining health. The East India Company's agents stated that they were loath to "lose a Man of his distinguished Abilities," but by October 1773 he was back in Britain. He then spent some time advising the East India Company's Court of Directors on how best to fortify its defenses in India.[18]

After returning from six years in India, which had been quite lucrative, Campbell decided to settle down as a Highland Laird (large landowner) in his native Argyllshire. As a self-described "Scotsman through and through," he was proud of his Highland roots. Since he had "acquired additional marks of distinction from his Sovereign, and an independent fortune, with an unblemished reputation," in 1773–74 Campbell became the proprietor of the estates of Inverneill and Danna. Later on he would consolidate his position as one of only two proprietors who held all of the land in North Knapdale.

In 1774 Campbell was elected as an MP for the Burgh of Stirling. He served his constituency in this position until 1780 and again in 1789. During this period he began his courtship of Amelia Ramsay, the daughter of the renowned painter Allan Ramsay of Kinkell, and granddaughter of Allan Ramsay the poet. Campbell and Amelia Ramsay were later married on July 7, 1779. As Campbell settled down to life in Scotland as the laird of a large Highland estate and as an MP, the deteriorating political situation in Britain's North American colonies demanded his immediate return to the army.

Campbell rejoined the army in 1775 as lieutenant colonel of the second battalion of the 71st (Fraser's) Highlanders, which was raised by General Simon Fraser, the master of Lovat. Fraser's father, Lord Lovat, had been hanged for his part in the Jacobite Rebellion of 1745-46, and his estate had been forfeited to the Crown. The young master of Lovat fought hard to get his family's estate restored, and when he finally succeeded, he raised Highland troops to fight for the Crown out of gratitude to the King. The original Fraser's Highlanders (the 78th Regiment) played a heroic part in the bloody attempt to capture Fort Ticonderoga from the French during the Seven Years War, and served with distinction for the duration of that conflict.

When war broke out in North America against the American patriots in 1775, General Fraser once again raised Highland troops, "warmly assisted by his officers, of whom no less than six, beside himself, were chiefs of clans." Two battalions with a combined strength of 2,340 men were raised, and assembled "first at Stirling, and afterwards at Glasgow, in April 1776." When the two battalions reached Glasgow, they joined with the 42nd Highlanders. Known for their fine appearance and model discipline, the combined force of nearly 6,000 Highlanders was stationed in the city.

The 71st Highlanders sailed for North America with a full naval escort on seven transports, including the *George* and *Annabella*. The convoy faced fierce storms in a passage that lasted seven weeks. Campbell sailed on the *George* along with Major Menzies, 108 soldiers from the first battalion, the adjutant, the quartermaster, two lieutenants and five gentleman volunteers, while Captain MacKenzie, two subalterns, two volunteers and 82 men from the first battalion were aboard the *Annabella*. The severe weather scattered the convoy, and these two lightly armed transports arrived unescorted outside Boston Harbor on June 17, 1776. They immediately fell victim to incompetence, which was all too pronounced for the British in the early days of the escalating crises in the colonies.

Incredibly, when the British under General William Howe hastily evacuated Boston on the previous March 17, they failed to take the precaution of leaving behind a small naval force to patrol the coastal waters and warn other British ships of the city's evacuation. The result was that Campbell arrived outside Boston Harbor on June 17 completely unaware that the city was now in enemy hands. Campbell and his men were captured after an intense naval battle in which their two lightly armed transports engaged a fleet of heavily armed patriot vessels. The *George* and *Annabella* were armed with six cannons and two swivel guns respectively. The six patriot privateers, on the other hand, had 40-man crews and each carried eight cannons and 12 swivel guns. Despite such heavily uneven odds, the battle raged for most of the day, with the British transports successfully beating off successive patriot attacks.

This fierce naval battle turned decisively in the patriots' favor as the light faded, and the patriots were reinforced by the brig *Defence*, armed with 16 cannon, 20 swivel guns and a crew of 117 men; and by a schooner carrying eight cannon, 12 swivel guns and 40 men. With the arrival of these reinforcements, the transports attempted to dash for what they believed to be the sanctuary of Boston Harbor. Indeed, according to Campbell's account of the action, it was only when the transports came under fire from patriot shore batteries that the British realized that control of Boston had somehow changed hands. Disoriented by this unexpected development, the transports anchored at St. George's Island and awaited the resumption of hostilities. The conclusion of the battle was particularly intense, as Campbell tried to steady his men in the face of the patriots' renewed onslaught. Campbell's men continued to fight until their ammunition was exhausted, and further resistance was deemed futile.

The capture of Campbell, and detachments of the 71st Highlanders, came to the attention of Major General Artemus Ward in a letter to George Washington dated June 20th, in which the former described Campbell "as a member of parliament, and a gentleman of fortune." Archibald Campbell remained a prisoner of war for just under two years, during which he faced in captivity one of the greatest challenges of his life. His resolve and strength of character that he showed during the engagement, in captivity, and afterward, earned him the respect on both sides. Indeed, it won Campbell the personal regard of both King George III, and General George Washington, in almost equal measure.

After his controversial confinement at Concord jail, "lodged in a dungeon, without a bed, allowed nothing but bread and water, denied the use of pen, ink, and paper, his servant refused admittance, and in this unhappy situation did he continue many months," Campbell and five other Hessian officers were released in exchange for patriot prisoner Lieutenant Colonel Ethan Allen on May 6, 1778, at Staten Island. Not long after the exchange, Campbell rejoined his old regiment, the 71st Highlanders. He was soon involved in British operations that routed the patriot privateers at Old Tappan on September 28, 1778. It was around this time that Clinton named Campbell to lead the British expeditionary force to attack Georgia.[19]

As Campbell prepared his expeditionary force, General Prevost was ordered by Clinton to proceed to the St. Mary's River to await the arrival of Campbell. Prevost sent two expeditions into lower Georgia. He sent his son, Lieutenant Colonel Mark Prevost, to collect cattle in the Newport and Midway settlements, while he sent Lieutenant Colonel Lewis V. Fuser's force via inland waterway to attack Sunbury. This force of some 400 Regulars, Rangers and Indians arrived in the area of the Altamaha River in mid–November.

A British New York expedition of this size would surely not go unnoticed for too long, and such was the case. A South Carolina loyalist who had been in New York informed Henry Laurens of the proposed British expedition to the South. Laurens was suspicious of the value of this intelligence, but military steps were taken anyway. The Continental Congress requested Virginia to send 1,000 troops to support South Carolina and Georgia. North Carolina was asked to supply an additional 3,000 men. North Carolina quickly complied as it collected troops and started southward under General John Ashe. Later 2,000 troops were also sent. Laurens sent dispatches warning of the British expedition, which were laid before the Georgia Executive Council on November 19.

Alerted to the British threat in southern Georgia, Major General Robert Howe had no choice but to react, even as he knew Lincoln would soon replace him. He sent notice to the Congress that he was taking his force to engage and hoped that his action would be accepted. On the evening of November 18 Howe departed Charles Town with his Continentals, hoping to intimidate the enemy into moving back into Florida. Three days later, Howe received a letter outlining that the Florida invaders "destroy everything they meet in their way. They have burnt all the houses on the other side of Newport Ferry, within 4 miles of Sunbury. Our present stand is at Midway Meeting house."[20]

On the way to Midway, the British were engaged by Colonel John Baker, who had gathered up some local militia to stop Prevost. Baker met the enemy at the junction where the Savannah and Darien roads crossed Bulltown swamp. A short skirmish ensued, and Baker had to retreat. Continental colonel John White, with 100 men and two artillery pieces, built a breastwork across the road near the Midway Meeting House. Before Prevost appeared, White was joined by General James Screven and 20 militiamen. White abandoned the site and moved to the church to set up an ambush about a mile and a half south of Midway where the road was bordered by thick woods. Colonel Daniel McGirth, a loyalist who had previously been a patriot scout, knew the country well and suggested that same place to Prevost for an ambush.

Both forces arrived at nearly the same time as the engagement began. Screven was wounded and taken prisoner by the British. Colonel Prevost's horse was shot from under him and the patriots thought he was killed. Prevost promptly mounted another horse and advanced. Overwhelmed by larger numbers, the patriot force retreated after destroying the bridges across the swamp until they reached Midway Meeting House. Here White wrote a letter to himself purporting to be sent from Colonel Elbert. The fake letter ordered him to retreat to draw the enemy toward Savannah so that the cavalry could attack the British from the rear.

The fake letter left for Colonel Prevost worked and the British stopped their advance some seven miles beyond Midway. Meanwhile, Colonel McGirth, who was reconnoitering toward Sunbury, learned that Fraser's force had not arrived. He abandoned the pursuit of the patriots to return towards St. Augustine. On his way back Prevost burned Midway Meeting House and all buildings in his path as his men plundered the region.[21]

Meanwhile, Howe's Continentals arrived at Zubly's Ferry some 30 miles upstream from the capital on the Savannah River on the morning of the 27th. Howe was near frantic by this point. He hurried correspondence down to Moultrie in Charles Town revealing the "dreadful situation" in Georgia while urging him to exert himself "to the utmost to hasten up the troops under the command of Colonel Huger ... baggage at this time is not to be considered ... let the men force on." Colonel Isaac Huger was ordered by Howe to gather additional troops to follow. He also authorized the deputy quartermaster general to request the South Carolina president to use his power to impress wagons and horses. Howe wanted 5,500 pounds of gunpowder, with 5,000 pounds of lead, and a surgeon along with medical supplies.[22]

Colonel Fuser's water-bound force failed to reach the area of Sunbury until December 1 due to headwinds. Finally, Fuser sailed up the Midway River with his ships containing 500 men, a battering cannon, light artillery and mortars. Fuser occupied the town of Sunbury without a shot being fired. His force then moved to nearby Fort Morris, which was commanded by Lieutenant Colonel John McIntosh, the younger brother of George, William and Lachlan McIntosh. McIntosh had a force of 100 Continental troops, militia and a handful of local citizens from the town. Fuser sent a threatening letter to McIntosh demanding that he surrender. McIntosh responded with a defiant reply: "come and take it." Fuser hesitated attacking the mud fort as he awaited the report of his scouts. When Colonel Fuser learned that Colonel Prevost had returned to St. Augustine, he gave up the siege and returned to the St. Johns River. On the way, Fuser left a detachment at St. Simons Island to repair the fortifications there.

Meanwhile, as Prevost and Fuser blamed each other for the failed incursion into Georgia, Howe gathered his scattered forces at Sunbury. With the immediate threat past, Howe settled in to devise a plan to defend Georgia as best he could. He sent detachments to positions along the coast for early warning of any British incursion. He sent a galley to Warsaw, and another one to Tybee Island, to stand guard. Howe maintained a detachment at Midway to allow the locals to remove remaining valuables not already stolen by the British. As the patriot force patrolled the region looking for the enemy, Howe instructed them to "take every measure in your power to aid and assist the inhabitants of this state," and to "prevent wicked and designing men from Maruding [sic] the Inhabitants & encreasing their distress."

Howe continued to be frustrated by the lack of a defensive structure and preparations in Georgia, as he complained in writing to Moultrie for needed supplies. As Howe remained in an ill humor, a fleet under Commodore Hyde Parker sailed from Sandy Hook. The British Georgia Expedition force of Lieutenant Colonel Archibald Campbell was now under sail and on its way to the South. On December 6 a deserter from the British transport *Neptune*, off Tybee Island, reported to Governor Houstoun of the British fleet's sailing from New York. This intelligence confirmed that the British were heading to Savannah.[23]

As Campbell's fleet was sailing to Georgia, Major General Benjamin Lincoln arrived at Charles Town on December 4 to the warm welcomes of the citizens. The local establishment was excited to have a new face in charge of the Southern Department. Edward Rutledge wrote to thank General Washington "for introducing to my acquaintance a gentleman of his character and merit." The socializing soon ended as the harsh reality of the military situation in the South became apparent. As indeed General Howe had warned, the quartermaster reported there were almost no supplies in Georgia or South Carolina. Not even the six Continental fieldpieces were actually fit for service. To add to his desperate condition, the 3,000 Virginia militia promised to him were being withheld until "more authentic evidence of the enemies designs against South Carolina should be obtained." Lincoln expected some 1,000 militia from North Carolina, but their enlistment was scheduled to end in only four months.

General Howe wrote Lincoln explaining that the Continental troops were ill clothed, ill paid and hungry. He also confessed, "Destitute as we have been of a military chest the army has been in a state of abject dependence upon the civil authority for every shilling they receive." Lincoln responded as he wrote, "I hope things will be better settled and that I never shall be driven to hard necessity of altercating with the civil power, then which nothing [could] be more disagreeable." But it would only be a few days before Lincoln was in conflict with South Carolina president Rawlins Lowndes over army supplies.[24]

From the day General Lincoln had arrived in Charles Town he had faced the issue of active British aggression. With General Howe already in the field, the only thing he could do was plead for militia from the southern governors as he prepared the available Continentals to march to Howe's aid. With the news of the British sailing from New York, the

Georgia Executive Council initially ignored sending notification to Howe in favor of dispatching agents to Charles Town to appeal to Lincoln for help. Howe immediately left Sunbury, leaving Major Joseph Lane in charge of Fort Morris as he returned to Savannah with 600 men.

On December 23, 1778, Campbell's Georgia Expedition Fleet arrived off Tybee Island. The fleet had actually weighed anchor at New York on November 12, but heavy winds had driven it back to Staten Island as several vessels were damaged. The fleet sailed the second time on November 27. By December 17 the fleet was off Charles Town, and positioned off Tybee on December 23. General Howe reported there were 26 British sail at anchor off Cockspur Island, just 14 miles below Savannah.[25]

Howe was acutely aware of the desperate situation he was in defending the citizens of Savannah. Returning from Sunbury, he camped his forces southeast of town and prepared to defend the town. Howe had at his disposal 600 Continentals; half were from South Carolina, commanded by Colonel Isaac Huger, and the other half the Georgia Continentals under Colonel Samuel Elbert. Howe ordered these troops to take up positions around Savannah until the specific movements of the enemy were evident.

As Howe prepared as best he could for the attack, but there were very few Georgia militia present to support the defense of the state. It was not until the evening of December 24 that Governor Houstoun agreed to place the militia force of just over 100 men under Continental command. The troops were welcomed into the defensive force as the Continental troops were reminded to treat the militia with "Consideration and Respect." Colonel George Walton, as the commander of the Georgia Militia, was to be "respected and obeyed."[26] Howe also directed that his adjutant general send words of encouragement to the citizens of Sunbury, promising to rush to their aid at the earliest opportunity if the threat moved their way.

Howe proceeded to visit all the possible British landing sites in an attempt to guess where the British might strike and determine possible defensive positions. Placing small parties of militia at each potential site, he detached 50 Continentals at the most likely disembarkment landing spot at Girardeau's Bluff, located two miles below the town. Howe called a council of war composed of the field commanders to advise him on whether they should defend Savannah or surrender it. Despite the estimated four-to-one advantage of the British, the patriot council voted in a majority to defend it to the end.

On the night of December 27, a company of Highlanders light infantry under Sir James Baird was put ashore at Wilmington Island in two flatboats to seize a few inhabitants in the area. The idea was to gain intelligence about the rebel defenses and troop strength. Two persons were apprehended and taken to Campbell for interrogation. Campbell gained "the most satisfactory intelligence concerning the state of matters at Savannah." Armed with this information, Campbell came to a conclusion regarding where to land his force and the type of force and defenses he would encounter. Though he was under orders to join with General Prevost for the attack, Campbell was now confident that he had the forces to take Savannah without assistance.[27]

At noon on December 28 the British fleet sailed up the Savannah River, but at 4 P.M. the ships came to an abrupt halt when one of the transports ran aground. At sunset, Howe rode out with some of his officers to Brewton's Hill on Girardeau's Plantation, a rice plantation, to view the fleet. Since that seemed the best British landing site, he posted troops at a bridge over a small creek on the main road southeast of town, feeling it was "the most defensible I could find."

At daybreak the next morning, scarlet and white uniforms were everywhere as

Campbell put his troops ashore as expected at Girardeau's Plantation. The invasion force was led by his 1st Division consisting of all the light infantry, the loyalist battalion of the New York Volunteers, and the 1st Battalion of the 71st Highlanders. The light infantry marched off immediately down the causeway that led from the landing to the Girardeau house on the bluff. Girardeau Plantation was located on a 40-foot bluff about three-fourths of a mile from the river. A long and narrow causeway stretched through the broad rice fields from the riverside. A dispatch later sent from Campbell to Clinton described the success-ful British charge against the patriots' forward positions:

> The Highlanders under Captain Cameron were the first ashore, and with their usual impetuosity rushed against the house, which was defended by about fifty Rebels, who opened a smart fire of musketry upon them. These they instantly drove into the woods, without giving them time to repeat their fire, and happily secured a landing for the rest of the army. Captain Cameron, a spirited and most valuable officer was killed, and seven sol-diers killed or wounded.[28]

When the British reached the Girardeau house, these 50 patriot pickets from South Carolina under Captain J.O. Smith opened fire on the advancing Highlanders. The brisk fire killed Captain Cameron and two men, and wounded five other troops before the High-landers charged with bayonets, driving the patriots away from the house. No further conflict occurred as the rest of Campbell's troops offloaded the transports and marched up.

Meanwhile, General Howe with his force of some 700 men took up position at Fair Lawn Plantation, about a half mile southeast of town. From Girardeau's house a road lead-ing to Savannah passed through Fair Lawn. It was at Fair Lawn that Howe found the nat-ural defensive characteristics he felt afforded his troops the best way to engage the British. The road toward Savannah was bordered on the left by swamps and on the right by the river. The rice fields, due to low rainfall, were so hard Howe's troops could easily move across them. With the American position on high ground, with supposedly impassible swamps on his right, Howe had chosen the best place to defend the approach to Savannah that was possible with his small force.

On Howe's left flank, extending almost to the river, was Colonel Elbert's Georgia Brigade. Howe commanded the center of the formation as his force was astride of the road to Savannah. On his right were the South Carolina regiments under the command of Colonels Huger and William Thompson, which extended to a wooded swamp guarded by the small force of the Georgia Militia under Colonel Walton.

Howe had been concerned over the rumors that there were paths through the swamps to his right. As a result, he ordered Walton and other officers to maintain careful surveil-lance of the swamp. French engineer Jean Baptiste Ternant, serving as the inspector gen-eral of the Southern Department, was one of the men who was dispatched to search for any pass through the swamp. Neither Ternant nor any of the other Georgia militia officers were able to find any paths through the swamp. Colonel Leonard Marbury reconnoitered the swamp on two occasions and was unsuccessful. After three failed attempts at finding any openings, the right flank of the American line was declared impassible as the party departed to Fair Lawn after leaving a small detachment of militia to guard the swamp.

At 10 A.M. Howe called together a council of war and decided that the patriot posi-tions should be held, but if they were forced to retreat, they would do so through a pass to the south of and around Savannah. Orders were given to the troops, along with the retreat instructions. It was felt prudent to discuss the possibility of retreat with the threat of some 3,000 British soldiers out there in front of the American patriot force. It was quite likely that they would have to carry out this most difficult maneuver. Howe attempted to encourage the troops by assuring them that a major relief army from Charles Town was on the way, but few believed they would be saved in time.

As his redcoats progressed from Girardeau's, Campbell reconnoitered the American lines. When he discovered they were drawn up and supported with only a few fieldpieces, he advanced, feeling "it expedient, having the day before me, to go in quest of the enemy, rather than give them an opportunity of retiring unmolested." Campbell left a battalion of the 71st and the First Battalion of Delancey's Provincials to cover the landing place as he moved his forces toward Savannah. Campbell's advance continued down the road toward the center of the American line at Fair Lawn with his light infantry, followed by the New York Provincials and 1st Battalion of the 71st. The two battalions of the Hessians were bringing up the rear.[29]

As Campbell's force reached a point approximately 100 yards in front of the patriot line, the column halted. The American force had already thrown up a barrier trench to act as an obstacle. Behind that was a marshy rivulet running parallel to the entire American line. Howe's forces had destroyed a bridge that had existed over the creek. As Campbell reflected on the terrain in front of his troops, he became aware of a deserted slave named Quamino Dolly who wandered into the scene and informed Campbell of a private path through the swamp to the American rear. With this incredible intelligence, Campbell decided to feint against the American left position as he sent a flanking force through the swamp pass. He hoped to be able to strike Howe's force in two points simultaneously.

With bagpipes playing, the 1st Battalion of the 71st moved off forward as the light infantry under Sir James Baird angled off to their right in the feint to the American left. When the infantry had moved to a point where the Americans could not see them, they doubled back to the rear and moved undetected into the swamp path. Following them were Colonel Trumbull's New York Volunteers. Campbell had his artillery moved into a concealed position until the proper moment. Howe's force responded to the British maneuvers with sporadic firing from their field guns, but remained in place. Campbell had Baird's infantry quickly moved through the swamp path and burst out, shocking Colonel Walton's Georgia militia.

When Campbell heard the firing in the rear of the Americans, and was certain that Baird's force had fully engaged the patriots' right wing, he ordered the artillery to open fire, and a general advance of all his forces:

> I commanded the line to move forward briskly. The well aimed fire of the artillery, and the rapid advance of the troops caused the Enemy to disperse instantly. As the Light Infantry under Sir James Baird came out of the Swamp, the scattered remains of the Carolina and Georgia Brigades ran across his front, and he dashed forward on their flank, and with his usual gallantry terminated the Fate of the Day with a brilliant success.[30]

As Baird's men came out of the swamp, with Campbell's field pieces firing, and a general British troop advance underway, Walton's Georgia militia fled in complete panic. Realizing his forces were caught from forward and at the rear, Howe ordered an immediate withdrawal. The Continentals moved in a fairly orderly manner in column using the designated retreat path to the south of Savannah. The center and right moved out first with Colonel Elbert. Elbert changed the retreat to a file formation from a single column formation to provide greater protection from the cannon fire. Unfortunately, the formation change served to add to the confusion.

As the Americans retreated, the British gained on them. With Campbell's main column firing from their rear, and the infantry pressing in from the right, the Georgia brigade broke and fled for town. Colonel Owen Roberts, using a few field guns, held off the advancing forces long enough to allow General Howe and the South Carolina Continentals to escape to the retreat path as planned. Soon Roberts moved his artillery to safety.[31]

Elbert's Georgia brigade raced through the streets of Savannah, pausing only to seek protection at the courthouse. When a local citizen mentioned that they could escape via a foot log across Musgrove Creek at Yamacraw just west of the town, Elbert hastily led his men toward the creek. To their surprise, there was no log in sight. The tide was high. Led by General Elbert, his troops jumped into the murky chilled waters and attempted to swim to the opposite bank. Elbert swam to safety, but most of his men could not swim and were trapped. Some tried to swim but ultimately 30 drowned in the swollen creek. The remaining patriot force surrendered to the British. By 3 P.M. the British captured most of Elbert's force. One prisoner later wrote of the capture at the creek recalling, "being caught, as it were, in a pen, and the Highlanders keeping up a constant fire on us, it was thought advisable to surrender ourselves, which we accordingly did, and which was no sooner done than the Highlanders plundered every one amongst us...." Many had fled without even firing a shot. It would be difficult to call it a battle. It was really a rout.[32]

After successfully evading the British in retreat around Savannah, a South Carolina officer wrote a note to his father from Ebenezer explaining, "we effected a retreat thro' a very heavy fire of the Enemy for near a mile but I believe we have lost but a few men kill'd[.] I assure you it is wonderful how so many escaped as the Enemy six times more than our number. We have been compelled to retreat to this place & are still proceeding towards Augusta the river being so exceedingly high that we cannot cross over at Zubly's ferry & we being so exceedingly weakened that it is impossible to withstand them should they approach."

By sundown on the 29th, Howe's forces had suffered a major defeat, with 83 killed, 11 wounded, and 38 officers plus 415 men captured.[33] The British lost only seven killed (two officers and five men) and 19 wounded (one officer and 18 men). The British had captured 48 cannons, 23 mortars and 94 barrels of gunpowder, a fort with all its stores, and the shipping in the harbor. The patriots had also lost the capital of Georgia. Colonel Walton's Georgia Militia had received the worst of the attack by Baird's forces. Walton was wounded, fell off his horse and was captured. Later Campbell reported to Lord Germain with pride that he had defeated the Americans and that the Georgia capital "fell into our possession before it was dark."

With only 150 remaining of the original 700 troops under his command, General Howe led his frazzled group northward for eight miles to Cherokee Hill. There he waited for stragglers. As Howe retreated from Savannah, he sent orders to Lieutenant Aaron Smith, commander of the Third South Carolina Regiment at Ogeechee Ferry, and to Major Lane at Sunbury, to evacuate their posts and join up with him immediately. Smith obeyed orders and returned with 20 men, but Lane was persuaded by the local citizens of Sunbury not to leave.

During the following two days, Colonel Campbell had Sir Hyde Parker to move his ships up to the town to load rebel prisoners. The heat was so bad that many prisoners died. In this operation, Parker captured 126 prisoners, three ships, and eight smaller vessels, with the loss of only one British seaman killed and five wounded.

Campbell continued to advance upriver even though his ships carrying his horses had not arrived. His men were forced to drag their guns and carts cross country with the help of a few animals they could round up. A number of locals volunteered to help Campbell, and were organized into militia. Small groups of Americans were encountered and overpowered. Colonel Campbell reached Cherokee Hill on January 1, 1779, shortly after General Howe had crossed the Savannah River into South Carolina.

At Ebenezer, loyalist the Reverend Christopher Triebner, the village minister who had taken an oath of allegiance to the king and accompanied Campbell's troops into Ebenezer, joined Campbell. Others of the Salzburgers' church joined the British. These loyalists even organized marauding parties, as they started on a campaign of burning and pillaging every patriot farm and plantation.

Campbell stationed a company at Ebenezer, and set up the Salzbergers' church as a hospital. Prisoners that had been rounded up were taken to Savannah under a guard of ten soldiers. On the way to Savannah, two patriots, Sergeant William Jasper and his friend Sergeant Newton, waited by a spring and attacked the British guards. Two British soldiers were killed and the other eight men were taken to the Americans' camp across the Savannah River. The spot was later named Jasper Springs.

Now that Campbell had possession of the countryside around Savannah, he intended to head toward Sunbury. He was soon to learn that General Augustine Prevost had already taken Sunbury. About 1,000 citizens of Sunbury watched as Prevost's men destroyed the town, burned the church and laid the crops to waste. Many locals retreated into South Carolina as refugees.[34] Major Joseph Lane commanding Fort Morris at Sunbury tried to defend the fort with but 200 men. General Prevost, who was delayed in arriving from East Florida, had sent his brother, Lieutenant Colonel James Mark Prevost, to attack, which he did on January 6, 1779, with some 2,000 men. When the British moved up artillery to bombard the fort on January 9, Lane surrendered the fort. Lane had suffered 11 casualties, and Prevost only four.[35] Besides the 212 prisoners taken by the British, the patriot forces gave up 40 guns with ammunition and supplies.[36] Lane was later exchanged for a British prisoner, and returned to be court-martialed. He was dismissed for disobeying his general's orders.

On January 10, 1779, Campbell returned to Savannah, and on the 17th General Augustine Prevost, who had endured a difficult march from East Florida, finally joined him. Now in command of all southern British forces at Savannah, Prevost too was without horses and his men had barely survived on oysters as they had come up through the swamps of Georgia.[37] Campbell immediately presented General Prevost with his plan for an offensive against Augusta to complete the reconquest of Georgia. Campbell appears to have removed any doubts that Prevost may have had by telling him that the capture of Augusta would make the general the first British officer "to take a stripe and star from the rebel flag of Congress."[38] This argument proved irresistible to General Prevost, and Campbell's dispatch to Sir Henry Clinton of January 16, 1779, confirms that he was preparing

> to march with all of the Light Troops and a Battalion of the 71st Regiment to Augusta, to capture that important Post on the Savannah River, and there give encouragement to his Majesty's loyal subjects in the Back Country of the Carolinas.

Campbell's dispatch referred to the difficulties of campaigning in Georgia, and confirmed that with his usual thoroughness he was making careful preparations before launching the offensive: "The country through which I must travel is little cultivated and thinly populated. Hence careful arrangements were necessary to reduce the Hazards of this expedition."[39]

Capturing Savannah had demonstrated that Campbell was indeed a bold and skillful officer, unlike many British officers of his day. He had planned well, executed with zeal and speed, improvised and exploited battlefield advantages. Above all he had shown his decisive and confident leadership style.[40] Soon the news of the spectacular British victory was delivered to the world. Captain John Jervis, a friend to Clinton, wrote him, "your coup in

Georgia, and the repulse of D'Estaing in his attempts upon St. Lucia have preserved the nation from despair and the Ministry from perdition. There never was a thing so well timed, as the Georgia business, which arrived on the eve of the opening the Budget, and of the arrangement of measures, and impeachment of men." Alexander Innes, who carried the news of victory to England, reported to Clinton in a letter dated February 20 that the positive events "had an astonishing effect" in London.[41] Finally, the British had possession of a southern port, and had won a decisive victory. Georgia was lost.

It was a particularly sad time for Major General Robert Howe, and history would show no mercy, as he would soon learn. The historical fate of Howe would turn out to be in stark contrast to that of Campbell. The patriot commander subsequently faced a court of inquiry into his defeat at Savannah, and he was cleared "with highest honours." It would appear, however, that some of Howe's contemporaries were less than impressed by the court's verdict, and Howe, provoked by the criticism of General Gadsden, later fought a duel with the latter. Both men survived, with Gadsden suffering a minor wound to his ear.[42]

General William Moultrie also criticized Howe for attempting to stand up to such an overwhelming force. He wrote, "It was absurd to suppose that 6 or 700 men ... could stand against 2 or 3000 as good troops as any the British had ... Gen. Howe should have retreated." Light Horse Harry Lee in his memoir judged Howe for "his negligence betrayed by his Ignorance of the avenues leading to his camp." Perhaps Howe thirsted for a victory after enduring a year of frustrations in Georgia.[43] Whatever the case, Howe's image was forever tarnished for his loss of Savannah on that late December day in 1778.

10

Patriots Regroup and D'Estaing Arrives

"To astonish the enemy is almost to have conquered them...."

On January 4, 1779, on the banks of the Savannah River, and some 30 miles upriver at Purrysburgh, South Carolina, Major General Robert Howe finally met his replacement face to face, Major General Benjamin Lincoln. Surrendering his command to Lincoln now, Howe set about to brief him in detail on recent developments and the fall of Savannah. Howe had been ordered to report to General Washington's headquarters without delay, but he seemed to be in no hurry to head north. Moving to Charles Town, he stayed put. In early February, Howe promised he would depart immediately after completing the intelligence briefing to Lincoln. As another month passed, Howe confided to Thomas Sumter that he had suffered from "an inconvenient tho' not very painful disorder in stomach and bowels."

Later, on March 17, Howe signed a power of attorney giving Dr. William Keith, William Bull Jr. and Alexander Rose the power to collect all debts due him in Charles Town. The next day, Robert Howe, with his military aides, headed north in search of a new command. By April 5, he was in Halifax, North Carolina, reaching Philadelphia on the evening of April 26. Howe wished to present his account to the Continental Congress of the misfortunes of his southern command before heading to Washington, who was in winter quarters with his army at Middlebrook, New Jersey. Robert Howe's fate was now beyond the Southern Department.[1]

Meanwhile, at Purrysburgh, Lincoln had managed to gather some 1,400 troops consisting of militiamen from southern states and a handful of Continental soldiers. It was a pretty sad sight, but this was what Lincoln had to start his command with. Trying to get militia from South Carolina was like pulling teeth. South Carolina's president, Rawlins Lowndes, was not sympathetic and reported that "There is no law which obliged the militia to leave the State, and if there were a law made for that purpose, he was not without his doubts whether there was efficacy enough in the Government to execute it."

The real problem was that Lincoln needed money. He wrote Henry Laurens that, "The lack of military chest impedes progress and renders the military commander impotent." To Washington, Lincoln wrote, "I have met with almost every disappointment since I came into this department." The reality that Howe revealed to him was coming true. Somehow

Lincoln had to get more troops to stop the tide of British regulars consuming Georgia. Out of the compassion he felt for the family ideal of the homestead he had always known, Lincoln wrote of his frustration: "I have daily the unhappiness to see families of affluence fleeing before the enemy, reduced in a few hours to a state of want." To Washington, he recounted that his "wound which was nearly closed when I left camp, is opening again, and in a worse condition than it was seven months ago." For Lincoln, the new command and the new year for the war of American independence had opened with a dismal refrain.[2]

After the fall of Savannah and the British occupation was a reality, life changed for many of the local citizens. Campbell reported that after the battle his troops showed restraint. But the accounts of loyalists and patriots told another story. It was a story of looting, of mahogany tables and chairs scattered about the streets, of public records scattered in the sand, of feather beds ripped open and strewn in the wind. One French volunteer noted, "Robbery, incendiarism, rape, and murder were the fruits of that unhappy day." He told of patriot atrocities as fleeing American soldiers were "Plunging their bayonets into the sides of the unhappy wretches, they continued stabbing until, on withdrawing their blades, they tore out their victims' entrails."

The British occupying army took up residence in the large patriot barracks in the village of Yamacraw, and in the houses of patriot families throughout the town. Soldiers and their wives overran the courthouse where they broke up the bench and bar in the courtroom, and most of the window sashes for firewood. In time, many of the loyalist houses were appropriated for the British. For Lucy Tondee, her home became the quarters of the British troops and as the next years came, she saw nearly all her property, including slaves, furniture and carpenter's tools, sold at auction by the royal government. For patriots, and even some loyalists, Savannah was not a place to be as the British claimed the victor's spoils.[3]

As the month of January 1779 progressed, Lincoln was able to thicken the ranks of his militia force as they joined him at the various fords along the Savannah River to "prevent excursions into this state, and to cover our flanks." He expected more support and daily expected that General John Ashe and his North Carolina militia would arrive. Lincoln wrote a militia leader in the backcountry, "To hold the upper part of your state is of importance as thereby you will curb the disaffected, restrain the savages, give countenance to our friends and support the common cause."[4]

By the middle of January, a few hundred militia were gathering at Burke Jail under Lieutenant Colonel James Ingram, who was cooperating with Lincoln and the South Carolina militia. Unable to directly engage the British, Ingram used his force to attack small parties of British and loyalists. In the backcountry of Wilkes County, militias were gathering under the leadership of Colonels Elijah Clarke, John Twiggs and John Dooly. Since the British could not promise universal coverage, doubt began to pervade much of Georgia that it was not wise to take the king's oath.[5]

While Lincoln was regrouping, Campbell was busy consolidating his gains. In order to formally restore the Crown's authority, Campbell issued proclamations to the Georgia citizens requiring them to take oaths of allegiance to the Crown, as well as asking the fit to join the loyalist regiments. He also offered rewards for the capture of patriots raiding Georgia from their bases in South Carolina. To carry out the operational plan he had talked Prevost into, on January 22 Campbell and his troops marched out of Ebenezer toward Augusta, which was upriver some 100 miles away.[6]

On the trek to Augusta, Campbell was joined by loyalist militia, as the patriots could do nothing. Though the forces with Lincoln and Moultrie were just across the Savannah River at Purrysburg, they had an insufficient number of men to attack Campbell. To provide at least some resistance to Campbell's army, Lincoln sent Colonel Elbert and his Georgia troops to the upper part of South Carolina. Elbert skirmished with Campbell's force at the crossing at Briar Creek, but was forced to retire without stopping them. On January 29, Campbell marched into Augusta, the temporary seat of the Georgia government since 1776, unopposed. Hundreds of the local people gathered their household goods and cattle and fled into South Carolina.

With Augusta in British hands, on January 30 General John Ashe with 1,100 North Carolina patriot militia arrived at Charles Town. Spirits and moral improved dramatically with Ashe's arrival. A young Continental reflected on the new optimism and wrote, "Lincoln is anxious and uneasy at being obliged from the enemy's superiority, or at least equality of numbers, to remain so long inactive, and will assuredly take the first opportunity of paying them [the British] a visit." Now Lincoln sent General Ashe to the fords opposite Augusta to join General Williamson and Colonel Elbert in order "to digest a plan of defense for the country and future operations."[7]

As Lincoln and his leaders contemplated their next move, in another quarter British major Gardiner with some 200 troops made an amphibious landing on Port Royal Island from Commodore Hyde Parker's ships. Reacting to this raid of February 3, Lincoln sent General William Moultrie and Brigadier General Stephen Bull, with 300 South Carolina militia, to drive the British off the island. Moultrie, armed with three field guns, the militia troops and 10 Continentals, occupied Beaufort and positioned his men on both sides of the road in expectation of Gardiner's troops.

When Gardiner's force arrived, Moultrie fired his cannon, sending the British running for cover in the woods. After an hour of fighting, the Americans ran out of ammunition, but fortunately the British began to retreat. American dragoons took after the British, but they were able to take only a few British prisoners. Moultrie suffered 30 casualties, and British losses were unknown. The battle served to distinguish Major Thomas Grimball's Charles Town Battalion of Artillery, as well as the two companies under Captains Thomas Heyward and Edward Rutledge, both signers of the Declaration of Independence. Christopher Gadsden from Charles Town had previously organized this unit.[8]

With Savannah under British control, and Lincoln's army across the river in South Carolina, the Georgia partisans took to the field. One such well-respected loyalist partisan and a Scotsman, Colonel John Hamilton, was sent by General Prevost upriver to Augusta with 200 mounted infantrymen to encourage the locals to support the British. On February 10, Hamilton and his infantry at Carr's Fort were attacked by a combined force of some 350 militiamen from Colonel Andrew Pickens' South Carolina Militia and Captain John Dooley's Georgia Militia. At the point in the engagement when the Americans had the upper hand and appeared to be winning, news arrived that another loyalist militia force of around 700 North Carolinians under Colonel Boyd was heading south to join Hamilton. After considering his predicament, Pickens, in a gutsy move, decided to break off the battle and march to intercept and attack Boyd.[9]

Andrew Pickens was not the sort of man one would have thought of as a dour Presbyterian elder, but that he was. Born in 1739, he had grown up in an "atmosphere of rifle and religion" in Bucks County, Pennsylvania. In his youth, his Scotch-Irish family moved him to the Shenandoah Valley in Virginia, and then on to the Waxhaw community in upper South Carolina. By the 1760s, Pickens had settled in and married in the Long Canes district of South Carolina, located about 22 miles west of Ninety Six.

In business, Pickens prospered with his Indian trade and before long he had become quite a successful merchant. As evidence of his success, he had built a warehouse across the

Savannah River from Augusta for the purpose of storing goods acquired for sale down river. As a backcountry wealth holder, Pickens, and other successful men like him, shared the economic values with their fellow Tidewater plantation owners of the Carolinas and Georgia. With a vested interest in his business and his way of life, it was only natural that he would side with the patriot cause.[10]

Unaware of the presence of patriot militia, Colonel Boyd's force crossed the Savannah River on the 13th and camped at a farm on the north side of Kettle Creek, which was 50 miles northwest of Augusta. Meanwhile, Pickens' men crossed the river and made a complete circle to move in behind Boyd. After received a scouting report from Captain Hugh McCall of no threats in the area, Boyd's men turned their horses loose to graze as they slaughtered cows and parched corn.

The next day, Pickens' force attacked Boyd's loyalists with complete surprise from three directions simultaneously. The patriots advanced, firing as they went, as the loyalists formed up in a line behind a fence and fired back briskly. It took nearly an hour for Pickens' men to overcome the loyalists. In retreat, Colonel Boyd was killed when he was hit by three cannonballs, with two of them passing through his body. Boyd's troops fled across the creek and into a swamp, leaving their horses, baggage and arms behind, while Pickens led his men through the swamp to continue the battle on the other side of Kettle Creek. When the battle ended, 70 loyalists were dead, and another 75 were either wounded or captured. Pickens' force suffered only nine killed and 23 wounded.

As Boyd lay dying on the ground, Pickens ordered that his old acquaintance from the past receive all manner of available medical assistance. Boyd thanked Pickens for his act of chivalry and asked him who had won the battle. Learning the patriots had won, Boyd remarked that the outcome would have been different if he had not been wounded. He then asked Pickens to bury him, and also to send his wife his broach with an explanation of how he had died. Pickens agreed and it was done.

The Kettle Creek victory gave a solid lift to patriot morale, and it put added pressure on Campbell's forces in Augusta. The battle also had the effect of scattering many of the loyalists to as far away as Florida. Some returned home and some 200 headed to Augusta to join Campbell. Loyalist prisoners were taken to Lincoln at Purrysburg where they were tried for treason. Most were pardoned, but five were ultimately executed.[11]

On February 14, General Prevost wrote to Clinton noting that he had set up headquarters at Ebenezer, a location well suited for protecting Savannah, while supporting Campbell's operations in Augusta. Since Campbell had captured Augusta, Prevost had sent him reinforcements from the 2nd Battalion of the 71st Highlanders and three Grenadier companies.[78] Unfortunately for the British, the advance to Augusta and the other moves into the backcountry failed to rally the expected numbers of local loyalists to join the Crown forces. Without such reinforcements, Campbell's position in Augusta soon became vulnerable to attack from patriot troops who were massing on the Carolina side of the Savannah River. Patriot troops had already seized a sufficient numbers of boats to enable them to return almost at will to the western shore of the Savannah River and into Georgia.[12]

Even the promised Indians were reluctant to provide much support to the British. The British Indian superintendent, James Stuart, had promised that the Creeks and Cherokees would cooperate with the British upon arrival, but it never happened. Stuart had in fact been unable to accomplish much work due to a prolonged illness. Stuart died on March 21. Before long, the British government split his past responsibilities between two other men. Alexander Cameron, a deputy, was assigned to work with the Choctaws, Chickasaws, and other Indians along the Mississippi. The notorious Georgia loyalist and leader of the Florida

Rangers, Thomas Brown, was given the Creeks, Cherokees, Catawbas and other Indians along the middle Atlantic. At Augusta, Campbell saw few Indian allies and those who were present just wanted presents. Campbell held Augusta, but things were looking rather bleak.[13]

With patriot forces eager to engage the British, Lincoln sent a sizable force under General Ashe to retake Augusta. Ashe moved with his 1,400 North Carolina militia, 100 Georgia Continentals and 200 light-horse militia, toward Augusta.[14] Ashe wrote, "the motion of the British troops at Augusta ought to be attended to and opposed in force. I consider them as a snowball, that should they move any distance into the frontiers of this state, will collect all the lukewarm and disaffected in each of the Carolinas, and should they reach Camden will become so large, that no force can be raised in these parts ... would be sufficient to oppose their march to Charlestown."[15]

Before Ashe and his substantial force could reach Augusta, the British had departed the "Bad Post," as Prevost later called it. Campbell had determined that the town was not worth the potential loss of his army. In the early morning of February 14, the British departed Augusta, marched down the Savannah River, and camped at Hudson's Ferry, some 24 miles from General Prevost's main army at Ebenezer. The news of Campbell's retreat reached Lincoln on the 16th. He immediately sent off a dispatch to Ashe revealing his hope that Ashe had "crossed the first opportunity you had and that you will follow them with all the force you can muster and as quickly as you can." Lincoln said it was important that Ashe keep up the pressure on Campbell or he might attempt to cross the river in force at a lightly guarded ford farther downstream from Augusta in order to flank the American left.

Campbell's departure from Augusta was confusing to many patriot leaders, including General Washington. A letter from Washington to Henry Laurens confirmed how perplexed he was with Archibald Campbell's "precipitate retreat from Fort Augusta." The local Anglican priest in Augusta, the Reverend James Seymour, who had only two weeks before celebrated the arrival of Campbell's troops in Augusta, sadly lamented the scene before him as the British marched into the thick woods. He explained, "Our feelings at first on that Occasion cannot be easily described. We expected to be plundered of everything we had, and even that our Lives were in danger."[16] Though a surprise, it was a promising patriot development.[17]

On the 18th, Lincoln ordered Ashe to cross the river and move "with all the dispatch possible consistent with the precaution necessary to be observed in marching in an enemy country." Four days later, Ashe was ordered to remain at Briar Creek, upriver from Hudson's Ferry and Campbell. Lincoln thought the place would be "a good stand for you until some plan of cooperating be digested." Ashe was ordered to meet with him at Two-Sisters, a ford on the South Carolina side of the river, for a council of war.

Generals Ashe, Moultrie and Rutherford attended Lincoln's upbeat Two-Sisters' council of war. Lincoln later wrote to John Jay, the new president of the Continental Congress, that the favorable events for the patriot cause "gives great spirit to the upper country" and "blasts the hopes of the disaffected." Lincoln rightly noted that it would convince "the timid and deluded" that taking up with the British was foolhardy for the British could not protect them. With Ashe to protect Augusta, plans could be made to allow the citizens to return to their homes and reestablish the Georgia legislature for the reorganization of the civil authority. The council agreed that Briar Creek was a strong defensive location and that Ashe should be reinforced there. The patriot spirit was high again as a new hope was in the air.[18]

When Campbell had withdrawn from Augusta, he had crossed Briar Creek and stopped to burn the bridge there. On March 3, while troops from General Ashe's units were in the process of rebuilding the bridge, a force of some 900 infantry, grenadiers, dragoons and militia from Lieutenant Colonel Prevost arrived in the area. Prevost's forces began to cross the creek above Ashe's camp in an attempt to get behind the patriot forces. As the British attack began, Ashe's Continentals opened fire, which alarmed the militia so much they immediately began to scatter. Then, the Continentals, realizing they were in trouble, also retreated in disorder.

The untimely American retreat found many men throwing down their weapons and heading for the river. The shameful defeat left over 150 American patriots dead, while the British captured 11 officers and 162 troops. The British also captured seven cannons with ammunition and various supplies. Colonel Prevost's force suffered only 16 casualties. Of the defeat, the British publication *New York Gazette and Weekly Mercury* declared, "The panic occasioned by the terror of the bayonet, left them no alternative but that of plunging into the water ... few would have escaped if night had not come on soon."[19]

Lincoln wrote of the "very disagreeable news" of the defeat to John Rutledge, the newly elected president of South Carolina, reporting, "I thought him very secure." General Moultrie called the defeat a total rout, and one that would serve to lengthen the war by a year. Ashe described the event as being such a surprise that "the troops in my division did not stand fire for five minutes. Many fled without discharging their pieces." Most of the deaths were from drowning as the patriots struggled to swim across the river. The defeat was most complete. Of the 1,500 men Ashe commanded, no more than 450 ever served with the American forces again. Ashe was brought up before a court-martial a week after the defeat, but was found not guilty of personal cowardice. He was found to have failed to secure his camp and to gather intelligence of the enemy's movements.[20]

The defeat at Briar Creek was yet another setback for Lincoln and his plans to continue an offensive tactic. Lincoln held a critical council of war at Purrysburg and asked his Continental officers to give their opinions on what the next move should be. The patriots had some 1,800 rank and file, while it was believed the British had around 3,500. With the odds so in favor of the British, the decision was to concentrate the patriot forces at Purrysburg, and that no forward posts be established that were out of effective range of the main body of the army. They must delay until their forces could be recruited to replace those lost at Briar Creek.[21]

Shortly after Campbell set up his headquarters at Hudson Ferry, his health began to deteriorate. Unable to carry on with the campaign, Campbell relinquished his command to the brother of General Augustine Prevost, Lieutenant Colonel James Mark Prevost, and returned to Savannah. On March 12, Lieutenant Colonel Archibald Campbell sailed for Britain and out of Georgia history with Commodore Hyde Parker aboard the *Phoenix*.[22]

While Lincoln pondered the next move, on March 4 the civilian royal government had been restored with Colonel Prevost designated as the lieutenant governor. A complete slate of provincial appointees was also named, including a new council. All laws of 1775 were restored. Since the treasury was nonexistent, General Prevost drew on the British Treasury to fund expenses. Steps were taken to provide frontier defense and to regain Indian support. With a new temporary government in place, Georgia's old provincial leaders were ordered back to the colony. Former royal governor James Wright was to return to Georgia to restore the "Peace of the King" if possible. He was also instructed to call an assembly to convince the citizens that all was back to normal.[23]

Campbell's departure from Georgia was a serious blow to the British war effort in the South. From a strategic standpoint in the campaign, Campbell's departure marked the high-water mark of British offensive action in Georgia. Through the bold leadership of Campbell to take Savannah and secure much of Georgia for the British, Lord George Germain became convinced that all efforts should be concentrated on regaining control of South Carolina. On March 31 he wrote Henry Clinton requesting that Campbell be reinforced so he could take Charles Town.[24]

If the problems of maintaining an army in the field were not enough, it was even harder still to deal with recruiting. Lincoln spent an undue amount of time pleading with the governors of North Carolina and Virginia to extend the enlistment of their militias for three more months. Recruiting was a continual ordeal for the militia were always ready to leave. Lincoln noted a distinct change in the attitude of those that enlisted. He wrote, "Too many there are who content themselves with having done what they called their turn ... and pay little attendance either to the good of the service, justice to the public, or to a line of conduct which will promote a speedy termination of the present war." Conversely, for his Continentals, there was no going home until the war was won.

The frustration with the situation in the Southern Command, coupled with a festering and aching wound, carrying around a fever, and the extreme climate of the South, caused General Lincoln to seriously consider finding a way out. In a first move he authorized his aide, Everard Meade, to head to Philadelphia to suggest to the Continental Congress that his recall would be welcome. On April 12, Lincoln wrote his friend James Lowell a long letter summarizing the state of affairs and expressing a hope that "my friends will not suffer me to be kept here long." Lincoln feared that his reputation would be impacted forever by the lack of will on the part of the southern leaders to carry out the war. He wrote, "I hardly know how to reconcile myself to the Fabian principles," when Georgia is held "by the enemy with a force so inconsiderable compared to what might have been sent into the field by this and the neighboring states." Lincoln was sure that the Continental Congress was unaware of the true situation when it refused to send reinforcements.

While Lincoln waited for Congress to take action on his resignation request, the military situation improved somewhat. The recruiting effort was beginning to yield favorable results and soon allowed the patriot forces to outnumber the British and loyalists. Finally, Governor Richard Caswell of North Carolina and President John Rutledge of South Carolina provided militia replacements and extended the enlistment periods. From his headquarters at Black Swamp, Lincoln explained to Rutledge that "I think we might act offensively with every rational hope of success—Now seems to be the time for our greatest exertions—the weather is good, the season healthy & the enemy not reinforced."

With renewed strength, Lincoln's army left Black Swamp on April 23 and marched toward Augusta on the northern banks of the Savannah River. He took with him 2,000 troops and left General Moultrie with two regiments, the Second and Fifth, with another 220 men under Colonel McIntosh and Colonel Maurice Simon's brigade of Charles Town Militia, all totaling some 1,200 men. While Lincoln crossed the river and moved down the southern bank, Moultrie's orders were to act as a counter to the British forces at Ebenezer, Georgia, and to oppose any crossing and hold the strong passes behind him. If Lincoln's plan went well, he would protect Augusta so that the Georgia legislature could gather on May 1 while also forcing the British back toward Savannah.[25]

Just as the renewed patriot offensive was taking form, on April 24 Lincoln received intelligence that the British intended a move into South Carolina. Lincoln discounted the news as an attempt to draw him back from Georgia. Unfortunately, Lincoln's intuition was misguided. Seeing a real opportunity with Lincoln's absence, Colonel Mark Prevost took 2,000 men across the Savannah River on April 28 and marched toward Charles Town. The patriot garrison at Purrysburg under Lieutenant Colonel McIntosh retreated immediately and moved to Coosahatchie, where General Moultrie joined him. Moultrie sent dispatches immediately to General Lincoln, to Rutledge at Orangeburgh, and to Lieutenant Governor Thomas Bee in Charles Town notifying them of the dire situation.

Moultrie's forces fled back to Charles Town and by the evening of May 10, after fording rivers with pontoon bridges, plundering as he went, Prevost reached Ashley Ferry, only seven miles from the city. The next morning, his force crossed the river and appeared before the lines at Charles Town. After a failed attempt with heavy losses to slow the forward guard of the British with General Kasimir Pulaski's cavalry, Moultrie opened fire at Prevost's men with his cannon.[26]

Portrait of William Moultrie (Smithsonian Institution).

After repeated pleas from Moultrie about the seriousness of Prevost's drive to Charles Town, finally on the 10th General Lincoln moved his forces under forced marches in the relief of Charles Town. He wrote, "We are making every exertion. The inability of the men only will put a period to our daily marching."[27]

By the evening of the 11th, the opposing forces were in negotiation mode. Colonel Prevost was asking for surrender, while Moultrie with Governor John Rutledge was contemplating whether they should resist to the end or surrender. Moultrie had 3,180 troops, and believed, incorrectly, that the British had upward of 8,000 men. The civil authorities wanted to capitulate and ask for the terms for giving up Charles Town. After several days of negotiations, with many key patriot leaders seriously considering surrendering Charles Town, on the 12th Moultrie queried the gathered men and declared, "Gentlemen, you see how the matter stands; the point is this: I am to deliver you up prisoners of war or not." Some indicated a hearty, "Yes!" Then Moultrie exclaimed, "I am determined not to deliver you up prisoners of war. We will fight it out." Colonel Henry Laurens jumped up and declared, "Thank God, we are on our legs again." Prevost was notified that Charles Town would not be surrendered.

It was like a miracle, for at daybreak on May 13 the citizens of Charles Town awoke to great joy as many cried out, "The enemy is gone!" And so they were. Immediately after getting word that the patriots would not surrender and under the cover of darkness, Prevost pulled out his troops. Some light infantry had been left behind to make sure Moultrie did not move as the main force retreated under the cover of night. Pulaski proceeded to follow the British with his cavalry, but the British had already crossed the Ashley River before he could reach them.

Prevost had been alerted to the presence of Lincoln's force by an intercepted letter. When General Lincoln had received Moultrie's May 8 letter on May 10 at 4 P.M., within one hour he had shot off a reply to Moultrie. Lincoln's reply letter was taken by the British near the battle lines at Charles Town. In fact, by the afternoon of May 12, Lincoln was still

65 miles away from the city. Sadly for the patriots, Lincoln's progress was too slow to catch Prevost. Lincoln's force of over 5,000 men reached Dorchester on May 14, the day after Provost's army had crossed the Ashley River in retreat. Lincoln's perceived slow reaction to the plight at Charles Town would soon bring him significant criticism. Colonel Prevost likewise received criticism for his actions. Sir Henry Clinton called Prevost's attempt at taking Charles Town reckless.

The same day Prevost hurried away from the Charles Town peninsula, the Continental Congress, after a long debate, gave General Lincoln permission to retire and "resolved that Brig. Gen. Moultrie be commander in the absence of Maj. Gen. Lincoln of the Southern army during its continuance, to the southwest of North Carolina, with the allowance of a Major General on a separate command until the further order of Congress." Lincoln would learn of the approved request later on June 8 and the next day Moultrie responded to the affair with a sense of loyalty and respect for Lincoln by urging Lincoln not to retire. Lincoln then responded to Moultrie on June 10 that he would continue to render service to the state as long as his health held out. Lincoln acknowledged that Moultrie had the respect and confidence of the people. But, after receiving his permission to retire, and with the knowledge of his current unpopularity with many, Lincoln did not relinquish his command after all and the issue was dropped.[28]

As Prevost's forces moved away from the city and headed toward Savannah, pillaging and destroying plantations as they went, they became stretched out in a long line along the Stono River from Wapoo Cut to Stono Ferry. With few cavalry reconnaissance troops, Lincoln did not gain solid intelligence of Prevost's force situation until May 24. As Lincoln positioned his patriot forces at Stono River opposite Prevost's units, he was determined to regain the offensive and drive the British out of the Lowcountry, and eventually from Savannah. On June 15, Lincoln consulted with Rutledge and his council on an attack plan that involved having him attack the British entrenchments along the west side of Wappoo Cut as General Moultrie attacked on the rear of the British from James Island.

The next day, June 16, Lieutenant Colonel Prevost left Stono Ferry by boat for Savannah with the majority of the British force, including the Grenadiers of the Sixteenth Regiment. In addition, he took along all the vessels that had served the British to maintain a "bridge" from his post on the eastern shore of John's Island across to James Island. Prevost left behind Lieutenant Colonel John Maitland to defend the British rear with some 900 men of the First Battalion of the Seventy-first Regiment, loyalist militia and Hessians. Maitland's force spent from June 17 to 19 transporting the sick and wounded, blacks and Indians across the inlet with the baggage and horses of the garrison. Maitland also ordered the unnecessary buildings of the force destroyed in preparation for defense of the post.

On June 19, Lincoln ordered Moultrie to move on to James Island across from Charles Town as a show of force to the British on John's Island. Lincoln's plan was to have Moultrie take his boats up to Wappoo Cut to be in position to head off any retreating British and support action from Lincoln at Stono Ferry. Unfortunately, General Moultrie did not follow Lincoln's orders with speed. When Lincoln began his attack on Maitland at 7 A.M. on June 20, Moultrie had only half of his force of 700 men on James Island. Unfortunately, Moultrie's force did not reach Wappoo Cut until the battle was over.

Lincoln's forces arrived at the British defensive works about an hour after daybreak on the 19th after traveling the 18 miles from the Ashley River. On the next day, the attack on Prevost's force at Stono River was executed. Lincoln's force of 1,500 men formed in a pine wood some 400 yards from the British lines, and attacked at 7 A.M. The engagement lasted an hour as the patriots drove the British back to their lines. Unfortunately, Lincoln found the British to be much stronger than he anticipated and had to withdraw. Lincoln's main forces retired, and the battle at Stono Ferry was over by 8:30 A.M. Lincoln's retreating forces returned to Charles Town.[29]

Casualties were heavy on both sides, as the British suffered 26 killed and 103 wounded or missing. The patriot forces lost 34 killed and 113 wounded. Lincoln explained the battle to Rutledge, "Though we had not the wished for success; yet I think good will arise from the attempt." He noted, "Our men now see that little is to be feared either from musquetry or field pieces; they are full of spirit, & are sure they can beat the enemy on equal grounds at any time." Lincoln hoped to catch Prevost and defeat the British before they moved back to Savannah. But it was not to be.[30]

On June 24, having accomplished his mission of protecting Prevost's movement to Savannah, Maitland evacuated his post at Stono Ferry and marched southward along the seacoast, from island to island, to rejoin Prevost at Beaufort on Port Royal Island on July 8. Colonel Prevost then departed Beaufort for Savannah, leaving Lieutenant Colonel Maitland in command of a garrison of some 900 troops. The British could use Beaufort as a forward base of operations into the Lowcountry.[31] The British offensive campaign into South Carolina was now at an end.

After the attack at Stono Ferry, Lincoln had to again come to terms with many of his militia forces having reached the end of their enlistment periods. Soon he was left at his headquarters at Sheldon in the heat of the summer with about 800 Continental troops to watch the British forces at Beaufort, just 15 miles away.[32] The past six months since the loss of Savannah had not been kind to Lincoln or to the patriot cause. Lincoln reflected on his delayed offensive in Georgia, his lost opportunity to catch Colonel Prevost's forces at Charles Town, his defeat at Stono Ferry, and the loss of most of his militia. He also came to appreciate the brutal legacy of the British incursion into South Carolina. Some 3,000 black slaves were believed taken by the British as they left South Carolina. Many of them were shipped off to the West Indies and sold, while thousands of other slaves were left behind and suffered terribly under the British.[33]

There was also great loss of property for Lowcountry planters at the hands of the British. They smashed the furnishings of prominent Lowcountry planter Eliza Lucas Pinckney at Belmont. The Bull family's Ashley Hall was looted, Major Thomas Pinckney's home at Ashepoo suffered 19 slaves taken, along with the prize horses, sheep and poultry and the dwelling house burned.[34] Even with the aid of stolen horses taken from planters, the British could barely transport all the loot from the Lowcountry homesteads. More wealth was actually destroyed than was taken out by the British. The barbaric behavior to the slaves, the cruel treatment of horses and livestock, and the plundering of the Lowcountry was a British disgrace.

In Georgia, on July 14, 1779, Royal Governor James Wright, Lieutenant Governor John Graham, and Chief Justice Anthony Stokes returned to Savannah from England to take up their duties and restore the formal British civil government in Georgia.[35] When they arrived the situation was troublesome. Wright was concerned about the inadequate British troop strength in and around Savannah. In a letter to Germain dated July 31 he declared, "I shall look with the utmost Anxiety and Impatience for the Troops from New York and hope they will be in our Neighborhood early in October, for till then, as the Troops that were here are so much Scattered about, I shall not Consider this Province as safe." The reference to the month of October is significant because that was the most likely point when the French fleet under d'Estaing might appear off the Georgia coast, being the end of the hurricane season along the Atlantic seaboard. Clinton had admitted that he "had not received any accounts of the French fleet's operations on the American coast."[36]

Later, on August 9, Wright wrote to Germain, "The more I am able to see into the state of affairs here, the more I am convinced of the wretched situation this Province is in, and how nearly it was being totally lost while the army was carrying on their operations in South Carolina; and now, my Lord, the Rebels who went from hence into Carolina on the arrival of Colonel Campbell, with other Rebels of Carolina and this Province, are possessed of the Country at and about Augusta, and all above it, and I have the honor to inclose your Lordship the information I received from three Back Country People by which it appears that almost the whole settlements down to Briar Creek are broke up, or the inhabitants skulking about to avoid the Rebel Partys, and that the Rebels have collected upwards of 600 men and are going to establish a post with them somewhere in St George's Parish."[37]

Governor Wright had other concerns in Georgia. Wright, who had always been suspicious of the reliability of those locals who had taken the oaths of allegiance to the British after Savannah fell, found that the people were not ready for an assembly. Trade restrictions had been lifted only in Savannah, where some level of normalcy had returned. Due to the pressure exerted by British creditors desiring to collect debts from the citizens in South Carolina and Georgia, the ministry directed General Prevost to restore commercial relations "as your situation will admit." The British peace commissioners likewise issued a blank proclamation for use by Prevost to suspend the Prohibitory Act if possible. While the expectation of regaining full and effective civil governmental control of the recaptured colony of Georgia was present when Campbell won his easy victory at Savannah in the beginning, the British weakness in regaining civil management was a continual problem throughout the Revolution.[38]

With serious reflection of their perilous situation in the South as they attempted to drive the British out of the Lowcountry and Savannah, Governor John Rutledge, General Lincoln and Monsieur Plombard, the French consul at Charles Town, wrote letters to Admiral d'Estaing at Cape Francois in Hispaniola. They pleaded to him to come to the aid of the patriot forces at Savannah.[39] Another French supporter, a Colonel and Marquis de Bretigny, who was stationed at Charles Town, also urged the admiral to come to the Carolina coast. The colonel wrote to d'Estaing that "All here is in frightful confusion; very few regular troops, no help from the north, a feeble and badly disciplined militia and the greatest friction among the leaders." D'Estaing indicated that he had been told that the "American cause was in peril and all hopes were based on my early arrival."[40]

One year earlier, Admiral d'Estaing had withdrawn midway through a joint operation with patriot forces under General John Sullivan at Newport, Rhode Island, leaving them stranded and vulnerable to the British Army. The encounter had left bitter feeling on both sides. But now d'Estaing had just come off a successful expedition against the British in the West Indies. His fleet had captured the island of St. Vincent in June, took Grenada in July, and defeated British Admiral John "Foul Weather Jack" Byron in a major naval engagement during this 1779 summer. Coming off his victories in the Caribbean, and with the pleas from the southern patriots, d'Estaing saw an opportunity to improve his reputation and come to the aid of the American cause in retaking Savannah.[41]

It was 5 A.M. on August 13, 1779, when Phillipe Seguier de Terson set sail aboard the *Robuste* for Port de Paix, Haiti. It was a day with perfect weather for this proud captain of a company of the French Agenois grenadiers. Though the sea travel made him queasy, he loved his ground job. As they anchored at Haiti his stomach felt settled again. On the 14th, the ship's captain, Commodore de Grasse, entertained some 30 persons from Port de Paix for dinner. The commodore had many relatives on the island from his wife's side of the family. Among the guests were four women who were "neither young nor pretty." Captain

Portrait of Vice Admiral Charles Henri Jean-Baptiste, Comte d'Estaing. Taken from *Dead Towns of Georgia*, C.C. Jones, Jr., Vol. I, opposite page 200 (Hargrett Rare Book and Manuscript Library, University of Georgia Libraries).

de Terson went ashore and found the place to be nice and worthy of his garrisoning there if it ever came to be.

While de Grasse remained to hold more dinners at Port de Paix, on the 15th d'Estaing sailed from Cape Francois, Hispaniola, with 24 men-of-war, 12 frigates, four flutes, and several armed merchantmen. His fleet was escorted out of the channel by the *Protecteur*, the *Fier*, two frigates and two flutes. The next day, de Grasse sailed at dawn, following the coastline, and stopped at the latitude of the French island of Tortue, off the northern coast of Haiti, to wait for d'Estaing's fleet. At noon a sailor fell overboard, but was rescued without incident. That afternoon, de Grasse sighted the fleet division under de Vaudreuil that had departed Port au Prince a week before.

On the 17th, de Grasse sighted the first frigate from d'Estaing's fleet and the next day at 4:30 P.M. he joined with d'Estaing's main fleet. Frigates were sent to bring de Vaudreuil's ships to join. By the following dawn, all of the wayward units of d'Estaing's fleet were assembled. The fleet sailed toward Savannah and d'Estaing provided orders to all units to be prepared to supply the troops with at least three days rations upon landing. On the last day of August, d'Estaing dispatched two frigates escorted by two men-of-war under Major General Carnie to Charles Town to meet with General Lincoln to gather intelligence, gather pilots and make necessary arrangements for provisions for the upcoming campaign.

On September 1, the fleet anchored off the St. Johns River at Florida. The next day, the fleet became dispersed as it encountered a "squall that lasted thirty-six hours." Many vessels received damage, lost cannon and "some rudders were shattered."[42]

On the 3rd, at the lighthouse on Tybee Island, Georgia, d'Estaing's advance vessels were spotted by the British. Captain Brown of the British ship *Rose* sent out Lieutenant Lock aboard a pilot boat to confirm the French presence. The next day, General Prevost received intelligence from Lock declaring that the mystery ships were French and included two ships of the line, two frigates and a sloop. The French ships sailed on toward Charles Town as d'Estaing had ordered.

On the next day, Viscount De Fontanges, the adjutant-general of the army, arrived aboard the French frigate *Amazon* in Charles Town with dispatches for Lincoln. These dispatches revealed that the French fleet was then off the Savannah bar, with a fleet made up of 21 ships of the line, eight frigates, and five smaller armed vessels. Aboard the fleet were 5,000 men, including troops, marines and seamen. The dispatch also indicated that while the admiral was ready to cooperate with the Americans to retake Savannah, he urged that actions be taken with much dispatch, as he was concerned about remaining too long on the coast during this hurricane season.[43]

The news of the presence of the French fleet caused great excitement in South Carolina. The South Carolina legislature, which was in session, immediately adjourned to consider the military issues.[44] Boats were immediately sent to assist the French in landing troops, ordnance and stores. Lincoln ordered his aide, Colonel Thomas Pinckney, Colonel Cambray of the engineers, Captain Gadsden and several other intelligence officers to return with Viscount De Fontanges to support d'Estaing with the Georgia landing operation. On September 4, Lincoln ordered all officers to rejoin their regiments and sent off correspondence to McIntosh to gather all troops possible within 24 hours and march them to Ebenezer, where he would meet him on the 11th. An initial plan of action was developed and agreed upon. Lincoln hoped to collect 1,000 troops and march into Georgia, down the south bank of the Savannah River to Savannah.[45] At Ossabaw Sound, d'Estaing was to be joined by Colonel Joseph Habersham to advise the Admiral on the ideal location to debark his troops.[46] There was a sense of exhilaration among the patriot forces in Charles Town.

The British looked on with total shock at the arrival of the French fleet off Savannah. Wright declared that nobody "could have thought or believed that a French fleet ... would have come on the Coast of Georgia in the month of September."[47] On September 4, a dispatch rider was on the road from Savannah with a letter from General Prevost to Lieutenant Colonel Maitland at Beaufort ordering him to keep his detachment in readiness to march to Savannah at short notice, since it was possible that the French fleet might attempt to cut off communications by going into Port Royal Bay. Maitland was soon ordered to move over to Tench's Island, a promontory of Hilton Head Island, where he was to proceed toward Savannah if not receiving others orders along the way.

Confusing the situation, at that time Prevost was not sure if the French force was intended for Savannah or Charles Town. A British officer that had been sent with Prevost's order "was taken by the Rebels, going through Skull Creek. This accident was then judged of no consequence, as the French disappearing, and their coming on the coast being hoped, for various reasons, to be accidental. Colonel Maitland was next day directed to remain; but embarking all his baggage and other encumbrances, to hold himself in constant readiness to come away on the shortest notice."[48]

So it was that on the evening of September 4, the French fleet disappeared from view off Tybee Island. Promptly General Prevost issued countermanding orders for Maitland to hold his force at Beaufort. Maitland was instructed to have his heavy baggage embarked, and if he had other intelligence that was more accurate, he was to use his own judgment in taking no risk and return to Savannah. Lieutenant Colonel Cruger was ordered to evacuate Sunbury and march by land to Savannah. The sick and invalids were to embark in small armed vessels and to proceed by the inland navigation to Savannah under the care of Captain French. Because of headwinds, Captain French's vessels could not reach the pass until the French forces had already taken possession of it.

Changing plans, Captain French sailed up the Ogechee River, but finding the land occupied by the patriots, he landed and fortified a camp just 15 miles south of Savannah. French fortified his camp with his four armed vessels up front, each equipped with one 14-pounder and three 4-pounder guns. With 40 able seamen, and 111 regular troops who were mostly sick, French set about to fight off the patriots. Captain French and his force never did reach Savannah.

On September 5, Lincoln ordered all his officers and men to join their regiments. American patriot forces with General Lincoln were garrisoned at Sheldon, located on the north shore of the Savannah River and some 15 miles from Beaufort. That same day, Lincoln sent a dispatch to General Lachlan McIntosh in Augusta declaring, "You will excuse my pressing the matter in such strong terms—I do not mean to call into question your zeal and dispatch, but to convey my own ideas how necessary I take the measure—Saturday next (the 11th) I have engaged that the Troops shall be collected near Ebenezer—the good of my Country and my own honor demand from me a fulfillment of the engagement."

After the battle at Stono, Brigadier General Pulaski had been sent with his cavalry to a post located 50 miles northeast from Augusta for forage and provisions and to be at Augusta and Charles Town for support operations. Now Pulaski was ordered to join General McIntosh at Augusta. McIntosh was sent to Ebenezer as discussed.[49] McIntosh advanced past Ogechee Ferry and proceeded to Millen's Plantation, three miles from Savannah, to wait for Lincoln's forces to join him.

The next day, Lieutenant Whitworth, the commander of the *Keppel* armed brig, was sent aboard a tender to New York with dispatches alerting Sir Henry Clinton of the presence of the French fleet off Savannah. Whitworth was unable to evade seven French vessels chasing him and had to return to port. On the evening of the 7th, Whitworth tried again to escape and this time he was successful. In the river channel the British naval forces were engaged in recording soundings as they moved the *Rose, Keppel* and *Germain* into their moorings.[50]

On September 6, the French fleet reappeared off the Savannah bar at Tybee. Prevost decided that it was necessary to strengthen the works at Fort Tybee and increase the number of troops deployed there. He ordered Captain Moncrief to reinforce the post with 100 infantry. For the first time, Prevost was aware of the actual size of the French fleet and the danger his forces were in. He ordered Maitland to march to Savannah with haste, and assigned alarm posts at the appropriate locations to ensure communications of any approaching attack.[51]

The mysterious disappearance of the French fleet had been caused by rough seas and high winds that had scattered the fleet until the 6th. With the entire French fleet now off Tybee Island, the British warships *Rose, Fowey, Keppel, Germain*, and the *Comet*, along with a galley and several smaller vessels lying in Tybee Roads, weighed anchor and sailed to Five Fathom Hole and immediately anchored.

The British at Fort Tybee opened fire on the French Squadron offshore. Fort Tybee, located near the lighthouse on the northern edge of Great Tybee Island, had been built to guard the entrance to the Savannah River. The fort now contained one 24-pounder gun and an eight-and-a-half-inch howitzer, now manned with British troops under Captain Moncrief. After having no effect upon the French fleet operations off Tybee and recognizing their hazardous position, Moncrief ordered the guns spiked, and the entire British garrison at Fort Tybee to abandon it, escaping from the island the next morning.[52]

D'Estaing had come to America to perform "some action advantageous to the Americans, glorious for the arms of the King, and fitted to show the protection which his Majesty extends to his allies." The admiral had discussed his plans at great length with Conrad A. Gerard, the French ambassador to the United States. It was Gerard who had accompanied the admiral on the 85-day and first voyage to America that ended at the mouth of the Delaware River on July 7, 1778. He gave clear advice, "Promptitude is the first quality ... to astonish the enemy is almost to have conquered them; it is this which is desirable, which perhaps will be shown, and to reach which we shall surely do all that is possible.... A combination of rapid operations might overcome the ordinary firmness of the British troops.... The least act of feebleness or timidity might be very fatal." Sadly, it was d'Estaing's lack of following his own advice for "rapid operations" that would come to critical focus during the coming campaign at Savannah.[53]

11

Siege Forces Gather at Savannah

"[T]he evening gun to be fired ... at an hour before sundown
shall be the signal for recommencing hostilities."

Charles Henri d'Estaing had remained at anchor off Tybee Island on his 74-gun flagship, the *Languedoc*, since he had arrived on September 6, 1779. The admiral had already decided on his plan for attacking the British as he received the various regimental commanders aboard his flagship. Experienced pilots from Charles Town had finally arrived to assist the French admiral in navigating the Savannah River channel and bar. To relieve the respective ship captains of any responsibility for possible damage to their hulls while crossing the bar, on the 9th d'Estaing boarded the lead frigate, *Chimere*, and waited for his orders to be carried out.[1]

That day at 4 P.M., d'Estaing crossed the Savannah bar trailed by three other frigates and later the rest of his squadron. On the sight of the French maneuver of the four lead frigates, the British ships "*Fowey, Keppel* and *Comet*, ran up the Savannah River as far as Long Beach," which was "the end of the island on the inland side of the river." The *Fowey* ran aground on White Vester Bank, and the *Keppel* and *Comet* came to her assistance "with boats, anchors." The *Fowey* was unable to sail away until high tide as the tension mounted. As the French moved closer inshore to Tybee Island, the American pilots seemed unable to know where to land d'Estaing's ships at Tybee. As night came on, the admiral directed that 24 soldiers be put ashore to reconnoiter. The news was that the fort had been "abandoned and burnt...."[2]

To gain further intelligence on the British, d'Estaing directed Chevalier Trolong Durumain to lighten his frigate and sail up the Savannah as far as possible to establish a blockade to bombard the town. On Saturday, September 11, d'Estaing's fleet rendezvoused in Ossabaw Sound, an inlet a few miles south of the Savannah River entrance to the sea. That night, Captain Louis Antione de Bougainville of the *Guerrier* and Commandant Dampierre dined together and discussed the strategy. They were not particularly impressed with d'Estaing's plans as they reflected on the upcoming events. De Bougainville had gained fame as an explorer when he circumnavigated the world during 1766–1769. After dinner, the 23-year-old Louis Marie, the Viscount de Noailles, and Arthur, Viscount de Dillon, came aboard to see de Grasse and discussed the various disadvantages that existed for the operation.

At 4 P.M., the French regiments received their final orders for the landing. Positioned at the entrance to the Vernon River, which empties into Ossabaw Sound, the troops boarded longboats and canoes from all the selected ships by 8 P.M. By 9 P.M., the entire landing party had gathered between d'Estaing's *Languedoc* and the *Annibal*. D'Estaing had left the greater part of his fleet to guard the river entrance as he deployed five men-of-war up the river. First aboard the *Alerte* cutter, then to a rowboat, and over to a "prize *Victory*," d'Estaing led the boats over the bar and toward the designated landing area. Unfortunately, the hand-picked American pilot became confused and the troops had to spend the night in their boats, crowded in bad weather at the "greatest risks of running on the reefs."

At midnight on the 12th the troops were still anchored in the same place they had been all night and still no orders to proceed had come. The troops were incredibility impatient, as might be expected. At "12:30 [A.M.] the *Alerte* and M. d'Estaing appeared. He issued orders and set out with several longboats. A cannon shot gave the signal for the rest to follow him. Now all the boats weighed anchor and followed without further orders. Several boats were with the *Alerte* and very close to land. But only a few volunteers landed as a scouting party; d'Estaing posted sentinels to watch the paths by which the enemy could approach."

There were only five British — a captain and four soldiers— at the former residence of Colonel William Stephens at Beaulieu Plantation on the Vernon River that evening to oppose the landing. Beaulieu was 12 miles from the capital. On the appearance of the French landing, the small force of British fled, leaving the French landing entirely unopposed. With 300 men, d'Estaing advanced up the Savannah Road three miles to the fork that led to the town of Savannah. There, off the road, he noted the American "orphan house," locally known as George Whitefield's Bethesda Orphanage. Here he placed a detachment as protection to the landing force.

D'Estaing reconnoitered a house "for a post for his detachment to occupy. The master of the house was in Savannah, but the wife nonetheless claimed to be an enthusiast for the American cause. I was impressed by a picture, seven feet high with a most magnificent gilded frame Hanging in a most ostensible place, it represented liberty in the person of Milady Abingdon. She trampled a crown under her feet. In her hand she held a crown of thorns and walked in the midst of precipices and aloes-wood. It was very symbolic. It seemed to me that this well-executed painting had recently been put on display and was not in its usual place. I asked two children of the house, eight and ten years old, how long had this painting been there? They answered, 'since yesterday.' I also asked what party they belonged to. They told me, 'Royalists.'"

Unknown to d'Estaing until later, on the 11th the 36-gun French frigate *Amazon*, commanded by the famous navigator Perouse, was successful at capturing the 24-gun British warship *Ariel* after a gallant resistance by the British captain. The *Ariel* had been patrolling along the Atlantic Coast out from Charles Town in complete ignorance of the presence of the French. Two weeks later, the British 52-gun warship of 12-pounders, *Experiment*, was on a passage from New York to Savannah, having lost her bowsprit and masts in a gale wind and became separated from the convoy. She was accompanied by the navy victualer *Myrtle,* and the storeship *Champion*. Likewise unaware of the French navy, the *Experiment*, *Myrtle* and *Champion* were captured by four French vessels that surrounded her, including the *Sagittaire*.[3] She was carrying the equivalent of 750,000 francs for the Savannah British garrison. Together with the other prizes taken during the siege, "she was valued at four million francs."[4]

By the day's end on the 12th, 1,200 French troops had landed at Beaulieu. The next two days were occupied in disembarking the remaining troops, artillery, ammunition, provisions and entrenching tools. During the French disembarkment, high winds, including a gale, had delayed the work. Several vessels had slipped their cables and sailed out to sea in an attempt to avoid damage. Several vessels sustained severe damage, and it was not until the 15th that the winds calmed enough to complete the operation. D'Estaing wrote, "A constant rain troubled us, even more so because we had no tents. The two houses were not sufficient to shelter the munitions; arms, cartridges and cartridge pouches got wet. This superabundance of water from heaven provided nothing to slake our thirst. The water from the river was sandy and salty. One well and a single pump, which luckily worked, was our sole supply."[5]

The majority of the French troops bivouacked as best they could in the rainy conditions at Beaulieu. They built huge fires where they cooked their meat and made their soup. There was no salt and bread was rationed, but there was some rice. There were few cooking utensils and many of the men used washing pots to make soup for all. With the rain and poor sleeping environment, the French regiments were in poor shape. On the 14th at 4 P.M. "the rain stopped for a while which made everyone rejoice. The soldiers cleaned and repaired their muskets; a quantity of soaked cartridges had gotten too wet to be used."[6]

On the 15th, d'Estaing marched a force of 2,400 men nine miles to "invest Savannah." Six hundred men "took the right-hand road and proceeded to occupy a position on Wright Hill, on the left of the city. From there we dispatched another party to Brewton Hill, near the Savannah River. The rest of the army followed the left-hand road and camped three miles from the city, the right wing on the road which ends in front of the barracks, the center at Minis house, the left stretched out as far as the St. Augustine road."

D'Estaing expressed his surprise that the British made no effort to encumber the French forces. They did not destroy the bridges over the small streams or creeks, and "totally neglected a road easily obstructed by an abates, and a multitude of other ways of stopping, delaying of harassing our march." He noted, "At that point I was also convinced that Savannah's resistance would be very weak."[7] This would prove to be quite untrue.

By 6 P.M. that day, d'Estaing's force, totaling over 3,000 French troops, was now encamped three miles southeast of Savannah in three groups, with the admiral in the center, on the right was de Dillion, and to the left was de Noailles.[8] As the French had moved up to their encampment, they had confiscated 13 steers, 10 cows, five sheep, 39 hogs, 50 fowl and 20 gallons of Jamaican rum from the Georgia citizenry.

Meanwhile, as d'Estaing was landing and deploying his forces at Savannah, General Lincoln was trying to get his forces to Savannah as fast as possible. Back on the morning of September 8, Lincoln departed Charles Town "to join the army and lodged at Captain Sander's." He reached his designated gathering location of Sheldon at around 4 P.M. on the 9th, an hour after the army had marched out of town. The army moved with ease until they reached the bridge at Coosahatchee River, which had been burned. The troops halted until the next morning while the bridge was being repaired. Lincoln stayed at Mr. Heyward's home.

The troops were able to finally march across the repaired bridge at 10 A.M. the next day. That day they were able to march nine miles to Mr. Praho's home, which was nine miles from Zubly's Ferry and the place where they planned to cross the Savannah River. In preparation for the river crossing, the previous day Lincoln had directed Colonel Laurens to reconnoiter the area and obtain boats to cross at Zubly's. Laurens was able to locate only "one small canoe, a rowing boat, and one flat which was sunk in the river one mile below Purysburg." Lincoln was forced to wait for boats from Augusta. He wrote of his plight with the Savannah River noting, "tho narrow yet one of the most difficult to pass on the Continent." He also lamented, "The land adjoining is mostly swamp and often overflowed from 2–4 feet deep, the breadth of them is generally 2 miles on both sides."

On the 11th, while d'Estaing was gathering his fleet in Ossabaw Sound, Lincoln directed that Count Pulaski's mounted cavalry cross the river to reconnoiter Ebenezer and the road leading to it. The count returned "towards night" and reported that the British had withdrawn toward Savannah. He noted the bridges and roads through the swamp were "out of repair." After some men knocked together a raft, on the morning of the next day, Lincoln's army started crossing the river. On the first attempt the raft sank. An unfinished flatboat was discovered, which Lincoln ordered completed with timbers and boards from several buildings. Two large canoes were found by noon, one from McClay's Creek that would hold 30 men, which helped to move the troops with a faster pace. By nightfall the majority of the men were across the Savannah River. The next two days were busy bringing over the artillery and supply wagons, as the local bridges were repaired.[9]

General McIntosh crossed the river and joined Lincoln on the 13th just before evening came. Anxious to learn of d'Estaing's situation, that day Lincoln sent off two detachments to find the admiral. Major Harleston, with two pilots, was sent toward Beaulieu, but they ran into a "party of the enemy in the night" and had to return. Count Pulaski was directed to attempt to reach d'Estaing by another path. On the way to Savannah, Pulaski ran into forward pickets, killing and wounding five men, and capturing five privates and a subaltern. Pulaski's cavalry pressed on toward Beaulieu in a driving rain to find d'Estaing. Pulaski was looking forward to joining up with the French, since he had come to find the Americans without continental culture.[10]

When Pulaski finally arrived at Beaulieu, d'Estaing "cordially embraced and expressed mutual happiness at the meeting." Pulaski was then informed by the admiral that he intended to move on Savannah without waiting for Lincoln's force to arrive, and that "he counted on his Legion to form his van." Captain Bentalou recorded that "In pursuance of this wish, we set out immediately and reached Savannah some time before D'Estaing, where we engaged and cut off an advanced picket of the enemy's infantry."

Count Kasimir Pulaski was a unique addition to Lincoln's force. He had been born in Poland in 1747 to a noble family, and had fought with his father's troops against the Russians and served in the Turkish army. In Paris he had become a friend to Benjamin Franklin, who encouraged him to go to America and join the patriot cause. With Franklin's recommendation to Congress in hand, he arrived in America in 1777. He became an aide to General Washington at the Battle of Brandywine, and based on a suggestion from Washington, Congress offered Pulaski a commission as brigadier general of a newly authorized cavalry unit.

After ineffective efforts at Germantown, General Pulaski spent the winter with Washington at Valley Forge. He, like many of the European mold, was highly egotistical and difficult to get along with. He was known to quarrel with his American subordinates, and once brought up his second-in-command for not showing proper respect to him, as a noble Pole. He resigned from his cavalry unit in 1778 and was allowed to raise his own "elite" corps, made up of former British deserters and prisoners. The Pulaski Legion had not yet shown any great brilliance in the war.[11]

On September 14, Lincoln sent off two more expresses toward Savannah and d'Estaing. He also received a note from Captain Washington that he had seen General Pulaski at Beaulieu with "a number of troops on shore." The next day the entire patriot force moved to Cherokee Hill, which was just eight miles from Savannah. En route, Lincoln finally received a letter from Pulaski from a returning express.

On the 15th, while d'Estaing was surrounding Savannah, the united forces of Lincoln and McIntosh were encamped at Cherokee Hill.[12] This force of some 3,000 troops was made up of the Continental regiments from South Carolina and Georgia, and every militia unit that could be rallied. The heat of the day was suffocating, with temperatures reaching to 100 degrees. These were an interesting and diverse array of patriot men who marched down the road toward Savannah. There were so many different styles of "uniforms" that one officer commented, "Makes them appear more like wild savages than soldiers." Stretched out for miles was this patriot army, which included not only generals Lincoln and McIntosh, but also the soon-to-be-renowned "Swamp Fox," Francis Marion; John Laurens and his regiment; Charles Cotesworth Pinckney; Thomas Heyward Jr., a signer of the Declaration of Independence; and the Huguenot leader, General Issac Huger.[13] All these men were aching for the opportunity to take Savannah back from the British, and proudly restore Georgia to patriot control.

Meanwhile, as the allied forces were gathering around Savannah, the British were busy preparing defenses and redeploying troops in expectation of the coming attack. When the French had first arrived off Tybee Island, the British had only 23 cannons mounted on the works around Savannah. On the first day of the actual American and French assault, there were 100 more cannons deployed. Since the capture of Savannah back in December of 1778, the British had not materially strengthened the works around Savannah. The works, built by the Americans originally, were intended to protect the southern, eastern and western exposures of the town.

Beginning on September 11, the British warships were stripped of most of their cannons, which were deployed along the earthen works. The British ended up with 13 substantial redoubts and 15 gun batteries. Batteries were manned by sailors and marines from the vessels *Fowey*, *Rose* and *Keppel*. In addition to the gun batteries from the warships, field pieces were fixed at intervals. The British ships *Rose* and *Savannah*, and four transports, were sunk in a narrow channel of the river three miles below the town to prevent any French or American vessels from getting close enough to the town for direct support of infantry operations. Above the town, small craft were sunk and a boom was stretched across the river to stop any vessel from passing up the North River, around Hutchinson's Island, to attack from the northwest. Entrenchments were also dug to cover the British regular and reserve troops. The strengthening of the Savannah's fortifications was an impressive undertaking, and worthy of significant praise for the engineering officer in charge, Captain James Moncrief.[14]

To upgrade the works around Savannah, Prevost put some 500 black slaves to work on the lines.[15] Moncrief ordered the construction of a semicircular line of fortifications about 1,200 feet long on the level plain south of the town. A British seaman wrote, "The General, ever attentive to increase the defenses of the town, with Captain Moncrief, our principal engineer, was now, indefatigably, night and day, raising new works and batteries." The barn and other agricultural buildings on Governor Wright's plantation just outside Savannah were dismantled and the lumber used for cannon platforms. Houses were destroyed at the edge of the town to prevent the attackers from having any place to cover them as they approached across an open area of several hundred yards.[16]

In Savannah were civilians and Major General Augustine Prevost with his garrison of 1,700 men. Colonel Maitland's force of 800 men was now heading toward Savannah. On the 10th, Lieutenant Colonel Cruger arrived in Savannah with his detachment from the fort at Sunbury. When the French had surrounded Savannah on September 15, Prevost and the British were in no shape to hold off any kind of attack from both d'Estaing's French troops, now outside Savannah to the southeast, and General Lincoln's troops, coming up to join in the attack from the northwest.[17] Without Maitland's forces, even the superior defensive fortifications now constructed could not prevent a patriot victory.

Having encountered no opposition to his landing or his move up to Savannah, and with supreme confidence in his situation, Admiral d'Estaing decided not to wait for General Lincoln before engaging the British. On the 16th d'Estaing sent a summons to General Prevost as follows:

> Count D'Estaing summons his Excellency General Prevost to surrender himself to the arms of his Majesty the King of France. He admonishes him that he will be personally answerable for every event and misfortune attending a defense demonstrated to be absolutely impossible and useless from the superiority of the force which attacks him by land and sea. He also warns him that he will be nominally and personally answerable henceforth for the burning, previous to or at the hour of attack, of any ships or vessels of war or merchant ships in the Savannah River, as well as of magazines in the town.

Prevost was evasive in response as he acknowledged receipt of d'Estaings demand for surrender and wrote, "I hope your Excellency will have a better opinion of British troops and me than to think either will surrender on general summons without any specific terms."

Then, d'Estaing countered that "it is the part of the Beseiged to propose such terms as they may desire, and you cannot doubt of the satisfaction I shall have in consenting to those which I can accept consistently with my duty." D'Estang warned Prevost of the expected arrival of the American forces that day.

To this new message, Prevost responded with his infamous request for a delay in the proceedings:

> SIR, I am honored with your Excellency's letter in reply to mine of this day. The business we have in hand being of importance, there being various interests to discuss, a just time is absolutely necessary to deliberate. I am therefore to propose that a cessation of hostilities shall take place for twenty-four hours from this date: and to request that your Excellency will order your columns to fall back to a greater distance and out of sight of our works or I shall think myself under the necessity to direct their being fired upon. If they did not reconnoitre anything this afternoon, they were sure within the distance.

Without any consideration for the importance of his decision on future events, and for the advantage it gave General Prevost and the British, Admiral d'Estaing agreed to a truce for another 24 hours with the words, "SIR, I consent to the truce you ask." Under the confident assumption the French were in control and clearly able to take Savannah regardless of the British maneuvers, he later wrote, "It was a matter of very little importance to me."[18] D'Estaing had also joked "that a girl who made compromises was very close to surrender."[19] As history would soon reveal, d'Estaing's decision to allow the British to delay would turn out to be the fatal error.[20]

Meanwhile, General Lincoln left Cherokee Hill on the morning of the 16th, unaware that d'Estaing was negotiating with the British without him. The patriot commander joined d'Estaing "about noon, having been led into the wrong route." By that time, Prevost's first response to the surrender demand had arrived in the camp. Lincoln "then remonstrated to the Count against his summoning them to surrender to the arms of France only, while the Americans were acting in conjunction with him." D'Estaing agreed that all future negotiations would be conducted as joint arrangements.[21]

The Americans were in high spirits as they took their positions in a temporary camp "in the rear of the French troops." But the real event of the day was with the British force from Beaufort. On the evening of the 16th, Lieutenant Colonel Maitland arrived at Dawfuskie

Island. The French had positioned ships outside the mouth of the Broad River, which separates Port Royal Island from Hilton Head Island. Since no ships were stationed behind Hilton Island, Maitland's force of 800 men was able to cross into Calibogue Sound in small boats and on to Dawfuskie. Due to the shortage of small boats, the ships and galleys under Captain Christian of the Royal Navy were left behind with some of the Beaufort garrison on Dawfuskie, erecting shore batteries. His force was so strong that neither the French nor Americans attempted to engage his defensive forces during the entire siege of Savannah.[22]

From their location on Dawfuskie, Maitland could see the masts of the French warships in the entrance to the Savannah River. All seemed to be lost until a black Gullah fisherman told Maitland about a narrow passage through the marsh behind Dawfuskie Island, called Wall's Cut. Wall's Cut was through Skull Creek, and emptied into the Savannah River upstream of the French ships. Maitland, who was quite ill with bilious fever, led his men through Wall's Cut at high tide, in places wading up to their waists and dragging their boats through the mud. The tide and the thick fog had made the passage secure.[23]

On the morning of the 17th, Maitland's force reached the shore of the Savannah River, in sight of town across the river on the southern shore. Using 14 boats, Maitland's force crossed the river. By midday the entire force had disembarked at Savannah. "The acquisition of this formidable reinforcement," said a Captain McCall, "headed by an experienced and brave officer, effected a complete change in the dispirited garrison. A signal was made and three cheers were given, which rung from one end of the town to the other."[24] A loyalist women explained, "Our men ... suffered from fatigue and want of rest, but in the height of our despondence Colonel Maitland effected a junction in a wonderful manner ... thus giving new life and joy to the worn-out troops."[25]

Bolstered by the presense of Maitland's force, General Provost decided to "assemble the field officers, sea and land, and with the Governor and Lieutenant Governor in camp." They were "unanimously determined to defend ourselves to the last man." Provost then sent the following letter to Admiral d'Estaing on September 17:

> SIR, In answer to the letter of your Excellency which I had the honor to receive about twelve last night, I am to acquaint you that having laid the whole correspondence before the King's civil Governor and the military officers of rank, assembled in Council of War, the unanimous determination has been that though we cannot look upon our post as absolutely impregnable, yet that it may and ought to be defended: therefore the evening gun to be fired this evening at an hour before sundown shall be the signal for recommencing hostilities agreeable to your Excellency's proposal. I have the honour to be, &c.
>
>   A. Prevost.

While Maitland was sneaking into Savannah, Lincoln and d'Estaing toured the Brewton's Hill area. Lincoln noted that they "had here a pretty good view of the left of the town and of the vessels off Brewton's Hill." D'Estaing's account of his visit to Brewton's Hill was to "confirm with my own eyes the report of the night before. We saw still crossing the river a string of small boats loaded with troops, a sight so vexatious that I began to bemoan bitterly the impossibility of stopping a reinforcement that was going to give the expedition extreme difficulty. General Lincoln, who could and should have prevented this misfortune, saw it and fell asleep in an arm chair. The haughtiness of the English general's letter surprised General Lincoln a little, not, however, to the point that he gave up hoping for a surrender."[26]

There was general disappointment in the American ranks that the British had not taken the road to surrender. Having let the British have enough time to parley and, thus, reinforce Savannah, had proven to be a key mistake on d'Estaing's part. Some British officers felt the town could have been taken with little or no bloodshed, without artillery, in 10 minutes if the French admiral had moved at the first opportunity. In d'Estaing's defense, he was not provided with the necessary intelligence to have made such a judgment earlier in the operation.[27]

According to d'Estaing's journal, Lincoln tried to "exculpate himself" from Maitland's return with his Beaufort garrison "by accusing [Major General] de Fontanges of not telling me what had been decided at the Council held in Charleston. The American general claimed that it had been ordered and acknowledged that it was the French responsibility to prevent the evacuation of Beaufort by anchoring vessels up the river. This complaint, contrived after the fact, seemed to me another of our allies' unjust recriminations."

D'Estaing was outraged that Lincoln would "assume that an officer of advanced rank, experienced, well informed and intelligent, could have forgotten the primary purpose of a mission as important as the one I entrusted to M. de Fontanges." The French admiral noted: "The letter from the French consul at Charleston, dated September 23, removes all doubt. It asserts unequivocally that the Council did not discuss anchoring men-of-war off Beaufort." The consul, the Marquis de Bretigny, declared that in fact Lincoln "was personally ordered by the Council to stop with his troops the evacuation of the Beaufort garrison and the reinforcing of Savannah." D'Estaing wrote that Bretigny assumed that Lincoln "took it upon himself to abandon the mission ... and that he crossed the Savannah River for personal reasons, mainly jealous, and in order to play a part in the capitulation and capture of the capital of Georgia."[28]

With any idea of an all-out direct assault on Savannah considered foolhardy with Maitland's reinforcements now in town, d'Estaing resolved to approach the taking of Savannah gradually by siege. The French frigates moved up within gunshot of the town as the British ships took shelter under the battery. D'Estang's and Lincoln's forces moved up closer to Savannah and were situated within 1,200 yards of the English lines. Both sides were busy making preparations for an upcoming battle. Savannah is situated on the southern bank of the river of the same name, thus, securing the northern front. To the west was a thick swamp and woody morass. The south and east were open ground with few trees for some distance from the town.[29]

American troops, numbering some 2,127 men under General Lincoln, were on the western front, resting on the swamp bordering the town. They consisted of 1,003 Continental troops, including the Fifth Regiment of the South Carolina Infantry, 65 men from Heyward's Artillery, 365 men of the Charles Town Volunteers and Militia, 212 troops from General Williamson's Brigade, 232 men of the Georgia Militia regiments under colonels Twiggs and Few, and the 250 men of the cavalry of Brigadier General Count Pulaski.

On the Americans' right came the division of the Viscount de Noailles with 900 men of the regiments of Cambresis, Auxerrois, Foix, Guadelope, and Martinique. To Noailles' right, in the direct southern front of the town, was d'Estaing's division of 1,000 men of regiments of Cambresis, Hainault, the Volunteers of Berges, Agenois, Gatinois, the Cape, and Port au Prince. On the eastern front, on d'Estaing's right, ready to attack were the forces of de Dillon's division comprising some 900 men of the regiments of Dillon, Armagnac, and the Volunteers Grenadiers. On Dillon's right were the powder magazine, cattle depot, a field hospital and the quarters of the 50 dragoons of Conde and of Belzunce, under command of M. Dejean. On their right were the dragoons of M. de Rouvrai with the 750 men of the Volunteer Chasseurs. To their right and in advance some 200 yards were the 156 Grenadier Volunteers with another 200 men of mixed regiments under M. des Framais. The total French forces at Savannah, including an estimated 500 sailors and marines from off the ships, came to 4,456 men.[30] This combined French and American force of some 6,583 fighting men now enclosed the entire semicircle around Savannah, from west to east.

The British forces of some 2,500 men were deployed behind the substantial defensive works that had been under construction for some time. There were a line of works, with the right and left defended by redoubts and in the center by seamen's batteries. The entire works were surrounded with abatis. On the right toward the swamp were three redoubts, manned in the center by two companies of militia supported by the North Carolina loyalist regiment under Lieutenant Colonel Hamilton. On their right were the South Carolina King's Rangers under Captains Raworth and Wylie. Captain Tawse commanded the dismounted corps of provincial dragoons on the redoubt on Hamilton's left known as the Spring Hill redoubt. South Carolina loyalists under Lieutenant Colonel Thomas Browne supported Tawse.

Between the Spring Hill redoubt and the center of the British lines were batteries under the command of Captain Manby, with Lieutenant Colonel Glazier's Sixteenth Regiment grenadiers and the marines from the ships. The entire force on the right, which would be forced to take the brunt of the attack, was under the command of Lieutenant Colonel Maitland. The left lines were defended by two redoubts, which were strongly constructed of heavy green and spongy palmetto trees filled by sand, with heavy cannons deployed. Lieutenant Colonel Cruger and Major James Wright, with his Georgia loyalists, each commanded a redoubt. Behind these defensive works were impalements and transverses in the center with two regiments of Hessians, two battalions of the Seventy-first Regiment, the New York Volunteers, a battalion of Skinner's Brigade, a battalion of DeLancey's and the light infantry unit under Major Graham.[31] The British were now ready for the promised attack on their positions and the town of Savannah.

Savannah, always considered to be a healthy town from its earliest days of settlement, was now an armed camp. Like Charles Town, it was a refuge during the summer and autumn months from the fevers incident to the swamps for rice planters from the nearby Lowcountry. The dense forests on Hutchinson's Island and to the east and west of the town had once shielded the citizens from "the noxious vapors and malarial influences" of the Lowcountry rice fields. But after the trees had been cut down to convert more land for rice plantations, the town was now more susceptible to the winds from the east and north carrying unhealthy ill vapors to the inhabitants.

In 1779, Savannah was a town of some 430, mostly wooden, houses built out from the rivers wharves and bluffs. The wharves below the bluffs had been well constructed according to a design provided by Surveyor-General DeBrahm in 1759. DeBrahm recommended "to drive two Rows of Piles as far asunder as he desired his Wharf to be wide, and as far towards the River as low Water Mark; secure their tops with plates, and to trunnel Planks within on the Piles; this done, then brace the insides with dry Walls of Stones intermixed with willow Twigs, and in the same manner to shut up the Ends of the two Rows with a like Front along the Stream; to build inside what Cellars he had occasion for; then to fill up the Remainder with the Sand nearest at hand out of the Bluff or high shore of the Stream under the Bay." Now this well-constructed town of Savannah was under siege, which could mean its possible destruction.

On Wednesday, September 22, Savannah was completely isolated on the land side. The French frigate *La Truite,* armed with 9-pounder guns, and two galleys with 18-pounders moved up river within cannon shot of the town "within 1500 yards of the city." To ensure all communications routes were blocked, the frigate *La Chimere* and store ship *La Bricole* were posted before the river islands. Both armies were now ready for the final struggle. The

French fleet offloaded their naval guns at Thunderbolt and transported them to their batteries outside Savannah.[32] On the next day, one could see the allied forces making fascines and building batteries at their positions opposite Savannah. During 12 days, some 53 artillery pieces and 14 mortars had been moved up by the French and mounted for the siege.[33] Soon the battle would be real.

12

The Siege of Savannah

"I think that this is the greatest event that has happened the whole war."

On Wednesday, September 22, de Guillaume, of Noailles' division, with 50 hand-picked men, set out to capture an advanced British position, but was forced to turn back by heavy musket and artillery fire at Savannah. At 3 P.M. the next day, the French opened a trench to a point just 300 yards from the British lines. After the fog finally lifted the next morning, the British sent a sortie at 9 of three companies of light infantry under Major Graham to capture the French position. With a loss of 21 men killed or wounded, Graham retreated with two columns of French on his heels. The French were finally drawn off when they had come close enough to British batteries to receive accurate firing.[1] The French loss was 48 killed or wounded.[2]

Though d'Estaing complained that they were "scarcely sufficient," Lincoln agreed to supply tools for trenching, which he gathered from the local homes outside the town. At 7 P.M. on September 23, some 300 workers, supported by "600 grenadiers and chasseurs," began digging the trenches in the sandy soil. The British fired some cannon shells at random near them, but "despite their close proximity and the bright moonlight, they did not detect our presense." They dug one 206-yard trench and a parallel one 80 yards long, which was only 300 yards from the British defensive works. Concerned over the closeness, at dawn the next day, Chevalier de Neufi, the engineer officer from the Royal Corps, ordered half the trench workers replaced by guards.[3]

At around 8 A.M. that day, after a light cannonade from the British, some 400 enemy troops ambushed the French on the left. The French temporarily abandoned the trench and took up position on the flank while returning musket fire. After an intense engagement, the British were repelled and pursued by Lieutenant Colonel Thadee Humphrey O'Dunne of the Irish Regiment up to the abatis with 200 men. The British battery opened fire on his troops as they were forced to retreat. Later de Fontanges moved forward six companies of grenadiers to hold back the potential for another attack. A truce was called to remove the dead from the field of battle. Four officers lay dead, nine wounded, some 25 chasseurs and grenadiers killed and 66 wounded. The British loss was thought to be similar to O'Dunne's losses.[4]

Work continued on the trenches on the night of the 24th as the French were supposed to continue the trenches in parallel toward the barracks, with the American's digging a second parallel. With tools in short supply, d'Estaing ordered a battery constructed just behind the communications trench located 425 yards from the barracks. The communications

Plan of the Siege of Savannah, with the joint attack of the French and Americans on the 9th of October 1779. Drawn by Faden, 1779 (Hargrett Rare Book and Manuscript ibrary, University of Georgia Libraries).

trench between the headquarters and the siege lines was deemed so unsafe, that d'Estaing ordered perpendicular trenches behind the first ones.

On September 25 at 7 A.M., a French artillery commander, de Sane, opened fire on the town of Savannah with his two 18-pounder guns. He was firing from a newly erected battery with 150 men. During the firing the "bright young officer" de Sane was killed by a British cannonball and grapeshot. On inspection, d'Estaing ordered the battery re-configured and armed with twelve 18 and 12-pounder guns, and called for construction of another battery just to the right of the trench to contain 13 18-pounders. Other batteries erected were a battery holding six 16-pounder guns manned by Americans, and a bomb battery 200 yards to the left of the trench with nine mortars. D'Estaing ordered that no more firing would occur until these artillery batteries were completed.

That evening, 100 "Americans dug a communications trench between the main siege line and the left battery." The two other such trenches started the previous night were also completed. During the night there was a false alert in the communications trench. The "pickets seized arms," and six companies of grenadiers "flew from the camp through the slanted communications trenches hidden in the marsh and at the edge of the pine thicket which protected the camp's outskirts." D'Estaing dressed down Regimental Major de Browne for the false alert and wasted powder.[5]

While the allied armies were in final preparation for a grand assault on the British works at Savannah, the French sailors of the 32-ship fleet were suffering at anchor offshore. The conditions of the fleet were miserable. An officer told of being anchored offshore at the mercy of southeastern winds driving the ships ashore, causing damaged rudders, lost anchors, and crippled rigging. The poor sailors suffered from scurvy, no refreshments for the sick, little adequate clothing or shoes, no linen, and little to eat except salt provisions, which created severe thirst. The bread, which had been stored for two years, was decayed and worm-eaten, and so inedible that even the domestic animals would not touch it. Food was rationed severely as it was felt the engagement might last for a significant period. An average of 35 dead French sailors were thrown overboard on a daily basis. Those sailors who did survive were almost too weak to complete even a simple shipboard task. With the French admiral's attention focused on the siege, there seemed to be no compassion for the average French sailor.[6]

On the night of the 26th, the allied work continued on the left battery by the allies. All the batteries had been placed at exactly 425 yards, except for the mortar batteries that were set at 640 yards. On the next night, British major Archibald McArthur, with a detachment of the 71st Regiment, attempted to sortie against an allied battery where heavy cannons were being mounted. After a vigorous attack, McArthur's men retreated suddenly and with great silence. Confusion between the French on the right flank and the Americans on the left resulted in several friendly-fire causalities for the allies.[7] The French account of the incident revealed that twice during the night the troops in the trenches had believed they had seen the enemy on the approach, and had presented heavy fire by mistake on the working parties. Seventeen men were reported to have been killed or wounded.[8] If it had not been for the "firmness and good conduct" of the captain of the Grenadiers in the Foix Regiment, de Segoyer, "the loss would have been greater, as the whole right was firing on the left."[9]

On September 28, the French frigate La Truite moved up and anchored in the North Channel. The ship fired several cannon shots toward the town with little effect. The following day, General McIntosh asked General Lincoln for permission to send a flag of truce to General Prevost to request that his wife and family, and any other women and children as might desire, to leave the besieged town before the battle. Lincoln agreed, and Major John Jones, who was aide to McIntosh, took the flag and request to Prevost. Prevost refused the request feeling that the presence of McIntosh's family might tend to restrain the shelling on the town.[10] This was not to be the case.

A rather interesting and brave event occurred on the night of October 1, when patriot Colonel John White, with Captains George Melvin and A.C.G. Elholm, a sergeant and three privates set out to reconnoiter the position of Captain French. French and his 111 regular troops, with five vessels and crew, had been cut off from reaching Savannah and had taken refuge in the Great Ogeechee River. Approaching French's camp on the left bank of the river, Colonel White had a number of fires built to give the impression that a large force was in the area. Colonel White summoned Captain French to surrender his forces. Thinking he was outnumbered, French complied with White's summons. The British were disarmed of their stand of 130 weapons and the troops were marched to the allied camp.

On that same day, the frigate *La Truite*, commanded by Chevalier Durumain, and two armed American galleys sailed up to within a mile of Savannah. Positioned in the North Channel, they opened fire on the southeastern end of the town. The shelling prompted the British to build a new battery "with 8 nine-pounders" to strengthen the defensive works on that side of the town. The next day was a rainy one, with wind from the east north east, as the French and Americans continued to build their batteries and trenches. In the morning, the French ships which had moved up the previous day fired some cannons "into the rear of the [British] camp without doing execution." The British *Thunderer* returned fire but the sea battery was silent. From deserters, one from Pulaski's legion and one from the French regiment, the British learned that the batteries were nearly ready. There was more firing in the afternoon from the French frigate as the British returned a few rounds at the French works.[11]

Having completed all the necessary artillery batteries, d'Estaing ordered the bombardment of Savannah, which began at midnight of Sunday, October 3, 1779. D'Estaing noted, "We fired 300 firebombs on the city and the enemy fortifications ... deserters said that they caused distress; however, the ground was all sand in the city and the streets were not paved. We chose to begin firing the firebombs at night in order to make them more terrifying." That day d'Estaing "wanted all the batteries to fire at the same time so that they could protect each other, and have greater effect or at least cause alarm."[12] François d'Auber de Peyrelongue, a second lieutenant in the Royal Corps of Artillery, wrote, "At first the enemy seemed surprised at the rate of our fire. Then shortly afterwards they responded by a salvo every hour on the quarter hour, thus showing that we were superior."[13]

This initial shelling ceased two hours later the next morning after an assessment of the poor accuracy of the cannoneers. The artillery troops were believed to have been under the influence of too much rum. Shells fell at a rate of more than one per minute. The Savannahians fled in terror in the darkness to get away from the explosions. The firing finally ceased and most people slipped back into their homes. But just before dawn another battery of cannons commenced firing. This was the start of five days of continual shelling.

A French journal recorded that first day's results of the shelling:

October 4th, Monday. At four o'clock in the morning, the enemy's beat of drum at daybreak furnishes the signal for unmasking our batteries on the right and left trench, and that of the Americans to the left of the mortar battery, and we begin to cannonade and bombard the town and the enemy's works with more vivacity than precision. The cannoneers being still under the influence of rum, their excitement did not allow them to direct their pieces with proper care. Besides, our projectiles did little damage to works which were low and constructed of sand. The effect of this very violent fire was fatal only to the houses and to some women who occupied them.

Protected by their entrenchment, the enemy could not have lost many men, if we may judge the effect of their fire upon our works which had been hastily constructed and with far less skill and care than theirs.

All our batteries ceased firing at eight o'clock in the morning that we might repair our left battery which had been shaken to pieces by its own fire. A dense fog favors our workmen. We open fire again at ten o'clock in the morning and continue it with little intermission until four o'clock after midnight.[14]

The allied bombardment of the 4th had opened up with nine mortars and 37 guns from land and 16 shipboard cannons. This shelling caused considerable damage to the town and some lives were lost.[15] The bombardment terrified the occupants. The loyalist chief justice of Georgia, Anthony Stokes, whose house was burned by a shell and his library and manuscripts destroyed, described the events: "I had some distance to go before I got out of the line of fire, and did not know the way under the Savannah bluff, where I should have been safe from cannon balls, and therefore, whenever I came to an opening of a street, I watched the flashes of the mortars and the guns, and pushed on until I came under cover of a house, and when I got to the Common and heard the whistling of a shot or shell, I fell on my face."

Stokes continued, "The appearance of the town afforded a melancholy prospect, for there was hardly a house which had not been shot through, and some of them were almost destroyed.... In the streets and on the Common there was a number of large holes made in the ground by the shells.... The troops in the lines were safer from the bombardment than the people in the town.... In short, the situation of Savannah was at one time deplorable. A small garrison in an extensive country was surrounded on the land by a powerful, enemy, and its seacoast blocked up by one of the strongest fleets that ever visited America. There was not a single spot where the women and children could be put in safety, and the numerous desertions daily weakened that force which was at first inadequate to man such extensive lines, but the situation of the ground would not permit the able engineer to narrow them. However, with the assistance of God, British valor surmounted every difficulty."[16]

To avoid the cannonade, Governor James Wright and Lieutenant Governor John Graham moved out of the town itself and stayed in a tent next to Colonel Maitland, located on the right of the British lines. Ensign Pollard of the Second Battalion of General DeLancey's Brigade was killed by a bomb from the allied nine-mortar battery. Mrs. Thompson's daughter was killed by a shot. General Prevost's aide-de-camp, T.W. Moore, described the shelling as tearing the town to pieces, to the "shrieks of women and children" on every side. He added that "Many poor creatures were killed in trying to get in their cellars, or hide under the bluff of Savannah River." According to Rivington's *Royal Gazette*, on October 5 a mulatto man and three negroes were killed in the lieutenant governor's cellar. That evening, Mrs. Lloyd's home near the church was burned by a shell and seven blacks lost their lives. Also that night, a shell fell on Mr. Laurie's house on Broughton Street, killing two women and children.[17]

A patriot soldier recorded the details given by a deserter who told him a stirring account of the shelling of Savannah:

> Poor women & children have already been put to death by our bombs & cannon; a deserter is this moment come out, who gives an account that many of them were killed in their Beds and amongst others, a poor woman with her infant in her arms was destroyed by a Cannon Ball; they all got into Cellars but even there they do not escape the fury of our Bombs, several having been mangled in that place of security.[18]

There were over 1,000 shells fired on Savannah, as they shattered roofs, riddled walls, and kicked up the sand on the streets until there were craters everywhere. The pounding could be felt as far away as Tybee Island. Many died in the foray. The barracks master was killed in his house on the bay, and four members of one family, including the mother, daughter, grandmother and niece, died from a single shell as it landed in the middle of the home. Another girl was struck and killed as a shell exploded through a wall, crossing the room to nearly cut her in half. Even horses fell victim as they died in the Common from the shelling.

Some brave black slave children learned to rush unexploded bombs, throwing sand on the fuses to snuff them out. After the balls cooled, they sold them to the British for 7d each. With the shells lofted into the town, ironically the safest place to be was in the British lines where Wright and other leaders took refuge along with other officers wives.

On October 6, and the third night of shelling, with women and children in tears, both black and white assembled at the large home of Moses Nunez at the west end of Yamacraw, and ferried over to Hutchinson's Island for protection. Eventually most of the families were moved over. Fifty-seven female refugees crowded into Lachlan McGillivray's rice barn, and a single male, Dr. Johnston. By this point in the shelling, there was "hardly a house that had not been shot through."

The shelling of Savannah on the 6th was rather weak, with long intervals between firings. At 1 A.M. Prevost beat for a parley and the following message was delivered to d'Estaing, asking to allow women and children, including his own wife and children, to "embark on board a ship or ships and go down the river under the protection of yours until this business is decided." D'Estaing refused to support Prevost's request, noting in his response that he had warned him at the outset that he alone would be responsible for the consequences of not surrendering to the allied forces. D'Estaing wrote, "Perhaps your zeal has already interfered with your judgement ... and we deplore the fate of those persons who will be victims of your conduct, and the delusion which appears to prevail in your mind."

On the next day, the French began firing incendiary bombs at Savannah. The patriots outside the town, looking on, expected that "the whole will be in flames" by nightfall, but at the end of the following day, only a few homes had burned. This was due to the excellent work of the firemen, the serious rain of the previous day, and the various vacant tracts of land and open squares around Savannah.

After five days of shelling without surrender from the British, d'Estaing and Lincoln considered their options. The cannonade attack had not driven the British to give up Savannah and surrender as was hoped. Having been on the Georgia coast for over a month, with his naval forces in poor condition, with disease now in the French camps, an appearance of the British fleet always possible at any point, a continuing threat of hurricanes coming up the coast, and with little hope of inflicting greater cannon damage on the British at Savannah, d'Estaing was convinced that it was indeed time to begin the direct frontal attack.[19] His true sentiments were squarely for leaving Savannah and he noted that, "If I had been by myself, I would not have attempted it at all." D'Estaing's engineers felt the British had supplies for two more months and time was not on the French side. D'Estaing wrote of the situation:

> The needs of the fleet, the scarcity of water, the advanced season, the necessity before then of having the wheat and biscuit from Philadelphia delivered, and the importance of sending back to Europe immediately the Toulon ships so that there would be time to repair them for sailing in the spring, all these were matters more important to the king, and even to his allies, than a useless persistence before Savannah.

D'Estaing lacked much conviction that a direct attack would succeed either. He wrote, "To mount a new regular attack ... was entirely an American idea." The only viable option left to the allied forces was to engage in a frontal assault. Lincoln convinced the admiral to stay and support the assault. He recorded, "I am fully of the opinion that a more determined mode of attack must be adopted before Savannah is ours." On the morning of the 8th, d'Estaing was our reconnoitering "the right side of the Spring Hill redoubt," the place designated to be the focal point of the frontal attack on the British. As Lincoln and d'Estaing planned the upcoming operation, a French officer recorded developments for Friday the 8th in his journal: "We cannonade and bombard feebly. The enemy does little more. He seems to be husbanding his strength for the anticipated attack. Informed of all that transpires in our army, he is cognizant of the trifling effect produced by his fire upon us in our trenches."[20]

At 11 P.M. on October 8 General Lincoln and Admiral d'Estaing issued the orders for the allied attack on Savannah. The time of the attack was set for 4 A.M. Peyrelongue wrote of the attack strategy: "Finally, a direct assault was decided upon, in spite of everyone's advice, especially that of M. de Noailles who did all he could to change the general's mind. We [Royal Corps of Artillery] were supposed to hit the enemy's first bastion on the right, although while advancing our batteries could not fire such an enormous distance.... Imagine what disorder there was! Here was our strategy. There was supposed to be two false attacks: one by 300 troops from the trenches; another by a like number from the galleys under [M. le chevalier] Durumain's orders who were to debark, enter the city from the rear. Set a fire, and complete the assignment by penetrating as far as the lines if possible."[21]

Orders to the American forces directed that:

> The infantry destined for the attack of Savannah, will be divided into two bodies: the first composing the light troops [South Carolina regiments] under the command of colonel Laurens: the second, of the continental battalions [1st and 5th South Carolina Regiments, and some Georgia Continentals all under General Lachlan McIntosh] and the first battalion of Charleston militia, except the grenadiers, who are to join the light troops. The whole will parade at one o'clock, near the left of the line, and march by the right, by platoons.... The cavalry under the command of count Pulaski, will be at the same time with the infantry, and follow the left column of the French troops, and precede the column of the American light troops: they will endeavour to penetrate the enemy's lines between the battery on the left of the Spring-hill redoubt, and the next toward the river. Having effected this, they will pass to the left toward Yamacraw, and secure such parties of the enemy as may be lodged in that quarter.... The artillery will parade at the same time; follow the French artillery, and remain with the corps de reserve, until they receive further orders....
>
> The militia of the first and second brigades, general Williamson's and the first and second battalions of Charlestown militia, will parade immediately under the command of general Isaac Huger, after drafting five hundred of them; the remainder will go into the trenches and put themselves under the command of the commanding-officer there. With the five hundred, he will march to the left of the enemy's lines and remain as near them as he possibly can, without being discovered, until four o'clock in the morning, at which time the troops in the trenches will begin the attack upon the enemy: he will then advance and make his attack as near the river as possible; thought this is only meant as a feint, yet should a favorable opportunity offer, he will improve it and push into the town.[22]

The watch word was "Lewis."

The French troops were to form in three columns, with two attacking and one held in reserve. The first column under Dillon would be commanded by d'Estaing himself. The second column would be commanded by the colonel of the infantry, Steding. The third column of French reserves was under Viscount de Noailles.[23] The leaders of the French forces under d'Estaing, who were about to fight their arch rival, the British, were a most distinguished group of well-placed aristocrats. Count Arthur Dillon was the son of Henry, the 11th Viscount Dillon in the Peerage of Ireland. His father was a colonel in the French Army, and his grandfather Arthur was in the French Army and commanded an Irish Regiment after his father. The regiment Count Dillon commanded at Savannah had been passed down from his grandfather through his relatives to him. Dillon was involved with the French Revolution and was killed under the guillotine in 1794.[24] Curt Louis Christophe, Count von Steding was a Swedish officer in the French service. The Viscount Louis-Marie de Noailles was a 23-year-old aristocrat and the brother-in-law of the Marquis de Lafayette.[25] Now all were in position for the fateful attack.

Unfortunately for the allied forces, the actual details of the coming attack were given to Prevost on the night of the 8th. James Curry, a sergeant major of the Charles Town Grenadiers, deserted to the British and revealed the plan. Prevost and his forces at Savannah were now well prepared for the upcoming attack. With this most timely and accurate intelligence, Prevost moved many of his troops from the left works to the right works near Spring Hill redoubt under Lieutenant Colonel Maitland.

The battle was supposed to start around 4 A.M. but thick fog shrouded the dawn. At 5 P.M. the allied troops were still forming below the southwestern battery when the eerie sound of bagpipes from behind the British lines pierced the mist of the morning. Count Pulaski called the strange music a "mournful harmony: that tended to dispirit him and eroded the morale of his men.[26]

The French engineer, Antoine Francois Terrence O'Connor, recounted the particulars of the attack. He wrote:

> On the 9th at midnight the army took up arms; at 3 A.M. we marched toward General Lincoln's camp where M. le general ordered a halt to wait for the scouts that were obliged to furnish us. The American general could provide only one, and at 4 A.M. the two armies set out together for the Spring Hill redoubt, a mile away. Coming out of the woods a half mile from the enemy, a halt was called to close up the columns in accordance with the manner stipulated in the orders. The vanguard, commanded by M. le comte de Bethisy, moved to the right to take up a position opposite the principal angle of the redoubt. M. le comte de Dillon's column was to the rear of it, and a little to the left. M le baron de Steding's column, where M. le general was, stationed itself on the same high ground; the American column, commanded by General Lincoln and preceded by General Pulaski's cavalry, turned to place itself onour left. The reserve corps, commanded by M. le vicomte de Noailles, advanced as far as an old Jewish cemetery, and we placed on its right and a little to the rear the four 4-pounders.
>
> At 4:30 A.M. the army began to march, in that order. Toward five o'clock we heard the musket fire of the diversionary attacks on the enemy's left. M. le comte de Bethisy'e *avant-garde* penetrated to the abates and chopped through it with hatchets. Immediately the enemy was within pistol range. A single volley of musketry and one round of cannon fire caused a great disorder. However, the vanguard jumped into the ditch which lay before them and uselessly climbed up the side. The cannon pieces which defended this ditch took a frightful toll. M. le comte de Dillon arrived with part of his vanguard, and Colonel Laurens with his light company. General Pulaski went through with some of his horsemen, and he was dangerously wounded. M. le comte de Bethisy was wounded by two balls, M. Browne, major in the Dillon regiment, killed, M. le baron de Steding wounded, and shortly afterwards M. le general himself was wounded in the arm. Brisk grapeshot fire directed toward our left pushed part of the troops into the marsh. All of this created the greatest confusion, and the vanguard troop, realizing they had no support, were forced to fall back. They charged a second time without success.
>
> Disorder increased; most of the officers were wounded; part of the troops coming out of the marsh crowded into the others and confused the order of attack. However, M. le general

partially rallied them, and the vanguard charged a third time, supported by the troops that M. le general had just reassembled. The charge lasted a long time; the enemy cannon exacted heavy losses; the fire of the Scotch Regiment which protected the redoubt was particularly galling. M. le general, wounded a second time by a ball through his leg and witness to the confusion which began again, ordered the retreat. M. le vicomte de Noailles covered it at the head of the reserve. Our troops suffered greatly in the retreat. M. le viconte de Noailles formed the rear guard, and the enemy, who came out of their abates, did not dare a sortie when they saw the determination and discipline of our rear guard, exposed to their cannon loaded with grapeshot.[27]

The Americans fared no better than the French in their attacks. The American right column under Colonel Laurens, preceded by Pulaski's unit, assaulted the Spring Hill redoubt with much determination, and at one point had planted the colors of the Second South Carolina Regiment on the exterior slope. British firing was too heavy, and Laurens' group was driven back. Confusion was caused during the retreat by Pulaski's cavalry passing through the ranks of the infantry also in retreat from hellish fire.

The second column of Americans under General McIntosh arrived at Spring Hill Redoubt at a moment of severe confusion as d'Estaing had been wounded in the arm. Although speaking no French, McIntosh was given verbal orders to move his fresh units more to the left and to not interfere with the attempts by the French to rally and attack. In taking that course, the troops were too much to the left and ended up in the wet, boggy Yamacraw Swamp, where they received cannon grapeshot from the British galley deployed there. With the Spring Hill redoubt fighting off all the attackers, and with the grapeshot killing his men in droves, McIntosh ordered a retreat.

During the raging attack, Count Pulaski attempted to take 200 of his cavalry, made up of his legion accompanied by some Georgia Cavalry, between the British works to penetrate the town and pass behind the enemy's rear to the British camp. Pulaski's cavalry attacked at full speed, but were stopped by the abatis, where they received heavy crossfire from surrounding batteries. Pulaski was wounded by canister shot in the groin and right thigh, and unhorsed. His men took him from the battlefield.

After the terrible frontal attack at Savannah, the battlefield was covered with the slain. On the right of the British lines were 80 men dead in the ditch, and at the parapet of the first redoubt attacked were some 93 killed. Many troops were hung in the abatis, along with disfigured men slain by grapeshot everywhere in the open.[28] The gallant attack on the Spring Hill redoubt had seen two American standards planted. But the effort was in vain as the British resistance was too strong.[29] The allied forces were repulsed at every location, and the British prevailed to a hard-fought victory.

The violent attack had lasted just short of an hour. D'Estaing reported the allied men killed and wounded at Savannah as 760 French soldiers, 61 French officers, and 312 Americans. General Moultrie reported, "Our troops remained before the lines in this hot fire fifty-five minutes; the Generals, seeing no prospect of success, were constrained to order a retreat, after having six hundred and thirty-seven French and four hundred and fifty-seven Continentals killed and wounded." Because of the attack plan intelligence, incredible defensive works and gallant battlefield behavior, the British suffered few casualties. General Prevost reported 40 killed, 63 wounded, four missing and 48 desertions during the Savannah battle. Captain T.W. Moore, Prevost's aide, estimated the losses to be 163 men, including desertions.[30] Regardless of the actual counts, it is obvious that the allied French and Americans suffered roughly ten to one losses versus the British and loyalists who were able to fight off the attack with brilliant success. It was a clear patriot disaster.

The sight of the battlefield after the allied attack prompted Prevost to write:

Our loss on this occasion was one captain and fifteen rank and file killed, one captain, three subalterns, and thirty-five rank and file wounded. That of the enemy we do not exaggerate when set it down from 1000 to 1200 killed and wounded. We buried within and near the abatis 203 on the right, on the left 28, and delivered 116 wounded prisoners, the great part mortally. They themselves, by permission, buried those who lay more distant. Many no doubt were self-buried in the mud of the swamp, and many carried off.

A number of well-known military men were among the brave killed or wounded at Savannah. D'Estaing had been shot in the arm and in the calf of his right leg.[31] French major general D'Fontanges, along with Colonels de Betizi and de Steding, were wounded. The Americans lost Sergeant Jasper, Lieutenant Gray, and Lieutenant Bush. Majors Pierce Butler and John Jones were aides to Brigadier General McIntosh. The brave Brigadier General Count Pulaski, wounded in the groin and right thigh, was taken aboard the United States brig *Wasp* heading for Charles Town. Forced to remain for several days in the Savannah River due to headwinds, Pulaski was attended by surgeons from the French fleet. In spite of the efforts of the surgeons, Pulaski died as the *Wasp* was leaving the river. Colonel Bentalou reported that Pulaski's corpse was so offensive that they were "compelled, though reluctantly, to consign to a watery grave all that was now left upon earth of his beloved and honored commander."[32] Funeral rites were performed in Charles Town with military honors.

After the battle d'Estaing wrote, "On the day of the attack I notified General Lincoln that I was under the ineluctable necessity of raising the siege. He agreed to it; I asked him what he wanted us to do to safeguard his retreat. He asked only that our troops remain at Savannah for twenty-four hours after he left. I agreed to that, and that plan, which was later put in writing, was then ordered."[33] The siege was at a formal end.

On October 10, d'Estaing ordered the dismantling of the batteries and return of the guns on shipboard. The embarkment location was set for Castion's Bluff, with 292 men detailed from regiments of Armagnac and Auxerrois and the marine unit to guard the retreat, deploying at three points to the east of the town. On the 15th, de Bretigny arrived from Charles Town to ask d'Estaing if he would send 900 French troops to protect Charles Town. The French admiral refused. Also, that day the militia of Georgia, Virginia and the Carolinas withdrew.

On the 18th at 10 A.M., the tents and camp were placed in wagons and transported to the embarkment point. At 11 the remaining American forces moved to the left and the French to the right, as the allied force broke off. General Lincoln's forces moved toward Zubly's Ferry and on to Ebenezer. Lincoln then left his force and headed to Charles Town. The French had traveled only two miles toward Causton's Bluff when the darkness of night overtook them. The next morning at 5, Tuesday the 19th, the French reached the bluff and began loading. A French journal recorded that "Causton's Creek and all Georgia are evacuated."[34] All was loaded aboard the French fleet by October 20, but adverse winds forced the French to stay until November 1. On that date, the French ships passed over the bar, and the next day the fleet sailed away from Georgia. Almost immediately, d'Estaing's fleet encountered a violent gale that dispersed the vessels. It was another displeasure to add to all the other disappointments the admiral had endured in the southern colonies.

There was much disappointment and near despair in all patriot quarters over the failure of French and Americans to retake Savannah. But General Lincoln had good things to say about d'Estaing. In his letter to Congress he said, "Count D'Estaing has undoubtedly the interest of America much at heart. This he has evidenced by coming over to our assistance; by his constant attention during the siege; his understanding to reduce the enemy by assault, when he despaired of effecting it otherwise; and by bravely putting himself at the head of his troops and leading them to the attack. In our service he has freely bled. I feel much for him; for while he suffering the distress of painful wounds on a boisterous ocean, he has to combat chagrin. I hope he will be consoled by an assurance, and those of America; we regard with high approbation his intentions to serve us, and that his want of success will not lessen our ideas of his merit."[35]

Most of the blame for the defeat at Savannah went in the direction of d'Estaing. First, he had let the British delay to reinforce with Maitland's force from Beaufort, and, second, pushing for the frontal attack on the defensive works at Savannah. Perhaps the arrogance that d'Estaing showed by believing that it would be easy to take Savannah tended to taint the whole of his actions and his relationships with the Americans. John Harris Cruger, a loyalist officer, described the lack of Franco-American cooperation, "They came in so full of confidence of succeeding, that they were at some loss where to lay the blame, each abusing the other for deceiving them. We are all hands sufferers by this unfortunate invasion. The difference is we have acquired glory and our Enemies, Disgrace."[36]

It was reported that some French officers informed General Prevost, with their apologies, that the Americans were to blame for not allowing the women and children to leave the town by ship as Prevost had requested.[37] General Lincoln was also deserving of some culpability for his lack of a prompt troop movement to join up his forces with d'Estaing's earlier in the campaign. It was seven days before Lincoln joined the French after d'Estaing had landed. If Lincoln had rushed to the side of the French, it is very likely that the truce would have been rejected and Savannah taken before Maitland arrived.[38]

D'Estaing offered a most comprehensive critique of the Savannah attack from his perspective. He wrote:

> 1st. The enemy was not surprised. Surprise was the capital point, it was most essential and important. Everything depended on it in my opinion.
>
> 2nd. The columns direction was changed by the fire from the trenches; instead of marching to the right, after having marched to the left as it was prescribed..., they continually and incessantly veered toward the left, in spite of the example, exhortations, entreaties and threats of many officers. The marsh attracted them; they soon ended up by plunging into it....
>
> 3rd. Only two of the first vanguards showed great ardor....
>
> 4th. The vanguards were insufficiently supported because, as was said, the direction of the columns was altered....
>
> 5th. The troops led by M. Gauthier, aide-major general *des logis*, were on the verge of taking the battery.... They had to sustain the most withering fire on their flank....
>
> 6th. The attack started too late.... I made a mistake by waiting for the one [scout] from the Americans....
>
> 7th. The feint attack from the seigeworks was not executed as the orders specified and attracted little attention from the enemy because he was informed of the real point he had to defend. The worthlessness of the diversion of the Americans who wandered back to their camp, and the failure of the one from the river which did not take place.... This was the result of a treacherous bribe of 400 dollars given to a sailor, who then managed to get away. Obviously the three diversionary attacks, so essential to the real one, would have been of great assistance.[39]

While it is appropriate to place most of the fault upon d'Estaing, it does not diminish the valor and courage that he and his men demonstrated in their attempts to aid the struggling American patriots. One of d'Estaing's naval officers wrote the following about their leader:

Count d'estaing was unable to resist a desire, rising superior to the hazard, to attempt to add new triumphs to those which he had already achieved. If zeal, activity, eagerness, and ambition to accomplish great deeds are worthy of recompense, never will France be able sufficiently to acknowledge, he possesses the enthusiasm and the fire of a man twenty years of age. Enterprising, bold even to temerity, all things appear possible to him. He fancies no representations which bring home to him a knowledge of difficulties. Whoever dares to describe them as formidable is ill received. He wishes every one to view and to think of his plans as he does. The sailors believe him inhuman. Many died upbraiding him with their misery and unwilling to pardon him; but this is a reproach incident to his austere mode of life, because he is cruel to himself. We have seen him, sick and attacked with scurvy, never desiring to make use of any remedies, working night and day sleeping only an hour after dinner, his head resting upon his hands, sometimes lying down, but without undressing.

Thus have we observed Count d'estaing during this campaign. There is not a man in his fleet who would believe that he has endured all the fatigue which he has undergone. When I am now asked if he is a good General, it is difficult for me to respond to this inquiry, He committed much to chance, and played largely the game of hazard. But that he was energetic, adventurous almost to rashness, indefatigable in his enterprises which he conducted with an ardor of which, had we not followed him, we could have formed no conception, and that to all this he added much intellect, and a temper which imparted great austerity to his character, we are forced to admit.[40]

The English savored their new victory. To commemorate the victory over the allied forces, Governor Wright and his council set aside October 29 as a day of thanksgiving and prayer. In St. Augustine, Colonel Fuser, the commanding officer, gave a ball in honor of the deliverance of Savannah.[41] When the news reached London, guns were fired at the Tower of London and the date of the battle was celebrated as the "Glorious Ninth."[42] Henry Clinton wrote, "I think that this is the greatest event that has happened the whole war." Governor Wright gave the credit for the victory with his words, "Give me leave to mention the great ability of Captain Moncrief, the Chief Engineer who was Indefatigable day & Night and whose Eminent services contributed vastly to our defense and safety." It was another crowning achievement for Lord North and George Germain's southern strategy, while it did show the weakness in British sea power in colonial waters.

Wright told Germain, "The Southern parts of No. America are now in Your Lordships Power, whereas had the French got Footing here, I fear they wou'd have been Lost."[43] Later, the next April, in Savannah 60 government officials and loyalist citizens sent an address to the king testifying their devotion with the "most grateful Thanks for sending a Body of Your Forces here, which relieved this Colony from such a Scene of Tyranny, Fraud and Cruelty as would have disgraced any Asiatic Country."[44]

Major General Augustine Prevost was most impressed with the victory as he wrote the king, "tho' on the great scale of the war the transactions of a distant corner like this may not be of great importance, yet to us who were on the spot they were interesting." He wrote of his noble troops: "The noble and steady perseverance manifested by all ranks in exposing themselves to every fatigue and to every danger, the cheerful yet determined spirit with which they set all the threats of the enemy at defiance and their firm resolution of abiding to the last man by every consequence of an obstinate will I hope meet with the approbation of his Majesty and do them honor with their country.

Prevost also had a prediction about the future for the Carolinas, as Georgia was in hand:

> And my real opinion, now more than ever, is that if the Carolinas are not powerfully reinforced from northward or from Europe, they [the Americans] will not make a great resistance to any adequate force that is sent against them.[45]

"The disagreeable news from Genl. Lincoln, that our army have not succeeded against Savannah," reached Philadelphia on November 10. General Washington called the news a "mortification." Sadly, the Congress had the "most sanguine expectations of success," which were not to be. One congressman invoked the Lord writing, "Providence by another Striking Instance has ... tumbled our Towering Expectations to the ground." Some blamed the French for the disaster. A young man noted that there was more than a grain of truth that "this continent is certainly hostile to the Monsieurs." A Philadelphia Quaker wrote with satisfaction that the defeat was "remarkably providential in preventing the French from Getting footing on this continent."[46]

The patriot tragedy of the siege of Savannah was perhaps most exemplified in the words of a "sensitive American officer" like John Jones. A Sunbury, Georgia, planter and rice merchant, Jones had joined the militia in 1778 when Prevost invaded Georgia. Though the British had confiscated his house, lands, slaves and business, he regretted the plight of the women and children in the besieged Savannah. Jones was like most of the allied forces when the cannons first opened fire, but his optimism faded as the days of shelling seemed to show no signs of capitulation on the part of the British. When the orders to assault were given, Jones told his wife, Polly, that he would die in action. Jones wrote, "every ... soldier's wife should religiously believe in predestination"; and "if it is my fate to survive this action, I shall; if otherwise, the Lord's will be done." His gloomy Calvinism came out when he told his friends just before the attack that he expected to die. Unfortunately he was right. John Jones was killed in the assault on the Spring Hill Redoubt, and was buried on the field of action.[47]

Regardless of the best of intentions and great bravery on the part of the allied French and Americans to retake Savannah, the British continued to hold it. The surviving patriot army had retired to South Carolina and the British continued to reestablish their civil administration. What remained of the Georgia patriot government was now at Augusta. With no present threat to their existence, the arrogant loyalists now demonstrated their cruelty upon those who had supported the patriot cause with more pronouncement than even before the French had landed. The loyalists took to plundering the homes of the defeated. They took slaves, furniture, stock, clothing and anything of value from the patriot families of Georgia. Being under the protection of the British was of little conciliation to those suffering at the hands of these loyalist activitists. General McIntosh's family was reduced to poverty, Colonel Twigg's home was burned and a young man killed, and Colonel Elijah Clarke's home was fired and his family ordered to leave the state. The obscene language and personal insults were extreme and the cruelties toward these fellow Georgians were beyond that of a civilized people. Savannah and Georgia were lost!

13

An Occupied Georgia

"In the evening the town was illuminated."

After the British victory over the allied French and patriot forces, Savannah was initially swarming with troops—British, Hessian and loyalists. Not one patriot house was without troops being quartered there. Even Governor Wright and the chief justice were complaining that General Prevost had taken "all the Houses called Rebel's Houses, which are the most in number and the best Buildings in Town." The courthouse had been taken already so court had to be held in the upstairs room in Lachlan McIntosh's home. Most patriot families saw their possessions and property attached and sold at action.[1]

In order to "check the spirit of rebellion," Governor Wright pressed the citizens "to give a very circumstantial account of their conduct during the siege." He excluded locals who were not deemed "material culpable" but others were forced to furnish security service for their behavior for 12 months. They had to have bonds issued for £100 sterling with two sureties, each with the sum of £50. They were also required to swear their allegiance to the Crown.

On October 29, 1779, Wright issued a proclamation to all Georgians to lay down their arms and submit to the Crown. Many took him up on the oath with the hope of returning to a peaceful and normal life. The marks of the previous battle were everywhere. The mortars from the allied army had taken their toll. In addition, churches and public buildings had been turned into hospitals, storehouses and barracks. Some facilities were so polluted by the presence of troops and slaves that careful attention was a matter of first order with Wright. The "wretched conditions" were so poor that before long smallpox appeared. The slave population that had been engaged during the siege by being armed and working in the trenches was showing more resistance to return "to obedience and former servitude." With inoculations and harsh measures, Wright was able to restore the community to health and some level of security.

On November 15, Chief Justice Anthony Stokes and Attorney General James Robertson reported that "writs of election ought to be issued in the usual form for all the parishes and districts that sent members to the last Assembly." They recommended that "if there should be any parish ... without freeholders qualified to elect, or if through the invasion or vicinity of the rebels the provost marshall cannot venture to proceed to an election, then the provost marshall must return ... the writs of election, and verify it by affidavits." The Commons House did meet but only 15 members appeared at Savannah.[2]

Sir Henry Clinton, the commander of British forces in North America, had been trading correspondence with Lord Germain about further British operations in the South for most of 1779, even as events proceeded around Savannah. It was not until October 8 of that year that Clinton first learned that d'Estaing was on the Georgia coast and the siege of Savannah was underway.[3] When the news reached Lord Germain in London, there was nothing to do but wait for the results. Word that the siege was lifted in a grand British victory reached Clinton on November 19. He immediately made plans to attack Charles Town as he awaited news of the status of d'Estaing's fleet. One month later, Clinton learned the good news that the French fleet had departed the American coast. The critical continuation of the Southern Campaign was about to begin.[4]

On the day after Christmas, at 10 A.M., Clinton sailed from Sandy Hook aboard Vice Admiral Arbuthnot's 96-ship fleet. The voyage from New York to Charles Town would prove to be an ordeal. What should have taken some 10 days sailing time proved to be a much more untimely ordeal. The New York winter of December 1779 had been so cold that heavy guns could be taken across the frozen Hudson River. The wind, high sea conditions and icehindered operations so much that the British lost seven transports before they could leave New York Harbor.[5] With 6,975 troops loaded aboard 80 transports, the fleet sailed southward.[6]

After enduring storms with cold winds and heavy seas for 36 days, the British fleet gathered off Tybee Island. Captain Hinrichs reported that of the 36 days of the voyage, 15 days were with a storm and 25 were with a "contrary wind" during the sailing of some 1,851 miles.[7] Some 16 ships were off Tybee Island on February 1, and the remainder of most of the fleet, including Lord Cornwallis, arrived by late the next day. After resupplying for the upcoming operation, lead vessels sailed north from Tybee toward Charles Town at noon on February 9. Some units stopped at the 10-mile-long, pine-covered Trench Island (Hilton Head Island) to wait for the rest of the vessels to leave the Savannah River and Tybee.[8]

On February 10, the British fleet of 62 vessels sailed north from Tybee Island along the South Carolina coast toward North Edisto Inlet. On the next day, the fleet came in at North Edisto with the transports anchoring behind Deveaux Bank off Simmons Island (Seabrook Island) in "five and one-half fathoms of water." Part of the fleet was sent around to block the harbor sea entrance while the troops disembarked. Four battalions of light infantry and the grenadiers landed at Simmons Point on Seabrook Island, some 30 miles south from Charles Town, and marched inland across John's Island and James Island. The area was reported to be "desolate and salty, and full of cabbage trees."[9]

As the siege of Charles Town was about to begin, Clinton stripped Georgia and East Florida of most of their British troops. This left most of the territory outside the immediate environs of Savannah to patriot partisans and the militia. Governor Wright was bitter, and complained vigorously to London that Georgia was wide open. The patriot assembly could meet in Augusta and elect a full state government, as patriots raided to within a few miles of Savannah.

Wright was fairly precise about the number of troops he needed to defend British interests in Georgia. He wanted 500 in Savannah, 500 in Augusta, 1,500 to 2,000 patrolling between Augusta and the South Carolina back country, 200 at Ebenezer or Hudson's Ferry, 150 at Zubly's Ferry, and 70 mounted troops to patrol in the Savannah area. He also required several armed galleys to cruise the coast. Sadly for Wright, the British military authorities deemed his troop requirements as inflated and he would never see those troops materialize.

Clinton was not the only one to remove troops from Georgia. General Lincoln, over the pleas of Georgia's patriot leaders, removed the Georgia Continentals from the state for service at Charles Town. Georgia was able to get General Andrew Williamson's brigade of South Carolina militia to be stationed at Augusta from late March of 1780 until the following May 29.[10]

In Charles Town, as Lincoln prepared to defend the fourth-largest city in the colonies while he pleaded to Congress for more troops, Clinton and his forces continued their offensive operations. Since they had landed on John's Island on February 11, the British had consolidated their control of most territory south of the Ashley River. At 8 A.M. on March 29, Clinton's troops crossed 200 yards of water of the Ashley and began to move down the Charles Town Neck.[11] Charles Town was just 14 miles away. On the afternoon of March 31, the British "broke ground ... from ten to twelve hundred yards" from the patriot line, as they prepared lines across the neck to lay siege.[12]

Though Lincoln received additional support with the arrival of General James Hogan's brigade of 600 North Carolina Continentals, General William Woodford's 750 Virginia Continentals, and some 2,500 militia and volunteers, his force of around 5,000 men was no match for the British force. The British forces had swelled with Lord Rawdon's 3,000 reinforcements who had arrived on April 12 to over 10,000 regulars.[13] On April 10, the British started their cannon bombardment of Charles Town. Overwhelmed with no hope of a patriot victory, at 11 A.M. on May 12, 1780, "Lincoln limp'd out at the Head of the most ragged Rabble" and surrendered to the British.[14]

It was a staggering defeat for the patriots and the American cause at Charles Town. The 42-day siege yielded a British loss with 76 killed and 189 wounded, but they captured 5,466 armed men, 391 artillery pieces, 5,916 muskets, 33,000 rounds of small arms ammunition, 8,000 round shot, 376 barrels of powder and 49 American ships. The patriots lost 89 killed and 138 wounded, with 20 civilians killed.[15] Clinton wrote, "By this very important acquisition there fell into our hands seven generals and a multitude of other officers, belonging to ten Continental regiments and three battalions of artillery, which, with the militia and sailors doing duty in the siege, amounted to about six thousand men in arms."[16]

After the surrender of Charles Town, Clinton sailed away on June 8 for New York, taking part of his army back with him, leaving the balance of the British forces with Lord Cornwallis. Throughout 1780 and 1781, the fighting in the South between Cornwallis's force and patriot troops under Gates, and then Nathanael Greene, would occur in the Carolinas. The fate of Georgia and Savannah was now set with the loss of Charles Town. Both the British and American military leaders ignored Georgia. British troops that were taken from Savannah were never returned. As Cornwallis moved into North Carolina in the fall of 1780, the backcountry patriots felt safer than ever. Over the objections of the state government, Georgia patriot leaders received no consideration for additional troops during this period.

After General Williamson evacuated Augusta in May of 1780, loyalist troops under Colonels Thomas Brown and James Grierson soon took possession of the town. During that summer, Brown and Wright thought that resistance in Georgia would come to an end. Though many people took the oath of allegiance to the king in Georgia, there was never any great love for the British. By July it was reported that most of the upcountry had submitted to the British except for some 800 to 900 patriots in Wilkes County and the upper part of Richmond County. Discouraged, many patriots moved to South Carolina and other states to the north.

Back in Savannah, on September 25, 1780, Governor Wright convened a session of the General Assembly and explained that the spirit of the rebellion was not yet crushed and that "rigorous measures were still required to subdue certain portions of the province."

Wright pushed the group to act on compelling those in Savannah and Augusta to give an account of the male slaves they owned between the ages of 16 and 60, and to send some of them with tools to "work upon and complete the fortifications of those towns." Those who did not own slaves were to provide themselves for work or act as overseers.

Wright also tried to pass an act to give certain people the authority to impress horses, carts, and teams for service for the public defenses. He also called for revising the laws over the militia to make them more effective and "stringent." The assembly accomplished little and suffered from absenteeism and the conflict between the two branches of government. After some long adjournments, Wright finally gave up and adjourned the Commons House on November 15. Curiously, some of the merchants coerced Wright to gather the assembly members on December 11 to consider building a 60- to 70-foot armed galley to defend against the rebel cruisers intercepting cargo off Savannah and Sunbury. After consideration of the costs for such a vessel and provisions, the group determined that funding the galley was financially beyond the reach of the province. They adjourned without taking any action.

Various attempts to establish an effective royal assembly in Georgia during this period were "spasmodic, partial, feeble, and futile." Though the governor retained his seat and carried out some of his rightful duties, his correspondence shows that he was always "opposed by a sense of insecurity." Wright would, on occasion, send a letter back to England telling his majesty that a few of his faithful officeholders would "use their utmost to promote an attachment to his person and government and the welfare of the British Empire;" and they "would not fail to put up their prayers to Almighty God that He would pour down His Blessings upon his Majesty, his Royal Consort, and his numerous offspring, and that He would give him a long and happy reign and that his posterity might sway the scepter of the British Empire till time should be no more." This correspondence would likely be followed by a letter presenting the sad condition of the defenses of the province and how with more troops he could "scour the country and repel the rebel cavalry who were plundering the governor's plantations on the Ogeechee and thundering at the gates of Savannah."

Taking action where he could, Wright did take advantage of the October 30 act that passed and sent out 400 slaves to work on the defences at Savannah. He wrote, "We are making five Redoubts & Batterys, & there is to be a Parapet made of Facines & Earth from the River at each end & on the back of the Town. The Parapet is 10 foot wide & 7 foot high, with a Ditch on the outside 15 foot wide at top, 10 foot deep, & sloping to the bottom 3 foot. I think the Redoubts will be finish'd & each Parapet about half done, or say whole 4 foot high by Christmas...."[17]

Military activities were now driven by the personal inclination of both patriot and loyalist leaders in and around Georgia. The patriot partisan units were led by Elijah Clarke, John Twiggs, Benjamin and William Few, James Jackson and John Dooly. Loyalist units were directed by James and Daniel McGirth, Thomas Brown and James Grierson. The usual operational scenario for patriot partisans was to gather to attack the loyalists and then disperse after the sortie to return to their homes to renew their frontiersman lifestyle until called out again. It was not unusual for these patriots fighters to return to find their homes and crops burned at the hands of loyalists.

Probably the most famous Georgia partisan to emerge to some prominence during this period was Elijah Clarke. He and his men in mid-August of 1780 joined up with North Carolina patriots and attacked Musgrove's Mill in North Carolina. Clarke's party then returned to their homes in Georgia after passing through loyalist-held South Carolina. Ten days later, Clarke and some 300 patriots reassembled and headed toward Augusta. In mid-September, Clarke attacked Thomas Brown's loyalist' force at Augusta, but he could not force the loyalists to surrender as word of reinforcements from Colonel Cruger forced Clarke to retreat. Clarke's force moved to Little River where they discovered that 400 women and children were attempting to flee for their safety to the patriot area of the Watauga Valley in North Carolina. Clarke's men on their return helped to support the attack and victory over British major Patrick Ferguson's force at the Battle of Kings Mountain on October 7.

By April of 1781, it was obvious that Major General Nathanael Greene, the new commander of the Southern Department, wished to go on the offensive in Georgia and the Carolinas. Under the command of Micajah Williamson and Clarke, Georgia and South Carolina militia began the siege of Augusta. Joined by Continental troops under General Andrew Pickens and Lieutenant Colonel Henry Lee on May 21, these patriots captured Augusta on June 5 as Brown's loyal-

Portrait of Elijah Clarke (Hargrett Rare Book and Manuscript Library, University of Georgia Libraries).

ist forces laid down their arms in surrender. Ten days later, Greene reported that the British had evacuated every post in the upcountry they had held except Ninety Six, South Carolina, which was abandoned on July 3.

As the patriots took control of the backcountry in Georgia, the military situation had totally changed. Many loyalists soon fled to British-controlled areas around Savannah. By December 1781, Lieutenant General Alexander Leslie, who was the commander of British forces at Charles Town, and Governor Wright in Georgia felt the situation was so bad that Clinton authorized Leslie to abandon Georgia if he thought it best. By this time, the British troops available for duty in Georgia totaled 970 soldiers. Most of these men were loyalists, two-ninths were Hessians, and less than one-ninth were British regulars. The troop situation would essentially remain the same until the end of the Georgia occupation.

The British troops in Georgia complained dearly of the oppressive climate. It was not unusual to see as many as one-third of the men sick, and at times there were as many as 50 percent. The Hessian commander in Georgia, Lieutenant Colonel Friedrich von Porbeck, complained perhaps the most during the occupation. He described strange diseases caused by the dreadful climate and the poor drinking water and sewage disposal system in Savannah. Porbeck later recorded that some 500 to 600 whites died of fever each year he lived in Georgia. He appealed several times to obtain a transfer to the North, but was always turned down, as his morale deteriorated.[18]

Wright tried to get along with the military commanders in Savannah, including General Prevost. Prevost had come in 1779 after the British capture and he was not to leave until May of 1780. He was replaced by Lieutenant Colonel Alured Clarke, who commanded Georgia as well as East Florida. In April of 1781, Clarke took part of the troop contingent and moved to St. Augustine as fears of Spanish aggression surfaced. He left Lieutenant Colonel Porbeck as the senior military officer in Georgia. Until Clarke returned on June 7, Porbeck continued to complain about the civil government along with many other complaints.

Wright's relationships with these officers was strained at times, largely because Wright had the interest, as he understood it, in the welfare of the people of Georgia. He was also convinced that he had to have more British troops to maintain control of the province, even if that was only 500 to 1,000 men. Wright was frustrated by London's inaction toward Georgia. Many British leaders would have agreed with the remarks of Lieutenant Colonel Balfour who called Wright and his council "the most Absurd of all People." Wright eventually lost all hope as he expressed in the record:

> The Generals &c. have always Set their faces against this Province, as I have frequently Wrote you, and I can't tell why, unless it is because the King has thought Proper to Reestablish his Civil Government here — which the Military Cannot bear — and I have long Seen they will do Nothing for us, without a Positive order from Home & which may now be too late.[19]

Wright had always wanted a mounted force in Georgia, but Clinton, and later Cornwallis, refused to support him. In early 1781, Wright and his council approved three patrols of 20 mounted militiamen each, plus later a unit of horsemen to protect the backcountry.

Wright and the British were not the only leaders having trouble getting troops. The patriot cause also suffered in Georgia in this regard. The Continental Congress had authorized four battalions of infantry and one regiment of light dragoons for Georgia, but only the first battalion of infantry and the dragoons were actually raised in Georgia. The other battalions were gathered in the Carolinas, Virginia and Pennsylvania. These battalions of out-of-state troops complained about serving in Georgia because of the hot climate, poor valuation of Georgia's currency, low pay and their distance from home. In 1779, Congress ordered a reduction to one infantry battalion and a regiment of horse. In early 1780, it was recommended that two battalions of blacks be formed, but these troops were never raised.

The weak and irregular Georgia state government could do little to support the military cause from the fall of Savannah until mid–1781. Once the British and loyalists were essentially run out of the upcountry, the state government was able to form and take up the cause. The best known of militia units raised by Georgia was the Georgia State Legion, also known as Jackson's Legion. This unit was commanded by Lieutenant Colonel James Jackson at the suggestion of General Greene in the summer of 1781.[20]

State troops were no more successful than other militia had been in Georgia. The key problem was that the state government could pay little to nothing. As a result, these troops resorted to taking land, horses, slaves, clothing, food, or anything else they could get their hands on. When Augusta was captured, some militia reported that had been in the field for over a year without pay. Militia who stayed in the field for long periods were likened to the partisans for they stayed out of their hatred of the British, the respect they had for their leaders, or they found militia life safer than being a civilian. The chief reason most militia did not remain in the field for long periods was the necessity to work their farms.[21]

At this point in the war in 1781, the British maintained only two major defensive outposts in the lower South — Augusta and Ninety Six — other than Charles Town and Savannah. After the battle at Camden, Greene decided to head for Ninety Six while he ordered operations against Augusta, where loyalist Colonel Thomas Browne commanded his Florida Rangers in their strong entrenchment. Greene sent Lieutenant Colonel Henry Lee with his legion, and the newly promoted Brigadier General Andrew Pickens, commanding his South Carolina Militia, to take Augusta.

Loyalist Colonel Browne had constructed three forts around Augusta for defense — Galphin, Cornwallis and Grierson. On his way to the Augusta area for offensive operations, covering some 75 miles in three days from Fort Granby, Lee had sent out strong patrols under Captain Ferdinand O'Neale. O'Neale discovered that the annual British gift to the Indians had just arrived at Fort Galphin, only 12 miles away. The gift consisted of powder, balls, small arms, liquor, salt and blankets. Seeing this opportunity before him, Lee brought his forces around Fort Galphin.

On the morning of May 18, Lee sent a detachment of mounted militia to the front gate in open defiance. He had also sent a unit of his legion infantry through cover of the woods to approach from the opposite direction in the hopes of catching the loyalist militia if they came out to pursue the mounted patriots. The loyalists took the bait, and as most of the garrison came out to pursue the horsemen, the concealed infantry charged the open gate from the other side and took the fort with only a single casualty — a sunstroke victim. The British lost four killed, and a few wounded out of the 126 prisoners taken. Now the gift supplies were in the hands of the patriots.

On the evening of May 21, Lee crossed the river and moved toward Augusta. Arriving, he joined with Pickens and Elijah Clarke commanding his Georgians to take on the two remaining enemy-held Augusta forts. Fort Cornwallis was located in the middle of the town and Fort Grierson was a mere one-half mile away up the river across a narrow creek swamp. Pickens ordered his artillery to construct batteries midway between the two forts. At Fort Grierson was Colonel Grierson, a hated loyalist, with a garrison of 80 loyalist Georgia militia. From their encampment on the west of town, Lee, Pickens and Clarke decided to attack the weaker enemy garrison at Grierson first. At Fort Cornwallis on the river bank, Colonel Browne commanded 320 Provincial regulars with two artillery pieces. Supporting this facility were some 200 slave laborers who maintained the fortifications. The plan was to attack Grierson and prevent his militia from joining with those at Fort Cornwallis.

The attack on Fort Grierson began on May 23. Pickens and Clarke attacked from the north and west, while Major Eaton with the North Carolina Continentals engaged from the south along a swamp. Lee's legion of infantry and artillery moved up from the swamp with Eaton. Captain Eggleston with the legion cavalry was positioned in the woods to the south of Lee with orders to support by attacking Browne's rear if he advanced toward Lee. When Colonel Brown noticed Lee's movements on the edge of the swamp, he came out of his fort with infantry and artillery. After a long-range and ineffective bombardment between Lee and Browne, Browne retreated back inside the fortification. The garrison fell quickly at Fort Grierson with the coordinated attack. The loyalists lost 30 killed, and many of the remaining wounded. American casualties were light, but among them was the promising young officer Major Eaton.

To the south of the swamp was a creek which flowed into the river, and a large brick mansion belonging to a prominent loyalist. Here Lee took up his legion while Pickens and Clarke positioned the militia in the woods on the left of Fort Cornwallis. Since the fort was near the Savannah River, its banks allowed the Americans to operate rather freely. The siege works began around the left and rear, as Browne continued strengthening his defensive works. In an attempt to dislodge the Americans, Browne sent out a British assault unit just before midnight on May 28 to attack the trenches next to the river. The unit was able to drive the surprised Americans out, but a fierce battle led by Captain Handy fought off the British. That same night, Browne sent out another detachment. Likewise, this force was driven back by Captain Michael Rudolph of the legion and troops who used bayonets and hand-to-hand combat to win.

Since the area around the fort was a flat river plain, Pickens, Lee and Clarke decided that a Maham tower, like the one used by Marion and Lee at Fort Watson, should be built. The timbers for the tower arrived on May 30 as construction began, hidden by an old house. The frame for the tower was raised, steadied by a foundation of earth, stone and brick rubble. Anticipating that Browne would try to destroy the tower, Lee and Pickens placed a company of infantry around the tower to guard it. The night the tower was raised, Browne did come out and attacked Pickens' militia, in the rear of Fort Cornwallis. Captain Rudolph's men fought off the river attackers as Captain Handy's troops swung around and came to the aid of Pickens' militia under bayonet attack from Browne. With losses on both sides, Browne finally retreated into the fort.[22] On the 31st, a summons to surrender was sent to Browne, but he refused.[23]

Realizing the danger of the Maham tower, Browne erected a tower opposite the American tower. On his tower he mounted two of his heaviest artillery pieces. The British fired at the American tower even as it was nearing completion. The American tower was completed on June 1, with a single 6-pounder cannon mounted on the top. At dawn the next day, counter-fire commenced immediately by the Americans with good effect. By noon, the Americans had dismounted the two British cannons on the tower, and were sending cannon and musket shot into the fort in all locations, except at the British tower, which was out of range.

Browne was getting desperate, but he would not surrender. He sent a Scottish sergeant into Lee's camp pretending to be a deserter. The deserter told Lee that he knew where the British powder magazine was located. If red-hot cannon shot was fired at it, the whole place would go up in smoke. Apparently the mission of the Scottish sergeant was to set fire to the house before the tower, in the hopes that it would reach the tower itself. Lee became suspicious and removed the sergeant from the tower platform and placed him under guard. In frustration at the lack of success of the sergeant, Browne came out and burned two empty log cabins on the outside of the fort. The Americans commanders could not understand why Browne had spared two other houses. Pickens ordered a party of militia to prepare to occupy the tallest house on the early morning of June 4 to cover a planned attack. At about 3 A.M. that selected house was destroyed by a violent explosion. Apparently Browne had positioned a mine at the house and blew it up. It was fortunate for the designated party that they had not moved yet to occupy the house that morning.

At 9 A.M., Lee and Pickens were positioned to attack the fort. First they sent a letter to Browne asking him to surrender the fort. Initially he refused, but later a white flag was seen and negotiations began. Since June 4 was the British king's birthday, Browne would not surrender on that day. So, on the next day at 8 A.M., Browne's 300 troops marched out of their fort and laid down their arms. Captain Rudolph then marched in and raised the American flag. Augusta was now in American hands.[24]

Knowing of the hatred toward Browne and some of his officers, Browne was sent directly to Lee's headquarters for protection. Lee recorded, "This precaution suggested by the knowledge of the inveteracy with which the operations in this quarter have been conducted on both sides turned out to be extremely fortunate; as otherwise, in all probability, the laurels acquired by the arms of America would have been stained by the murder of a gallant soldier...." Pickens sent a heavy escort of the North Carolina Militia with the prisoners to Savannah to be paroled. This mission was successfully accomplished.

In Georgia in 1781, the actions of the state government were not unlike those of the other southern states. After the patriot victory and retaking of Augusta in that June, General Greene sent Joseph Clay, his paymaster general, to the town in an attempt to reestablish the Georgia government, which had all but dissolved. The Georgia Assembly met on August 17 in Augusta with representatives from all the Georgia counties except Camden. This body elected Dr. Nathan Brownson as governor along with the other state officials, county officers and congressional representatives. The assembly extended expiring laws and regulations, and set about dealing with the issues surrounding the loyalists and citizens' rights.[25]

On January 1, 1782, the assembly again met in Augusta. By this point, all of Georgia was clear of British control except Savannah. Like their fellow representatives in the neighboring states, the legislature passed an act allowing confiscation of property, both real and personal, belonging to those who had joined with the British. These loyalists were banished forever from the state by this act. The plan called for property to be sold and all proceeds to be credited to the state treasury. Funds from the credit were issued in the form of certificates totaling some £22,100 sterling to meet government obligations. The certificates were redeemable in par value for gold or silver coin or Spanish milled dollars. The assembly took other actions, including appointing the executive and judicial officers, with their salaries fixed and paid in certificates. Certificates worth £15,000 were also allocated to pay in arrears the salaries due to the state militia.

After the surrender of Lord Cornwallis's forces on October 19, 1781, at Yorktown, in early January 1782 Brigadier General Anthony Wayne was ordered to Georgia as the Continental commander for the state. At that time the British had a total of some 1,000 men in Georgia compared to the 500 or so patriot forces. Early in February 1782, Wayne was ordered to Ebenezer with 100 of Colonel Moylan's dragoons under Colonel Anthony Walton White to join with Colonel James Jackson's Georgia State Legion. Soon they were also combined with Colonel Posey's 300 Continental troops. Even with this strengthened force, General Wayne had to limit his activities to defending the countryside around Savannah from foraging and plundering parties from the British out of Savannah.

A most pressing problem for Wayne was feeding the army and assisting others west of Augusta who were in dire need. The need was so great that John Werreat used his own slaves and boats to ship rice upriver to help the citizens of the interior. When the British under Brigadier General Clarke were ordered in from other outposts to defend Savannah as a result of Wayne's move to Ebenezer, he directed that all food and goods they were unable to bring with them to the town were to be destroyed. The conflagration was so successful that for many miles from the coast to Sunbury and Savannah,

Portrait of Anthony Wayne (National Park Service).

the rice farms were in ruin. These British and loyalist actions forced Wayne to feed and supply his army from South Carolina.

Some of the British and loyalist foraging parties were active even after most of the Savannah area was in patriot hands. On February 13, Colonel Jackson was attacked at his camp at Cuthbert's Sawmills at 11 A.M. by 50 loyalists and Indians from Savannah led by Colonel Hezekiah Williams. The patriots rallied after the attack, but not before three of Jackson's men were wounded. Unfortunately, Williams' force was able to escape back toward Savannah.

Wayne turned his attention to the extensive amount of rice being stored on Hutchinson's Island opposite Savannah. Rice fields had been ordered cultivated by Governor Wright. Unable to gain possession of the rice because of the number of cannons pointed in that direction, Wayne decided to have it destroyed. On the night of February 26, Wayne detached Major Barnwell of South Carolina with 50 men in boats down the north river to burn the rice on the island, as well as any available on the mainland. Meanwhile, Colonel Jackson was ordered to take 30 dragoons to Governor Wright's rice plantation. Jackson's mission was successful at burning all the rice without any casualties. Unfortunately, Major Barnwell's detachment was not so successful. The enemy found out about the plan and ambushed his force on the island. Barnwell lost two men killed and four were wounded. One of his boats ran aground and three of his men were taken prisoner.

Armed incidents continued around Savannah during the first six months of 1782. One action was prompted by the movement of a party of Indians passing through Savannah from the Creek Nation with horses stolen from patriots in Liberty County. Major Francis Moore, with 15 men, chased the Indians and overtook them at Reid's Bluff. Finding the Indians well settled in a log cabin, Moore attacked the superior numbers anyway with no success. Moore was killed and another wounded on the first trade of musket fire. The patriots were forced to retreat.

Realizing the value in using the local Indians to supplement his forces, General Clarke sent representatives to the Creek and Cherokee nations to enlist their support. A general gathering was planned for May 15 on the southern frontier, but disagreements with the Indian councils delayed the movement. Though the grand council of the Cherokee and Creek nations did not sanction the British alliance, some 3,000 Creek warriors under Guristersigo set out for Savannah in June. Using white guides, the Indians moved down the southern frontier of Georgia to the vicinity of Wayne's encampment at Joseph Gibbon's Plantation some seven miles from Savannah. The white guides alerted Guristersigo to the patriot camp position as they changed their path to avoid Wayne's camp.

Fortunately, Wayne moved his camp on the afternoon of the 23rd to avoid being detected by foraging parties from Savannah, not realizing that an enemy force was coming from the opposite direction. The Indian force had some 15 miles to cover and did not reach Wayne's location until 3 A.M. on June 24. Guristersigo sent out a party to kill the sentinels while he moved his force into the rear of Wayne's camp. The Indian warriors were able to reach the patriot camp undetected. Captain Parker realized the situation he was in and ordered a retreat behind Gibbon's house. General Wayne sprang to his horse and ordered a bayonet defense calling out "victory or death." Wayne's horse was shot out from under him. Wayne continued to advance with sword raised in hand toward the attacking Indians. His men were able to regain their field cannon, as the tide of the conflict turned in favor of the patriot forces. When it was all over, 17 warriors were dead plus Guristersigo. The remaining Indians fled and were pursued. Twelve warriors were captured while retreating. Wayne's force suffered four killed and eight wounded.[26]

With these and other small engagements, the area around Savannah was more in patriot control as the year of 1782 progressed. The Georgia government and executive spent most of their time securing food and supplies for itself, the militia and for many of the citizens who had no hope for supply until the next crop could be harvested. In May, the assembly moved to Ebenezer where Wayne had his encampment. In Georgia, the focus now centered around determining when the British would finally leave the fair town of Savannah.

As the war carried on, Governor Wright saw the number of British troops dwindle away. Chronic lack of cooperation between the civil and military officials was the new norm, as Wright's pleas to London for reinforcements produced no results. The royal control over Georgia had shrunk to the town of Savannah as patriot raids approached within a mile or two. Wright noted that "Since the Unfortunate affair of Lord C., ... the Military ... every where give the matter up...."[27]

Meanwhile, back in England, the Parliament's Christmas recess had lasted until January 21, 1782. The opposition forces to Lord North's administration led by Charles James Fox, Lord Rockingham and Lord Shelburne had been busy during the recess, gathering support for ending the war. After Lord North met with King George III in March for over an hour, word spread of the curious event. Uncharacteristically, some 400 members of Parliament were present at 5 P.M. when Lord North entered the hall in full dress, showing his ribbon of the Order of the Garter on his coat. The members scrambled to their seats while North moved to address the chair. The members were in pandemonium while North stood trying to talk in vain above the roar. Finally he was able to speak with the permission of the opposition. North declared, "His object was to save the time and trouble of the House by informing them that the administration was virtually at an end; that His Majesty had determined to change his confidential servants; and that he should propose an adjournment, in order to allow time for the new ministerial arrangements which must take place."

The opposition cried out in triumph with frantic cheers. Wraxall wrote, "a more interesting scene had not been acted within the walls of the House of Commons since ... Sir Robert Walpole retired from power." With incredible dignity, North continued to remain as the body recessed for the night. From his waiting coach, North spoke these words to his friends: "Good night, gentlemen, you see what it is to be in the secret." The 12 years of the North government had come to an end.[28]

When the North ministry ended, Lord George Germain and Sir Henry Clinton resigned to the king. On April 27, Clinton opened a letter revealing that the king had accepted his resignation. He was to turn his command over to Major General James Robertson, the royal governor of New York, until the permanent commander, Sir Guy Carleton, could assume command.[29]

Carlton received his orders and sailed from Portsmouth, England, on April 8 for America. His primary orders were to evacuate all forces and equipment to Halifax from New York, Charles Town, Savannah, as well as to determine whether St. Augustine should also be abandoned. He was also ordered to provide for all loyalists who wanted to leave the colonies. On May 5, Carleton arrived at New York to be greeted by Clinton, Major General Robertson, and Admiral Robert Digby, who commanded all British naval activities in North America. Clinton wrote:

> Sir Guy Carleton being in consequence sent out to New York to relieve me, I had the happiness of resigning to him on the 8th of May the chief command of His Majesty's forces in North America-a command which I had neither solicited nor coveted but accepted with reluctance, and which I was afterward compelled to retain for four years, although I had each year prayed to be released from it from the thorough conviction of the impossibility of

my doing anything very essential toward extinguishing the rebellion without more troops than I had the direction of, and a cooperating naval force constantly superior to that of the enemy.[30]

During some 10 days of briefings from these and other officials, Carleton gained a clear view of the discouraging situation before him. With limited troops and few vessels, Carleton had his work cut out for himself.

Reports from the southern colonies were likewise depressing. Before Clinton departed from the Chesapeake Bay after discovering that Cornwallis had already surrendered, he had ordered Lieutenant General Alexander Leslie to move to Charles Town to assume command of the troops in the Carolinas, Georgia and East Florida. Soon after Leslie arrived at Charles Town on November 8, he realized that the British were in an extremely weakened condition. He immediately ordered Craig to abandon Wilmington, North Carolina, and bring his troops back to Charles Town. Leslie reported the troops on duty in the South to be down to 4,576 at Charles Town, 691 at Savannah, and 476 at St. Augustine. Clinton could not spare any significant numbers of troops from New York as Leslie requested, but he did send 537 officers and men who belonged to units in the South.

Information from Savannah was most distressing. Wright and Brigadier General Alured Clarke believed that the town could not be defended from an assault unless they received additional troops from New York. The request for troops was refused. If Savannah were attacked, Leslie would have to provide assistance from Charles Town. To complicate matters in the South, 2,000 troops had been ordered sent to Jamaica to assist in the defense of that island. Leslie refused to send that number, but was able to send 1,300 men in May of 1782.

Though the British were indeed weakened, General Greene, who was outside Charles Town, and his subordinate, General Anthony Wayne, at Savannah, had insufficient troops to assault the two southern towns. Their operations against the British were confined to intercepting foraging parties and preventing supplies from reaching Savannah.

On May 7, 1782, two days after he arrived in New York, Carleton directed a survey of the number of transport vessels in the colonies. The results revealed that the British had only 32 transports and victuallers, and one hospital ship at New York; only seven transports at Charles Town, and five other vessels engaged in other operations in the South. It was a severe blow to realize that it would impossible to remove all the British garrisons in America in 1782.

The years of the war had resulted in the loss of nearly 2,000 transports and victuallers in North America. During most of the period from 1775 until 1781, the movement of British troops and supplies in amphibious operations had been hampered by the lack of transports, but the North administration had failed to secure adequate vessels for America. Although the new Rockingham government had hoped that the colonies could be evacuated as soon as possible, it likewise had no interest in providing additional seaborne transportation to accomplish the movements. Evacuating the British forces and other supporters from the American colonies would indeed be a complex and prolonged task.

On May 23, Carleton issued directions to General Leslie to abandon Savannah and St. Augustine. All troops, stores and supplies were to be sent to New York. No specific instructions were included telling him where to send the loyalists, except that he was not to bring them to New York. Carleton was of the opinion that not many loyalists would desire to leave the southern colonies. Carleton also directed that plundering be strictly forbidden. After both the towns were evacuated, Leslie was directed to leave Charles Town. After receiving these instructions from Carlton, Leslie immediately forwarded orders to Wright at Savannah and Patrick Tonyn, the royal governor of East Florida, at St. Augustine.

When Wright received his orders to evacuate Savannah, he was absolutely shocked. While it was true that the British influence around Georgia had extended only to the immediate fortifications around Savannah during the previous six months, Wright felt that he needed only some 500 reinforcements to shore up his force to maintain control in the colony. Governor Tonyn was also outraged, and with support of the Assembly of East Florida, they protested to Leslie and Carleton. As it turned out, only four days after he had issued his evacuation orders to Leslie, Carleton had conferred with a naval officer, Captain Keith Elphinstone, who told him that there were an insufficient number of transports to evacuate both towns. Since it was believed that Savannah could be reinforced from Charles Town, Carleton decided to delay departing from St. Augustine before Charles Town. Carleton notified Wright that he could send loyalists to East Florida if it was necessary since he directed that no one would be allowed to land at Charles Town.

As the world fell apart around him, in June, during the customary celebration of the king's birthday, Wright gave "an elegant entertainment (provided by Mr. Lewis at his own house and Mrs. Tondee's) to a more numerous company than was ever assembled on the like occasion in this place.... In the evening the town was illuminated, and every mark of respect shewn that is due from subjects to the best of Kings." A victualer, James Lewis, supplied the food for the celebration and Mrs. Tondee supplied her sizeable Long Room for the festivities.[31]

On June 20, 34 transports and victuallers sailed into Charles Town harbor. By early July, these same vessels reached Tybee Island at the mouth of the Savannah River. Wright directed General Clarke to prepare the fortifications at Tybee for protection during the embarkation there. On July 11, the British troops, along with 3,200 loyalists and 3,500 blacks, departed Savannah and camped at Tybee Island in preparation to sail away.

Unfortunately the evacuation was a slow one, lasting over three weeks. Even after Lieutenant Governor John Graham hired on five private ships, there were not enough vessels to carry those fleeing Georgia. Some 5,000 loyalists whites and blacks had to travel to St. Augustine overland or in small boats and canoes along the Georgia inland waterways. After getting approvals from Leslie, on July 20 six transports with 10 white families and 1,568 blacks onboard sailed to Jamaica. Two days later, seven ships departed for St. Augustine with 580 loyalists and 748 blacks. The last 24 ships left for New York carrying 1,996 British, German and provincial troops with all stores and equipment. They arrived in New York in early August.

With the British out of Savannah on July 11, General Wayne immediately occupied the town. He chose not to interfere with the slow embarkation at Tybee. Before the British had departed, Wayne had promised protection to all loyalists who wished to stay in Savannah, as well as allowing the merchants to have six months to dispose of their goods. Additionally, Wayne permitted anyone who had supported the British to regain their citizenship by serving for two years in the Georgia Continental Army. As it turned out, Wayne did not stay at Savannah for long. After a brief period, Wayne marched his army back to Charles Town where Greene was nervously waiting. Greene was concerned that troops from Savannah would land at Charles Town and join the forces there to reengage in offensive operations. Thankfully, Carleton's plan did not include landing troops at the city. The evacuation of Charles Town did not begin until December 18 and involved the use of 126 vessels.

During 1782, records indicated that 5,090 whites and 8,285 blacks from Georgia and South Carolina traveled to East Florida, where the population swelled from 4,000 to 17,375 souls. Counts made in East Florida in December of 1782 showed that 911 white loyalists and 1,786 blacks had come from Georgia. Wright requested transportation of slaves from

Georgia to Jamaica and General Carleton later recorded that 10 families and 1,568 Negroes traveled there from Savannah. The slaves of Wright, William Knox and other loyalist men of wealth were reported to be in Jamaica.

Though the preliminary peace treaty ceding East Florida to Spain was signed on January 20, 1783, it was not until November 1785 that the British and loyalists from East Florida completed the evacuation. Those East Florida loyalists who did not wish to stay under Spanish rule were resettled in Nova Scotia, the Bahamas, Jamaica, and England, and some 421 whites and 2,561 blacks came back to the United States. The final British evacuation from the South was accomplished.[32]

After only two days following the British evacuation, the patriot Georgia Assembly met at Christ Church, Savannah, and elected James Habersham as the speaker. It also directed that the filature be "immediately fitted up and Put in order for the use of the General Assembly." They moved to Mrs. Tondee's and on the 5th of August they voted her £15 "for the use of her room which the Assembly Occupied during their Present Session." The Georgia governor, John Martin, better known as "Black Jack," was directed by the assembly to give her the funds "out of the first moneys which shall come into the Public Treasury." Two years later, Mrs. Tondee was still waiting for her money.[33]

Among the many local Savannahians who welcomed the returning patriot army were the destitute widows and orphans. Soon after the Executive Council took control of the town once again, it ordered provisions to be issued to them. During the period from mid–August to mid–October, Lucy Tondee received rations for herself and her four children. The 35 weekly food allotments amounted to 44 pounds of beef, 35 pounds of bread and three/fourths of a pint of salt.

In mid–August, Lucy Tondee also put her signature to a petition to Governor Martin and the council to allow loyalist Doctor Andrew Johnston to be released from jail so as to continue his medical practice. Dr. Johnston had been previously listed among the 280 loyalists to be banished from Georgia, but because of his "inoffensive Life and useful Talents," the petition signers pledged to answer for the parole "until an Opportunity offers of having him freed by the Legislature from the Present Penalties." The petition contained 26 signatures including former governor John Habersham, Lachlan McIntosh, John Milledge Jr. and his mother, Ann. After years of vacillating between banishing him and letting him stay, in 1785 Dr. Johnston and 16 others were removed from the List of Banishment and Confiscation. The dear doctor died in 1801 "after a tedious and severe illness" having resided in Georgia for 48 years "eminent in his profession as a physician."

The situation with Dr. Johnston was typical of the government's actions trying to sort out patriots and traitors after the Revolution. Often the former loyalists were simply overlooked out of deference to their age. This was the case for John Oates, who was not named on the list, although Inigo Jones, the younger brother of Noble Wimberly and the son of Noble, was listed. Though clearly a loyalist, Inigo had taken no part in the war and was able to resume his normal quiet life afterward. Some escaped by sheer strength of their reputation like Moses Numez. When Moses died in 1787 at age 82, his obituary read that he had lived in Georgia for many years "with an irreproachable character."

Other loyalists did not fare so well after the war even though they had powerful relatives. Mordecai Sheftall's half-brother Levi, John Milledge's cousin Wiliam Stephens, and even Nobel Wimberly Jones's son-in-law John Glen were listed as enemies of the state by both the British during the occupation and by the Americans after the evacuation. Sheftall and Glen had signed oaths to the Crown during the dark days of the siege of Savannah and the fall of Charles Town, and were not exonerated until 1785. Stephens was cleared only after a special act of the legislature. Five years later, Stephens served as representative of Chatham County, along with Joseph Habersham, at the convention in Augusta, which ratified the U.S. Constitution. Both Stephens and Glen were later to serve as mayors of Savannah.[34]

After the North ministry dissolved in England on March 20, 1782, the Marquis, Lord Rockingham, was successful at forming a government. Shelburne became the secretary of state for the new Southern Department over home, Irish and colonial affairs, with Fox as the secretary of state for the Northern Department heading foreign affairs. From the outset, confusion reigned over which British secretary was responsible for handling the treaty negotiations. Shelburne opened negotiations with the Americans, but both secretaries sent emissaries to the endless meetings held in Paris and Versailles and occasionally in London and Madrid. Spain, France and Holland were also parties to the treaty along with America. The British wanted a separate peace with America, to support the potential of breaking the French-American alliance. But Congress decided that it would not set aside the alliance indicating that "Congress will not enter into the discussion of any overtures for pacification but in confidence and in concert with his Most Christian Majesty."

In the middle of the complex peace negotiations, Lord Rockingham died and Shelburne became prime minister. While it was an initial setback for the Americans, as the secretary was an advocate for American independence, the American negotiators Benjamin Franklin, John Adams, Henry Laurens, and the New York lawyer John Jay, were eventually able to obtain a satisfactory agreement. On November 30, 1782, in Paris, the preliminary articles of peace between England and America were signed. The agreement stated that the treaty was not actually in effect until an agreement between England and France was completed.

After the treaty was signed and sealed, American negotiators rode out to Passy to have dinner with Franklin. At dinner, some Frenchmen joined them, one of whom expressed to the British of "the growing greatness of America" and exclaiming that "the Thirteen United States would form the greatest empire in the world." Caleb Whitefoord, who was the secretary to the British commissioners, responded, "Yes, sir, and they will all speak English; every one of 'em."

The articles of peace between Britain, France and Spain were signed on January 20, 1783, while Holland's peace truce was delayed several months.[35] The official text of the Treaty of Paris arrived in the United States with Joshua Barney of Baltimore on March 12, 1783, aboard the ship *Washington*. The official announcement of the ratification of the treaty was published on April 19, 1983, exactly eight years after the war started at Lexington and Concord.[36]

The American Revolution was formally at an end, and Georgia was free.

14

A Fifty Year Colonial Legacy

"Georgia must, I think, in a few years be
one of the Richest States in the Union."

On May 1, 1783, the citizens of Savannah celebrated the war-ending Treaty of Paris. The *Georgia Gazette* recorded that "His Honour the Governor was received by respectable Strangers, and the governor then reviewed the troops, who had for that purpose marched to their former position, and fired a 'feu de joie' [musket salute]. The behavior of the Regulars was admirable, and the appearance of the Virginia line thought equal to that of the most disciplined and veteran Europeans." Toasts went to Holland, the kings of Spain and France, King George III, Charles Fox, George Washington and the American ladies.[1]

The war had indeed taken a toll on Savannah. Damage from the siege had not been repaired and the churches, hospitals and public buildings showed the signs of distress everywhere. Even as there was destruction and ruin all around, on July 8, 1783, Governor Lyman Hall opened the Georgia Assembly for a state finally in territorial control for the first time since December of 1778. Without question, the focus of the session had to be sorting out the chaos from the war and British occupation. It was a daunting task. Hall delivered to the assembly an impressive executive briefing, which provided a comprehensive perspective of the condition of the state, along with suggested recommendations for action.

How would the state rebuild the damaged structures, deal with pressing matters in Indian affairs, capture funds through new taxes, pay the war debts of the state, establish schools, secure all confiscated property, handle disputed land grants, issue criminal warrants and reestablish the court system, establish organized religion, restore morale and more? Even defining the value of the money was an open issue for resolution. When the state's former colonial agent in London, Ben Franklin, requested payment for his past services, there was so little specie available that they had to pay him with a land grant of 3000 acres. In short, these legislators had the task of reimplementing a government in Georgia almost from scratch.[2]

Just trying to gather the governmental records was a significant undertaking. The colonial records of Georgia traveled much during the Revolution. After the fall of Savannah, they were moved to Charles Town, but with the British threat the records were moved to New Bern, North Carolina, in wagons by Captain John Milton. When the British came to North Carolina, they were moved on to Maryland, where they remained until the end of the war. Eventually they were returned to Savannah.[3]

Now that the war was formally ended, Georgia was different. The social fabric was forever changed as the older upper class, living in the coastal region, lost ever more control to the upcountry folk. The effect of British control around Savannah had fostered a sense of greater independence in the upcountry, from Augusta and westward. The English model of a society dominated by the aristocracy gave way to a social order with greater equality between free men.

Though Savannah again became the capital of Georgia after the British evacuation, the loss of political preeminence in the coastal region led to shifts in the capital location. Between 1783 and 1785 the capital actually shifted ten times between Savannah and Augusta, as the executives held their legislative sessions in one city then the next.

There was at least one bright spot in Georgia life for many after the war. The economy soon flourished as the demand for goods prompted the ports to open almost from the day the British left the town of Savannah. Trade increased dramatically, first with the West Indies, Jamaica and Cuba, and eventually with Britain. Though still in the shadow of the port of Charles Town, goods flowed with speed into Georgia. The citizens needed all types of supplies, tools, textiles, clothing, farm implements, and others as merchants exported naval stores, masts, spars, staves, shingles, and lumber. There was little exporting of agricultural products as the crops were in such demand for the settlers of the state. The shortage of slaves to be used as field hands tended to suppress the quick recovery of the plantation economy. But agricultural expansion did occur in Georgia as Joseph Clay, a Savannah merchant, observed when he noted that there was three times more land planted in 1784 than in the previous year.

As loyalist land was auctioned off and the state government regained control, land availability was the best it had ever been in Georgia. In 1782, land in the coastal areas cost £2 to £8 per acre, and the next year quotes per acre had raised to £12 for unimproved swampland. By the end of the decade the land prices had declined significantly. The highest price for confiscated loyalist land recorded in Georgia sold for £10 per acre for a tract of 2,500 acres. Information on the land prices in the upcountry has not been discovered.

Land allowed under the headright system was increased in early 1783 to 200 acres free, excluding administrative and survey fees, for the heads of families. In April 1783, some 500 families had moved in the previous six months to the backcountry of Georgia. It prompted a man from North Carolina to write, "Georgia must, I think, in a few years be one of the Richest States in the Union, and Where I've no doubt, you may live happy and secure a lasting and Valuable Estate for your self & family."[4]

At the end of the war, land was granted to officers who served in a military capacity. General Greene was granted 5,000 guineas, which was used to purchase the confiscated estate of former Lieutenant Governor John Graham, Mulberry Grove, located just outside Savannah. General Wayne took possession of Alexander Wright's estate. One hundred guineas was granted to every officer in the Georgia Continental Line, issued in certificates used to gain confiscated estates. Colonel Elijah Clarke, Lieutenant Colonel James Jackson and other militia and state officers were also granted estates.

Pensions were also granted to veterans of the war. Maimed veterans received an annual pension of £5 for the loss of an eye, £30 for the loss of both eyes or hands, and widows of veterans were granted £10 a year plus four shillings for each child under the age of 14. Disabled Continental and state officers living in Georgia were granted half pay at the recommendation of the Continental Congress, while troops received five dollars per month.[5]

The social order in Georgia was changing indeed. Now the "budding aristocracy and the established church were gone." The disestablishment of the Anglican Church in 1777 was an obvious change. After the war, organized religion was at a low ebb. But as the 1780s progressed, the Methodists and Baptists would become the leading religious denominations.

Education made more progress in the postwar era than religion. The Georgia Constitution of 1777 required that "Schools shall be erected in each county, and supported at the general expense of the state." Soon property was granted for schools. The Assembly laid out land at Augusta in lots to be sold and the proceeds used for a church and seminary of learning. One thousand acres of land in each county in Georgia was authorized for the establishment of free schools. In 1785, the University of Georgia was chartered with oversight of all publicly supported schools in the state. That same year, the Richmond Academy in Augusta, the oldest public school in Georgia, began operation in new buildings. Soon schools and academies were set up in the counties of Washington, Chatham, Lincoln and Glynn.

The push for a University of Georgia was spearheaded by two Yale-educated men from New England, Governor Lyman Hall and Abraham Baldwin. The assembly set up a university governing organization of seven trustees in 1784. In Baldwin's address to the trustees, he pointed out that there was no university south of Virginia and that it was inappropriate to send the state's children to foreign lands to be trained. Though there was considerable work at establishing the bold dream of the university in Georgia, it did not open for operations until 1801.

An important part of creating an enlightened people was through the freedom of the press. Near the end of the war, the only colonial newspaper editor in Georgia was on the list of confiscation and banishment, James Johnston. He was taken off the list in August of 1782, and six months later he reclaimed his printing equipment, secured a contract as the state printer, and brought out the first issue of the *Gazette of the State of Georgia* (later renamed the *Georgia Gazette*). Johnston was not a radical loyalist and his political beliefs never interfered with his journalistic treatment in the paper. In the summer of 1785, Greenberg Hughes started the second paper in Georgia, the *Augusta Gazette*.[6]

Georgia's social consciousness toward the poor was revealed after the war. It was necessary to have the state government procure and distribute food because the number of refugees and destruction the war had created. Postwar salt procurement was a special problem. By 1784, private agencies like the Savannah Philanthropic Organization, the Union Society, and others grew up. The care of orphan children continued to be a priority in Georgia.

Though there are no specific records of the medical activities of doctors in Savannah or elsewhere in Georgia after the war, there is ample reason to believe there was coverage during this period. The first recorded drugstore in Savannah, Bond & Company, was started in 1786 and sold medicines and compound physician prescriptions, along with medicine boxes for plantations and ships.

Life in Georgia was not all work after the war. Entertainment in Georgia consisted of a variety of activities. A local theater opened in 1783 and was staffed by local gentlemen who worked to bring actors and entertainers to Savannah. Tragedies and comedies were presented and some one-act plays. Prices ranged from three to five shillings per seat. From October 1783 to June 1784 there were nine plays using local actors in Savannah, of which seven were charity benefits.

Based on the number of liquor licenses in existence after the war, drinking of alcoholic beverages was a favorite pastime in Savannah. In the fall of 1785, a coffee house opened on the bay and advertised its hours to be from 7 A.M. to 9 P.M. daily, also serving breakfast, lunch and dinner. There were also music and dancing schools during this period in Savannah and Augusta. A Charles Francis Chevalier advertised a dancing and fencing school in Savannah in 1783.

Social clubs were also the order of the day. In Savannah, a hunting club with 21 charter members was established in December 1783. Every member had to furnish a beagle for use by the club and a horse for himself. At the meetings, held every second Saturday of the month, bread, beef or ham and a case of liquor were provided by the club. Fraternal orders were another form of social interaction. The Masonic order flourished and by 1787 there were six lodges in the state. Annual meetings of the order were held in Savannah with celebrations held on all saints days and especially St. John's Day. These celebration days involved a trip to church, followed by dinner and conversation. The fraternal order of the Georgia Society of Cincinnati was organized in August of 1783 with General Lachlan McIntosh as its first president. In 1789 General Anthony Wayne took McIntosh's place as president. Their quarterly meetings were in Savannah or Augusta and consisted of a dinner with numerous toasts and drinking.

Certainly most social life was not recorded in newspapers or personal letters of the day. There were private parties, dinners, literary and musical sessions, horse races, and the usual fun events of a somewhat frontier environment. Over time, new celebration days replaced those British celebrations of old. As time moved on, the major changes in the entertainment were associated with commercial recreation resulting from the increased population.[7]

The first 50 years in colonial Georgia were the most profound, and perhaps the most unique, among all the 13 original colonies. When the founding settlers landed at Savannah in February of 1733, the first permanent English colony on the banks of the James River in Virginia had already been established for 126 years. No other British colony moved from founding to realizing independence in such a short period of only 50 years.

From the dream of Oglethorpe, the founder, to the reality of conflict in 1776, the overall objectives of Georgia Charter and the Crown Province had been accomplished even though it had not come without much strife, some deaths, hard work, administrative failures, military effort and money. The settlers had indeed come and started a life for their families "by cultivating the lands at present waste and desolate." They had been able to "increase the trade, navigation, and wealth," had fought off "the neighbouring savages," and had been able to "protect all our loving subjects" in South Carolina. It was true that they had "settled and established in the southern territories of Carolina" a new colony called Georgia.[8]

Oglethorpe's passion for establishing a place in the New World to settle those from debtors prison yielded the first and only altruistic colony in the history of the world. Yet history has given James Oglethorpe mixed reviews about the results of his colonial experiment. Some saw Oglethorpe's dream as a genuine failure, while others saw it as a grand attempt to establish an ideal and wholesome community environment without the evils of slavery or liquor. Though his efforts were without question noble, even as Oglethorpe fought off the Spanish and held the Indians at bay, the economic decline of the 1740s left the colony crippled. Even before Oglethorpe saw his last Georgia sky in July of 1743 with his final sailing to England, the course toward decline was in evidence. Prosperity and growth in South Carolina and Charles Town in those days was in such stark contrast to neighboring Georgia, many settlers departed Georgia for greener pastures over the border. Who would have believed that after 20 years of settlement from the founding, by 1753 the population of Georgia would have been only 2,381 whites and 1,066 blacks?

As the Trustees' charter was surrendered in May 1752, and Georgia became a royal province, life in the southernmost colony slowly began to improve. By the time the second and successful royal governor, Henry Ellis, had sailed back to London in November 1760, the economic growth in Georgia had been revived, as trade flourished and the population of the province had more than doubled to 7,000 souls.

Georgia was a flourishing colony as the royal period continued. The colonists planted rice, indigo, corn, peas, tobacco, wheat and rye. With forests in abundance, many sawed lumber, made pitch, tar, turpentine, shingles and staves. Cattle, mules, horses and hogs were raised. Deer and beaver skins were obtained mostly from the Indians. As evidence of the economic growth, in 1755 Georgia filled 52 ships with products for foreign ports valued at £15,744. By 1773, the exports filled 225 ships that sailed away with £121,677 in goods. To Europe, the ships sailed with rice, indigo, and skins, and to the West Indies with lumber, horses and provisions.[9]

Perhaps the royal governors had done more in Georgia by contributing to the establishment of a relatively stable government under English law. In a publication available in 1783 titled *A View of the Constitution of the British Colonies*, authored by Anthony Stokes, the chief justice of Georgia under the royal administration, the case for that very royal government was made:

> Georgia continued under the King's Government to be one of the most free and happy countries in the world — justice was regularly and impartially administered — oppression was unknown — taxes levied on the subjects were trifling — and every man that had industry, became opulent — the people there were more particularly indebted to the Crown, than those of any other Colony — immense sums were expended by Government in settling and protecting that country — troops of rangers were kept up by the Crown for several years — Civil Government was annually provided for by vote of the House of Commons in Great Britain, and most of the inhabitants owed every acre of land they had to the King's gift: in short, there was scarce a man in the Province that did not lie under particular obligation to the Crown.[10]

Though the events that pushed Georgia into the American Revolution would sour the royal success, there is much that can be said for Stokes' account. Regardless, the royal period was a success story for Georgia. Though somewhat slow to join their fellow patriots in the other colonies against the British, the fact that Georgia's leadership made any move toward independence was in some measure a testament to that royal success.

With the 15-year period of leadership and solid governmental oversight by the third and last royal governor, Sir James Wright, Georgia had developed into a good place to live and prosper. Through the legacy of success of the legislative institutions in Georgia, and the confidence it gave the leaders of the province, the ultimate move toward independence was possible. Though the American Revolution had taken a toll on the state and its people, the aftermath would set the stage for a new legacy of economic advancement and successful government that would yield what we see today in the latter decades of the third century of its creation.

To the singing of *He Comes, the Hero Comes* and the cheers of the citizens, on May 12, 1791, President George Washington stepped onto the wharf to start a four-day visit to the capital city of the state of Georgia, Savannah. The distinguished visitor was met by the official greeting party of the old Liberty Boys — Joseph Habersham, Noble W. Jones, John Houstoun, Joseph Clay and Lachlan McIntosh, along with Anthony Wayne, James Jackson and the mayor of Savannah, Thomas Gibbons. From his gala parade, followed by a dinner with 15 toasts at Brown's Coffee House on Bay Street, to his last parting event, Washington offered a clear interest in all that had happened during the war. It was a fitting end to an era—from founding to a respected southern state in a new United States of America.

Though he was laid to rest in an obscure grave in Essex, England, certainly the success of Georgia today is a living memorial to all that James Edward Oglethorpe dreamed of. Great civilization is possible only with the efforts and sacrifices of great leaders. Thankfully, colonial Georgia had such men during its first 50 years.

Selected Biographies

After the American Revolution, those most prominent men who had influenced the destiny of Georgia moved on to changed lives and new roles throughout the world.

Thomas Browne

Defeated in May 1782 by Anthony Wayne, Browne, who was fiercely hated by the colonists, escaped and lived out his life in the British West Indies.[11]

Archibald Campbell

After the capture of Savannah and his attempt at holding Augusta, Archibald Campbell turned his command over to Lt. Colonel Mark Prevost. On March 12, 1779, he sailed back to England as a hero as the king promoted him to full colonel for his "judicious and gallant conduct."

After taking some time off, he married Amelia Ramsey. Returning to the army, Campbell was sent to Jamaica as the lieutenant governor in July 1781. There he participated in two successful actions against the Spanish. Promoted to major general the next year, he was also appointed to be the king's aide.

In Jamaica Campbell took steps to improve the island's defences to repulse any French attack. He raised a militia, supported the training of British recruits and took every measure he could to provide intelligence and support to British operations in the West Indies. He made a significant contribution of his most skilled marines in the successful fleet action of Admiral Rodney against French Admiral de Grasses off Saints Passage in April 1782. For his outstanding support in the Caribbean, Campbell was knighted by King George III on September 30, 1785.

Campbell stayed in Jamaica as the military governor until 1784 and then returned to England to a new assignment as the governor of Madras. Named commander in chief of Madras in 1786, Campbell set out to reorganize the forces of the East India Company in India. He was instrumental in trying to resolve a dispute over the debts of the nabob of Ascot. After a treaty he brokered was ultimately rejected by the board of directors, Campbell resigned his command in 1787. Staying in India for two more years writing military training manuals and training troops, he took command of the 74th Highlanders.

Campbell returned to England in 1789 and was reelected to serve as member of Parliament for Stirling Burgh. By this time in his life, the strain of his active career of service had taken its toll on his health. He died at age 52. The inscription on his tomb at Westminster Abby reads, "He died in 1791, regretted and admired for his eminent civil and military services to his country. He was possessed of distinguished endowments of mind, inflexible integrity, unfeigned benevolence, with every social and amiable virtue."

Archibald Campbell was one of the rare British commanders in the American Revolution who increased his reputation as a result of the war. He was remembered for his bold courage, leadership skills and superior tactics.[12]

Elijah Clarke

After the Revolution, Elijah Clarke was granted an estate by county and state authorities of Georgia. He then took off in a series of dubious adventures. He negotiated with the Indians and later fought against them, defeating them at Jack's Creek in Walton County. In 1793, he entered the service of France as a major general with a salary of $10,000 in planning actions against the Spanish. In 1794, he established the TransOconee State across the Oconee River in Creek territory with Georgia volunteers. President Washington ended the action, but later Clarke was suspected of continued involvement in designs against West Florida and the Yazoo Land Fraud deal. He died at age 66 in Wilkes County, a popular hero, on January 15, 1799.[13]

Samuel Elbert

Colonel Samuel Elbert was held prisoner until the fall of Charles Town when he was exchanged and went to the North to offer his services to General Washington. At Yorktown, he was in command of the Grand Deposit of Arms and Military Stores. In recognition of his military service, Elbert was promoted by the state of Georgia to the rank of major general and became a brevet brigadier general in the Continental Army. After the end of the war, he returned to his commercial pursuits.

Elbert became governor of Georgia in 1785 and was able to run a "clean, energetic and business-like" administration marked by the passage of the bill creating the state university. After serving as governor, he was elected sheriff of Chatham County in Savannah. He died on November 2, 1788, at age 48 with honors of all the military of Savannah, the Masonic Lodge and the Society of Cincinnati in attendance at his funeral. He was buried at the private cemetery of the Rae family, located just outside Savannah.[14]

Henry Ellis

Even before Ellis arrived in London from his return trip in stormy weather from Georgia via New York, Lord Halifax had assigned him to the governorship of Nova Scotia. Halifax hoped to reward Ellis, for he needed a man with good administrative skills who could transform French Arcadia to British Nova Scotia. On June 26, 1760, Ellis asked the secretary of state William Pitt, for a year's leave of absence. He reasoned that he had been back in England for only a month, his health was "far from being established," and he needed to settle certain matters before he sailed to his new assignment.

Ellis extended his leave of absence in 1762 even though his health had improved as a frequent visitor to Bath. By this time Ellis had become indispensable to Pitt's replacement. Since it was critical that a governor be in Nova Scotia, Ellis resigned, naming Lieutenant Governor Montague Wilmot as governor on October 23, 1763. When Pitt resigned in October 1761, the position was offered to George Grenville, but he recommended his brother-in-law, Charles Wyndham, Lord Egremont. Ellis served as Egremont's consultant on all matters of colonial and international affairs.

To provide an income to Ellis, Egremont allowed Ellis a choice of offices. Ellis chose a combination of small offices in Canada: secretary of the province, clerk of council, commissary general, and clerk of enrollments for registering deeds and conveyances. Ellis received a total stipend of £1,012 annually for life. Ellis now made more than a royal governor. In April 1763, Egremont gave Ellis the positions of provost marshall and marshall of the admiralty for Granada, St. Vincent, Dominica and Tobago with the £1,650 annual salary.

Ellis influenced the course of American history in his most unique role as advisor. He helped to see to it that governments were established in Canada, in the two Floridas, and in the West Indies. Nova Scotia was enlarged with Cape Breton and Prince Edward Island, and new boundaries were set in Florida and Georgia. An Indian reserve was established with a new trading policy. French Orleans became Spanish; and the Mississippi and Iberville rivers became the southern limits of British North America.[15]

Ellis served Egremont successfully because his lordship needed a man like Ellis with background knowledge and creative ideas in formulating foreign policy. Ellis likewise needed a man like Egremont to translate his ideas into actual policy. It was in this mutual relationship that Ellis and Lord Egremont were able to achieve so much together, culminating in the Proclamation of 1763, which defined the boundaries of the postwar North America.

At 8 P.M. on August 20, 1763, Egremont died of a stroke of apoplexy from overindulgence at Egremont House on Piccadilly. With his unexpected death, Ellis was prepared to assist Lord Halifax as vigorously as he had Egremont. But Halifax was not the kind of secretary that inspired a man like Ellis. Without a patron interested in policy, Ellis could not influence events. Ellis soon commented to William Knox that "I already begin to feel the insignificance of an idle man." Ellis stopped taking an active interest in debates over American policy.[16]

In 1768, Henry Ellis left public service and became a gentleman of the world. As a reputed expert on the New World to the British powerful, a former governor twice over, a membership in the Royal Society of scientists and a man of wealth, Ellis was prepared for his new role. His poor health caused him to visit resorts like Bath and Tunbridge Wells where he visited with his friends and fellow aristocrats. When he suffered with "rheumatic complaints" Ellis began to spend less time in England and more time in summer places. In the 1780s he spent the winters in Marseilles. The 1790s saw him, likewise, in Pisa, and after that, winters were in Naples. He had a special carriage built in Brussels to travel between there and Marseilles, and to Pisa.

As a gentleman elite, Ellis enjoyed his life in retirement. In a book describing famous contemporaries, it was written that he was "a rich old bachelor, one of the greatest humourists I ever knew." In his travels in France, Ellis visited such renowned men as Tissot and Voltaire. His dinners in Marseilles were famous for he had rare boar from Algiers, wines from Greece, liqueurs from Trieste and Venice, and tea from his friends the Twinings of London. Ellis was a great entertainer, a man with "uncommon talents" for socializing.

With his travel routine passing like a bird from London or Bath in the summer, Marseilles or Pisa in the winter, and Spa in the spring, Ellis was one to "give prudent and proper lessons to genteel travelers." One of his friends wrote him in Marseille: "Since your departure a fortnight ago, we have lived in the greatest loneliness. Comforts of every kind are gone with you. No cheerful morning teas, no friendly and pleasing dinners, no social evenings have taken place, much less enlightened, gay and sprightly conversation." In 1780,

Ellis wrote to Knox that his status as a celebrity was becoming inconvenient. While visiting at Spa, the king of Sweden asked to be introduced to the famous Governor Ellis. He met with the king in a large hall with a raised platform overlooking 150 guests.

In a letter to a friend in 1796, Ellis wrote from Pisa: "I enjoy a kind of still life here in a good climate and tolerable good society which at my years is all I ought in reason to expect." Ellis lived his good life funded by his governor's pension and supplemented by his Irish estates he inherited from his father who died in June of 1776.[17]

The coach trips between Spa and Marseilles ended in 1789 with the French Revolution. For safety, Ellis moved to northern Italy until the French Army invaded Tuscany. He then moved to Naples and became involved in one of the greatest dramas in British history. The British colony at Naples focused around King Ferdinand and Queen Maria Carolina. These rulers were expectedly nervous because of the beheadings of Louis XVI and Marie Antoinette at the hands of the revolutionaries and were seeking the protection of the British. Ellis would become acquainted with Lord Horatio Nelson in Naples and Sicily as the great British naval hero won the Battle of the Nile. Nelson also had an affair with Emma Hamilton, the second wife of the British minister to the Kingdom of Two Sicilies, Sir William Hamilton.

In Naples on July 26, 1805, there was a violent earthquake and Vesuvius thrust out mounds of lava. Ellis suffered a bad fall and had a paralytic stroke that prevented him from speaking for several weeks. He recovered by September but died the following January 21, 1806, in the eighty-fifth year of life. Ellis was generous in his will, leaving a lifetime annuity from the rents on his Irish estates, and £10,000 to his primary beneficiary, nephew Francis; £2,000 to Francis's brother, Henry; and £2,000 to each unmarried niece. Among other smaller distributions, his estate provided £3,000 for the Monaghan Hospital and a like sum to the poor fund of the county.[18]

Ellis was a unique man of his day. He was a man of letters, an explorer, a scientist, and leader of two colonies. He was overlooked by history even though he did more than any other royal governor to influence British American policy.[19]

Charles Henri d'Estaing

Comte Charles Hector Theodat d'Estaing returned to France in 1780, and in 1783 at Cadiz he was involved in organizing fleet operations for the West Indies when the war ended. He was elected to the Assembly of Notables in 1787 when he returned to France. He was made commandant of the National Guard at Versailles when the French Revolution broke out in 1789. In 1792, he was promoted to admiral. Though he was in favor of reforms, he continued to support the king and defended Marie Antoinette. For his actions, he was tried and was guillotined in Paris during the Terror on April 28, 1794.

The Georgia General Assembly was so impressed with the service given to their cause that it granted 20,000 acres of land to Admiral d'Estaing and gave "him all privileges, liberties and immunities of a free citizen of the State."[20]

John Habersham

Major Habersham worked with Lieutenant James Jackson under General Greene to maintain the town of Savannah after the British evacuation. In 1784, he was elected as the president of the Executive Council. During the period 1785–1786, he was a member of the

Continental Congress and in October of 1786 was chairman of the commission appointed by Georgia to make a treaty with the Indians at Shoulder Bone Creek in Hancock County. He successfully negotiated with the 59 chiefs and warriors of the Creek nation to resolve various boundary issues. In 1787, Habersham was appointed as one of the commissioners from Georgia to settle the dispute of the boundary between Georgia and South Carolina. That year he also married Ann Sarah Camber and together they had seven children.

Residing in Savannah after the war, he was elected to the first Board of Trustees of the state university and in 1789 was appointed to be the collector of the Port of Savannah. He died a respected patriot and public-spirited man of character on November 19, 1799, at age 45.[21]

Joseph Habersham

After the war, Joseph was elected to the General Assembly of Georgia and twice served as the speaker of the House. He was a delegate to the Continental Congress in 1785–1786 and in 1788 became a member of the convention that ratified the Federal Constitution. He served as a member of the Savannah City Council in 1790–1791 and in 1792 was elected to be the mayor. In 1795, Habersham was appointed as the postmaster general of the United States.

After service in the cabinet, he was (1802–15) president of the Georgia branch of the Bank of the United States in Savannah. He died on November 17, 1815. Habersham had married Isabella Rae of Branton Plantation near Savannah. They had ten children.[22]

Robert Howe

Ordered to return to Washington's forces after relinquishing the Southern Command to Benjamin Lincoln, General Howe departed Charles Town on March 18, 1779, and headed north. Moving through Baltimore on April 23, he arrived in Philadelphia three days later. After debriefing the Continental Congress over the sad circumstances of his former command, Howe soon joined Washington's army in their winter quarters near Middlebrooke, New Jersey.

With some 6,000 troops, Clinton left New York City on May 30 and began to move up the Hudson River valley. His purpose was to push the rebels away from their fortifications and split the American colonies, thereby cutting communications between New England and the Middle colonies. Washington moved his forces to the Highland area around West Point and set up his headquarters at New Windsor on the west bank of the Hudson. Howe supported numerous operations against the British around New York for Washington as one of his division commanders throughout 1779 and 1780. Howe shared Washington's low risk strategy against the British. Howe once wrote, "I am from nature devoted to enterprise, but rashness is my utter aversion, all conformable to the first I shall do, all dictated by the latter renounce."[23]

Howe served as the president of the court-martial of Major General Benedict Arnold, which ended January 26, 1780. He also headed up the force that put down the mutiny in the Pennsylvania and New Jersey Continental regiments. For his latter service, Howe was given great praise for his work by the commander in chief. Howe took an extended leave in Rhode Island, Massachusetts and New Hampshire during the spring of 1781 and did not return to West Point until early June. Washington then placed Howe in command of the Highland defenses.

As Washington's forces settled around a planned offensive against New York, word came that a French fleet under Comte de Frasse had departed the West Indies for the Chesapeake. Unfortunately for Howe, Washington gave the command of the Virginia Campaign to attack Lord Cornwallis in Virginia to General Benjamin Lincoln. Having obtained a verbal understanding with Washington that he would be able to accompany any operation into the South, Howe was upset when he was left behind with the explanation from Washington that "the matter turned up merely from the common routine of duty." Lincoln had seniority over Howe and, thus, with Washington participated in the victory over Cornwallis at Yorktown on October 18, 1781.

To add insult to injury, Howe was ordered to attend his court-martial at City Tavern in Philadelphia at 10 A.M. on December 7 to answer charges from Georgia delegates for his conduct during the surrender of Savannah in 1778. Howe was acquitted in January with "highest honors."[24]

Howe remained with the army as fighting ended. In June 1783 Howe was again called on to lead a detachment and marched against a group of Pennsylvania troops who were mad over the failure of Congress to "redress their grievances." The resistance collapsed and Howe set up his command in Philadelphia at the request of Congress.

After the Continental Army disbanded in late 1783, Howe returned to his Kendall Plantation. His finances were in disrepair to the extent that he had to mortgage his plantation. He received some funds from Congress that helped him recover some level of prosperity. He was received in North Carolina with honor and celebration, and a week of parties. Howe then slowly made the transition from soldier to planter. His major focus was in replanting his rice fields that bordered the Cape Fear River. He also took part in local affairs including the project to build a lighthouse on Bald Head Island at the entrance to the Cape Fear.

In 1786 Howe ran for a spot in the North Carolina General Assembly from Brunswick County. He took a liberal position against prominent conservative lawyers over the treatment of former loyalists. By campaigning hard for support, Howe was victorious in the election, but unfortunately came down with bilious fever. After a short period recovering he decided to travel to Fayetteville to the opening session of the General Assembly scheduled for November 20 to assume his duties. Traveling upriver and stopping at the home of Brigadier General Thomas Clark at Point Repose Plantation near Hood's Creek, Howe had a relapse of the fever and died on December 14, 1786. Howe's burial site has never been confirmed.[25]

John Houstoun

In 1784, John was elected governor of Georgia for the second time. He was named a member of the Board of Trustees of the state university. In 1786, he became the chief justice of the state. The following year, with Major John Habersham and General Lachlan McIntosh, he was elected to settle the boundary disputes with South Carolina and Georgia. In 1787, he was the justice of Chatham County. In 1790, he was elected mayor of Savannah and in 1792 became the judge of the Superior Court of the Eastern Circuit of Georgia. Houstoun died at the old family home at White Bluff on July 20, 1796.[26]

James Jackson

He was the first American soldier to enter the town of Savannah with the evacuation of the British. After the war he went back into his law practice. In 1785, he married Mary Charlotte Young and they had four children who gained considerable success in state and federal government. He was elected to the state legislature from Chatham County and in 1786 he was made brigadier general, grand master of the Grand Lodge of Masons of Georgia and an honorary member of the Society of Cincinnati. In January 1788, at age 30, he became governor of Georgia, which he declined modestly because of his age. He was engaged in military operations against the Creek Indians and in 1789 he was elected to the Senate. He served as governor of Georgia from 1798 to 1801 and was elected as a Republican to the United States Senate. He died in Washington, D.C., March 19, 1806, and is interment in the Congressional Cemetery.[27]

Nobel Wimberly Jones

Jones was captured in the fall of Charles Town in 1780 and was a prisoner at St. Augustine until he was released on an exchange the next year in a transfer to Philadelphia. There he practiced medicine under Dr. Benjamin Rush and served as a Georgia delegate to the Continental Congress until 1782. That year he returned to Savannah and his practice and in 1783 was elected as the speaker of the House of Assembly. In that role Jones was injured with a sword wound putting down a disorderly mob. He resigned his position and moved to Charles Town for five years.

Returning to Savannah in 1788, Jones supervised the celebrations associated with the visit of President George Washington in 1791. In 1795 he also officiated over the convention to amend the Georgia Constitution of 1789. In 1804 Jones helped create the Georgia Medical Society and served as its first president. Though in poor health, Jones continued to practice medicine in Savannah until his death on January 9, 1805. He is buried in Bonaventure Cemetery.[28]

Benjamin Lincoln

Benjamin Lincoln became the secretary of war in 1781 and in 1788 served as lieutenant governor of Massachusetts. He was the collector for the port of Boston from 1789 to 1809. At age 77 on May 9, 1810, Lincoln died at his homestead in Hingham, Massachusetts. Two days later in Boston, bells rang out for an hour and flags in the harbor were at half mast. His funeral was at the Hingham meetinghouse before a large crowd of friends, local citizens and dignitaries. His honorary pallbearers were John Adams, Robert Treat Paine, Cotton Tufts and Thomas Melville. The governor of Massachusetts, Christopher Gore, attended as the members of the Society of Cincinnati had their left arms draped with black crepe in tribute to their late president. The day after Lincoln died, the *Boston Gazette* printed a testimony to the fallen leader: "The death of General Lincoln is not common misfortune. His great revolutionary services; his irreproachable moral character; his incorruptible integrity; and the solidity of his political sentiments, conspire to render his loss, a public calamity."[29]

John Maitland

On October 25, 1779, the brave and resourceful Lieutenant Colonel John Maitland of the 71st British Scots Regiment, and a member of the House of Commons, died suddenly at Savannah from convulsions from excessive drinking, one of his bad habits.[30]

Lachlan McIntosh

General Lachlan McIntosh was held by the British as a prisoner of war as a result of the surrender of patriot forces at the Siege of Charles Town. After he was released he moved to Virginia with his family. He remained in Virginia until the British vacated Savannah in 1782. His estate in Georgia was in poor condition upon his return and for the rest of his life he remained under some financial strain.

McIntosh was promoted to major general in 1783, joined the Society of the Cincinnati the next year and was elected to serve in Congress. McIntosh died in Savannah at age 79 on February 20, 1806. He is buried in the Colonial Cemetery in Savannah.[31]

James Edward Oglethorpe

When Oglethorpe sailed away from Georgia on July 22, 1743, for the last time, he did not know it but it would be represent the apex in his career and in his life. The 60-day voyage was a pleasant and tranquil experience aboard the *Success*. The day he landed in England on September 28, he was rested and only 46 years old. Immediately after landing, he hurried to South Carolina governor James Glen's residence to demand a retraction and apology for Glen's outspoken and public criticism of Oglethorpe's expedition to St. Augustine.

After confronting his detractor, Oglethorpe settled down at Westbrook and in London for the next six weeks. Soon Parliament was pondering the evidence concerning the monies Oglethorpe claimed he had spent in the interest of Georgia from September 1738 to 1743. While his colleagues were deciding Oglethorpe's financial fate, military officials called on him to help them handle the pending invasion of the Young Pretender, Bonnie Prince Charles, and his forces. Oglethorpe was asked to prepare to defend the realm. He was formally commissioned to raise a regiment of Hussars to aid in defending his German sovereign against the army of the Stuarts.

On March 21, 1744, the House of Commons referred the estimates of Oglethorpe's expenses to the Committee of the Whole. The next day, Oglethorpe was awarded £66,109 and some change "on Account of extraordinary Services incurred in Georgia ... and not provided for by Parliament." For Oglethorpe, this meant that he would receive an immediate and full refund for his expenses in Georgia.

As the House of Commons debated the funding for the mercenary troops from Germany, they were insistent that better intelligence be gained about the anticipated sailing of the French invasion fleet of the Young Pretender. At a time when it was high treason to hold correspondence with the Pretender's sons, the Commons debated the suspension of habeas corpus in an attempt to deal with the chaos that an invasion would bring.[32]

The issue of a trial to answer the 19 formal charges leveled by Lieutenant Colonel William Cooke against his commander as the second in command of his regiment in Georgia was about to start. The most significant charge had been that Oglethorpe had habitually defrauded his men "by making them pay for the provisions the Government sent them over gratis." The hearing that was held in June came down to whether they should believe a lieutenant colonel or a brigadier general. After a few hours of discussion, Lord Mark Kerr and seven generals ruled that the article of complaint was "either frivolous, vexatious, or malicious, and without foundation." The report of the military body also recommended the dismissal of Cooke.

Oglethorpe was delighted to have the cloud over his life removed, but he was impatient to take action on his military assignment. He was also ready to clear up the rumors that always surrounded him regarding his bachelor state. In London, stories surfaced that Oglethorpe was interested in marrying a wealthy bride, Lady Elizabeth Sambrooke. In fact, he had become interested in a woman of lower station of childbearing age. His fancy was for Elizabeth Wright, the daughter of a baronet. She was not poor and actually had an annual income of £1,500, which was substantially more than Oglethorpe's. She also stood to inherit the fine estate of her bachelor brother.

Oglethorpe was married to Elizabeth Wright in the King Henry VII Chapel at Westminster Abbey on September 15, 1744. Six months later, he was promoted to major general just as the opportunity to command men again surfaced. Bonnie Prince Charles's troops landed at Scotland and were preparing to attack England's heartland. Oglethorpe's regiment was ordered to Yorkshire to help repel the invaders.

In December 1745, the first significant bloodshed of the uprising occurred, known in Britain as The Forty-Five. Soon Charles was defeated and retreating. Oglethorpe's troops were in a position to hamper the retreat, but they did not. The end of Charles Stuart's invasion was at the battle of Culloden, Scotland, on April 16, 1746. There the Hanoverian forces defeated the invaders. Never again would a Stuart offer a serious military threat to the stability of England. In the battle, the commander, the third son of King, George II the Duke of Cumberland, was not satisfied with victory as he slaughtered Highlanders on the field and became known as the "Butcher."

Cumberland came to accuse Oglethorpe for his strange indecisiveness that seemed to be confirmed when his half-hearted pursuit allowed Bonnie Prince Charlie's retreating army to escape near Penrith. As a well-placed former Jacobite with clear family history of support, Oglethorpe was ripe for suspicion. He went to court-martial on September 1746 charged with "having disobey'd or neglected his orders." In spite of the Duke of Cumberland's great influence, Oglethorpe was acquitted, but his reputation would never recover. Although Oglethorpe was promoted to lieutenant general in 1747, and to full general in 1765, he was never again allowed to serve on the active list. For years in his old age he was the senior ranking officer in the British Army living as a "half-pay general."[33]

Oglethorpe played no role in the final activities of the Georgia Trustees. He did not attend sessions of the common council of the Trust after January 19, 1749, and attended his last session that March 16. He wanted no part of the changes that were voted in to transform the colony to one that he had strived to prevent.

As the years came Oglethorpe's life became ever more inactive and frustrating. At the marriage of Elizabeth Wright, he added her country seat at Cranham Hall in Essex to his at Westbrook in Godalming. In 1752, he lost his seat in Parliament from Haslemere and afterward had little to do. He was elected as a Fellow of the Royal Society because he was thought to be "well versed in Natural History, mathematics and all branches of polite literature." Later he was expelled for not paying his subscription fees. He played a central role in founding the British Museum in 1753 with his spirited support of a national lottery to raise funds, but because of the jealousy of some of his colleagues, he was not made a Trustee.[34]

When the Seven Years' War (French and Indian War) broke out in 1756, the English government refused to give Oglethorpe any military command, so Oglethorpe took an extraordinary action by going off incognito to join the forces of Britain's ally, Frederick the Great of Prussia. He was able to do this because of his acquaintance with the Jacobite soldier of fortune, James Keith, whom he had met as a young man at the Paris Academy and who had ended up a field marshal in the Prussian army. Oglethorpe served under various false names and was apparently known to Frederick the Great as "Jacques Rosbif." At the Battle of Hochkirch in 1758, it was said that it was into Oglethorpe's arms that Field-Marshal Keith fell when shot dead from his horse.

In 1761, Oglethorpe returned to England still hoping to get back into politics. He vainly courted the prime minister, the Earl of Bute, and wrote letters to William Pitt to no avail. In 1768, he made a last and unsuccessful attempt to regain his Parliamentary seat at Haslemere. Mostly he kept up some of his humanitarian interests and spent time writing letters to the newspapers.[35]

When the American Revolution began, Oglethorpe showed a strong sympathy with the colonists and supported a peace plan designed to keep the Americans in the empire by giving them full rights as Englishmen. After the war on June 1, 1785, King George III formally received John Adams as the first ambassador to the Court of St. James's from the United States of America. Three days later, Oglethorpe, at age 88, called on Adams with a sincere welcome. Oglethorpe's courtesy to Adams was a milestone in British history, and one that Edmund Burke called one the most thrilling of that century.[36]

Though he lived a more reduced life than he desired as an old aristocrat, Oglethorpe became a most interesting and lively conversationalist. He became a patron of the literary circle that revolved around Samuel Johnson when he subscribed to his poem called "London." In 1768, he startled the young 28-year-old James Boswell by calling unannounced to say how much he admired his recently published *Account of Corsica* by announcing, "My name, Sir, is Oglethorpe, and I wish to be acquainted with you."

Oglethorpe regularly had Boswell, Johnson and the writer Oliver Goldsmith to dinner. On one occasion, Goldsmith sang them Tony Lumpkin's song "Three Jolly Pigeons" from his new play, *She Stoops to Conquer*. In this company, Oglethorpe met David Garrick, the actor, and Sir Joshua Reynolds, who later painted his portrait. Boswell greatly admired Oglethorpe's "vivacity of mind: "In his society I never failed to enjoy learned and animated conversation."

As the 1780s arrived, Oglethorpe had become quite the figure on the London literary scene, and, likewise, a success with the women. To the ladies he was a gallant old world leader. In London and at his estate in Westbrook, he was a man to know. One to whom he talked politics with often, Edmund Burke, thought Oglethorpe to be a most extraordinary man: "for that he founded the province of Georgia; had absolutely called it into existence, and had lived to see it severed from the empire which created it, and become an independent state." Despite the death of his companion, Samuel Johnson, in 1784, Oglethorpe lived a vigorous existence during the last two years of his life. With Goldsmith and Johnson gone, he became a close friend and admirer of Hannah More, who was a poetess. She once told her sister that Oglethorpe was "quite a preux chevalier, heroic, romantic, and full of gallantry."[37]

Always able to endure great physical hardships, Oglethorpe was a very spry man for his old age. By lifelong habit he had always gotten out of bed and exercised on the floor. Horace Walpole called him "alert, upright, [with his] eyes, ears, and memory fresh." Though at age 88 he had no teeth, he could read a book without wearing glasses. He always had a great zest for life and incredibly, only a month before he died he wrote excitedly to Boswell to reveal that he had two tickets for an ascent by Lunardi, the Italian balloonist.

Oglethorpe as a personality presents a most complex array of characteristics. He was vain, quarrelsome, hot-tempered, and at times quite violent. His ideals were honorable and he fought to make them true. In 1722 he wrote, "An untarnished reputation is dearer to every honest man than life." In discussion with Johnson and Goldsmith some 50 years later, Oglethorpe declared, "a man had a right to defend his honour." He was also one of the most benevolent, generous, and compassionate Englishmen in history.

Nothing that Oglethorpe ever did was perhaps more remarkable than his prohibition of black slavery in the new colony of Georgia. It happened 130 years before its abolition in America. Oglethorpe was against slavery primarily on moral grounds, for he denounced it as an "abominable and destructive custom." In 1732, he had intervened to rescue an educated slave who had escaped from Maryland and personally paid for him to be returned to Gambia. To the Trustees, Oglethorpe declared that to allow slavery would "occasion the misery of thousands in Africa." He said, "If we allow slaves, we act against the very principles by which we associated together, which was to relieve the distressed."[38]

Oglethorpe's contributions to Georgia were its founding, its settlement, its protection and its leadership. He kept the Spanish at bay and attempted to guide the province to the idealistic and passionate pursuit of peasant proprietorship, silk and wine production, with no slaves or rum, and a government with paternalistic qualities. James Edward Oglethorpe died on June 30, 1785, at his wife's estate and was buried at the Parish Church of All Saints, Cranham Hall in Upminster, Essex, about 30 miles from the heart of London. His wife, Elizabeth, was buried beside her husband at her death two years later. They had no children. The burial site was neglected and for decades lost, but in 1923 the president of Oglethorpe University, Thornwell Jacobs, rediscovered it.[39]

There is no great monument to mark the final resting place of the most important man in the history of Georgia — only a bronze plaque and a tablet on the wall.[40] The real monument to the career of James Edward Oglethorpe is the living legacy of Georgia today and the inspiration that such a man really existed. A rare, confident and proud man with a zest for life, and on a mission to make the world a better place.

In July of 1743, the month that Oglethorpe planned to sail away from the New World he helped to create in Georgia, a severe thunderstorm raged in Savannah. On the 3rd of July a bolt of lightning "Shattered our Flag Staff into Small pieces," as William Stephens observed. A week later, as Oglethorpe was preparing to leave, another lightning strike blasted two of the trees left standing on the bluff where the founder had originally landed and where he had "pitched his tent." According to Stephens the trees had remained "as a Standing Monument" to Oglethorpe and the act of settlement, but now they were gone.[41]

Andrew Pickens

For his contribution to the patriot victory at Cowpens the Continental Congress awarded him a sword, and was promoted by the State of South Carolina to brigadier general. After the Revolution Pickens purchased land and built his home, Hopewell, on the Keowee River on the South Carolina frontier. He served as the representative for Ninety-Six in the State House of Representatives from 1781 until 1794. In 1787 he served as one of the commissioners named to settle the boundary conflict between Georgia and South Carolina.

Pickens participated in the State constitutional convention in 1790, and served in the Third Congress from 1793 to 1795. In 1795 he was promoted to major general of the State militia. He ran for a United States Senate seat in 1797, but was unsuccessful. From 1800 to 1812 Pickens served in the State house of representatives. He died suddenly on August 11, 1817 at Tomassee in the Pendleton District of South Carolina, and was buried in the Old Stone Churchyard near Pendleton, South Carolina. The county of Pickens was named in his honor in 1826.[42]

Augustine Prevost

After the siege of Savannah, General Prevost sailed back to England, where he died in 1786. Augustine was a skillful professional soldier who found himself fighting less-experienced leaders in the southern theater. He was one among other distinguished Swiss expatriates, including Bouquet, Haldiman, Meuron, and Watteville, who won fame in service to Britain in North America.[43]

John Reynolds

John Reynolds sailed from Georgia in February of 1757, but en route to London his ship, the *Charming Martha*, was taken by a French privateer. He was taken to the port of Bayonne where he was treated with some courtesy, but his journal and all his papers were taken from him. When he finally did reach England on July 7, he found himself a hostage to the Board of Trade as he awaited their review. The board finally informed Reynolds of various charges against him on March 8, 1758. The board heard Reynolds's lengthy response to the charges on April 17, but it had no impact on the ultimate decision, for Lord Halifax had already made up his mind to replace Reynolds.[44]

Reynolds resumed his career with his old post in the Royal Navy, and advanced up the longevity ladder. Just before the outbreak of the American Revolution, Reynolds was promoted to rear admiral. He became a full admiral in 1787 at age 74, even though he was incapacitated by a stroke. A year after that promotion, on February 3, 1788, he died in London.[45]

Anthony Stokes

He went to Charleston, South Carolina, after leaving Georgia, and at the evacuation of that city he returned to England. He published "View of the Constitution of the British Colonies in North America and the West Indies" (London, 1783), "Narrative of the Official Conduct of Anthony Stokes" (1784), and "Desultory Observations on Great Britain" (1792). Stokes died in London on March 27, 1799.[46]

Anthony Wayne

Wayne was lauded for his command leadership when the British evacuated Savannah in July 1782. The next year he was promoted to major general and returned home in poor health to Pennsylvania. He served in the state legislature in 1784 and then moved to Georgia to use an award of 3,900 guineas from the Georgia government for his service during the Revolution to acquire an estate. He would run into debt trying to improve the property, and the estate was later foreclosed. In 1788, he was a delegate to the state convention that ratified the Constitution of the United States.

Wayne then served in the U.S. Senate in 1791 but was forced to give up his seat as a result of his residency qualifications. He did not run for re-election. On March 5, 1792, Congress created a new army, Legion of the United States. President Washington named Wayne as the commander. After working to train his troops and building ten forts, Wayne was sent to the Northwest Territory to put down armed resistence from the confederation of the Miami, Shawnee, Delaware and Wuandot Indian tribes lead by Blue Jacket of the Shawnees and Little Turtle of the Miamis.

On August 20, 1794, Wayne's Legion defeated the Indian confederation in the Battle of Fallen Timbers, Ohio. The next year the Treaty of Greeneville was signed, which established the peace and opened up the Northwest Territory to settlement. On his way back from accepting the surrender of Detriot in 1796, Wayne suffered a severe attack of gout and died at Fort Presque Isle, Pennsylvania, on December 15. He was buried beneath the flagpole. In 1809 his son brought his remains to the family cemetery at St. David's Church in Radnor, Pennsylvania.[47]

John Wesley

After spending three years in Georgia, Wesley returned to England in early 1738. In a meeting room in Aldergate Street in London on May 24 that year he experienced a revelation and outpouring of assurance from God that he had been forgiven for his sins. He was so impressed he even reencountered the moment it happened, "about a quarter to nine." With his inner struggle somewhat lifted, Wesley joined with renowned preacher George Whitefield in Bristol.

Wesley's passionate sermons were innovative and so disturbing to the complacency of the Anglican Church and its followers that he was often barred from speaking in the parish churches. Wesley was forced to preach in the open air, and the common people came from miles around to hear his message about God's salvation. He formed his followers into "societies," the first in Bristol, then London (1740) and later in Newcastle (1742). Each society was subdivided into "classes" of a dozen or so followers who would meet weekly for prayer. Over time the disciplined followers created orderly congregations. Soon his societies were given the name "Methodist" because of the method of his organized movement.

Wesley traveled throughout the country, showing compassion for the laborers and delivering his message of God's love, asking that they "be saved and made holy." He spoke of the need to work hard and cease gambling and drinking. Wesley's unique approach to his faith often met with angry mobs throwing stones and bent on attacking him and his associate preachers. In support of the suffering and poor, Wesley founded an orphan house and several schools, including the Kingswood School in Bristol, to teach the children of miners.

Over the last 52 years of his life, it has been estimated that Wesley delivered 40,000 sermons and traveled some 225,000 miles on horseback on difficult roads and at times in bad weather. His first sermon of the day was often at 5 A.M. He usually gave two sermons per day, and often three or more. His energy and dedication was more than astounding. He also found time to author a significant number of books and founded the *Methodist Magazine*. As his fame grew over the years, the crowds turned to admiration for this selfless man of God.

John Wesley died on March 2, 1791. The last words on his lips were, "Best of all, God is with us." At his death he left behind some 75,000 followers.[48]

Sir James Wright

After the Revolution, Wright returned to England and in 1783 became the head of the Board of Agents of the American Loyalists, whose property had been confiscated by the American government. Wright's contributions to his beloved Georgia were economic growth, new settlements, population growth, successful farms and plantations, and moreover, a most efficient government. Wright died on November 21, 1785, at his Westminster home and was buried in the North Transept at Westminster Abbey.[49]

Appendix A.
The First English
Settlers to Georgia

The list below includes all 114 of the first English settlers who embarked on the ship *Anne* for Oglethorpe's new colony of Georgia. The 35 families are grouped together, with indented entries for wives, children, and servants after the head of household.

A list of the persons sent to Georgia on the [Anne] by the trustees for establishing the colony there, 16 November 1732, by Captain Thomas

Paul Amatis, understands the nature &
  production of raw silk, aged ___

Timothy Bowling, potashmaker, aged 38

William Calvert, trader of goods, aged 44
  Mary, his wife, aged 42
  William Greenfield, his nephew, aged 19
  Charles Greenfield, his nephew, aged 16
  Sarah Greenfield, his neice, aged 16
  Elizabeth Wallis, his servant, aged 19

Richard Cannon, calendar & carpenter,
  aged 36
  Mary, his wife, aged 33
  Marmaduke, his son, aged 9
  James, his son, aged 7 months [died 26
    NOV 1732]
  Clementine, his daughter, aged 2½
  Mary Hicks, his servant, aged ___

James Carwell, peruke maker, aged 35
  Margaret, his wife, aged 32

Thomas Causton, callicoe printer, aged 40

Thomas Christie, merchant, aged 32
  Robert Johnston, his servant, aged 17

Robert Clarke Taylor, aged 37
  Judith, his wife, aged 29

Charles, his son, aged 11
John, his son, aged 4
Peter, his son, aged 3
James, his son, aged 9 months [died 22
  DEC 1732)

Henry Close, clothworker, aged 42
  Hannah, his wife, aged 32
  Ann, his daughter, aged under 2

Joseph Coles, miller & baker, aged 28
  Anna, his wife, aged 32
  Anna, his daughter, aged 13
  Elias Ann Wellen, his servant, aged 18

Joseph Cooper, writer, aged 37

William Cox, surgeon, aged 41
  Frances, his wife, aged 35
  William, his son, aged above 12
  Eunice, his daughter, aged 2¾
  Henry Loyd, his servant, aged 21

Joseph Fitzwalter, gardener, aged 31

Walter Fox, turner, aged 35

John Gready, understands farming, aged 22

James Goddard, carpenter & joyner, aged 38
  Elizabeth, his wife, aged 42

John, his son, aged under 9
Elizabeth, his daughter, aged 5

Peter Gordon, upholstereer, aged 34
Katherine, his wife, aged 28

Richard Hodges, basketmaker, aged 50
Mary, his wife, aged 42
Mary, his daughter, aged 18
Elizabeth, his daughter, aged 16
Sarah, his daughter, aged 5

Joseph Hughes, in the cyder trade & understands writing and accompts, aged 28
Elizabeth, his wife, aged 22

Noble Jones, carpenter, aged 32
Sarah, his wife, aged 32
Noble, his son, aged 10 months
Mary, his daughter, aged 3
Thomas Ellis, his servant, aged 17
Mary Cormock, his servant, aged 11

William Littel, understands flax & hemp, aged 31
Elizabeth, his wife, aged 31
William, his son, aged under 2
Mary, his daughter, aged 5

Thomas Millidge, carpenter & joyner, aged 42
Elizabeth, his wife, aged 40
John, his son, aged 11
Richard, his son, aged 8
James, his son, aged 1½
Sarah, his daughter, aged under 9
Frances, his daughter, aged 5

Francis Mugridge, sawyer, aged 39

James Muir, peruke maker, aged 38
Ellen, his wife, aged 38
John, his son, aged 18 months
Elizabeth Satchfield, his servant, aged 25

Joshua Overend, aged 40

Samuel Parker, a heelmaker & understands carpenter's work, aged 33
Jane, his wife, aged 36

Samuel, his son, aged 16
Thomas, his son, aged under 9

John Penrose, husbandman, aged 35
Elizabeth, his wife, aged 46

Thomas Pratt, aged 21

John Samms, cordwainer, aged 42

Francis Scott, a reduced military officer, aged 40
John Richard Cameron, his servant, aged 35

Joseph Stanley, stockingmaker & can draw & reel silk, aged 45
Elizabeth, his wife, aged 35
John Mackay, his servant, aged 25

George Symes, apothecary, aged 55
Sarah, his wife, aged 52
Anne, his daughter, aged 21

Daniel Thibaut, understands vines, aged 50
Mary, his wife, aged 40
James, his son, aged under 12
Dianna, his daughter, aged under 7

John Warrrin, flax & hemp dresser, aged 34
Elizabeth, his wife, aged 27
William, his son, aged 6
Richard, his son, aged 4
John, his son, aged 1½
one son to be baptized aged 3 weeks
Elizabeth, his daughter, aged 3

William Waterland, late a mercer, aged 44

John West, smith, aged 33
Elizabeth, his wife, aged 33
Richard, his son, aged 5

James Wilson, sawyer, aged 21

John Wright, vintner, aged 33
Penelope, his wife, aged 33
John, his son, aged 13
Elizabeth, his daughter, aged 11

Thomas Young, wheelwright, aged 45

Reference: E. Merton Coulter, *Georgia Historical Quarterly*, 1947.

Appendix B.
Georgia Constitution of 1777

Whereas the conduct of the Legislature of Great Britain for many years past has been so oppressive on the people of America that of late years they have plainly declared and asserted a right to raise taxes upon the people of America, and to make laws to bind them in all cases whatsoever, without their consent; which conduct being repugnant to the common rights of mankind, hath obliged the Americans, as freemen, to oppose such oppressive measures, and to assert the rights and privileges they are entitled to by the laws of nature and reason; and accordingly it hath been done by the general consent of all the people of the States of New Hampshire, Massachusetts Bay, Rhode Island, Connecticut, New York, New Jersey, Pennsylvania, the counties of New Castle, Kent, and Sussex on Delaware, Maryland, Virginia, North Carolina, South Carolina, and Georgia, given by their representatives met together in general Congress, in the city of Philadelphia;

And whereas it hath been recommended by the said Congress, on the fifteenth of May last, to the respective assembles and conventions of the United States, where no government, sufficient to the exigencies of their affairs, hath been hitherto established, to adopt such government as may, in the opinion of the representatives of the people, best conduce to the happiness and safety of their constituents in particular and America in general;

And whereas the independence of the United States of America has been also declared, on the fourth day of July, one thousand seven hundred and seventy-six, by the said honorable Congress, and all political connection between them and the Crown of Great Britain is in consequence thereof dissolved;

We, therefore, the representatives of the people, from whom all power originates, and for whose benefit all government is intended, by virtue of the power delegated to us, do ordain and declare, and it is hereby ordained and declared, that the following rules and regulations be adopted for the future government of this State:

Article I. The legislative, executive, and judiciary departments shall be separate and distinct, so that neither exercise the powers properly belonging to the other.

Article II. The legislature of this State shall be composed of the representatives of the people, as is hereinafter pointed out; and the representatives shall be elected yearly, on the first Tuesday in December; and the representatives so elected shall meet the first Tuesday; in January following, at Savannah, or any other place or places where the house of assembly for the time being shall direct.

On the first day of the meeting of the representatives so chosen they shall proceed to the choice of a governor, who shall be styled "honorable;" and of an executive council, by ballot out of their own body, viz: two from each county, except those counties which are not yet entitled to send ten members. One of each county shall always attend, where the governor resides, by monthly rotation, unless the members of each county agree for a longer or shorter period. This is not intended to exclude either member attending. The remaining number of representatives shall be called the house of assembly; and the majority of the members of the said house shall have power to proceed on business.

Article III. It shall be an unalterable rule that the house of assembly shall expire and be at an end, yearly and every year, on the day preceding the day of election mentioned in the foregoing rule.

Article IV. The representation shall be divided in the following manner: ten members from each county, as is hereinafter directed, except the county of Liberty, which contains three parishes, and that shall be allowed fourteen.

The ceded lands north of Ogechee shall be one county, and known by the name of Wilkes.

The Parish of Saint Paul shall be another county, and known by the name of Richmond.

The Parish of Saint George shall be another county, and known by the name of Burke.

The Parish of Saint Matthew, and the upper part of Saint Philip, above Canouchee, shall be another county, and known by the name of Effingham.

The Parish of Christ Church, and the lower part of Saint Philip, below Canouchee, shall be another county, and known by the name of Chatham.

The Parishes of Saint John, Saint Andrew, and Saint James shall be another county, and known by the name of Liberty.

The Parishes of Saint David and Saint Patrick shall be another county, and known by the name of Glynn.

The Parishes of Saint Thomas and Saint Mary shall be another county, and known by the name of Camden.

The port and town of Savannah shall be allowed four members to represent their trade.

The port and town of Sunbury shall be allowed two members to represent their trade.

Article V. The two counties of Glynn and Camden shall have one representative each, and also they, and all other counties that may hereafter be laid out by the house of assembly, shall be under the following regulations, viz: at their first institution each county shall have one member, provided the inhabitants of the said county shall have ten electors; and if thirty, they shall have two, if forty, three; if fifty, four; if eighty, six; if a hundred and upward, ten; at which time two executive councillors shall be chosen from them, as is directed for the other counties.

Article VI. The representatives shall be chosen out of the residents in each county, who shall have resided at least twelve months in this State, and three months in the county where they shall be elected; except the freeholders of the counties of Glynn and Camden, who are in a state of alarm, and who shall have the liberty of choosing one member each, as specified in the articles of this Constitution, in any other county,

until they have residents sufficient to qualify them for more; and they shall be of the Protestant religion, and of the age of twenty-one years, and shall be possessed in their own right of two hundred and fifty acres of land, or some property to the amount of two hundred and fifty pounds.

Article VII. The house of assembly shall have power to make such laws and regulations as may be conducive to the good and wellbeing of the State; provided such laws and regulations be not repugnant to the true intent and meaning of any rule or regulation contained in this constitution.

The house of assembly shall also have power to repeal all laws and ordinances they find injurious to the people; and the house shall choose its own speaker, appoint its own officers, settle its own rules of proceeding, and direct writs of election for supplying intermediate vacancies, and shall have power of adjournment to any time or times within the year.

Article VIII. All laws and ordinances shall be three times read, and each reading shall be on different and separate days, except in cases of great necessity and danger; and all laws and ordinances shall be sent to the executive council after the second reading, for their perusal and advice.

Article IX. All male white inhabitants, of the age of twenty-one years, and possessed in his own right of ten pounds value, and liable to pay tax in this State, or being of any mechanic trade, and shall have been resident six months in this State, shall have a right to vote at all elections for representatives, or any other officers, herein agreed to be chosen by the people at large; and every person having a right to vote at any election shall vote by ballot personally.

Article X. No officer whatever shall serve any process, or give any other hindrances to any person entitled to vote, either in going to the place of election, or during the time of the said election, or on their returning home from such election; nor shall any military officer, or soldier, appear at any election in a military character to the intent that all elections may be free and open.

Article XI. No person shall be entitled to more than one vote, which shall be given in the county where such person resides, except as before excepted; nor shall any person who holds any title of nobility be entitled to a vote, or be capable of serving as a representative, or hold any post of honor, profit, or trust in this State, whilst such person claims his title of nobility; but if the person shall give up such distinction, in the manner as may be directed by any future legislation, then, and in such case, he shall be entitled to a vote, and represent, as before directed, and enjoy all the other benefits of a free citizen.

Article XII. Every person absenting himself from an election, and shall neglect to give in his or their ballot at such election, shall be subject to a penalty not exceeding five pounds; the mode of recovery, and also the appropriation thereof, to be pointed out and directed by act of the legislature: Provided, nevertheless, That a reasonable excuse shall be admitted.

Article XIII. The manner of electing representatives shall be by ballot, and shall be taken by two or more justices of the peace in each county, who shall provide a convenient box for receiving the said ballots: and, on closing the poll, the ballots shall be compared in public with the list of votes that have been taken, and the majority immediately declared; a certificate of the same being given to the persons elected, and also a certificate returned to the house of representatives.

Article XIV. Every person entitled to vote shall take the following oath or affirmation, if required, viz:

"I, A B, do voluntarily and solemnly swear (or affirm, as the case may be) that I do owe true allegiance to this State, and will support the constitution thereof; so help me God."

Article XV. Any five of the representatives elected, as before directed, being met, shall have power to administer the following oath to each other; and they, or any other member, being so sworn, shall, in the house, administer the oath to all other members that attend, in order to qualify them to take their seats, viz:

"I, A B, do solemnly swear that I will bear true allegiance to the State of Georgia, and will truly perform the trusts reposed in me; and that I will execute the same to the best of my knowledge,for the benefit of the State, and the support of the Constitution thereof, and that I have obtained my election without fraud or bribe whatever; so help me God."

Article XVI. The continental delegates shall be appointed annually by ballot, and shall have a right to sit, debate, and vote in the house of assembly, and be deemed a part thereof, subject, however, to the regulations contained in the twelfth article of the Confederation of the United States.

Article XVII. No person bearing any post of profit under this State, or any person bearing any military commission under this or any other State or States, except officers of the militia, shall

be elected a representative. And if any representative shall be appointed to any place of profit or military commission, which he shall accept, his seat shall immediately become vacant, and he be incapable of reelection whilst holding such office.

By this article it is not to be understood that the office of a justice of the peace is a post of profit.

Article XVIII. No person shall hold more than one office of profit under this State at one and the same time.

Article XIX. The governor shall, with the advice of the executive council, exercise the executive powers of government, according to the laws of this State and the constitution thereof, save only in the case of pardons and remission of fines, which he shall in no instance grant; but he may reprieve a criminal, or suspend a fine, until the meeting of the assembly, who may determine therein as they shall judge fit.

Article XX. The governor, with the advice of the executive council, shall have power to call the house of assembly together, upon any emergency, before the time which they stand adjourned to.

Article XXI. The governor, with the advice of the executive council, shall fill up all intermediate vacancies that shall happen in office till the next general election; and all commissions, civil and military, shall be issued by the governor, under his hand and the great seal of the State.

Article XXII. The governor may preside in the executive council at all times, except when they are taking into consideration and perusing the laws and ordinances offered to them, by the house of assembly.

Article XXIII. The governor shall be chosen annually by ballot, and shall not be eligible to the said office for more than one year out of three, nor shall he hold any military commission under any other State or States.

The governor shall reside at such place as the house of assembly for the time being shall appoint.

Article XXIV. The governor's oath: —

"I, A B, elected governor of the State of Georgia, by the representatives thereof, do solemnly promise and swear that I will, during the term of my appointment, to the best of my skill and judgment, execute the said office faithfully and conscientiously, according to law, without favor, affection, or partiality; that I will, to the utmost of my power, support, maintain, and defend the State of Georgia, and the constitution of the same; and use my utmost endeavors to protect the people thereof in the secure enjoyment of all their rights, franchises, and privileges; and that the laws and ordinances of the State be duly observed, and that law and justice in mercy be executed in all judgments. And I do further solemnly promise and swear that I will peaceably and quietly resign the government to which I have been elected at the period to which my continuance in the said office is limited by the constitution. And, lastly, I do solemnly swear that I have not accepted of the government whereunto I am elected contrary to the articles of this constitution; so help me God."

This oath is to be administered to him by the speaker of the assembly. The same oath to be administered by the speaker to the president of the council.

No person shall be eligible to the office of governor who has not resided three years in this State.

Article XXV. The executive council shall meet the day after their election, and proceed to the choice of a president out of their own body; they shall have power to appoint their own officers and settle their own rules of proceedings.

The council shall always vote by counties, and not individually.

Article XXVI. Every councillor, being present, shall have power of entering his protest against any measures in council he has not consented to, provided he does it in three days.

Article XXVII. During the sitting of the assembly the whole of the executive council shall attend, unless prevented by sickness, or some other urgent necessity; and, in that case, a majority of the council shall make a board to examine the laws and ordinances sent them by the house of assembly; and all laws and ordinances sent to the council shall be returned in five days after with their remarks thereon.

Article XXVIII. A committee from the council, sent with any proposed amendments to any law or ordinance, shall deliver their reasons for such proposed amendments, sitting and covered, the whole house at that time, except the speaker, uncovered.

Article XXIX. The president of the executive council, in the absence or sickness of the governor, shall exercise all the powers of the governor.

Article XXX. When any affair that requires secrecy shall be laid before the governor and the executive council, it shall be the duty of the governor, and he is hereby obliged, to administer the following oath, viz:

"I, A B, do solemnly swear that any business that shall be at this time communicated to the council I will not, in any manner whatever, either by speaking, writing, or otherwise, reveal the same to any person whatever, until leave given by the council, or when called upon by the house of assembly; and all this I swear without any reservation whatever; so help me God."

And the same oath shall be administered to the secretary and other officers necessary to carry the business into execution.

Article XXXI. The executive power shall exist till renewed as pointed out by the rules of this constitution.

Article XXXII. In all transactions between the legislative and executive bodies the same shall be communicated by message, to be delivered from the legislative body to the governor or executive council by a committee, and from the governor to the house of assembly by the secretary of the council, and from the executive council by a committee of the said council.

Article XXXIII. The governor for the time being shall be captain-general, and commander-in-chief over all the militia, and other military and naval forces belonging to this State.

Article XXXIV. All militia commissions shall specify that the person commissioned shall continue during good behavior.

Article XXXV. Every county in this State that has, or hereafter may have, two hundred and fifty men, and upwards, liable to bear arms, shall be formed into a battalion; and when they become too numerous for one battalion, they shall be formed into more, by bill of the legislature; and those counties that have a less number than two hundred and fifty shall be formed into dependent companies.

Article XXXVI. There shall be established in each county a court, to be called a superior court, to be held twice in each year.

On the first Tuesday in March, in the county of Chatham.

The second Tuesday in March, in the county of Effingham.

The third Tuesday in March, in the county of Burke.

The fourth Tuesday in March, in the county of Richmond.

The next Tuesday in the county of Wilkes.

The Tuesday fortnight, in the county of Liberty.

The next Tuesday in the county of Glynn.

The next Tuesday, in the county of Camden.

The like courts to commence in October and continue as above.

Article XXXVII. All causes and matters of dispute, between any parties residing in the same county, to be tried within the county.

Article XXXVIII. All matters in dispute between contending parties residing in different counties shall be tried in the county where the defendant resides, except in cases of real estate, which shall be tried in the county where such real estate lies.

Article XXXIX. All matters of breach of the peace, felony, murder, and treason against the State to be tried in the county where the same was committed. All matters of dispute, both civil and criminal, in any county where there is not a sufficient number of inhabitants to form a court, shall be tried in the next adjacent county where a court is held.

Article XL. All causes, of what nature soever, shall be tried in the supreme court, except as hereafter mentioned; which court shall consist of the chief-justice, and three or more of the justices residing in the county. In case of the absence of the chief-justice, the senior justice on the bench shall act as chief-justice, with the clerk of the county, attorney for the State, sheriff, coroner, constable, and the jurors; and in case of the absence of any of the aforementioned officers, the justices to appoint others in their room pro tempore. And if any plaintiff or defendant in civil causes shall be dissatisfied with the determination of the jury, then, in that case, they shall be at liberty, within three days, to enter an appeal from that verdict, and demand a new trial by a special jury, to be nominated as follows, viz: each party, plaintiff and defendant, shall choose six, six more names shall be taken indifferently out of the box provided for that purpose, the whole eighteen to be summoned, and their names to be put together into the box, and the first twelve that are drawn out, being present, shall be the special jury to try the cause, and from which there shall be no appeal.

Article XLI. The jury shall be judges of law, as well as of fact, and shall not be allowed to bring in a special verdict; but if all or any of the jury have any doubts concerning points of law, they shall apply to the bench, who shall each of them in rotation give their opinion.

Article XLII. The jury shall be sworn to bring in a verdict according to law, and the opinion they entertain of the evidence; provided it be not repugnant to the rules and regulations contained in this constitution.

Article XLIII. The special jury shall be sworn to bring in a verdict according to law, and the opinion they entertain of the evidence; provided it be not repugnant to justice, equity, and conscience, and the rules and regulations contained in this constitution, of which they shall judge.

Article XLIV. Captures, both by sea and land, to be tried in the county where such shall be carried in; a special court to be called by the chief-justice, or in his absence by the then senior justice in the said county, upon application of the captors or claimants, which cause shall be determined within the space of ten days. The mode of proceeding and appeal shall be the same as in the superior courts, unless after the second trial, an appeal is made to the Continental Congress; and the distance of time between the first and second trial shall not exceed fourteen days; and all maritime causes to be tried in like manner.

Article XLV. No grand jury shall consist of less than eighteen, and twelve may find a bill.

Article XLVI. That the court of conscience be continued as heretofore practiced, and that the jurisdiction thereof be extended to try causes not amounting to more than ten pounds.

Article XLVII. All executions exceeding five pounds, except in the case of a court-merchant, shall be stayed until the first Monday in March; provided security be given for debt and costs.

Article XLVIII. All the costs attending any action in the superior court shall not exceed the sum of three pounds, and that no cause be allowed to depend in the superior court longer than two terms.

Article XLIX. Every officer of the State shall be liable to be called to account by the house of assembly.

Article L. Every county shall keep the public records belonging to the same, and authenticated copies of the several records now in the possession of this State shall be made out and deposited in that county to which they belong.

Article LI. Estates shall not be entailed; and when a person dies intestate, his or her estate shall be divided equally among their children; the widow shall have a child's share, or her dower, at her option; all other intestates estates to be divided according to the act of distribution, made in the reign of Charles the Second, unless otherwise altered by any future act of the legislature.

Article LII. A register of probates shall be appointed by the legislature in every county, for proving wills and granting letters of administration.

Article LIII. All civil officers in each county shall be annually elected on the day of the general election, except justices of the peace and registers of probates, who shall be appointed by the house of assembly.

Article LIV. Schools shall be erected in each county and supported at the general expense of the State, as the legislature shall hereafter point out.

Article LV. A court-house and jail shall be erected at the public expense in each county,where the present convention or the future legislature shall point out and direct.

Article LVI. All persons whatever shall have the free exercise of their religion; provided it be not repugnant to the peace and safety of the State; and shall not, unless by consent, support any teacher or teachers except those of their own profession.

Article LVII. The great seal of this State shall have the following device: on one side of a scroll, whereon shall be engraved "The Constitution of the State of Georgia;" and the motto "Pro bono publico." On the other side, an elegant house, and other buildings, fields of corn, and meadows covered with sheep and cattle; a river running through the same, with a ship under full sail, and the motto, "Deus nobis haec otia fecit."

Article LVIII. No person shall be allowed to plead in the courts of law in this State, except those who are authorized so to do by the house of assembly; and if any person so authorized shall be found guilty of malpractice before the house of assembly, they shall have power to suspend them. This is not intended to exclude any person from that inherent privilege of every freeman, the liberty to plead his own cause.

Article LIX. Excessive fines shall not be levied, nor excessive bail demanded.

Article LX. The principles of the habeas-corpus act shall be a part of this constitution.

Article LXI. Freedom of the press and trial by jury to remain inviolate forever.

Article LXII. No clergyman of any denomination shall be allowed a seat in the legislature.

Article LXIII. No alteration shall be made in this constitution without petitions from a majority of the counties, and the petitions from each county to be signed by a majority of voters in each county within this State; at which time the assembly shall order a convention to be called for that purpose, specifying the alterations to be made, according to the petitions preferred to the assembly by the majority of the counties as aforesaid.

Reference: *Watkins' Digest of the Laws of Georgia*, pp. 8–16.

Appendix C.
Colonial Georgia
Timeline, 1733–1783

This is a chronology of major events in the history of Georgia in the first 50 years.

1733

January 13 — The *Anne* arrives in Charleston with James Oglethorpe, a doctor, a pastor and 114 colonists.

January 19 — Oglethorpe, along with the settlers, set sail for Beaufort, South Carolina.

January 20 — The *Anne* arrives in Beaufort, South Carolina.

January 21 — Oglethorpe, Peter Gordon, Colonel William Bull and others set sail to find a site to settle south of the Savannah River.

January 24 — Benjamin Lincoln born in Hingham, Massachusetts.

January 29 — Sailing from Beaufort on six smaller boats, the settlers head for the site on the Savannah River selected by Oglethorpe.

January 30 — After a storm forces them to land in South Carolina, the colonists once again set sail for Oglethorpe's site.

January 31 — The Trustees demand the resignation of three trustees, who had used funds they raised for chartering a vessel and allowing Jewish colonists to go to Georgia.

February 1 — Oglethorpe and the settlers land at the site of present-day Savannah.

February 9 — First structure in Savannah.

May 2 — The *James* docks at Port Royal.

May 14 — The *James* arrives in Savannah with supplies, store and people for the colony.

May 21 — Oglethorpe signs treaty with the Creek Indians.

June 9 — Oglethorpe returns to Charles Town to thank the colony for its kindness.

July 7 — Oglethorpe organizes the administration of Georgia.

October 18 — Treaty between the Creek and Oglethorpe ratified by the Trustees

November 27 — Salzbergers arrive in Rotterdam

December 15 — Trustees approve assisting the Salzbergers move to the colony of Georgia

December 21 — Salzbergers arrive in Dover and find the Trustees willing to help with the expense of sailing to Georgia

December 21 — First land allotment takes effect. Although the land had been designated in July, the deeds were not executed until this date. Included in the designation are recently arrived Jewish colonists.

1734

January 8 — Salzbergers set sail for Georgia in the ship *Purysburg*

January 23 — James Oglethorpe, Captain Ferguson and 16 men head out to explore the coast and name various geographic features

January 27 — Heading south along the coast, Oglethorpe stops at St. Simons Island, where he spends the night. It is during his stay on the island that Oglethorpe decides to build Fort St. Simon, Fort Frederica and New Inverness

January 28 — Oglethorpe names Jekyll Island in honor of his friend Sir Joseph Jekyll

February 21— First Masonic meeting in Georgia held at Fort Morris in Sunbury.

March 7 — Salzbergers arrive in Charles Town, where they are personally greeted by James Oglethorpe

March 12 — First group of Salzburgers arrives in Savannah, aboard the *Purysburg*

March 17 — The site of the Salzberger settlement (Ebenezer) is selected

March 23 — James Oglethorpe, Tomochichi, Toonahowie, and others leave Savannah on a journey to England

March 27 — Oglethorpe arrives in Charles Town on the first leg of a trip that will take him to England. With him are Tomochichi and other Indians

April 7 — James Oglethorpe leaves for England on the *Aldbourough*

June 16 — The *Aldbourough* arrives at the Isle of Wight

August 1— The king of England receives Tomochichi, his wife and son and other Indians at his palace in Kensington

December 27 — The ship *Prince of Wales* arrives in Savannah. On board are James Oglethorpe, Tomochichi, Toonahowie, and others who visited England, and Salzburgers who are moving to Georgia. The Salzburgers are directed by Oglethorpe to Ebenezer.

1735

April 6 — First Morovians land in Georgia.

October 14 — John and Charles Wesley set sail to Georgia

October 18 — Sailing from Inverness on the *Prince of Wales*, Scots under the command of Hugh Mackay head for Georgia

1736

December — George Galphin (sometimes spelled Golphin) establishes a trading post at Ogeechee Old Town.

January 10 — Scottish Highlanders under the command of Hugh Mackay arrive in Savannah on the *Prince of Wales*.

January 19 — Highlanders arrive at New Inverness (Darien)

February 5 — *Symond* and *London Merchant* arrive at Tybee Roads. Among the passengers are Charles and John Wesley

February 6 — The Wesleys disembark on the Peeper (now Cockspur Island)

February 18 — Oglethorpe arrives at St. Simon

February 19 — Oglethorpe begins work on the fort that will anchor the town of Frederica

February 22 — Oglethorpe crosses the bay from Frederica to Darien and visits the Highlanders in New Inverness. He approves the construction of a fort on the site of Fort King George and the name of the fort (Fort Darien). He allots land to the male heads of households for farming and lays out a city.

March 7 — John Wesley gives his first sermon (not in a church) in Savannah

March 13 — John Wesley's first church service in Savannah is attended by some 20 worshippers

March 18 — Oglethorpe heads south from Frederica to continue scouting the coast

March 23 — A battery of cannon is mounted at Fort Frederica

June 14 — Oglethorpe orders Noble Jones to survey Augusta.

July 25 — Work begins on a road between Fort St. Simon and Fort Frederica. The road is usable in three days.

September 10 — Responding to the threat of Spanish troops, General Oglethorpe writes his friend Sir Joseph Jekyll and mentions that Spain has 1,500 regulars in St. Augustine while there is only militia in Georgia

November 29 — Oglethorpe returns to England to petition the crown for money to defend Georgia

December 3 — Charles Wesley arrives in England at the end of his return trip from Georgia

1737

December 2 — John Wesley returns to England

1738

May 7 — George Whitfield arrives in Savannah. He begins work on establishing the orphanage known as Bethesda

May 8 — King George II instructs James Oglethorpe to learn and report the designs of the Spanish in Florida

June 2 — Unpaid bills for the colony of Georgia reach £5,000.

June 7 — Thomas Causton, magistrate of Savannah, is replaced by Henry Parker. A review of the records reveal gross mismanagement of funds

June 15 — Oglethorpe reports that the Spanish are attempting to bribe the Creek Nation to attack the Georgia colony

October 10 — Oglethorpe returns to Savannah from Frederica

October 19 — In a letter to the Trustees, Ogle-thorpe accuses Thomas Causton, former magistrate of Savannah, of "squandering the resources of the colony," and continues to state "If this had not happened the Colony ... [would be] in a flourishing condition"

October 25 — Oglethorpe sails for Frederica

1739

January 14 — George Whitefield ordained a minister in the Church of England

January 14 — First Convention of El Pardo. England signs a preliminary agreement with Spain, leaving to a board of commissioners to be appointed by both countries the determination of the Spanish-English border (Georgia-Florida). England never ratifies the agreement

July 17 — Oglethorpe starts a journey to the Creek capitol of Coweta, accompanied by Lieutenant Dunbar, Ensign Leman and Cadet Eyre. They left Savannah, headed to Uchee Town, north of Ebenezer, then headed west along the old Creek Trading Path.

August 11— Creek Indians greet General Oglethorpe at a "great council"

August 21— Creeks confirm their cession of land to Georgia in a second treaty

October 5 — Chief Tomochichi dies

October 19 — England declares war on Spain. Commonly called the War of Jenkins Ear. Robert Jenkins lost his ear to Spanish raiders who boarded his ship, the *Rebecca*, in 1731. After addressing the Lower House in 1738, and holding up a bloody ear, war was declared on Spain.

November 5 — In preparation for war, Oglethorpe returns to Frederica

November 15 — A party of Spanish regulars lands on Amelia Island and conceals themselves in the woods. The following day they kill two of Mackay's Highlanders

1740

January 1— At the head of a massive fleet that includes some 15 boats, General Oglethorpe decides to raid two Spanish forts. He enters the St. Johns River and burns Fort Picolata and quickly captures Fort St. Francis de Papa, just over 20 miles from St. Augustine. He is nearly killed in the battle.

March 25 — George Whitefield "laid the foundation" for Bethesda Orphanage

May 9 — Oglethorpe, confident after his successful raid earlier in the year, begins a move on Fort Francis de Papa and Fort Diego.

May 17 — Oglethorpe is joined by Capt. McIntosh and a company of Highlanders and some Carolina troops

June 5 — Oglethorpe prepares to attack St. Augustine, but Spanish defense proves difficult. Oglethorpe decides to invest the town

June 13 — Oglethorpe begins to lay siege to St. Augustine

July 4 — With a large force of Spanish regulars to his rear (they had come from Havana), General Oglethorpe decides to withdraw from St. Augustine.

1741

April 12 — The Rev. Johann Martin Bolzius holds two services for the Salzburgers

April 15 — The Trustees divide Georgia into two counties, Savannah, with William Stephens as executive, and Frederica, with James Oglethorpe as executive

May 12 — Oglethorpe reports a contingent of 800 Spanish regulars arriving at St. Augustine

1742

July 7 — Battle of Bloody Marsh

July 14 — Parliament repeals the "rum act," directing the Trustees to allow importation of rum into the colony

1743

February 13 — Oglethorpe promoted to brigadier general

March 22 — The magazine at Fort Frederica is blown up.

July 11–December, — William Stevens becomes president of the state of Georgia

July 22 — Oglethorpe returns to England for the last time

1744

September 15 — Oglethorpe marries Lady Elizabeth Wright

1745

November 1— The Rev. Bartholomew Zouberbuhler is appointed the minister of Established Church

1747

March 19 — Mr. Cretien Von Munch and the Rev. Sauel Urlsperger, of Augsburgh, are chosen as "corresponding members" of the trust established to manage Georgia. They never attend a meeting, but correspond information about German immigration

July 20 — Thomas Bosomworth, with the queen of the Creek, Mary Musgrove, march into Savannah.

1749

January 10 — President Stevens sends a petition suggesting that the prohibition against slavery be repealed

May 19 — Trustees petition the king to allow the repeal of the prohibition of slavery

May 29 — Oglethorpe's regiment at Frederica is disbanded

1750

July 26 — Henry Parker is made vice president and James Habersham is made secretary

1751

January 1 — Slavery officially becomes legal in Georgia

January 15 — A provincial assembly is called to convene in Savannah. One of the major discussions will be the annexation of Georgia into South Carolina

April 1 — Culminating an effort to revive the silk industry, a reeling plant is completed in Savannah

April 8 — Henry Parker becomes president of the state of Georgia

April 8 — Henry Parker is appointed president of Georgia, succeeding Col. William Stephens

June 13 — Captain Noble Jones and 220 members of the Georgia Militia parade in Savannah.

1752

June 23 — A deed of reconveyance returns control of Georgia to the crown from the Trustees

September 2 — The Gregorian calendar goes into effect. This date becomes September 14, and September 2–13 never exist. New Year's Day was moved from March 25 to January 1 at the same time.

1754

December — Henry Yonge and William Gerard De Brahm are appointed surveyors-general

October 30 — Captain John Reynolds becomes the first royal governor of Georgia

1755

January 7 — Georgia officially transitions from Trustee control to a royal colony

1756

1757

February 16 — Henry Ellis becomes royal governor of Georgia

October 25 — Georgia Governor Henry Ellis and South Carolina Governor William Lyttleton meet with various Chiefs in an effort to preserve the peace during the war with France

December — William Gerard De Brahm (1718–1799?) designs the community of Ebenezer

1758

March 15 — Seven parishes established

1760

May 13 — James Wright commissioned lieutenant governor of Georgia

October 31 — James Wright becomes royal governor of Georgia

November 2 — Henry Ellis leaves Georgia to become royal governor of Nova Scotia.

1762

January 5 — John Stuart receives the title royal superintendent of Indian affairs, Southern District of North America

1763

February 10 — Treaty of Paris ends the French and Indian War and reduces Georgia's western boundary from the Pacific Ocean to the Mississippi River

April 5 — South Carolina governor Thomas Boone begins to grant Georgia land south of the Altamaha, mostly to speculators but also some to wealthy friends.

May 30 — The Board of Trade, the ruling English authority in the matter, instructs South Carolina governor Thomas Boone to cease granting Georgia land and withdrawing the land he had already granted

August 16 — Thomas Boone receives the communiqué from the Board of Trade

October 7 — King George III issues the Proclamation of 1763

November 10 — Creek Indians cede coastal land from the Altamaha River to the St. Mary's River to Georgia.

1764

January 20 — King George III defines Georgia's boundaries, extending them to the St. Mary's River

April 5 — Revenue Act of 1764 (Sugar Act)

June 6 — The northern boundary of western Florida is moved to the mouth of the Yazoo River

October 9 — Archibald Bulloch marries Mary de Veaux

1765

March 22 — Parliament passes the Stamp Act

May 14 — Samuel Bowen, who had been imprisoned for four years while in China, purchases a tract of land in Thunderbolt. He had already asked Heny Yonge, a friend, to plant the soybean seeds he brought with him from China

September 4 — John and William Bartram arrive in Savannah.

September 24 — John and William Bartram dine with Royal Governor James Wright

September 30 — Heading south, the Bartrams cross the Ogeechee River

October 1 — During their stay at Fort Barrington, John and William Bartram discover Franklinia, Fevertree, and Ogeechee Lime

October 5 — The Bartrams head south from Fort

Barrington, following the King's Road to St. Augustine

November 1 — Official date the Stamp Act was to go into effect

November 5 — Demonstration of sailors in Savannah to protest the new Stamp Act

November 6 — First meeting of the Sons of Liberty at MacHenry's Tavern in Savannah

November 19 — The Rev. John Martin Bolzius, a leader of the Salzbergers, dies

1766

January 2 — Governor Wright personally turns back the Sons of Liberty at the gate of the governor's mansion.

January 3 — Stampmaster George Angus serves a single day in the port of Savannah, making Georgia the only colony to actually have a stampmaster.

March 18 — Parliament passes the Declaratory Act.

March 18 — Parliament repeals the Stamp Act, official as of May 1.

November 19 — *Georgia Gazette* reports that Samuel Bowen meets King George III

1767

June 26 — First Townshend Act

June 29 — Second Townshend Act

July 2 — Third Townshend Act

1768

February 1 — Forfeit date for the land granted to Wrightsboro Quakers. They were required to have 10 families to keep the grant. They had 40.

December 6 — Wrightsboro residents petition Royal Governor James Wright for additional land

1769

November 15 — Wright refuses to order elections for four newly established parishes along Georgia's southern coast.

1770

January 28 — George Whitefield delivers a sermon to the royal governor, his council and the General Assembly in Savannah, Georgia

February 22 — Royal Governor James Wright dissolves the Lower House because of its refusal to accept the governor's actions as precedent

July 10 — James Habersham receives rhubarb seeds from John Ellis and distributes them to local growers, including Samuel Bowen, who successfully grows the first rhubarb crop in America (generally attributed to Benjamin Franklin)

September 30 — George Whitefield dies in Newburyport, Massachusetts

1772

December — Oldest remaining Baptist church organized in Columbia County (Kiokee)

December 6 — James Wright made a baronet for his accomplishments as royal governor of Georgia

1773

April 11 — William Bartram arrives in Savannah

April 16 — William Bartram leaves Savannah, heading south on the King's Road to Darien

April 24 — William Bartram leaves Darien, following the River Road northwest to Fort Barrington

May 1 — William Bartram heads to Augusta, Georgia, to participate in meetings with the Creek Indians

May 10 — Tea Act

June 3 — Royal Governor James Wright and British Indian Agent John Stuart conclude a meeting to resolve boundary disputes with the Treaty of Augusta, which ceded some 675,000 acres to the state of Georgia

June 7 — William Bartram leaves Augusta as part of a team sent to survey the "New Purchase"

June 21 — William Bartram leaves Wrightsboro, heading north to the Tugaloo River

1774

January 17 — Georgia House appoints a "committee of correspondence" to handle communication with the other colonies on matters of interest.

March 24 — Britain passes the "Intolerable Acts."

July 14 — The *Georgia Gazette* publishes an invitation to a meeting at the "liberty pole" at Tondee's Tavern signed by George Walton, John Houstoun, Noble W. Jones and Archibald Bullock

July 24 — Meeting at Tondee's Tavern to organize Georgia for the rebellion.

August 10 — Meeting at Tondee's Tavern to vote on eight resolutions, including calling the Intolerable Acts "contrary to the British constitution." The Radicals did not elect representatives to the First Continental Congress, although the proposal did receive much of the meeting's attention.

September 5 — First Continental Congress convenes with representatives from 12 of the 13 colonies. Only Georgia is absent.

December 6 — St. John's Parish elects Lyman Hall as its representative to the First Continental Congress. He does not attend because he had not been elected by the provincial congress.

December 6 — St. John's Parish votes to join the Continental Association

1775

January 17 — Lower House called to order in Savannah

January 18 — Provincial congress called to order in Savannah

March 2-March 3 — Battle of the Rice Boats

April 19 — Start of the American Revolution

June 4 — Patriots in Savannah spike cannons assembled to celebrate the king's birthday

June 5 — Liberty pole erected in front of Peter Tondee's tavern in Savannah

June 21 — Council of Safety established to make decisions when the provincial congress is not seated. Its leader serves as Georgia's executive

July 3 — Heading west to Creek country from Silver Bluff on the Savannah River (near Augusta), William Bartram spends the night at Ocmulgee Old Fields (now Ocmulgee Mounds National Park).

July 4 — Archibald Bulloch elected president of Georgia's provincial congress

July 7 — The Second Provincial Congress elects Archibald Bulloch, John Houstoun, the Reverend John Zubley, Noble Wimberly Jones and Lyman Hall as delegates to the Continental Congress

October 7 — Georgia seizes British ship

December — George Walton elected president of the Council of Safety

December 22 — Prohibitory Act

1776

January 1— The Continental Congress recommends an attack on Florida

January 7 — Lachlan McIntosh appointed colonel of Georgia troops

January 14 — William Bartram returns to Augusta, Georgia

January 22 — Archibald Bulloch elected president of the Council of Safety

February 11— Royal Governor James Wright, who had been placed under house arrest in January, flees the governor's mansion in Savannah. He remains with the British fleet, then anchored off the coast near the Savannah River

February 27 — The Continental Congress creates the Southern Military Department of Virginia, the Carolinas, and Georgia.

March 1— Major General Charles Lee is appointed head of the Southern Department

April 15 — Georgia passes the Rules and Regulations, a document generally viewed as the first constitution of the state.

May 1— Archibald Bulloch elected first executive of Georgia, president of the Council of Safety

May 1— 200 Creek Indians meet with representatives of the Georgia government in Augusta.

May 21— Button Gwinnett and Lyman Hall arrive in Philadelphia to attend the Second Continental Congress

June 28 — Before the signing of the Declaration of Independence, Lt. Colonel Thomas Sumter, under the command of William Moultrie, aids in the defense of Sullivan's Island and Fort Moultrie.

July 4 — Declaration of Independence is printed on broadsides for distribution to the states and George Washington

August-October — First Florida Expedition

August 2 — Button Gwinnett, George Walton, and Lyman Hall sign the Declaration of Independence

August 8 — Declaration of Independence read to Council of Safety in Savannah

August 10 — Declaration of Independence read to citizens in Savannah

September 9 — Major General Charles Lee is replaced as commander of the Southern Department by Robert Howe, who is promoted to major general

October 1— State convention to create constitution held in Savannah

October 22 — Lachlan McIntosh orders William McIntosh to build a fort (Fort McIntosh) on the Satilla River to protect settlers from the Florida Rangers

1777

February 5 — Burke, Camden, Chatham, Effingham, Glynn, Liberty, Richmond, Wilkes counties created

February 5 — State constitution agreed upon unanimously

February 17-February 18 — Battle of Fort McIntosh

February 19 — Benjamin Lincoln promoted to major general

February 22 — Archibald Bulloch given the powers of the executive branch of the government; he dies under unusual circumstances the next day

March 4 — Button Gwinnett elected president of the Council of Safety

May 1— Overshadowed by the McIntosh-Gwinnett feud, Elbert departs from Sunbury heading south to the Georgia-Florida border

May 1— McIntosh, recalled from the Florida expedition as is his nemesis, Button Gwinnett, addresses the General Assembly, denouncing Gwinnett. Gwinnett challenges him to a duel

May 8 — John Adam Treutlen becomes the first governor of Georgia

May 12 — Florida Rangers rout Georgians waiting to meet Samuel Elbert on the Florida side of the St. Mary River

May 16 — Button Gwinnett and Lachlan McIntosh square off in a duel

May 17 — Decisive battle of the 2nd Florida Expedition fought at Thomas Creek (presently the site of Jacksonville, Florida)

May 17 — Georgia Whigs ambushed at Thomas Creek, marking the end of the Second Florida expedition

May 19 — Button Gwinnett dies from wounds received in a duel with Lachlan McIntosh

May 26 — Second Florida Expedition returns to Savannah

June 17 — 400 Creek warriors, George Galphin, Robert Rae and the Georgia Indian commission meet at Ogeechee Old Town. From here the chiefs journeyed to Augusta and Charleston.

July 15 — Governor John Adam Treutlen places

a $100 reward on William Henry Drayton. Drayton had been advocating the creation of a single state from Georgia and South Carolina

August 6 — Continental General Lachlan McIntosh is ordered to report to George Washington.

September 10 — The state of Georgia authorizes printing of specie, paper money exchangeable for Continental dollars on demand

September 25 — Major General Robert Howe is replaced by Major General Benjamin Lincoln as commander of the Southern Department

October 10 — Lachlan McIntosh leaves Georgia to report to Continental Army Commander George Washington. Colonel Samuel Elbert takes command of the Georgia brigade

November 15 — The Continental Congress Committee of Thirteen, which included Button Gwinnett, proposes the Articles of Confederation. They request states be ready to ratify the Articles of Confederation by March 10

1778

January 6 — France enters the Revolution on the American side.

January 8 — John Houstoun elected governor

January 10 — John Houstoun becomes the first native-born Georgian to lead the executive branch.

May 26 — Lachlan McIntosh is ordered to Fort Pitt as commanding officer

June 14 — Britain declares war on France

June 25 — Edward Langworthy, who was the only delegate to the Continental Congress from Georgia that was present, informs the body that he has no instructions from his state, but he is certain that Georgia will ratify the Articles of Confederation.

June 30 — Decisive battle of the 3rd Florida Expedition fought at Alligator Creek. After breaching the outer perimeter, American forces under command of Col. Elijah Clark were routed by British Regulars and Florida Rangers.

July 13 — Edward Telfair arrives in Philadelphia with instructions to ratify the Articles of Confederation

July 24 — Georgia ratifies the Articles of Confederation

August — Edward Telfair and John Walton, who had arrived the previous day, sign the Articles of Confederation for Georgia. Edward Langworthy, who had left Philadelphia, signed the Articles in July

November 19 — Battle of Bulltown Swamp (near Savannah), Battle of Spencer's Hill

November 24 — Battle of Midway Church

December 23 — British force lands at Tybee Island

December 29 — British capture Savannah; Battle of Brewton Hill

1779

January 6-January 9 — Battle of Sunbury

January 31 — British take Augusta

February 14 — Battle of Kettle Creek

February 14 — British withdraw from Augusta

March 3 — Battle of Briar (Brier) Creek

March 4 — English Lt. Colonel James Mark Prevost appointed acting governor of Georgia, to serve until the arrival of James Wright

March 21 — British Indian agent John Stuart dies in Pensacola, Florida

June 28 — Battle of Hickory Hill

July 22 — James Wright returns as royal governor of Georgia

August 6 — John Wereat becomes president of the Executive Council

September 16 — General Benjamin Lincoln and Admiral Charles Henri D'Estang lay siege to Savannah

October 6 — Battle of Savannah

October 9 — William Jasper dies in Savannah, Georgia

November — George Walton elected head of the executive branch

1780

January 4 — Richard Howley begins term as governor

February 3 — Heard's Fort, built by Stephen Heard in 1774, is named capitol of Revolutionary Georgia

February 15 — George Wells is killed in a duel by James Jackson in Augusta, Georgia

February 18 — Stephen Heard begins term as governor

May 12 — Benjamin Lincoln surrenders his command in Charleston, South Carolina

May 12 — British regain control of Augusta

June 30 — Battle of Fort Anderson

August 16 — Battle of Camden, South Carolina

August 18 — Baron Dekalb dies while a prisoner of war from wounds he received during the battle of Camden, South Carolina

September 14 — Battle of Fort Grierson (Augusta)

September 14 — Battle of Fort Cornwallis (Augusta)

September 15 — Battle of the White House (Augusta)

September 18 — Battle of Augusta

October 6 — Thomas Sumter promoted to brigadier general by South Carolina governor Edward Rutledge

October 7 — Battle of King's Mountain, South Carolina

October 31 — Major General Benjamin Lincoln is replaced by Major General Nathanael Greene as commander of the Southern Department

November 20 — Battle of Blackstock (or Blackstock's Farm)

December 1 — George Gauphin (Galphin) dies in Savannah before his trial before British authorities for treason.

1781

January 17 — Battle of Cowpens, South Carolina

April 13 — Skirmish near Augusta

April 18 — Battle at Ebenezer

May 21 — Battle of Fort Dreadnought

May 21 — Battle of Fort Galphin, on Silver Bluff near Augusta

May 24 — Second Battle of Fort Grierson

June 5 — Augusta falls, having been under siege since April, by Elijah Clarke, Andrew Pickens, and Colonel "Light Horse" Henry Lee.

August 17 — Augusta becomes the capitol of Georgia

August 18 — Nathan Brownson begins term as governor

October 17 — Cornwallis, surrounded at Yorktown, surrenders

1782

December — John Treutlen dies in Mett's Crossroads, South Carolina

January 3 — John Martin begins term as governor

January 19 — Continental general Anthony Wayne arrives in Georgia with orders to rid the state of the British in spite of being outnumbered 2 or 3 to 1.

January 25 — General Wayne outwits a larger British force near Ebenezer

January 28 — General Wayne captures provisions intended for British Savannah from an outpost on the Altamaha River

February 9 — Lachlan McIntosh, captured Continental general, is exchanged for a British prisoner

June 14 — Royal Governor James Wright receives orders to abandon Savannah, which he does a week later.

June 23 — General Anthony Wayne intercepts a large force of Creek Indians attempting to relieve the British in Savannah. Unknown to General Wayne, he kills Creek Chief Emistesigo (leader of the tribe).

July 10 — British evacuate Savannah after successful campaign by General Anthony Wayne

July 11 — James Jackson and American forces enter Savannah

July 13 — Savannah becomes the capitol of Georgia

July 25 — Lt. Col. James Jackson, leading a group of Georgia militia, briefly engages British forces on Skidaway Island. This is the final action in the coastal war.

September 20 — British-inspired Chickamauga Cherokee led by Skyuka meet John Siever and a band of irregulars near the face of Lookout Mountain (called Chattanooga by the Chickamaugans). Although this battle was fought in Tennessee, many of the Cherokee came from Georgia. This is occasionally, and incorrectly, referred to as the last battle of the American Revolution.

1783

January 8 — Lyman Hall begins term as governor

February 4 — Formal cessation of hostilities with the United States by Great Britain, ending the American Revolution

May 1 — Word reaches Georgia of the Treaty of Ghent, ending the Revolutionary War

Reference: *Our Georgia History* (*www.ourgeorgiahistory.com*)

Chapter Notes

Introduction

1. Larry Worth, The Creek Indians of Georgia, Our Georgia History (http://www.ourgeorgiahistory.com).

1. Oglethorpe and the Georgia Inspiration

1. The Rev. William Bacon Stevens, *A History of Georgia, Vol. I* (New York: D. Appleton, 1847), pp. 85–86.
2. Amos Aschbach Ettinger, *Oglethorpe: A Brief Biography* (Atlanta: Mercer University Press, 1984), p. 6.
3. *Ibid.*, pp. 8–9.
4. Webb Garrison, *Oglethorpe's Folly — The Birth of Georgia* (Lakemont, GA: Copple House Books, 1982), pp. 16–18.
5. *Ibid.*, p. 22.
6. *Ibid.*, pp. 22–23.
7. Keynote Lecture of Sir Keith Thomas PBA, President of the Corpus Christi College at Oxford, England, on October 5, 1996, before the Oglethorpe Tercentenary Commission.
8. Garrison, *Oglethorpe's Folly*, pp. 24–25.
9. Ettinger, *Oglethorpe: A Brief Biography*, pp. 17–19.
10. *Ibid.*, pp. 33–34.
11. Garrison, *Oglethorpe's Folly*, pp. 28–29.
12. Mills Lane, *General Oglethorpe's Georgia, Vol. I* (Savannah: The Beehive Press, 1975), pp. xv–xvi
13. Ettinger, *Oglethorpe: A Brief Biography*, pp. 33–36.
14. *Ibid.*, pp. 36–37.
15. The Rev. William Bacon Stevens, *A History of Georgia, Vol. I* (New York: D. Appleton, 1847), pp. 476–484.
16. Ettinger, *Oglethorpe: A Brief Biography*, pp. 38–39.
17. Lane, *General Oglethorpe's Georgia, Vol. I*, pp. xvi–xvii.
18. William Northen, *Men of Mark in Georgia* (Atlanta: A.B. Caldwell, 1907), pp. xii–xiii.
19. Garrison, *Oglethorpe's Folly*, pp. 60–62.
20. Phinizy Spalding, *Oglethorpe in America* (Chicago: University of Chicago Press, 1977), p. 7.
21. Amos Aschbach Ettinger, *Oglethorpe: A Brief Biography* (Atlanta: Mercer University Press, 1984), pp. 41–42.

22. Amos Aschbach Ettinger, *Oglethorpe: A Brief Biography* (Atlanta: Mercer University Press, 1984), p. 42.
23. The Rev. William Bacon Stevens, *A History of Georgia, Vol. I* (New York: D. Appleton and Co., 1847), pp. 86–87.
24. Phinizy Spalding, *Oglethorpe in America* (Chicago: University of Chicago Press, 1977), pp. 8–9.
25. William Harden, *A History of Savannah and South Georgia* (Atlanta: Cherokee Publishing Company, 1969), p. 10.
26. Lane, *General Oglethorpe's Georgia, Vol. I*, pp. xix, 4, 8.
27. Stevens, *A History of Georgia, Vol. I*, pp. 87–88.
28. Lane, *General Oglethorpe's Georgia, Vol. I*, pp. xi, 3–5.
29. Stevens, *A History of Georgia, Vol. I*, p. 88.
30. *Ibid.*, pp. 88–89.
31. Harden, *A History of Savannah and South Georgia*, pp. 10–11.

2. The Founding of Savannah

1. Phinizy Spalding, *Oglethorpe in America* (Chicago: University of Chicago Press, 1977), p. 11.
2. *Ibid.*, pp. 11–13.
3. Webb Garrison, *Oglethorpe's Folly, The Birth of Georgia* (Lakemont, GA: Copple House Books, 1982), pp. 75–76.
4. Clifford Sheats Capps and Eugenia Burney, *Colonial Georgia* (New York: Thomas Nelson, 1972), pp. 50–51.
5. Garrison, *Oglethorpe's Folly*, pp. 74–79.
6. Spalding, *Oglethorpe in America*, p. 14.
7. *Ibid.*, p, 18.
8. Amos Aschbach Ettinger, *James Edward Oglethorpe, Imperial Idealist* (Oxford: Clarendon Press, 1936), p. 135.
9. Spalding, *Oglethorpe in America*, pp. 19–20.
10. *Ibid.*, pp. 15–17.
11. Garrison, *Oglethorpe's Folly*, pp. 80–81.
12. *Ibid.*, pp. 84–88.
13. Mills Lane, *General Oglethorpe's Georgia, Vol. I* (Savannah: The Beehive Press, 1975), pp. xxii, 22.
14. Capps and Burney, *Colonial Georgia*, p. 54.
15. *Ibid.*, p. 55.

16. Garrison, *Oglethorpe's Folly*, pp. 91–92.
17. *Ibid.*, pp. 109–116.
18. Capps and Burney, *Colonial Georgia*, pp. 55–56.
19. Spalding, *Oglethorpe in America*, pp. 24–25.
20. Garrison, *Oglethorpe's Folly*, pp. 121–122, 125–127.
21. Ettinger, *James Edward Oglethorpe, Imperial Idealist*, pp. 151–152.
22. *Ibid.*, p. 153.
23. Spalding, *Oglethorpe in America*, p. 25.
24. Ettinger, *James Edward Oglethorpe, Imperial Idealist*, p. 153.
25. Ettinger, *Oglethorpe: A Brief Biography*, p. 48.
26. Spalding, *Oglethorpe in America*, pp. 25–26.

3. The Spanish and Georgia

1. Phinizy Spalding, *Oglethorpe in America* (Chicago: University of Chicago Press, 1977), p. 26.
2. *Ibid.*, pp. 26–28.
3. Amos Aschbach Ettinger, *Oglethorpe: A Brief Biography* (Atlanta: Mercer University Press, 1984), pp. 49–51.
4. Webb Garrison, *Oglethorpe's Folly, The Birth of Georgia* (Lakemont, GA: Copple House Books, 1982), pp. 127–142.
5. Albert B. Saye, *New Viewpoints in Georgia History* (Athens: University of Georgia Press, 1943), pp. 84–85.
6. *Ibid.*, p. 84.
7. Phinizy Spalding and Harvey H. Jackson, *Oglethorpe in Perspective* (Tuscaloosa, AL: University of Alabama Press, 1989), pp. 83–86.
8. *Ibid.*, pp. 87–88.
9. Elfrida De Renne Barrow and Laura Palmer Bell, *Anchored Yesterdays, The Log Book of Savannah's Voyage Across a Georgia Century* (Athens: University of Georgia Press, 1923), p. 27.
10. Garrison, *Oglethorpe's Folly*, pp. 154–155.
11. Kenneth O. Brown, "Wesleys in America — What Went Wrong?," *Christian History Magazine*, Issue 69, Winter 2001, Vol. XX, No. 1, p. 14), Janine Petry, "The Matchmakers," *Christian History Magazine*, Issue 69, Winter 2001, Vol. XX, No. 1, p. 23.
12. J. Gordon Vaeth, *The Man who Founded Georgia* (New York: Crowell-Collier Press, 1968), pp. 42–43.
13. Garrison, *Oglethorpe's Folly*, pp. 143–159.
14. Spalding and Jackson, *Oglethorpe in Perspective*, p. 90.
15. *Ibid.*, pp. 90–95.
16. Barrow and Bell, *Anchored Yesterdays*, p. 31.
17. Garrison, *Oglethorpe's Folly*, pp. 160–166.
18. Barrow and Bell, *Anchored Yesterdays*, pp. 31–32.
19. Mills Lane, *General Oglethorpe's Georgia, Vol. II* (Savannah: The Beehive Press, 1975), p. 420.
20. *Ibid.*, pp. 451–453.
21. *Ibid.*, p. 454.
22. *Ibid.*, pp. 458–461.
23. Thaddeus Mason Harris, *Biographical Memorials of James Oglethorpe*, http://www.fullbooks.com
24. Luis Rafael Arana and Albert Manucy, *The Building of Castilo de San Marcos* (Eastern National Park and Monument Association, 1977), pp. 46–47.
25. Lane, *General Oglethorpe's Georgia, Vol. II*, p. 462.
26. Arana and Manucy, *The Building of Castilo de San Marcos*, pp. 47–49.
27. Lane, *General Oglethorpe's Georgia, Vol. II*, pp. 463–465.
28. Garrison, *Oglethorpe's Folly*, pp. 174–178.
29. Lane, *General Oglethorpe's Georgia, Vol. II*, pp. 485–491.

4. A Georgia Victory and Charter Surrender

1. William Stephens, *A Journal of the Proceedings in Georgia, Vol II (A State of the Province of Georgia)* (London: W. Meadows, 1742), pp. 509–533.
2. Albert B. Saye, *New Viewpoints in Georgia History* (Athens: University of Georgia Press, 1943), pp. 86–91.
3. Patrick Tailfer, Hugh Anderson, and Da. Douglas, *A True and Historical NARRATIVE Of the COLONY of GEORGIA* (Charles Town: P. Timothy, 1741), p. 80.
4. Mills Lane, *General Oglethorpe's Georgia, Vol. II* (Savannah: The Beehive Press, 1975), p. 579.
5. *Ibid.*, p. 585.
6. Webb Garrison, *Oglethorpe's Folly, The Birth of Georgia* (Lakemont, GA: Copple House Books, 1982), pp. 178–179.
7. Lane, *General Oglethorpe's Georgia, Vol. II*, pp. 618–619.
8. *Ibid.*, pp. 616–624.
9. Garrison, *Oglethorpe's Folly*, p. 184.
10. Lane, *General Oglethorpe's Georgia, Vol. II*, p. 646.
11. Garrison, *Oglethorpe's Folly*, pp. 186–189.
12. Saye, *New Viewpoints in Georgia History*, p. 89.
13. Garrison, *Oglethorpe's Folly*, p. 202.
14. Elfrida De Renne Barrow and Laura Palmer Bell, *Anchored Yesterdays, The Log Book of Savannah's Voyage Across a Georgia Century* (Athens: University of Georgia Press, 1923), p. 32.
15. Carl Solana Weeks, *Savannah in the Time of Peter Tondee* (Columbia: Summerhouse Press, 1998), pp. 81–85.
16. Saye, *New Viewpoints in Georgia History*, pp. 99–102.
17. Weeks, *Savannah in the Time of Peter Tondee*, pp. 36–40, 44–46, 50.
18. Saye, *New Viewpoints in Georgia History*, pp. 107–108.
19. Garrison, *Oglethorpe's Folly*, p. 205.
20. Weeks, *Savannah in the Time of Peter Tondee*, pp. 88–89.
21. Garrison, *Oglethorpe's Folly*, pp. 202–206.
22. Weeks, *Savannah in the Time of Peter Tondee*, p. 92.
23. Tim Stowell, *History of Georgia*, GAGenWeb, 17 May 2003.

5. The Royal Period Begins

1. Albert B. Saye, *New Viewpoints in Georgia History* (Athens: University of Georgia Press, 1943), p. 108.
2. Carl Solana Weeks, *Savannah in the Time of Peter Tondee* (Columbia: Summerhouse Press, 1998), pp. 81–82, 93–94.
3. W.W. Abbot, *The Royal Governors of Georgia, 1754–1775* (Chapel Hill, The University of North Carolina Press, 1959), pp. 1–2, 17.
4. *Ibid.*, pp. 40–43.
5. *Ibid.*, pp. 44–45.
6. *Ibid.*, pp. 45–46.
7. *Ibid.*, pp. 46–54.

8. Weeks, *Savannah in the Time of Peter Tondee*, pp. 97–98; Abbot, *The Royal Governors of Georgia, 1754–1775*, p. 54.

9. Weeks, *Savannah in the Time of Peter Tondee*, pp. 97–98.

10. Edward J. Cashin, *Governor Henry Ellis and the Transformation of British North America* (Athens: University of Georgia Press, 1994), p. 72.

11. *Ibid.*, pp. 1–13.

12. William Northen, *Men of Mark in Georgia* (Atlanta: A.B. Caldwell, 1907), p. 63; Weeks, *Savannah in the Time of Peter Tondee*, p. 101.

13. Abbot, *The Royal Governors of Georgia, 1754–1775*, pp. 57–60.

14. *Ibid.*, pp. 60–62.

15. *Ibid.*, pp. 65–67.

16. *Ibid* pp. 67–68.

17. Weeks, *Savannah in the Time of Peter Tondee*, pp. 101–104.

18. Cashin, *Governor Henry Ellis* pp. 142–143.

19. Abbot, *The Royal Governors of Georgia, 1754–1775*, pp. 8–13, 57–82.

20. *Ibid.*, pp. 17–18.

21. Weeks, *Savannah in the Time of Peter Tondee*, pp. 112–113.

22. Abbot, *The Royal Governors of Georgia, 1754–1775*, pp. 82–83.

6. The Wright Era and Patriot Crisis

1. W.W. Abbot, *The Royal Governors of Georgia, 1754–1775* (Chapel Hill: University of North Carolina Press, 1959), pp. 84–85.

2. Kenneth Coleman, "Oglethorpe and James Wright — A Georgia Comparison," in Phinizy Spalding and Harvey H. Jackson, *Oglethorpe in Perspective* (Oglethorpe and James Wright-A Georgia Comparison, Kenneth Coleman) (Tuscaloosa: University of Alabama Press, 1989), p. 126.

3. *Ibid.*, pp. 126–127.

4. Abbot, *The Royal Governors of Georgia, 1754–1775*, pp. 85–97.

5. *Ibid.*, pp. 100–103.

6. Kenneth Coleman, *Colonial Georgia* (New York: Charles Scribner's Sons, 1976), pp. 246–252.

7. Ellen Chase, *The Beginnings of the American Revolution* (New York: Baker and Taylor 1910), pp. 51–52.

8. Abbot, *The Royal Governors of Georgia, 1754–1775*, pp. 112–113.

9. Coleman, *Colonial Georgia*, pp. 247–248.

10. Abbot, *The Royal Governors of Georgia, 1754–1775*, pp. 113–117.

11. Berhard Knollenberg, *Origin of the American Revolution: 1759–1766* (New York: Macmillian, 1960), p. 235.

12. Kenneth Coleman and Milton Ready, eds., *Colonial Records of the State of Georgia, Vol. 28, Part II* (Athens: University of Georgia Press, 1979), pp. 132–134.

13. Coleman, *Colonial Georgia*, pp. 248–250.

14. Abbot, *The Royal Governors of Georgia, 1754–1775*, p. 123.

15. *Ibid*s., pp. 124–144.

16. Coleman, *Colonial Georgia*, pp. 258–262.

7. Georgia Heads to Revolution

1. Kenneth Coleman, *Colonial Georgia* (New York: Charles Scribner's Sons, 1976), pp. 258–262.

2. Samuel B. Griffith II, *In Defense of the Public Liberty* (New York: Doubleday, 1976), pp. 85–86.

3. L. Edward Purcell and David F. Burg, *The World Almanac of the American Revolution* (New York: Scripps Howard, 1992), p. 21.

4. John C. Miller, *Origins of the American Revolution* (London: Oxford University Press, 1943), pp. 358–359.

5. Charles Campbell, *Introduction to the History of the Colony and Ancient Dominion of Virginia* (Richmond: B.B. Minor, 1847), pp. 140–141.

6. Miller, *Origins of the American Revolution*, pp. 358–259, 367.

7. George White, *Historical Collections of Georgia* (New York: Pudney & Russell, 1855), pp. 45–46.

8. Coleman, *Colonial Georgia*, pp. 263–265.

9. W.W. Abbot, *The Royal Governors of Georgia, 1754–1775* (Chapel Hill: University of North Carolina Press, 1959), pp. 165–172.

10. Charles C. Jones Jr., *History of Georgia* (Boston: Houghton, Mifflin, 1883), p.177.

11. Coleman, *Colonial Georgia*, pp. 273–275.

12. Abbot, *The Royal Governors of Georgia, 1754–1775*, p. 179.

13. Mills Lane, ed., *Georgia: History Written by Those Who Lived It* (Savannah: Beehive Press, 1995), p. 32.

14. Abbot, *The Royal Governors of Georgia, 1754–1775*, p. 179.

15. Clark Howell, *History of Georgia, Vol I* (Atlanta: S.J. Clarke, 1926), pp. 353–354.

16. *Ibid.*, p. 354.

17. Jones, Jr., *The History of Georgia*, pp. 211–214.

18. *Ibid.*, p. 211.

19. *Ibid.*, pp. 222–231.

20. *Ibid.*, p. 235.

8. A Frontier War in Georgia

1. *Collections of the New York Historical Society for the Year 1872, The Lee Papers* (New York: New York Historical Society, 1872), pp. 114–117.

2. William Moultrie, *Memoirs of the American Revolution* (New York: David Longworth, 1802), pp. 184–185.

3. *Collections*, pp. 186–193.

4. Hugh F. Rankin, *The North Carolina Continentals* (Chapel Hill: University of North Carolina Press, 1972), pp. 76–78.

5. Clifford Sheats Capps and Eugenia Burney, *Colonial Georgia* (New York: Thomas Nelson, 1972), pp. 121–122.

6. Carl Solana Weeks, *Savannah in the Time of Peter Tondee* (Columbia: Summerhouse Press, 1998), p. 213.

7. *Collections*, pp. 200, 233–255.

8. John Richard Alden, *General Charles Lee* (Baton Rouge: Louisiana State University Press, 1951), p. 132.

9. Rankin, *The North Carolina Continentals*, pp. 78–79.

10. *Collections*, pp. 241–245.

11. *Ibid.*, pp. 205–207.

12. *Ibid.*, pp. 258–259.

13. Capps and Burney, *Colonial Georgia*, pp. 122–123.

14. Weeks, *Savannah in the Time of Peter Tondee*, pp. 215–216.

15. Kenneth Coleman, *The American Revolution in Georgia 1776–1789* (Athens: University of Georgia Press, 1958), p. 103.

16. Capps and Burney, *Colonial Georgia*, pp. 122–123.

17. Charles E. Bennett and Donald R. Lennon, *A Quest*

for Glory, Major General Robert Howe and the American Revolution (Chapel Hill: University of North Carolina Press, 1991), pp. 50–51.

18. *Ibid.*, pp. 51, 61.

19. Coleman, *The American Revolution in Georgia 1776–1789*, p. 103.

20. Bennett and Lennon, *A Quest for Glory*, p. 62.

21. Coleman, *The American Revolution in Georgia 1776–1789*, pp. 103–104.

22. Capps and Burney, *Colonial Georgia*, pp. 125–126.

23. Weeks, *Savannah in the Time of Peter Tondee*, pp. 215–217.

24. Coleman, *The American Revolution in Georgia 1776–1789*, p. 89.

25. Capps and Burney, *Colonial Georgia*, pp. 127–128.

26. Peter R. Johnston, *Poorest of the Thirteen — North Carolina and the Southern Department in the American Revolution* (Haverford, PA: Infinity, 2001), p. 127.

27. Bennett and Lennon, *A Quest for Glory*, pp. 50–51.

28. *Ibid.*, pp. 1–8.

29. *Ibid.*, pp. 28–29, 36–39.

30. Clark Howell, *History of Georgia, Vol I* (Atlanta: S.J. Clarke, 1926), p. 373.

31. Bennett and Lennon, *A Quest for Glory*, pp. 66–68.

32. Coleman, *The American Revolution in Georgia 1776–1789*, p. 106.

33. Bennett and Lennon, *A Quest for Glory*, pp. 68–72.

34. *Ibid.*, pp. 72–73.

35. Coleman, *The American Revolution in Georgia 1776–1789*, pp. 111–112.

36. Bennett and Lennon, *A Quest for Glory*, pp. 73–80.

37. *Ibid.*, pp. 80–86.

9. The Fall of Savannah

1. Paul H. Smith, *Loyalists and Redcoats* (Chapel Hill: University of North Carolina Press, 1964), pp. 82–84.

2. Henry Steele Commager and Richard B. Morris, *The Spirit of Seventy-Six* (New York: Harper & Row, 1958), p. 1075.

3. David Lee Russell, *The American Revolution in the Southern Colonies* (Jefferson, NC: McFarland, 2000), pp. 96–97.

4. Ulane Bonnel, *The French Navy and the American War of Independence, Cols Bleus Magazine*, November 8, 15, 1975 (www.xenophongroup.com).

5. James Breck Perkins, "The French Fleet" in *France in the Revolution* (Americanrevolution.org).

6. Ulane Bonnel, *The French Navy and the American War of Independence, Cols Bleus Magazine*, November 8, 15, 1975 (www.xenophongroup.com).

7. James Breck Perkins, "The French Fleet" in *France in the Revolution* (Americanrevolution.org).

8. L. Edward Purcell and David F. Burg, *The World Almanac of the American Revolution* (New York: Scripps Howard, 1992), p. 332.

9. Charles E. Bennett and Donald R. Lennon, *A Quest for Glory, Major General Robert Howe and the American Revolution* (Chapel Hill: University of North Carolina Press, 1991), pp. 87–88.

10. David B. Mattern, *Benjamin Lincoln and the American Revolution* (Columbia: University of South Carolina Press, 1998), pp. 57–58.

11. *Ibid.*, pp. 6–9.

12. *Ibid.*, pp. 57–58.

13. Kenneth Coleman, *Colonial Georgia* (New York: Charles Scribner's Sons, 1976), pp. 117–118.

14. Trevor N. Duprey, Curt Johnson, David L. Bongard, *The Harper Encyclopedia of Military Biography* (New York: HaperCollins, 1995), p. 611.

15. Christopher Hibbert, *Redcoats and Rebels* (New York: W.W. Norton, 1990), pp. 239–240.

16. Henry Lumpkin, *From Savannah to Yorktown* (New York: Paragon House, 1981), p. 28.

17. Robert A. McGeachy, *The American War of Lieutenant Colonel Archibald Campbell of Inverneill*, Archiving Early America, www.earlyamerica.com.

18. *Ibid.*

19. *Ibid.*

20. Coleman, *Colonial Georgia*, p. 89.

21. Clifford Sheats Capps and Eugenia Burney, *Colonial Georgia* (New York: Thomas Nelson, 1972), pp. 132–133.

22. Coleman, *Colonial Georgia*, p. 89.

23. Bennett and Lennon, *A Quest for Glory*, pp. 89–90.

24. Mattern, *Benjamin Lincoln and the American Revolution*, pp. 58–59.

25. Coleman, *Colonial Georgia*, p. 120.

26. Bennett and Lennon, *A Quest for Glory*, p. 91.

27. *Ibid.*, pp. 91–93.

28. "Lt. Col. Archibald Campbell to Sir Henry Clinton," 16 February 1779 ("Campbell of Inverneill's Dispatch"), quoted in Louis des Cognets, Jr., *Black Sheep and Heroes of the American Revolution* (Princeton: privately published, 1965), 146.

29. Bennett and Lennon, *A Quest for Glory*, pp. 91–96.

30. "Campbell of Inverneill's Dispatch," *Ibid.*, 147; *Annual Register* (1779), p. 33.

31. Bennett and Lennon, *A Quest for Glory*, pp. 96–97.

32. Dan L. Morrill, *Southern Campaigns of the American Revolution* (Baltimore: Nautical & Aviation, 1993), pp. 45–46.

33. Donald Barr Chidsey, *The War in the South* (New York: Crown Publishers, 1969), p. 60.

34. Capps and Burney, *Colonial Georgia*, pp. 136–139.

35. Purcell and Burg, p. 196.

36. Lumpkin, *From Savannah to Yorktown*, p. 29.

37. Hibbert, *Redcoats and Rebels*, p. 242.

38. Coleman, *Colonial Georgia*, p. 120.

39. "Lt. Col. Archibald Campbell to Sir Henry Clinton," 16 February 1779 ("Campbell of Inverneill's Dispatch"), quoted in Louis des Cognets, Jr., *Black Sheep and Heroes of the American Revolution* (Princeton: privately published, 1965), 149.

40. C.H. Metzger, *The Prisoner in the American Revolution* (Chicago: Loyola Univ. Press, 1971), pp. 51, 223–228.

41. *Scots Magazine*, xxxviii (Edinburgh, 1776), p. 427.

42. B. Barrs, *East Florida in the American Revolution* (Jacksonville, FL: Guild Press, 1932), p. 2.

43. Bennett and Lennon, *A Quest for Glory*, p. 98.

10. Patriots Regroup and D'Estaing Arrives

1. Charles E. Bennett and Donald R. Lennon, *A Quest for Glory, Major General Robert Howe and the American Revolution* (Chapel Hill: University of North Carolina Press, 1991), pp. 100–101.

2. David B. Mattern, *Benjamin Lincoln and the American Revolution* (Columbia: University of South Carolina Press, 1998), pp. 62–64.

3. Carl Solana Weeks, *Savannah in the Time of Peter Tondee* (Columbia: Summerhouse Press, 1998), pp. 220–221.

4. Mattern, *Benjamin Lincoln*, p. 64.

5. Kenneth Coleman, *Colonial Georgia* (New York: Charles Scribner's Sons, 1976), p. 122.

6. Dan L. Morrill, *Southern Campaigns of the American Revolution* (Baltimore: Nautical & Aviation, 1993), p. 48.

7. Mattern, *Benjamin Lincoln*, pp. 62–65.

8. Henry Lumpkin, *From Savannah to Yorktown* (New York: Paragon House, 1981), p. 30.

9. L. Edward Purcell and David F. Burg, *The World Almanac of the American Revolution* (New York: Scripps Howard, 1992), pp. 199–200.

10. Morrill, *Southern Campaigns of the American Revolution*, pp. 48–49.

11. Clifford Sheats Capps and Eugenia Burney, *Colonial Georgia* (New York: Thomas Nelson, 1972), pp. 139–140.

12. Robert A. McGeachy, *The American War of Lieutenant Colonel Archibald Campbell of Inverneill*, Archiving Early America, http://www. earlyamerica.com

13. Coleman, *Colonial Georgia*, pp. 123–127.

14. Morrill, *Southern Campaigns of the American Revolution*, p. 50.

15. Mattern, *Benjamin Lincoln*, p. 66.

16. Morrill, *Southern Campaigns of the American Revolution*, p. 50.

17. McGeachy, *The American War of Lieutenant Colonel Archibald Campbell of Inverneill*.

18. Mattern, *Benjamin Lincoln*, p. 66–67.

19. Capps and Burney, *Colonial Georgia*, p. 144.

20. Mattern, *Benjamin Lincoln*, p. 67.

21. *Ibid.*, p. 67.

22. This account of Campbell of Inverneill's retreat from Augusta, and of his relinquishing command is based on "Campbell of Inverneill's Dispatch,"p. 150–151.

23. Coleman, *Colonial Georgia*, pp. 124–125.

24. "Campbell of Inverneill's Dispatch," p. 149

25. Mattern, *Benjamin Lincoln*, pp. 67–69.

26. Edward McCrady, *The History of South Carolina in the Revolution 1775–1780* (New York: Russell & Russell, 1901/1969), pp. 357–360.

27. Mattern, *Benjamin Lincoln*, pp. 69–70.

28. McCrady, *The History of South Carolina in the Revolution*, pp. 360–384.

29. *Ibid.*, pp. 384–388.

30. Mattern, *Benjamin Lincoln* pp. 74–75.

31. Morrill, *Southern Campaigns of the American Revolution*, p. 54.

32. McCrady, *The History of South Carolina in the Revolution*, pp. 392–396

33. *Ibid.*, pp. 392–394.

34. Walter J. Fraser Jr., *Charleston! Charleston!* (Columbia: University of South Carolina Press, 1989), p. 158.

35. Capps and Burney, *Colonial Georgia*, pp. 144–145.

36. Morrill, *Southern Campaigns of the American Revolution*, p. 55.

37. Charles C. Jones, Jr., *The History of Georgia, Vol. II* (Cambridge: The Riverside Press, 1883), p. 373.

38. Paul Smith, *Loyalists and Redcoats* (Chapel Hill: University of North Carolina Press, 1964), pp. 106–107.

39. McCrady, *The History of South Carolina in the Revolution*, p. 399.

40. Morrill, *Southern Campaigns of the American Revolution*, pp. 55–56.

41. Lumpkin, *From Savannah to Yorktown*, p. 32.

42. Benjamin Kennedy, "Journal of Phillipe Seguier de Terson, Journal of Francois D'Auber de Peyrelongue," in Muskets, Cannon Balls & Bombs; (Savannah, Georgia: The Beehive Press, 1974), pp. 4–7, 28.

43. Captain Hugh M'Call, *The History of Georgia, Vol. 1* (Atlanta: A.B. Caldwell, 1909/1811), p. 427.

44. McCrady, *The History of South Carolina in the Revolution*, p. 403.

45. Mattern, *Benjamin Lincoln*, pp. 80–81.

46. Jones, *The History of Georgia, Vol. II*, p. 376.

47. Morrill, *Southern Campaigns of the American Revolution*, p. 56.

48. Kennedy, "Journal of Major General Augustine Prevost," in Muskets, Cannon Balls & Bombs, pp. 93–94.

49. Morrill, *Southern Campaigns of the American Revolution*, p. 56.

50. Kennedy, "An English Journal of the Siege of Savannah in 1779-Anonymous Naval Officer," (Muskets, Cannon Balls & Bombs), p. 81.

51. M'Call, *The History of Georgia, Vol. 1*, pp. 428–429.

52. Jones, *The History of Georgia, Vol. II*, pp. 376–378.

53. James Breck Perkins, "The French Fleet," France in the Revolution, in http://www.Americanrevolution.org.

11. Siege Forces Gather at Savannah

1. Benjamin Kennedy, "Journal of the Siege of Savannah-M. le compte d'Estaing," Muskets, Cannon Balls & Bombs (Savannah, Georgia: The Beehive Press, 1974), p. 46.

2. Kennedy, "Journal of the Siege of Savannah-M. le compte d'Estaing and An English Journal of the Siege of Savannah in 1779-Anonymous Naval Officer," in Cannon Balls & Bombs (Savannah, Georgia: The Beehive Press, 1974), pp. 46, 81.

3. Charles C. Jones Jr., *The History of Georgia, Vol. II* (Cambridge: The Riverside Press, 1883), pp. 376–378.

4. Kennedy, "Journal of Francois D'Auber de Peyrelongue," Muskets, Cannon Balls & Bombs, p. 31.

5. Kennedy, "Journal of Phillipe Seguier de Terson and Journal of the Siege of Savannah-M. le compte d'Estaing," Muskets, Cannon Balls & Bombs (Savannah, Georgia: The Beehive Press, 1974), pp. 9–10, 26, 47–49, 76.

6. Kennedy, "Journal of Phillipe Seguier de Terson," Muskets, Cannon Balls & Bombs (Savannah, Georgia: The Beehive Press, 1974), p. 11.

7. Kennedy, "Journal of the Siege of Savannah-M. le compte d'Estaing," Muskets, Cannon Balls & Bombs, p. 49.

8. Jones, *The History of Georgia, Vol. II*, p. 377.

9. Kennedy, "Journal of Major General Benjamin Lincoln," Muskets, Cannon Balls & Bombs, pp. 122–123.

10. Clifford Sheats Capps and Eugenia Burney, *Colonial Georgia* (New York: Thomas Nelson, 1972), p. 147.

11. L. Edward Purcell and David F. Burg, *The World Almanac of the American Revolution* (New York: Scripps Howard Company, 1992), pp. 362–363.

12. Jones, *The History of Georgia, Vol. II*, pp. 377–379.

13. Dan L. Morrill, *Southern Campaigns of the American Revolution* (Baltimore: Nautical & Aviation, 1993), pp. 56–57.

14. Jones, *The History of Georgia, Vol. II*, pp. 382–385.

15. *Ibid.*, p. 382.

16. Morrill, *Southern Campaigns of the American Revolution*, p. 57.

17. Edward McCrady, *The History of South Carolina in the Revolution 1775–1780* (New York: Russell & Russell, 1901/1969), p. 407.

18. David B. Mattern, *Benjamin Lincoln and the American Revolution* (Columbia: University of South Carolina Press, 1998), p. 82.

19. Kennedy, "Journal of Francois D'Auber de Peyrelongue," Muskets, Cannon Balls & Bombs, p. 30.

20. Jones, The History of Georgia, Vol. II, pp. 379–381.

21. Kennedy, "Journal of Major General Benjamin Lincoln," Muskets, Cannon Balls & Bombs, pp. 123–124.

22. McCrady, The History of South Carolina in the Revolution, p. 407.

23. Captain Hugh M'Call, The History of Georgia, Vol. 1 (Atlanta: A.B. Caldwell, 1909/1811), pp. 435–436; Morrill, Southern Campaigns of the American Revolution, pp. 58–59.

24. Jones, The History of Georgia, Vol. II, p. 383.

25. Morrill, Southern Campaigns of the American Revolution, p. 59.

26. Kennedy, "Journal of the Siege of Savannah-M. le compte d'Estaing and Journal of Journal of Major General Benjamin Lincoln," Muskets, Cannon Balls & Bombs, pp. 51, 124.

27. M'Call, The History of Georgia, Vol. 1, pp. 436–437.

28. Kennedy, "Journal of the Siege of Savannah-M. le compte d'Estaing," Muskets, Cannon Balls & Bombs, pp. 61–62.

29. McCrady, The History of South Carolina in the Revolution, p. 410.

30. Jones, The History of Georgia, Vol. II, pp. 384–385, 404.

31. McCrady, The History of South Carolina in the Revolution, pp. 410–411.

32. Jones, The History of Georgia, Vol. II, pp. 23, 388.

33. McCrady, The History of South Carolina in the Revolution, pp. 407–408.

12. The Siege of Savannah

1. Charles C. Jones, Jr., The History of Georgia, Vol. II (Cambridge: Riverside Press, 1883), p. 388.

2. Captain Hugh M'Call, The History of Georgia, Vol. 1 (Atlanta: A.B. Caldwell Publisher, 1909/1811), p. 438.

3. Benjamin Kennedy, Muskets, Cannon Balls & Bombs (Journal of the Siege of Savannah-M. le compte d'Estaing) (Savannah, GA: Beehive Press, 1974), pp. 54–55.

4. Ibid., p. 55.

5. Ibid., pp. 56–59.

6. Jones, The History of Georgia, Vol. II, pp. 388–389.

7. M'Call, The History of Georgia, Vol. 1, pp. 438–439.

8. Jones, The History of Georgia, Vol II, p. 389.

9. Kennedy, Muskets, Cannon Balls & Bombs, p. 58.

10. M'Call, The History of Georgia, Vol. 1, p. 439.

11. Kennedy, Muskets, Cannon Balls & Bombs, pp. 84–85.

12. Ibid., p. 61.

13. Ibid., p. 35.

14. Charles Campbell, Jr., History of Georgia Vol. II (Cambridge: Riverside Press, 1883), page 391.

15. Jones, The History of Georgia, Vol. II, pp. 390–391.

16. Esmond Wright, The Fire of Liberty (New York: St. Martin's Press, 1983), pp. 175–176.

17. Jones, The History of Georgia, Vol. II, pp. 391–392.

18. Dan L. Morrill, Southern Campaigns of the American Revolution (Baltimore: Nautical & Aviation, 1993), p. 60.

19. Jones, The History of Georgia, Vol. II, pp. 392–394.

20. Kennedy, Muskets, Cannon Balls & Bombs, pp. 64–65.

21. Ibid., p. 36.

22. M'Call, The History of Georgia, Vol. 1, pp. 441–443.

23. Jones, The History of Georgia, Vol II, pp. 394, 397.

24. Franklin B. Hough, The Siege of Savannah by the Combined American and French Forces under the Command of Gen. Lincoln and the Count D'Estaing in the Autumn of 1779 (Albany, GA: J. Minsell, 1866), p. 132.

25. Kennedy, Muskets, Cannon Balls & Bombs, p. 26.

26. Carl Solana Weeks, Savannah in the Time of Peter Tondee (Columbia, SC: Summerhouse, 1997), pp. 222–223.

27. Kennedy, Muskets, Cannon Balls & Bombs, pp. 67–68.

28. Jones, The History of Georgia, Vol. II, pp. 398–403.

29. Edward McCrady, The History of South Carolina in the Revolution 1775–1780 (New York: Russell & Russell, 1901/1969), pp. 415–416.

30. Jones, The History of Georgia, Vol. II, pp. 406–407.

31. Morrill, Southern Campaigns of the American Revolution, pp. 63–64.

32. Jones, The History of Georgia, Vol. II, pp. 402–403.

33. Kennedy, Muskets, Cannon Balls & Bombs, p. 74.

34. Jones, The History of Georgia, Vol. II, pp. 411–412.

35. M'Call, The History of Georgia, Vol. 1, pp. 454–455.

36. Wright, The Fire of Liberty, p. 177.

37. Henry Lumpkin, From Savannah to Yorktown (New York: Paragon House, 1981), p. 39.

38. McCrady, The History of South Carolina in the Revolution 1775–1780, p. 419.

39. Kennedy, Muskets, Cannon Balls & Bombs, pp. 69–71.

40. Jones, The History of Georgia, Vol. II, pp. 414–415.

41. Kenneth Coleman, The American Revolution in Georgia 1763–1789 (Athens: University of Georgia Press, 1958), p. 129.

42. Weeks, Savannah in the Time of Peter Tondee, p. 225.

43. Morrill, Southern Campaigns of the American Revolution, pp. 64–65.

44. Weeks, Savannah in the Time of Peter Tondee, pp. 226–227.

45. Kennedy, Muskets, Cannon Balls & Bombs, pp. 103–105.

46. David B. Mattern, Benjamin Lincoln and the American Revolution (Columbia: University of South Carolina Press, 1998), p. 87.

47. Kennedy, Muskets, Cannon Balls & Bombs, p. 129.

13. An Occupied Georgia

1. Carl Solana Weeks, Savannah in the Time of Peter Tondee (Columbia: Summerhouse Press, 1998), pp. 226–227

2. Charles C. Jones Jr., The History of Georgia, Vol. II, pp. 417–419.

3. Dan L. Morrill, Southern Campaigns of the American Revolution (Baltimore: Nautical & Aviation, 1993), p. 56.

4. Paul H. Smith, Loyalists and Redcoats (Chapel Hill: University of North Carolina Press, 1964), p. 126.

5. Franklin Wickwire and Mary Wickwire, Cornwallis, The American Adventure (Boston: Houghton Mifflin, 1970), pp. 125–126.

6. Bernhard A. Uhlendorf, The Siege of Charleston (Ann Arbor: University of Michigan Press, 1938), pp. 105–111.

7. Wickwire and Wickwire, Cornwallis, The American Adventure, pp. 125–126; Christopher Hibbert, Redcoats and Rebels (New York: W.W. Norton, 1990), p. 269; Uhlendorf, The Siege of Charleston, pp. 23, 111–141.

8. Uhlendorf, *The Siege of Charleston*, pp. 173–177.

9. *Ibid.*, pp. 177, 181.

10. Kenneth Coleman, *The American Revolution in Georgia 1763–1789* (Athens: University of Georgia Press, 1958), pp. 130–131.

11. Robert Middlekauff, *The Glorious Cause* (New York: Oxford University Press, 1982), p. 443.

12. Uhlendorf, *The Siege of Charleston*, pp. 231–233.

13. Edward McCrady, *The History of South Carolina in the Revolution 1775–1780* (New York: Russell & Russell, 1901/1969), pp. 470–471.

14. David B. Mattern, *Benjamin Lincoln and the American Revolution* (Columbia: University of South Carolina Press, 1998), p. 107.

15. Henry Lumpkin, *From Savannah to Yorktown* (New York: Paragon House, 1981), p. 49; McCrady, *The History of South Carolina in the Revolution*, pp. 504–506.

16. Morrill, *Southern Campaigns of the American Revolution*, p. 73.

17. Jones, *The History of Georgia, Vol. II*, pp. 424–427.

18. Coleman, *The American Revolution in Georgia 1763–1789*, pp. 135–137.

19. Coleman, *Colonial Georgia* (New York: Charles Scribner's Sons, 1976), pp. 137–138.

20. *Ibid.*, pp. 138–140.

21. *Ibid.*, p. 140.

22. Henry Lumpkin, *From Savannah to Yorktown* (New York: Paragon House, 1981), pp. 187–190.

23. John S. Pancake, *This Destructive War* (Tuscaloosa: University of Alabama Press, 1985), p. 202.

24. Lumpkin, *From Savannah to Yorktown*, pp. 190–191.

25. Coleman, *Colonial Georgia*, pp. 300–301.

26. Capt. Hugh M'Call, *The History of Georgia* (Atlanta: A.B. Caldwell, 1784, 1909), pp. 537–545.

27. Weeks, *Savannah in the Time of Peter Tondee*, p. 227.

28. Page Smith, *A New Age Now Begins, Vol. Two* (New York: McGraw-Hill, 1976), pp. 1721–1737.

29. William Seymour, *The Price of Folly* (London: Brassey's, 1995), pp. 231–236.

30. Sir Henry Clinton, *The American Rebellion* (New Haven: Yale University Press, 1954), pp. 361–362.

31. Weeks, *Savannah in the Time of Peter Tondee*, pp. 227–228.

32. Eldon Jones, W. Robert Higgins, ed. *The Revolutionary War in the South: Power, Conflict, and Leadership* "The British Withdrawal from the South, 1781–85," (Durham: Duke University Press, 1979), pp. 260–285.

33. Weeks, *Savannah in the Time of Peter Tondee*, pp. 227–228.

34. *Ibid.*, pp. 230–231.

35. Smith, *A New Age Now Begins, Vol. Two*, pp. 1721–1737.

36. Donald Barr Chidsey, *Victory at Yorktown* (New York: Crown Publishers, 1962), p. 158.

14. A Fifty-Year Colonial Legacy

1. Preston Russell and Barbara Hines, *Savannah, A History of Her People Since 1733* (Savannah: Frederic C. Beil, 1992), p. 73.

2. Kenneth Coleman, *The American Revolution in Georgia 1763–1789* (Athens: University of Georgia Press, 1958), pp. 189–195, 205.

3. Clifford Sheats Capps and Eugenia Burney, *Colonial Georgia* (New York: Thomas Nelsom, 1972), pp. 161–163.

4. Kenneth Coleman, *The American Revolution in Georgia 1763–1789* (Athens: University of Georgia Press, 1958), pp. 187–188, 209–211.

5. *Ibid.*, pp. 187–188.

6. *Ibid.*, pp. 221–230.

7. *Ibid.*, pp. 230–237.

8. The Rev. William Bacon Stevens, *A History of Georgia, Vol. I* (New York: D. Appleton, 1847), pp. 476–484.

9. Albert B. Saye, *New Viewpoints in Georgia History* (Athens: University of Georgia Press, 1943), p. 132.

10. *Ibid.*, p. 134.

11. *The Columbia Electronic Encyclopedia*, 6th ed. Columbia University Press, 2004. www.columbia.edu/cu/cup/ceelcec.html.

12. Robert A. McGeachy, *The American War of Lieutenant Colonel Archibald Campbell of Inverneill* (Archiving Early America, www.early america.com, 2001).

13. William Northen, *Men of Mark in Georgia* (Atlanta: A.B. Caldwell Publisher, 1907), pg 42–47.

14. *Ibid.*, pg 58–62.

15. Edward J. Cashin, *Governor Henry Ellis and the Transformation of the British North America* (Athens: University of Georgia Press, 1994), pp. 145–148, 152–171.

16. *Ibid.*, pp. 188–217.

17. *Ibid.*, pp. 221–236.

18. *Ibid.*, pp. 234–243.

19. *Ibid.*, pp. 145–241.

20. Jones, *The History of Georgia, Vol. II*, pp.414–415.

21. Northen, *Men of Mark in Georgia*, pp. 129–137.

22. *Ibid.*, pg 138–141.

23. Charles E. Bennett and Donald R. Lennon, *A Quest for Glory* (Chapel Hill: University of North Carolina Press, 1991), pp. 100–112.

24. *Ibid.*, pp. 100–112.

25. *Ibid.*, pp. 112–141.

26. Northen, *Men of Mark in Georgia*, pp. 167–172.

27. Northen, *Men of Mark in Georgia*, pp. 183–187; Biographical Directory of the United States Congress, http://bioguide.congress.gov/scripts/biodisplay.pl?index=J0000 17.

28. Biographical Directory of the United States Congress, http://bioguide.congress.gov/scripts/ biodisplay.pl?index=J000244, JONES, Noble Wimberly (1723–1805); Franklin, Benjamin. *Some Notes and Reflections Upon a Letter from Benjamin Franklin to Noble Wimberly Jones, October 7, 1772, by Malcolm Bell, III* (Darien, GA: Ashantilly Press, 1966).

29. David B. Mattern, *Benjamin Lincoln and the American Revolution* (Columbia: University of South Carolina, 1998), pp. 217–218.

30. Captain Hugh M'Call, *The History of Georgia, Vol. 1* (Atlanta: A.B. Caldwell, 1909/1811), p. 452.

31. Northen, *Men of Mark in Georgia*, pp. 251–256. www.ushistory.org/valleyforge/ served/mcintosh.html, abridged from the article by Charles William Heathcote, "General Lachlan McIntosh: Loyal American and Friend of Washington," *The Picket Post*, February 1957, published by The Valley Forge Historical Society.

32. Webb Garrison, *Oglethorpe's Folly, The Birth of Georgia* (Lakemont, GA: Copple House, 1982), pp. 189–202.

33. Keynote lecture of Sir Keith Thomas, president of the Corpus Christi College at Oxford, England, October 5, 1996, before the Oglethorpe Tercentenary Commission. www.cuiog.uga.edu/projects/jeo300/lecture.htm.

34. Garrison, *Oglethorpe's Folly, The Birth of Georgia*, p. 205.

35. Keynote lecture of Sir Keith Thomas.

36. Garrison, *Oglethorpe's Folly, The Birth of Georgia*, p. 219.

37. Amos Aschbach Ettinger, *Oglethorpe: A Brief Biography* (Atlanta, GA: Mercer University, 1984), p. 79.

38. Keynote lecture of Sir Keith Thomas.

39. Kenneth Coleman, "Oglethorpe and James Wright — A Georgia Perspective," in Phinizy Spalding and Harvey H. Jackson, *Oglethorpe in Perspective* (Tuscaloosa, AL: University of Alabama, 1989), p. 130.

40. J. Gordon Vaeth, *The Man Who Founded Georgia* (New York: Crowell-Collier, 1968), pp. 120–121.

41. Spalding and Jackson, *Oglethorpe in America* (Chicago: University of Chicago, 1977), p. 163.

42. G. Scott Withrow, park ranger, "*Andrew Pickens*," www.nps.gov/cowp/pickens.htm; http://bioguide.con gress.gov/scripts/ biodisplay.pl?index=P000320, "PICKENS, Andrew (1739–1817)"; Alice Noble Waring, *The Fighting Elder: Andrew Pickens, 1739–1817* (Columbia: University of South Carolina, 1962).

43. Tervor N. Dupuy, Curt Johnson and David L. Bongard, *The Harper Encyclopedia of Military Biography* (New York: Castle Books, 1992), p. 611.

44. Cashin, *Governor Henry Ellis and the Transformation of British North America*, pp. 71–72.

45. Carl Solana Weeks, *Savannah in the Time of Peter Tondee* (Columbia: Summerhouse, 1998), pp. 97–98.

46. Appletons Encyclopedia, *www. famousamericans. net/anthonystokes/*.

47. www.heidelberg.edu/Fallen Timbers/FTbio-Wayne.html, Commanding Generals and Chiefs of Staff," William G. Bell, 1992; "The Beginning of the U.S. Army," by James R. Jacobs, 1947, http://www.bbc.co.uk/dna/ h2g2/alabaster/A481682; General "Mad" Anthony Wayne, http://bioguide.congress.gov/scripts/biodisplay. pl?index =W000216, WAYNE, Anthony (1745–1796), Harry E. Wildes, Anthony Wayne, *Trouble Shooter of the American Revolution* (New York: Harcourt, Brace, 1941), www. bbc.co.uk/dna/h2g2/alabaster/ A481682, General "Mad" Anthony Wayne, http://en. wikipedia.org/wiki/Anthony_ Wayne, abridged from the article by Charles William Heathcoate, *The Picket Post*, Valley Forge Historical Society, July 1954

48. Richard M. Cameron, "John Wesley," *Collier's Encyclopedia* (Crowell-Collier Educational, 1969), pp. 411–412; *Christianity Today* International/ Christian History magazine, Christian History. Issue 69, Winter 2001, Vol. XX, No. 1, Page 10.

49. Coleman, "Oglethorpe and James Wright — A Georgia Comparison," in Spalding and Jackson, *Oglethorpe in Perspective*, p. 130.

Bibliography

Abbot, W.W. *The Royal Governors of Georgia, 1754–1775.* Chapel Hill: University of North Carolina Press, 1959.

Account of Campbell of Inverneill's Retreat from Augusta, and of his Relinquishing Command, Campbell of Inverneill's Dispatch. Annual Register, 1779.

Alden, John Richard. *General Charles Lee.* Baton Rouge: Louisiana State University Press, 1951.

Appletons Encyclopedia. *Anthony Stokes,* http://www.famousamericans.net.

Arana, Luis Rafael, and Albert Manucy. *The Building of Castillo de San Marcos.* Eastern National Park and Monument Association, 1977.

Barrow, Elfrida De Renne, and Laura Palmer Bell. *Anchored Yesterdays, The Log Book of Savannah's Voyage Across a Georgia Century.* Athens: University of Georgia Press, 1923.

Barrs, Burton. *East Florida in the American Revolution.* Jacksonville, FL: Guild Press, 1932.

Bennett, Charles E., and Donald R. Lennon. *A Quest for Glory, Major General Robert Howe and the American Revolution.* Chapel Hill: University of North Carolina Press, 1991.

Brown, Kenneth O. "Wesley's in America — What Went Wrong?" *Christian History Magazine,* Issue 69, Winter 2001, Vol. XX, No. 1.

Campbell, Charles. *Introduction to the History of the Colony and Ancient Dominion of Virginia.* Richmond: B.B. Minor, 1847.

Capps, Clifford Sheats, and Eugenia Burney. *Colonial Georgia.* New York: Thomas Melson, 1972.

Cashin, Edward J. *Governor Henry Ellis and the Transformation of British North America.* Athens: University of Georgia Press, 1994.

Chase, Ellen. *The Beginnings of the American Revolution.* New York: Baker and Taylor, 1910.

Chidsey, Donald Barr. *The War in the South.* New York: Crown, 1969.

_____. *Victory at Yorktown.* New York: Crown, 1962.

Clinton, Sir Henry. *The American Rebellion.* New Haven: Yale University Press, 1954.

Cognets, Louis des, Jr. "Lt. Col. Archibald Campbell to Sir Henry Clinton dated 16 February 1779 — Campbell of Inverneill's Dispatch," in *Black Sheep and Heroes of the American Revolution.* Privately published, Princeton, 1965.

Coleman, Kenneth, and Milton Ready, eds. *Colonial Records of the State of Georgia, Vol. 28, Part. II,* Athens: University of Georgia Press, 1979.

Coleman, Kenneth. *Colonial Georgia.* New York: Charles Scribner's Sons, 1976.

_____. *The American Revolution in Georgia 1763–1789.* Athens: University of Georgia Press, 1958.

Collections of the New York Historical Society for the Year 1872, The Lee Papers. New York: New York Historical Society, 1872.

Columbia Electronic Encyclopedia, 6th ed., *Thomas Browne,* Columbia University Press, 2004.

Commager, Henry Steele, and Richard B. Morris. *The Spirit of Seventy-Six.* New York: Harper & Row, 1958.

Dupuy, Trevor N., Curt Johnson, and David L. Bongard. *The Harper Encyclopedia of Military Biography.* New York: Castle Books, 1992.

Ettinger, Amos Aschbach. *James Edward Oglethorpe, Imperial Idealist*. Oxford: Clarendon Press, 1936.
_____. *Oglethorpe: A Brief Biography*. Atlanta: Mercer University Press, 1984.
Fraser Walter J., Jr.,*Charleston! Charleston!* Columbia: University of South Carolina Press, 1989.
Garrison, Webb, *Oglethorpe's Folly, The Birth of Georgia*. Lakemont, GA: Copple House Books, 1982.
Griffith, Samuel B., II. *In Defense of the Public Liberty*. New York: Doubleday, 1976.
Harden, William. *A History of Savannah and South Georgia*. Atlanta: Cherokee, 1969.
Harris, Thaddeus Mason. *Biographical Memorials of James Oglethorpe*. http://www.fullbooks.com.
Heathcoate, Charles William. "General Anthony Wayne" In *The Picket Post*. Valley Forge Historical Society, July 1954.
Hibbert, Christopher. *Redcoats and Rebels*. New York: W.W. Norton, 1990.
Higgins, W. Robert. *The Revolutionary War in the South: Power, Conflict, and Leadership — The British Withdrawal from the South, 1781–85*. Durham: Duke University Press, 1979.
Hough, Franklin B. *The Siege of Savannah by the Combined American and French Forces under the Command of Gen. Lincoln and the Count D'Estaing in the Autumn of 1779*. Albany, GA: J. Minsell, 1866.
Howell, Clark. *History of Georgia*. Vol. I. Atlanta: S.J. Clarke, 1926.
Johnston, Peter R. *Poorest of the Thirteen — North Carolina and the Southern Department in the American Revolution*. Haverford, PA: Infinity, 2001.
Jones, Charles C., Jr. *The History of Georgia*. Vols. I and II. Cambridge: The Riverside Press, 1883.
Kennedy, Benjamin. *Muskets, Cannon Balls & Bombs, An English Journal of the Siege of Savannah in 1779 — Anonymous Naval Officer*. Savannah: The Beehive Press, 1974.
Knollenberg, Berhard. *Origin of the American Revolution: 1759–1766*. New York: Macmillan, 1960.
Lane, Mills. *General Oglethorpe's Georgia*. Vols. I and II. Savannah: The Beehive Press, 1975.
_____. *Georgia: History Written by Those Who Lived It*. Savannah: The Beehive Press, 1995.
"Letter from Lt-Col. Campbell to General Howe." *Scots Magazine*, xxxviii. Edinburgh, 1776.
Lumpkin, Henry. *From Savannah to Yorktown*. New York: Paragon House, 1981.
Mattern, David B. *Benjamin Lincoln and the American Revolution*. Columbia: University of South Carolina Press, 1998.
McCall, Captain Hugh. *The History of Georgia*. Vols. I and II. Atlanta: A.B. Caldwell, 1811/1909.
McCrady, Edward. *The History of South Carolina in the Revolution 1775–1780*. New York: Russell & Russell, 1901/1969.
McGeachy, Robert A. . *The American War of Lieutenant Colonel Archibald Campbell of Inverneill, Archiving Early America*. http://www.earlyamerica.com, 2001.
Metzger, Charles H. *The Prisoner in the American Revolution*. Chicago: Loyola University Press, 1971.
Middlekauff, Robert. *The Glorious Cause*. New York: Oxford University Press, 1982.
Miller, John C. *Origins of the American Revolution*. London: Oxford University Press, 1943.
Morrill, Dan L. *Southern Campaigns of the American Revolution*. Baltimore: Nautical & Aviation, 1993.
Moultrie, William. *Memoirs of the American Revolution*. New York: David Longworth, 1802.
Northen, William. *Men of Mark in Georgia*. Atlanta: A.B. Caldwell, 1907.
Pancake, John S. *This Destructive War*. Tuscaloosa: University of Alabama Press, 1985.
Perkins, James Breck. *France in the Revolution*. http://www.americanrevolution.org.
Petry, Janine. "The Matchmakers." *Christian History Magazine*. Issue 69, Winter 2001, Vol. XX, No. 1.
Purcell, L. Edward, and David F. Burg. *The World Almanac of the American Revolution*. New York: Scripps Howard, 1992.
Rankin, Hugh F. *The North Carolina Continentals*. Chapel Hill: University of North Carolina Press, 1972.
Russell, David Lee. *The American Revolution in the Southern Colonies*. Jefferson, NC: McFarland, 2000.
Russell, Preston, and Barbara Hines. *Savannah, A History of Her People Since 1733*. Savannah: Frederic C. Beil, 1992.
Saye, Albert B. *New Viewpoints in Georgia History*. Athens: University of Georgia Press, 1943.
Seymour, William. *The Price of Folly*. London: Brassey's, 1995.
Smith, Page. *A New Age Now Begins*. Vol. Two. New York: McGraw-Hill, 1976.
Smith, Paul H. *Loyalists and Redcoats*. Chapel Hill: University of North Carolina Press, 1964.
Spalding, Phinizy, and Harvey H. Jackson. *Oglethorpe in Perspective*. Tuscaloosa, University of Alabama Press, 1989.

Spalding, Phinizy. *Oglethorpe in America*. Chicago: University of Chicago Press, 1977.

Stephens, William. *A Journal of the Proceedings in Georgia, Vol. II — A State of the Province of Georgia*. London: W. Meadows, 1742.

Stevens, the Rev. William Bacon. *A History of Georgia*. Vol. I. New York: D. Appleton, 1847.

Stowell, Tim. *History of Georgia*. GAGenWeb, 17 May 2003.

Tailfer, Patrick, Hugh Anderson, and Da. Douglas. *A True and Historical Narrative Of the Colony of Georgia*. Charles Town: P. Timothy, 1741.

Thomas, Sir Keith. *Keynote Lecture of Sir Keith Thomas PBA, President of the Corpus Christi College at Oxford, England on October 5, 1996, before the Oglethorpe Tercentenary Commission*.

Uhlendorf, Bernhard A. *The Siege of Charleston*. Ann Arbor: University of Michigan Press, 1938.

Vaeth, J. Gordon. *The Man Who Founded Georgia*. New York: Crowell-Collier Press, 1968.

Waring, Alice Noble. *The Fighting Elder: Andrew Pickens, 1739–1817*. Columbia: University of South Carolina Press, 1962.

Weeks, Carl Solana. *Savannah in the Time of Peter Tondee*. Columbia, SC: Summerhouse Press, 1997.

White, George. *Historical Collections of Georgia*. New York: Pudney & Russell, 1855.

Wickwire, Franklin and Mary Wickwire. *The American Adventure*. Boston: Houghton Mifflin, 1970.

Worth, Larry. *The Creek Indians of Georgia*. Our Georgia History. http://www.ourgeorgiahistory.com

Wright, Esmond. *The Fire of Liberty*. New York: St. Martin's Press, 1983.

Index

211